Center for Basque Studies
Basque Politics Series, No. 10

# Building the Basque City

## The Political Economy of Nation-Building

Nagore Calvo Mendizabal

Center for Basque Studies
University of Nevada, Reno
Reno, Nevada

This book was published with generous financial support from the Basque Goverment.

Basque Politics Series, No. 10
Series Editor: Xabier Irujo

Center for Basque Studies
University of Nevada, Reno
Reno, Nevada 89557
http://basque.unr.edu



Book design: Jose Luis Agote.
Cover illustration: Iñaki Crespo Calleja

Library of Congress Cataloging-in-Publication Data

Names: Calvo Mendizabal, Nagore, author.
Title: Building the Basque city : the political economy of nation-building / Nagore Calvo Mendizabal.
Description: Reno : Center for Basque Studies, University of Nevada, [2015] |
Series: Basque politics series ; no. 10 | Includes bibliographical references and index.
Identifiers: LCCN 2015039289 | ISBN 9781935709046 (pbk. : alk. paper)
Subjects: LCSH: Nation-building--Economic aspects--Spain--País Vasco. | Nation-building--Economic aspects--Spain. | Nationalism--Spain--País Vasco. | País Vasco (Spain)--Relations--European Union countries. | País Vasco (Spain)--Politics and government. | Spain--Politics and government--1982- | Spain--Economic policy.
Classification: LCC DP302.B53 C35 2015 | DDC 330.946/6--dc23 LC record available at http://lccn.loc.gov/2015039289

# Contents

# *List of Abbreviations*

| | |
|---|---|
| ACs | *Autonomous Communities* |
| ADIF | *Administrador de Infraestructuras Ferroviarias (Spanish National Railway Infrastructure Company)* |
| AHT | *Abiadura Haundiko Trena (Accronym for High Speed Train in Basque)* |
| AVE | *Alta Velocidad Española (Spanish High Speed Train Service)* |
| BAC | *Basque Autonomous Community* |
| CCOO | *Comisiones Obreras (Workers' Commissions trade union)* |
| *CEMAFE* | *Asociación Nacional de Constructores Españoles de Material Rodante (National Association of Spanish Rolling Stock Producers)* |
| DOT | *Directrices de Ordenación Territorial (Territorial Planning Guidelines)* |
| EC | *European Community* |
| EHNE | *Euskal Herriko Nekazari Elkartea (Basque Agricultural Association trade union)* |
| ELA | *Euskal Langileen Elkartasuna (Basque Workers' Solidarity trade union)* |
| ERDF | *European Regional Development Fund* |
| ERT | *Round Table of Industrialists* |
| ESDP | *European Spatial Development Perspective* |
| ETA | *Euskadi ta Askatasuna (Basque Country and Freedom)* |
| EU | *European Union* |
| FDI | *Foreign Direct Investment, Guiding Plan of Infrastructures* |
| FEVE | *Ferrocarriles Españoles de Vía Estrecha (Spanish Narrow Gauge Railways)* |

| | |
|---|---|
| FIAT | *Fabbrica Italiana Automobili Torino (Italian car manufacturer), the Italian Automobile Factory of Torino* |
| GDP | *Gross Domestic Product* |
| GIF | *Gestora de Infrastructuras Ferroviales (Spanish National Railway Infrastructure Management)* |
| HB | *Herri Batasuna (Popular Unity, radical Basque nationalist party)* |
| HST | *High Speed Train* |
| IBRD | *International Bank of Reconstruction and Development* |
| IMF | *International Monetary Fund* |
| INI | *Instituto Nacional de la Industria (state holding company)* |
| LAB | *Langile Abertzaleen Batzordeak (Patriotic Workers' Commissions trade union)* |
| LOAPA | *Ley Orgánica de Armonización del Proceso Autonómico (Organic Law for the Synchronisation of the Autonomous Process)* |
| MNC | *Multinational Corporation* |
| MOPT | *Ministerio de Obras Públicas y Transporte (Ministry for Transport and Public Works)* |
| NUTS | *Nomenclature of Territorial Units for Statistics* |
| OECD | *Organisation for Economic Co-operation and Development* |
| OEC | *Organisation for European Economic Co-operation* |
| PDI | *Plan Director de Infraestructuras (Master Plan for Infrastructures)* |
| PEIT | *Plan Estratégico de Infraestructuras y Transporte (Strategic Infrastructures and Transport Plan)* |
| PLAE | *Plataforma Logística Aquitania-Euskadi (Aquitaine-Euskadi Logistic Platform)* |
| PNV | *Partido Nacionalista Vasco (Basque Nationalist Party, moderate Basque nationalist party)* |
| PP | *Partido Popular (People's Party, Spanish centre-right party)* |

| | |
|---|---|
| PSE-EE PSOE | *Partido Socialista de Euskadi-Euskadiko Ezkerra, Partido Socialista Obrero Español (Basque Socialist Party-Basque Left, Spanish Socialist Workers' Party)* |
| PSOE | *Partido Socialista Obrero Español (Spanish Socialist Workers' Party)* |
| PTF | *Plan de Transporte Ferroviario (Spanish Railway Policy Plan)* |
| PTP | *Plan Territorial Parcial (Mid-term Territorial Plan)* |
| R&D | *Research and Development* |
| RENFE | *Red Nacional de los Ferrocarriles Españoles (Spanish National Railway Network)* |
| SEAT | *La Sociedad Española de Automóviles de Turismo (Spanish Passenger Car Company, founded by the INI, with FIAT's assistance, now a subsidiary of Volkswagen)* |
| SMEs | *Small and Medium Size Enterprises* |
| SP | *Spanish Constitution* |
| SPRI | *Sociedad para la Reconversión Industrial (Association for the Promotion of Industry, the Basque Business Development Agency)* |
| SOV | *Solidaridad de Obreros Vascos (Basque Workers' Solidarity trade union)* |
| TEN | *Trans-European Networks* |
| UGT | *Union General de Trabajadores (General Union of Workers trade union)* |
| WB | *World Bank* |
| WTO | *World Trade Organisation* |

# Acknowledgments

This book has not been an easy ride and could only be completed because of the support and encouragement of many people. The research would not have been possible had it not been for the very generous scholarship from the Department of Education, Universities and Research of the Basque Government that allowed me to study at Lancaster University. I owe a particular debt to Bob Jessop, whose intellectual support and personal encouragement have been critical for the completion of this work. During the years I have known him I have come to fully appreciate his vast knowledge as well as his generosity when it comes to sharing this with all his students. His patience and unfailing support have meant a lot to me. I am also grateful to Erik Swyngedouw and John Urry for their constructive criticisms and invaluable comments and suggestions. I would moreover like to thank Catherine Boyle, who as a head of the SPLAS Department at Kings College London made sure that I had sufficient time to complete the book. I would like to also show my deepest appreciation to Joseba Zulaika for his endless support and immense patience. The helpful comments by Daniel Montero and the anonymous reviewers helped me in clarifying and improving the argument.

I would like to also thank friends and colleagues who I have met over the years and who have always been there for me through good and bad times. I want to thank especially Adelina Angusheva-Tihanov and Galin Tihanov for their love and friendship. Also, Alan Metcalfe, Vicky Harper, Anna Vives, Sergey Khrychikov, Inna Khrychikova, Joo Hyoung Ji, Chia-Ling Lai, Anne Rogers, Dave Pilgrim. Their kindness, understanding and constant support have helped me to keep going in difficult times.

There are a number of people, too, who have contributed to this book in many other ways. They have given me valuable information, contacts as well as their own time. Without their ideas and thoughts, writing this book would not have been possible. I hope they read in these acknowledgements my appreciation to each and every one of them.

Lastly, I would like to thank my parents for always being there for me. Without their commitment and belief in education I would not have been where I am now. Finally, I would like to express my profound gratitude to Ivo. I firmly believe that without his love and his unconditional support, both intellectually and emotionally, this project would have never been completed. To him I dedicate this book.

# Introduction

In 2004 the Spanish centre-right party, the Partido Popular (People's Party, PP) was expected to win the forthcoming general elections comfortably after having governed the country since 1996. On 11 March, however, three days before the day of the elections, several bombs exploded on four commuter trains in Madrid killing 191 people and injuring over 1,000 more. Immediately after the news was announced in the media, the PP government representatives issued a series of statements. They all unequivocally blamed ETA for the terrorist attack and rejected any possible alternative explanations. The prime minister of Spain and leader of the PP, José María Aznar, declared: "The terrorists wanted to inflict a terrible pain. They have killed many people just for being Spanish. It is not the first time that they have tried to do so. . . We are on the side of the Constitution . . . and we cannot aspire to anything less but the complete surrender of terrorism" (Libertad Digital.es, 11 March 2004). In a statement quoted on the BBC, Spain's interior minister, Angel Acebes, made the link to ETA even more explicit: "There is no doubt ETA is responsible. ETA had been looking for a massacre in Spain" (BBC, 11 March 2004). These assertions were contrary to the patterns of previous ETA attacks and went against the opinions expressed by experts.

Soon after these initial reactions, evidence mounted that ETA was not, in fact, responsible. Nevertheless, the PP continued to hold ETA responsible until the day of the elections. Indeed, a focus on ETA had been a key aspect of the PP political platform for many years and one of the central issues in its 2004 electoral campaign. More generally, it seems that there is a strong consensus among the Spanish political and intellectual elite, as well as the media, within which the issue of ETA is overrepresented and tends to dominate political, economic and social debates—especially as regards any direct link between ETA and Basque nationalism (Woodworth 2004). Further, debates about nationalism in Spain tend to focus almost exclusively on the Basque Country, Catalonia and, to a lesser extent, Galicia. This is evident both in the media and academic works. Within this context, a terrorist attack in Madrid just before the elections could surely only have one outcome, namely, to strengthen the proponents of a hard line of non-negotiation and total disengagement with ETA. Yet, contrary to earlier expectations from opinion polls and the logic of the recent events, the PP lost the 2004 elections. While many complex factors contributed to this highly unlikely outcome (Chari 2004), the attempt to manipulate the media and withhold information was highly significant. Yet it was an unusual turn of events for a news item about a terrorist threat to work against the political status quo. Indeed, this counter-example was an important reason for my interest in the topic of political violence in the context of nation- and state-building.

Political violence is a key issue in (both academic and media) discussions of Spanish and Basque nation- and state-building. This holds both for explaining the presence of political violence (relatively unusual within Western Europe) and as a starting point and central aspect of almost all other social, economic and political debates. Political violence is endemic to all questions discussed within "Basque Studies." Thus, offering a broader perspective on the co-evolution of the Basque and Spanish nation and state formations could advance a more complex understanding of these processes. In this context, political violence could be seen as one (and not necessarily the most important) among many key factors for understanding nation- and state-building in Spain and the Basque Country. There are three closely interrelated features of how nation, state and nationalism are discussed (in the most visible academic accounts) in Spain:

First, there is a marked polarisation around dichotomies such as: whether one is for or against the Spanish Constitution and the Spanish state, whether one condemns or condones what is defined, alternately, as terrorism or the armed struggle, and whether one is classified as a democrat or a nationalist. Thus, in Spain as a whole, challenging the Constitution is likely to be interpreted as anti-democratic, anti-Spanish, nationalist and condoning terrorism. Intermediate positions would tend to be seen as impossible and/or dishonest. Both these positions tend to reduce the possibilities for political debate but also lead to a highly politicised society where open academic debate is also restricted.

Second, and relatedly, questions of nation and state formation and restructuring in Spain tend to be discussed as an "endemic problem" that is also historically over-determined and unlikely to be overcome. This is allegedly related to the specific historical path of Spain, especially its late and uneven development. Thus, the predominant accounts of the emergence and evolution of Basque and Catalan nationalisms are linked to the process of rapid industrialisation and urbanisation of three main urban areas in Spain in the late nineteenth century—Bilbao, Barcelona and Madrid—as well as the inability of the (Spanish) state to impose a common economic, political and cultural plan for the whole country.

Third, political, economic and social restructuring in Spain is often debated within rigid disciplinary boundaries. For example, nation- and state-building processes are located in the past and thus deemed to be best understood through historical accounts. Accordingly, academic discussions of crisis and restructuring are usually not well linked to understanding processes of nation- and state-building and evolution over time.

This book will critically engage with these perspectives but will also depart substantially from their key assumptions and the conceptual framework that they are using. Thus, I will argue that these perspectives are, first, overly Spain-centred and tend to overlook broader ongoing processes of global economic restructuring as well as the political processes within Europe. Second, I will contend that they tend to conflate the undoubtedly huge political achievements of the peaceful and democratic post-Franco settlement, on the one hand, with, on the other, a critical engagement with, and understanding of, the processes involved in this settlement. In this sense the discourse on democracy as the great achievement of the settlement obscures its concrete ideological expression: namely, as a vision for the fulfilment of one particular national and state project for Spain, while de-naturalizing alternative projects by branding them anti-settlement, anti-constitutional and anti-democratic. Furthermore, such alternative visions for Spain tend to be primarily discussed in political debates, the media and in academic literature as discussions about peripheral nationalism in Spain, and less so in relation to alternative visions for the role of the state and market in the context of the ongoing Post-Fordist restructuring and a growing significance of integration processes within Europe. Third, and related to the latter, it is my contention that the high level of politicisation of academic debates is an obstacle to broadening the discussion on the institutional legacies and the path-dependence of the transition, in which the continuities implied by the role of the Franco regime in building the modern Spanish nation and state are a part of the transition's "pact of silence."

As a result, the aim of this book will be to extend the debate on the nature of the ongoing political and economic restructuring of Spain, the relationship between the centre and regional authorities and the place of the Basque Country in Spain and Europe. With this aim in mind, the book will critically engage with debates on processes internal to Spain that shaped Spanish nation- and state-building, and will also contextualise the post-Franco restructuring within broader processes of global economic restructuring and the political restructuring of Europe. More specifically, I will problematize the taken-for-grantedness of the Spanish nation and state and the interpretation of the post-Franco national settlement as exclusively a "negotiated break with the past." While such an interpretation acknowledges some continuities with the more recent past, these continuities are rarely extended to acknowledging the role that the Franco regime played in building the institutions of the modern Spanish nation-state and in consolidating the vision for a Spanish nation that continues to be dominant at present.

In order to offer a broader context to these changes and to address questions of the economic and political crisis in Spain after the death of Franco, the book will further draw on debates on peripheral Fordism, rescaling and Post-Fordist restructuring, questioning taken-for-granted assumptions on territoriality. The latter has implications for understanding the process of regionalisation in Spain where institutional legacies, external economic and political pressures and national ideologies are closely interdependent. It is within this context that the book will explore the complex process of the co-evolution and co-shaping of Spanish and Basque nation- and state-building and will offer a multi-layered analysis of the processes involved. Thus, while ETA, Basque nationalism and their representation in the media and in academic literature played a very important role in my decision to study Basque nation- and state-building in the post-Franco period, they occupy a rather minor place in this book.

The book has four main aims. These are:

- in contrast to the predominant highly politicised and/or one-sided accounts on Basque nation- and state-building, to offer a multi-layered understanding of these processes
- to de-naturalise the taken-for-granted Spanish nation-state and discuss its co-evolution with other national projects within Spain
- to describe the complexities of nation- and state-building in Spain and the Basque Country over time
- to focus on current and ongoing debates in the Basque Country in order to offer a complex understanding of the strategies utilised and the coalitions developed by key players in the Basque national debate.

These themes will be discussed within the context of the debates, inter-institutional relationships and strategies surrounding the building of the High Speed Train (HST). The building of a HST is one of the most visible, controversial and widely debated topics concerning infrastructural development and is a point at which different economic and political agendas for the Basque Country, Spain and the EU (European Union) intersect. Indeed, the discussions about the HST started in the late 1980s and over the last 15–20 years the debate has grown and has included different sections of society as well as institutions operating on subnational, national and supranational level.

In this sense, the HST case study promises to offer insights into developments within the Basque Country, as well as relations between the Basque Country, Spain and the EU. It will allow me to look at the interdependences and contradictions of different scales, the co-evolution of nation and state discourses and institutional configurations and the reorganisation of the Spanish state, particularly in terms of the evolution of centre-periphery relations: legally, politically and economically.

Debates, negotiations and strategies related to the building of the HST will be useful in addressing questions of state restructuring in two ways: on the one hand, the HST is about links within Spain, as well as between Spain, the Basque Country and the rest of Europe. These links illustrate struggles over different economic and political articulations emerging within a context of uneven capitalist geography characterising the present stage of capitalist development (Harvey 1982; Brenner 1998, 2004). Thus, fast trains by their nature connect bigger units to each other and thereby prioritise connectivity between distant places over that between places located in close proximity to each other. High speed trains could be seen to connect Bilbao and other major cities in the Basque Country to one other, as well as to other major cities in Spain and EU, or alternatively they could be seen to be connecting the Basque Country to other regions in Spain and the EU. While the emphasis will have an impact on the economic and political rhetoric it will also have implications on prioritising one type of capital over another as well as the dominance of urban areas over rural areas and smaller towns.

The HST is also an inter-urban connectivity project and as such, it can be discussed in terms of the priorities and strategies employed by different stakeholders in the Basque Country and Spain. These strategies and imaginings on the national and regional level will be related to different visions of Europe that prioritise south-west–south-east and north–south links, the

Mediterranean zone (Barcelona–Trieste) and the Atlantic Arc (Glasgow–Lisbon). The book looks in more detail at specific EU policies (such as those related to cohesion, sustainability and competitiveness) and the subsequent institutions and funding bodies which support those policies in order to analyse the impact that such a myriad of institutional settings have had upon Spanish and Basque government political and economic priorities and strategies (for example, the Atlantic Arc, the Aquitaine-Euskadi logistic platform, and so on). In this sense, the HST debates offer further insights into the specific contradictions and complements between different institutional levels. These complex institutional interdependencies are explored throughout the book in terms of past legacies and ongoing negotiations of competencies.

Transportation is the sector where the strategy of the Basque government is most advanced (Franco 2004) in terms of position, policy, institutional and financial support. The area of transport infrastructure also offers a rich context within which to explore a variety of different changes that are currently taking place (for example, the expansion of the Port of Bilbao; the regeneration of the Port of Pasaia (Pasajes); the High Speed Train; the Euro City; the Aquitaine-Euskadi supra-region, and so on).

In this sense, the debates and strategies around the HST offer a number of different perspectives on political, economic and social restructuring in the Basque Country, Spain and Europe in the last twenty years. Thus, the HST is a specific mode of transport (an expensive and long-term investment), a symbol of modernisation, a way of connecting within/to Europe and a new technology. It offers new types of connectivity (between regions and cities) and could be a profitable business. Its introduction is closely associated with the introduction of neo-liberal reforms: specifically, privatisation and the restructuring of key state-owned companies. Consequently, the HST is particularly useful in order to study this specific case of the restructuring of the Basque Country and Spain as it has been central to political, economic and cultural processes, visions and strategies for the Basque Country, Spain and Europe as well.

## Structure of the chapters

Chapter 1 discusses the interdependencies of the political and economic aspects of the transition in Spain as a process embedded within broader processes of global restructuring and crises, but one that is also articulated through the specific historical, political, economic and social processes within Spain. My analysis draws on the regulation approach and economic geography and discusses the economic and political changes in Spain and the Basque Country as a transition from peripheral Fordism to a highly uneven Post-Fordist restructuring. It is argued that devolution in Spain needs to be seen as a complex process of economic, political and social restructuring while the emerging strategies of different actors (such as state and regional authorities) need to be seen as an aspect of the broader processes of rescaling and the changing role of the state.

Chapter 2 focuses on the specificities and the enduring legacies of nineteenth- and early twentieth-century Spain. This chapter suggests that, on the eve of the decline of the Spanish empire, given its maritime and military imperial structure over a multi-territorial space, the Spanish state and its myriad political and economic interests were mainly externally focused. This made it difficult to develop a desire and an ability to create a vision of a national economy centred on the territory of Spain, while the most significant social and economic centres in the country were integrated into different international markets. Further, although these regional centres had strong (mainly) political links with Madrid, they were very poorly interconnected. This shaped the direction and level of development as well as potential for industrialisation. The development of a modern capitalist economy was, therefore, highly uneven and likely to create strong tensions and contradictions articulated along class, identity and religious lines in the process of attempting to secure and impose a single national imagined community. Consequently, during the nineteenth and twentieth centuries, the high point of nation-state-building in Europe, Spain was a declining empire on the verge of losing its colonies and also relatively isolated from the rapid industrialisation taking place in other parts of Europe, as well as the new colonialism led by Great Britain.

Chapter 3 focuses mainly on the consequences of the Spanish Civil War (1936–39) and the subsequent Franco regime (1939–75). This period could be seen as an attempt on the part of Franco's elite to achieve national integration. This was a project unfolding within a context of poorly developed political and market institutions, an industrial sector that was very vulnerable to international competition and highly concentrated in a few urban areas, and a large and inefficient agricultural sector. These inherited legacies were only partially overcome. As a result, the highly uneven industrial structure persisted, while the poor institutional, economic and infrastructural links between different parts of Spain remained meagre and continued to be mediated through Madrid. The priorities in terms of economic restructuring and the organisation of the internal market were dominated by large foreign capital and international financial institutions. Further, Franco's nation-building project was based on clearly defined internal boundaries between friends and enemies. The latter comprised people and regions that were on the side of the Republican government during the civil war, while the former were made up of sympathisers for Franco's Spanish nationalists. Spain also remained relatively isolated from the two world wars, which only strengthened the significance of fighting the internal enemies of the regime as a part of the process of the Spanish nation-building project.

Chapter 4 addresses the process of post-Franco political and economic crisis that led to economic reforms, devolution and the introduction of autonomous communities (ACs), where central and regional powers remained to an extent separate. The chapter suggests, however, that these processes cannot simply be analysed at the national level and, in this sense, it relates the political and economic reforms that took place in Spain after Franco's death in 1975 to developments on the global, European and local levels. One of its central themes is how interpretations and experiences of this complex transition were mediated through the notion of crisis. More specifically, chapter 3 explores the political and economic crisis in Spain, which, as in the rest of Europe, started in the 1970s in the context of the oil crisis. However, unlike many other parts of Europe, with the exception of Greece and Portugal, the crisis in Spain was deeply affected by the death of Franco and the subsequent political reforms towards democratisation. This chapter argues that the latter events took precedence in the imagining and analysis of the restructuring of Spain. Thus "the Spanish transition" has widely been discussed and interpreted as a mainly political crisis that was overcome "successfully" in the early 1980s with the completion of what is usually referred as the "political devolution" (officially termed the State of Autonomies). Importantly, here the "successful" end of the political restructuring is also seen within the dominant discourse of post-Franco Spain as legitimising the Spanish state as a nation-state, therefore making any demands for further devolution problematic. Within the dominant discourse on the transition the political reforms are said to have been followed by a belated "realisation" of the need for an economic reform. In contrast, I will argue that these processes are highly interdependent and cannot be discussed as discrete events and clearly defined "cut points" that operate on the national level only. As such, chapter 3 also discusses the political and economic reforms that took place in Spain after Franco and how they were co-shaped by past legacies as well as changes on the global, European and local levels. More specifically, these include: the specificities of the terms of the "Consensus," devolution in Spain and the acceleration of the European integration process.

Chapters 5 and 6 argue that the building of a HST is a good illustration of the complex institutional interdependencies, contradictions and complementarities of the interests and strategies of different stakeholders. The main focus in these chapters is on two periods, 1986–1992 (chapter 4) and post-1993 (chapter 5), which marked significant shifts for all stakeholders in their HST agendas. Nevertheless, each period is better explored through changing the emphasis from developments within Spain (chapter 4) to changes and debates on the EU level (chapter 5).

Consequently, in chapter 5 the different agendas range from, for example, the priorities of the Spanish government as regards attracting new technology and knowledge, the internal integration of the country and showing the new "modern" face of Spain to Europe; to a focus on the EU level where the development of the HST was at that time mainly conceived as an integrationist project focusing on the "missing links" between states, overcoming national borders and the rationalisation and liberalisation of the transport sector, in general, and the railways, in particular (mainly the development of trans-European priority networks and creating a European transport policy). In the case of the Basque Country, the HST was related to establishing the limits of the competences of the new Basque authorities in relation to central political authority, as well as the legitimation of the new institutional structure within the boundaries of the newly created Basque Autonomous Community (BAC). Further, this chapter discusses the strategies deployed by the Basque government (to combat its peripheral status and develop the Atlantic Arc) in making the case for a specific shape of the HST line. Specifically, this plan envisaged linking the three provincial capitals of the BAC (which, due to its geographical form, came to be known as the "Basque Y"), as well as including the Basque Y as one of the priorities in Spanish modernisation plans as a whole and its incorporation as part of the EU Essen priority projects.

These themes are elaborated in chapter 6, which argues that, after the Single European Act came into effect in 1987, the HST became closely associated with further European integration and a more clearly defined neo-liberal agenda. Within Spain, the HST lost its appeal as a national integrationist project; a dynamic that was further accelerated by the declining significance of internal integration and a stronger emphasis on Spain in Europe (under the leadership of the PSOE (Partido Socialista Obrero Español), the Spanish Socialist Party and global Spain (under the leadership of the PP). Ultimately, then, the conception of the HST was reduced to that of a specific mode of transportation that would link different urban areas. HST debates in Spain after the early 1990s have been mainly dominated by issues of efficiency and value for money, of developing inter-urban links and of inclusion into trans-European networks – rather than serving as a focal point of national integration looking backward in history and aiming at national reconciliation. In contrast to the EU and Spain, in the Basque Country the HST became much more closely linked to Basque nation-building projects. The different imaginings of a Basque state and nation are well articulated around debates surrounding the building, potential route and expectations related to the HST. Chapter 6 explores this in greater detail.

More generally, chapters 5 and 6 advance an argument that Post-Fordist strategies of adaptation can be articulated through regional and city scales, both of which have affinities with different types of capital: production and financial, where it is either knowledge or information (respectively) that are crucial for successful adaptation. Region- and city-focused strategies therefore also have some affinity with different forms of infrastructural developments (such as enabling knowledge generation, exchange, retention and so forth, as opposed to access to information, enabling its mobility and so on). However, both city- and region-centred strategies are shaped by the relatively central or peripheral position that specific cities and regions occupy. Therefore, while the centre-periphery distinction has become far more complex, it is still very important for understanding strategies of adaptation, as well as their relative success or failure.

Chapter 7 focuses on the Basque Country and discusses the two emerging dominant imaginings of the Basque Country and nation (with a third less prominent vision of neo-liberal global integration). The first is associated with the metaphor of the Basque City and is dominated by the vision of the ruling PNV (the Basque Nationalist Party, Partido Nacionalista Vasco), in which the Basque Country is imagined as simultaneously a region in Europe, an AC in Spain and a city integrated through complex infrastructures prioritising fast connections between distant urban areas. The second vision could be called the "Basque Country of localities." It prioritises bottom-up integration and close interregional and inter-local cooperation, and builds on preserving small communities, prioritising short distance travel and well-being over competitiveness. The two imaginings could be closely associated with small and medium national capital and labour, respectively, while large national capital located in the Basque Country and associated labour are provisionally integrated or excluded on the peripheries of those imaginaries. It could be argued that neither of the two visions of the relationship between nation and state fit the ideal-type nation-state. The Basque City imaginary emphasises the significance of territorial cohesion, close integration and centralised authority over the territory of the country which is combined with a very flexible understanding of different scales, integrated within different institutional frameworks, and led by a highly flexible and strategically astute government. In contrast, the Basque Country of localities notion operates with a highly flexible and decentralised understanding of identity politics, but one that is combined with an imagining of the economy that is centred on the locality and to an extent sheltered from the influences of global markets. These visions for the Basque Country are not easily assigned along the traditional–modern–post-modern continuum as both are very highly integrated into global symbolic and material networks.

## Methodology

As mentioned earlier, my general research interest was in broad issues of political economy and nationalism, and how discussions about Basque nationalism and ETA in particular were portrayed in mainstream academic debates and media. My objective was to develop a more complex understanding of restructuring in Spain after Franco and of the formation and development of the Basque nation and its institutional expression.

Initially, I was unsure about a case study that could offer insights into these complex changes. I first examined academic and media discussions in the Basque Country and Spain more generally about key industries, policies and controversies and I also conducted some pilot interviews with representatives of trade unions and major companies in the Basque Country before deciding on my case study.

My first inclination was to examine the fishing industry because of: (a) its close links to changes at the EU level; (b) interesting questions posed through the representation of fishing interests by the Basque and Spanish governments; and (c) the material and symbolic importance of the fishing industry for the Basque economy and Basque identity. Key issues included labour mobility, foreign workers and labour legislation. However, while this provided a complex case, it concerned a declining and increasingly marginal industry for the Basque Country and would therefore be less relevant to the broader institutional and regional restructuring in Spain and Europe. It seemed that transport infrastructure provision was at least as complex, could be also studied over a long period and involved old and new stakeholders. The High Speed Train appeared particularly interesting as a significant transport infrastructure that also provided opportunities for an interesting comparison with road infrastructure, and over time. The HST was a flagship futurist project employing state-of-the-art technology and requiring large and risky investments. And in this sense, it was out of the ordinary even in relation to Spain, let alone a small area such as the Basque Country. Indeed, given the "Y" shape of the new railway system and the lack of clear material justification or popular support, the development of the HST was especially unlikely in the Basque Country.

In order to understand the HST debates I collected secondary material and conducted interviews with key informants. While most of the secondary data was available through UK libraries, more specialised material was collected in public libraries and research centres in the Basque Country. My fieldwork comprised a wide range of materials that included policy documents on transport infrastructures and particularly railways, environmental issues and sustainability, territorial planning and urban development. I looked at annual reports, workshop discussions and reports from government sources, chambers of commerce, banks, social movements (environmentalists and local political activists), trade unions, local councils and experts (academics, consultants); I researched archival material, local media sources and specialised Spanish journals on transport infrastructures and railways; I engaged with the Spanish and Basque legal frameworks concerning the competencies and powers each administration holds and how they are distributed generally, and more particularly in the case of transport and railways, as well as reviews of laws concerning transport agencies, transport liberalisation and privatisation, and the agreement reached between the Spanish and Basque government that approved the start of work on the Basque Y network in 2006. I also looked at the minutes of different parliamentary committees and debates in parliament, and online forums and publications produced by different organisations in the Basque Country.

The second set of sources included semi-structured interviews with different participants who had an interest in or had been involved with the HST and related issues of transport infrastructure and inter-institutional relations. Since the HST project, principally promoted by the Basque government, spans over twenty years, any government and/or former government officials I interviewed had been involved with it only for limited time periods. I therefore made a special effort to contact ministers who had been in office during the early days of the HST project but this proved impossible for various reasons. I nonetheless interviewed people who represented a wide range of opinions concerning the building of the HST and who also represented different interest groups and had different institutional affiliations. These interviewees included people from the Spanish and Basque Ministries of Transport and Public Works, the Transport Directory in Brussels, as well as former Basque government cabinet members, other government departments, Chambers of Commerce, business associations and representatives of Eusko Tren (the Basque railways agency). Other participants who perhaps had maintained an interest since its conception were environmental groups, experts (academics, consultants and journalists), local councils and trade unions. Getting access to this diverse group of informants required establishing different types of contacts. Getting access to government informants, in particular, was comparatively harder and it was facilitated through personal contacts and the fact that my study (towards a PhD) was funded by Basque government itself. In most cases, initial contact with potential key informants was established by letter or email but later I also relied on recommendations and references from those already interviewed. All interviewees were informed about the issues that my research aimed to address.

My objective was to develop a multi-layered understanding of the discourses and processes involved in the building of the HST in which my primary concern was the practical adequacy of both method and theory (Sayer 1992) in describing and explaining the phenomena under investigation. As such, I interviewed different stakeholders representing a wide range of political and ideological positions, as well as representing different institutions and interest groups. Respondents varied in the extent to which they simply replicated well established discourses for or against the HST in line with their position within specific organisations, or allowed themselves a broader and more critical engagement with the subject.

While one of my objectives was to develop a better understanding of the different ways of talking about the HST, another was to use the interview material as a source of more information on key developments, motivations and stakeholders. This was then followed through by either developing further contacts or by searching for archival material or more recent publications and campaigns. The latter also reflects the way in which quotes from interviews are used throughout the book as either primarily offering a narrative account of the complex interdependencies between the processes discussed or as an illustration of specific perspectives and positions on the development of the HST. While this eclectic use of the interview material might sometimes be confusing for the reader I felt that this has allowed me to better represent the complexly interwoven ideological positions, institutional affiliations and priorities in the presentation and interpretation of events, policies and controversies.

Being Basque, I was aware from the outset of the great politicisation of Basque society and I was regularly asked, often explicitly, to position myself regarding ETA and Basque self-determination. Moreover, practically all of my interviewees also felt obliged, although often reluctantly, to position themselves in these terms too. Despite my initial concerns, this did not prove a major obstacle to the research.

Another difficulty in interviewing government officials and policymakers was their tendency to talk in line with their official position. Asking them to talk through stories and to give specific examples was made more challenging by the need to comment and sometimes also make a judgment on their political position especially in relation to issues of Basque nationalism. Conducting research in different countries and over an extended period of time could sometimes feel a rather lonely process, which was not helped by the usual difficulties associated with such research like rescheduling interviews or the failure of interviewees to attend arranged meetings.

All interviews were conducted in a seven-month stay in Spain and a one-week visit to Brussels. This included face-to-face in-depth interviews and telephone interviews. Establishing contacts was initially difficult because transport and the HST were new research areas for me personally and therefore I was unfamiliar with the main stakeholders and gatekeepers for my project. This process became easier with time and I also gained confidence in my knowledge of the key issues as the interviews proceeded. I used different sources and entry points to start gathering information about the people it could be potentially interesting to interview. The interviews were conducted in Spanish, Basque and English and then transcribed and analysed. This created problems, for example, with the transcription of idiomatic expressions, which had to be interpreted when translating them into English.

Doing research is necessarily a process of learning and as a consequence some apparently exciting roads might often prove to be dead ends while others may lead the research in unexpectedly interesting directions. In addition, I am fully aware that improving my research skills requires making mistakes and reflecting on them. But there are still things that, with hindsight, I could and would like to have done differently. For example, looking back at the process of data analysis and having already overcome my initial fear of using qualitative software research packages such as NVIVO, the use of such tools would have proved helpful in generating a more systematic and better structured analysis of the interview material.

Moreover, I believe that my research could have benefited from adding further interviews with people who were involved with the HST project during different time periods and representing different political coalitions in Spain and within the BAC. However, there comes a point when the fieldwork had to stop and I believe that, given the purposes of my book, the accumulated material was sufficient. In the same way, although during the editing process of the book I did to some extent update the literature used therein, the literature review largely stopped during the writing up process.

Conducting original interviews raises ethical questions about disclosing the identity of interviewees and misrepresenting their opinions. Accordingly, all interviewees were informed about the aims of the research, which was done initially in the contact letter but elaborated on at the beginning of and during interviews. Names of the interviewees as well as associations within the interviews that might risk revealing their identity have been changed to ensure that their confidentiality remains protected. Further, working between different languages and using translated material only increases the danger of misrepresentation and overinterpretation of expressed opinions. All care was taken to avoid that through cross-referencing of information and opinions of other informants and secondary data.

# 1

# A Regulationist Approach: Re-Contextualising the Spanish Transition

The changes in Spain after the death of Franco in 1975 have for the most part been interpreted as a period of transition in which a predominantly political crisis was followed by economic restructuring. Moreover, the political crisis is mainly assumed to have originated from the "unhealed scars" of the civil war and the autocratic regime of Franco that suppressed its political opponents, which included "enemy" nations and regions within Spain. Further, the recovery is usually associated with the re-establishment of trade unions and political parties and the "reinstatement" of justice by granting autonomy to the "historic nations." In addition, economic restructuring is mainly seen as a rather separate development that followed the political transition and, indeed, was to some extent caused by it. In this sense, joining the EU in 1986 was seen as an important part of the "completion" of the political transition as well as the main reason for undertaking economic reforms to meet membership requirements. The political and economic transitions are thus discussed as largely separate processes that were mainly the outcome of an internal crisis.

In this chapter I will examine the interdependencies of the political and economic aspects of the transition in Spain and will situate them within both the broad processes of global restructuring and crisis and their articulation through the specific historical, political, economic and social processes within Spain. In particular, I situate discussion of the transition in Spain in debates about Fordism and Post-Fordism and argue, in contrast to Lapietz (1982; 1986), that Spain had a semi-peripheral status (Holman 1996) in relation to the core Fordist economies. The latter also explains why the restructuring in Spain cannot be understood purely in the context of the Post-Fordism literature. I further argue that the process of devolution in Spain cannot be narrowly defined just in political and administrative terms but, rather, should be understood as being closely interdependent with both the (Post-Fordist) restructuring of the (peripheral) Spanish economy (including the creation of a Basque economy) and the process of Spain's full integration into the European and global economy. In addition, the development of a new regional structure in Spain and the emerging strategies of both the Spanish state and regional governments need to be seen as an aspect of broader processes of rescaling and the changing role of the state (Jessop 2004; 2010). Later chapters elaborate on the historical legacies (chapter 2) and the different aspects and stages of the political and economic changes during the Franco regime and after a democratic political system was introduced (chapter 3).

## Fordism and Post-Fordism

The main aim of the Parisian Regulation Approach (RA) is to explain the crisis experienced by (primarily Western) capitalist societies during and after the 1970s (for example, Aglietta 1979; Boyer 1979; Lipietz 1987). Adherents of this approach argue that capitalist accumulation requires a series of institutions, habits, norms and so on in order to temporarily resolve its inherent contradictions and thereby produce relative stability in the medium-term. Regulationists define the relatively stable period of accumulation between the Second World War and the early 1970s as Fordism, at which point a crisis emerged characterised by stagflation, class struggles, new social movements and a crisis of international as well as national regulatory regimes. The set of strategies adopted to overcome this crisis and the resulting regime has likewise been loosely termed Post-Fordism.

There are, however, strong disagreements about the more specific connotations of the latter notion (Moulaert, Swyngedouw and Wilson 1988; Sayer 1989; Peck and Tickell 1994; Jessop 1992, 1994). On the one hand, it could be argued that Post-Fordism represents the beginning of a new era of accumulation under the auspices of flexible production and flexible forms of industrial organisation (Piore and Sabel 1984; Scott 1988; Storper and Scott 1989; Storper 1995). On the other, it has been argued that such changes do not amount to a radical break and, indeed, that an alternative to the previous regime of accumulation is yet to emerge (Amin and Robins 1990). More specifically, Jessop (1992, 1994) argues that the extent of this change can be assessed in relation to four analytical categories: labour process, regime of accumulation, mode of regulation and mode of societalisation. Jessop contends that, in order to convincingly argue that Post-Fordism represents a new phase of capitalist accumulation, one should be able to demonstrate that the contradictions and crisis generated in at least one of these dimensions can be successfully resolved.

However, while Fordism is generally associated with specific forms of labour process, regime of accumulation, mode of regulation and mode of societalisation, these appeared in different combinations in Western Europe. Thus, if Fordism comprises the combination of a semi-skilled labour force working in automatic assembly lines under the principles of Taylorist organisation, and the virtuous cycle of growth that guaranteed the smooth production-distribution-consumption of durable consumer goods based on wage-productivity increases, price control and investment, then it was not a universal form within Western Europe. Nevertheless, it is problematic to juxtapose Fordism and Post-Fordism as rigid and vertical as opposed to flexible and networked. For example, artisanal forms of production have long coexisted alongside more Fordist forms of production and certainly, such coexistence is not dissimilar to more recent developments (Sayer 1989; Amin and Robins 1990).

Accordingly, Jessop (1992, 1994) argues that it is changes in the mode of regulation rather than the labour process, accumulation regime or mode of societalisation that can best capture the shift to Post-Fordism. This claim should also be approached with caution as different forms of regulation could exist (Brenner, Peck and Theodore 2010) within Fordism, in some cases prefiguring features of Post-Fordist regulation (Jessop 2002). While global notions of Fordism and Post-Fordism must be used carefully, their sub-categories are nonetheless useful to open up the complexities of the crisis in the early 1970s.

## *Semi-Peripheral Fordism and Underdevelopment*

The US economy, which is the supposed archetype of Fordism, certainly differs from other European versions. While historical and institutional differences among countries make Fordism very context-specific, it is worth making a more general distinction between core and periphery, in which less developed countries experienced what could be called semi-peripheral Fordism (Arrighi 1985; Holman 1996, 2004). Less developed countries, such as Spain, were only integrated at the margins of North Atlantic Fordism and were thus also semi-peripheral to the cycle of virtuous growth.

As a consequence, the specific place of Spain within the general framework of North Atlantic Fordism under the hegemonic dominance of the US (Arrighi 1985; Tayfur 2003), can be best explored building on the concepts of "dependent state" (Poulantzas 1976;; Arrighi 1985)and semi-peripheral Fordism. Analysing developments within Spain as developments within a "dependent state" allows us to explore the role that Franco's regime played in relation to mediating the integration of Spain within North Atlantic Fordism as well as the uneven nature of such integration throughout the national space, thus accentuating the importance of the international division of labour as a mechanism affecting the spatial organisation of socio-economic relations within the territory of Spain. Therefore, the notion of "dependent state" offers an alternative to the more traditional set of distinctions around rural/urban and agriculture/industry that describe states in relation to the size of the agricultural sector and the degree of industrialisation and urbanisation. The latter has often been deployed in interpreting the socio-economic development of national formations, yet at the same time this has often been to the neglect of local specificities and the diverse patterns of the integration of regions, localities and states into the world market. Furthermore, and following Poulantzas (1976), Holman (1996) emphasises the importance of class formation as well as the role that particular forms of bourgeoisie played within the process of accumulation. This entails paying closer attention to the formation of a "domestic" bourgeoisie (in contrast to a *compradora* or "purchasing" bourgeoisie linked to foreign capital), which involves the constellation of economic interests around a set of stakeholders who consider the national state as a viable "entity" for representing their interests and reproducing their position (Jessop 1990).

### Spain as a Dependent State

Holman (1996), drawing on Poulantzas, argues that, in the late nineteenth and early twentieth century, Spanish industrial development was almost entirely focused on the extraction industry and was also dependant on foreign capital. The development of the railways, for example, was also closely associated with the business interests of British and French capital. In addition, key sectors such as shipbuilding and the steel industry developed only in connection to the extraction business, which then led to the economic integration of different regions of Spain (for example, the area around Bilbao) into the internationally expanding industrial markets (Harrison 1983, 1995). Financial, technical as well as organisational resources, know-how, and expertise from (mostly but not exclusively) European countries continued to play a crucial role in the pace and degree of industrial development in early twentieth-century Spain. The impact of these links was not only economic. To an extent, the presence of foreign interests in Spain helps to explain the geopolitical strategies that major European countries, such as Great Britain, adopted in relation to the Spanish Civil War in the 1930s (Barea and Barea 1945). Similarly, strategic sectors considered of national importance, such as the oil industry, also developed following the inclusion of Spain into international markets. By the early 1950s, these developments were strongly supported politically and economically by the US and were also closely linked to US public and private investment. Thus, the pace and degree of industrialisation in Spain was shaped by the conditions of its integration into the world economy. In the early twentieth century, some of these conditions were associated with a Spanish state that lacked capabilities and resources for internally driven development; it was characterised by a high level of social fragmentation, and traditional and modern forms of social and economic organisation still largely coexisted in the country. Broadly speaking, Spain was divided into an agrarian and feudal South and an industrial North-West and East (for example, the Basque Country and Catalonia). The coexistence of markedly different modes of production contributed to the development of highly fragmented labour and capital formations. As such, the olive oil and fruit producers of the South, the large and traditional industry of the North-West and the small and medium size textile industry of the North-East constantly competed for defining the balance between open markets and protectionism. Only interwar conditions, the outbreak of the Spanish Civil War and the subsequent establishment of a new ideological-military-economic regime created the conditions leading to the consolidation of a nationally orientated bourgeoisie. Consequently, while US financial and technical resources played a key role in creating the conditions for the development of modern industrial capitalist expansion during the 1960s and early 1970s, unlike in the early twentieth century, the state in Spain played a significant role in its development. The state had been successful in building strong public sector companies as well as supporting a nationally powerful financial-industrial coalition, which nevertheless also forged strong businesses alliances with US investors in the development of key sectors (Lopez III 1990). However, and in contrast to other less developed countries (for example, in most of Latin America), in Spain it was the state that had the overall control over the pace and degree of industrial expansion and thus had substantial leverage in terms of decisions over the overall economic direction and the broader compatibility between government policies, national interests and foreign investment (Holman 2004).

While uneven development is intrinsically characteristic to national industrial formations (Maasy 1984), the extent of disparities in Spain was so dramatic that it helps to explain the semi-peripheral position that the country came to occupy vis-à-vis core capitalist economies. Spain's national industrial structure was geographically limited to a few urban areas, particularly Bilbao, Barcelona and Madrid. Even more specifically, in the case of the Basque Country, the surrounding provinces, particularly Gipuzkoa and, later, to some degree, Araba (Álava), benefited from the spill-over effects of the development and expansion of iron and steel related industries, and shipbuilding (located in Bilbao in the province of Bizkaia). Thus many small and medium size enterprises (SMEs) were thriving by servicing the main industrial base in Bilbao. However, in contrast to core Fordist economies, Spanish industry was still dominated by a large primary sector while the secondary sector occupied the bottom of the (international) value chain. It thus remained dependent on foreign inputs, technology and capital, and was also very limited in terms of its scope and size. In addition, agriculture remained inefficient and it was not until the 1960s that it came to play a less significant role in the Spanish economy (Guillen 2001).

Another specificity of Spain is that US capital did not reach deep into the Spanish economic structure and, as a result, it had limited impact in terms of the pace and scope of changes introduced in the labour process. Moreover, the Spanish economy continued to be dominated by a large number of less efficient SMEs, which gradually came to be primarily associated with European investment and markets. As a result, Fraser (1976) observes that, during the early days of the transition, SMEs in the Basque Country and Catalonia began to develop coalitions and alliances involving trade unions, the Communist Party and other social groups favouring a strategy for a radical break with the former dictatorship in the wake of a crisis of political legitimacy coinciding with the death of Franco and a growing economic crisis.

### *The Consolidation of a Domestic Bourgeoisie in Spain and Institutional Restructuring*

As suggested earlier, Poulantzas (1976) distinguishes between two types of capitalist alliances, *compradora* and *doméstica*. He deploys this distinction in his analysis of Southern European dictatorships and, drawing on this distinction, identifies two types of capital. On the one hand, there was Spanish business that cooperated with the US, and, on the other, there was business that cooperated with European business partners. Whereas the former was dominant during the period of the autocratic regime, the latter became more dominant during the later years of the dictatorship and after the transition to democracy. As chapter 3 argues, the economic reform initiated by the PSOE was strongly supported by existing European links (for example, the strong influence of the German social democracy) and the direction of policy reforms more generally were strongly influenced by EU institutions as well as by Spain's desire for EU membership.

The differences between Spain and the core Fordist economies extend further into the institutional structure and the state's role in matters such as wage bargaining , state-sponsored social consumption and the management of aggregate demand. Unlike most other European countries, the institutional bargaining framework in Spain was confined to the state sponsored "vertical syndicate" that controlled wage settlements as well as the organisational capacity of workers. The corporate nature of industrial relations during the time of the dictatorship was aimed at reconciling and channelling capital-labour conflicts but, during the autarky period in the 1940s and early 1950s, it served, above all, as an efficient suppressor of wages and labour opposition (Richards 1998). The lack of effective structures for institutional cooperation and negotiation during this period has led some scholars to suggest that, in contrast to post-1945 democratic societies in Europe, corporatism in Spain could only be explained as an ideological phenomenon (Giner and Sevilla 1984; Martinez Alier and Roca 1987). Despite this lack of institutional engagement, however, Fowerarker (1987) has shown that the vertical syndicate provided, initially, a space for cooperative practices, albeit on the basis of clientelist relations. Moreover, the vertical syndicate became a vital mechanism for the distribution of resources, including jobs, in a period when welfare provision was poorly developed. In contrast, developments in the 1960s and 1970s, such as the state-led economic liberalisation and the 1958 labour reform, contributed to the reorganisation of the labour force outside of the institutional structures of the state, and to its transformation into a significant political force capable of challenging the stability of the regime (Fishman 1982). The change in legislation also became crucial when it came to creating the conditions for transforming the labour process and for linking wage rises to levels of productivity. Nevertheless, the attempt to introduce rational capitalist production practices throughout the whole economic structure of Spain failed, and the introduction of such practices was only successful in the core industries that were dominated by foreign capital. Furthermore, while a degree of corporatism was present in relation to economic planning and the labour process, the overall stability of the accumulation regime in Spain remained strongly centralist and highly bureaucratic, with decision-making powers concentrated in the hands of a very small minority of the upper echelons of the regime.

As far as state expenditure on health, social welfare and education is concerned, there was little state investment and where it did exist, it was fragmented (although investment in physical infrastructure was extensive). The lack of well-developed welfare policies was partly due to a poorly functioning and regressive fiscal system, as a result of which the state lacked the necessary financial resources to implement such policies. Under Franco's dictatorship, social provision was mainly available through Christian charities while the state only offered limited social benefits and then only to industrial workers (Moreno and Sarasa 1992). Indeed, the necessary administrative and legal system for the development of a modern welfare regime was only established after the post-Franco period (Rodríguez 2004). Nevertheless, while welfare spending increased substantially in the post-Franco period, social assistance for relieving poverty, the struggle against social exclusion as well as social integration of disability have all remained relatively low compared to the EU average and the scope of welfare services remains likewise more restricted (Navarro 2004).

In contrast to the core Fordist economies, the management of aggregate demand in Spain was not central to the coupling of production, distribution and consumption. While mass consumption was indeed important in Spain, it was nonetheless largely defined in terms of the consumption of imported goods, which were also very unevenly distributed and mainly benefitted the middle classes. In addition, the Spanish economy was mainly reliant on migrant remittances, the export of cheap manufactured goods and the expansion of tourism, with the latter too vulnerable to global competition and therefore offering the state little control over prices (Arestis and Paliginis 1995: 266).

### *Spain as a Case of Semi-Peripheral Fordism and Its Spatial Articulation*

The Spanish variant of Fordism first consolidated on a broad national scale during the period of rapid growth in the mid-1960s (Holman 1996, 2004). The economic expansion of the post-Stabilisation Plan (1959) was based on the relative expansion of mass production of durable consumer goods for domestic consumption (for example, car manufacturing), but above all the consolidation of public sector companies with the participation of foreign capital in key nationally strategic sectors such as iron and steel, oil companies, food processing and chemical and related products (Guillen 2001). While the economic boom was based on the expansion of the internal market, the Spanish economic model very much depended on the remittances of emigrants in Northern European countries (mainly in West Germany, France and Switzerland) as well as on income from the tourist sector. To an extent, the structures of the Fordist social formation in Spain, which appeared during the early 1960s, were the inevitable outcome of world market dynamics, the hegemonic power of the US (Hirst 1997) and an economic crisis that could have been fatal for the regime in the early 1950s (Preston 1990). The new economic model which improved consumer standards and raised productivity levels had been reoriented towards consolidating an industrial base economic growth model. The intention was that this economic model would be implemented nationally, and by the early 1960s the central government began developing plans to extend the benefits of "a growth industry" to other geographical areas of Spain.

However, the objective of expanding the growth benefits through the extension of industrial activities to other more "under-developed" areas in Spain ran into institutional and political impediments. Within a context where informal channels of clientalism worked better in terms of access to resources and influence, resources had little chance of being distributed further beyond the already established networks of industrial and financial circles that coincided with industrial interests linked to the geographical areas of Bilbao, Barcelona and Madrid.

More specifically, the dictatorship maintained fifty-two provincial administrations, which had been introduced in 1833 with the first impetus towards imposing a kind of centralist model in Spain (García Álvarez 2002). However, as already argued, the regime was governed by a highly centralist government as well as newly created institutional structures such as the urban corporations of Bilbao, Barcelona and Madrid, which together shaped the societal configuration of the late Fordist model in Spain. Thus, while local and provincial administrations fulfilled a merely administrative function, urban corporations worked in tandem with and closely following central government orders. Indeed, Bilbao, Barcelona and Madrid continued to grow as a result of the industrial expansion of the 1960s.

The objective of the "even" spatial distribution of industrialisation and urbanisation of Spain took centre stage within media propaganda as well as in government policies, particularly with the adoption of the French indicative policy and the so-called policies of growth poles. However, this strategy did not generally succeed as it did not lead to the industrialisation of rural areas while it also created additional pressure on the urban areas that were the traditional centres of industrial growth. As a result, the efforts to spatially distribute industrial growth hardly attenuated the specific historically developed patterns of uneven development in Spain. An important aspect of the historical legacies that have shaped the uneven development of Spain is the development of a physical transport infrastructure which simultaneously mirrors existing economic and political realities, conflicts, interests and visions for the future, as well as shaping the possible economic and political futures.

### *The Spatial Distribution of National Infrastructures: The Railways*

The railway network in Spain emerged some decades after similar expansion took place in the more developed European countries (for example, Great Britain, Belgium and France) (Bel 2010). The first railway linked Barcelona to Mataro (1848) and its purpose was entirely commercial, that is, it aimed to connect production and consumption markets in the region. During the period approximately between 1830 and 1855, most railway ventures came from private initiative with the purpose of benefiting local economic activities, except for the involvement of the Provincial Council of Bizkaia (Vizcaya), which constituted the first initiative of its kind in the country on behalf of a local authority in this regard; and whose objective was to link the wheat market of Castile to the Port of Bilbao. During this period, there were few state-led initiatiatives, particularly regarding planning and the availability of funding. Moreover, political instability prevented the completion and participation of the central government in such initiatives (Bel 2010: 85–122).

Things began to change around 1855 with the adoption of the General Law of Railways (*Ley General de Ferrocarriles*). From 1855 to the beginning of the 1900s, then, national government initiatives and funding supported in part railway development in Spain. The government commissioned a series of projects that would guide future government railway policy. The interesting feature about these projects was that defence and the political standing of Madrid, nationally and in Europe, took precedence when it came to informing national railway planning. The national government made vast amounts of funding available to priority railway projects, such as those linking, first, Madrid and the countries bordering Spain (Portugal and France) and, second, Madrid and the capital cities of the Spanish provinces. This created a railway infrastructure that could be described as politically driven with a vision of developing a consolidated national space centred on Madrid. This impetus led to an emerging railway infrastructure that took a radial shape with railway policies that were almost exclusively used in order to enhance the political centrality of Madrid nationally, and for developing links between Madrid-centred Spain with the rest of Europe. While commercial objectives and a process towards the spatial articulation of a national market were not entirely discarded (particularly within the new railway policy of 1864), these were always secondary considerations.

Another consequence of establishing these priorities in spatial infrastructural development in Spain was that they also restricted the possibilities for developing alternative political and economic territorialisations on the part of competing national projects, such as those associated with Basque and Catalan national ideologies and imaginings. Thus, the development of a railway connection between Madrid and France through the North-West (via Irun in the Basque Country) was undoubtedly subordinated to the primary objective of developing the radial shaped railway infrastructure within the territory of Spain. It also goes without saying that no government plans envisaged the objective of building a railway that would consolidate the links among the Basque provinces. To the extent to which such links did emerge, they were as a result of private and/or local initiatives (mostly by the Provincial Government of Bizkaia and, later on, by foreign capital primarily linked to the mining industry), and had a clear commercial rationale. However, they could also rely on support from local authorities through the revenues of locally collected taxes (since the provincial authorities of Bizkaia, Gipuzkoa and Araba, unlike other areas of Spain, enjoyed preferential fiscal treatment from central government).

It is worth noting that wherever private commercial interest in the development of railway infrastucture existed in that period, it was not supported through government involvement and policies, and this goes for the whole territory of Spain and not exclusively for the Basque Country. Accordingly, the national government's investment effort, unlike those in other European countries at that time, did not go towards supporting and expanding economic and market relations. Early transport infrastructure development has traditionally been associated with organising social and economic activities within a given geographical area, and has also been linked to supporting innovation and economic development more generally (Yago 1983; Holl 2007). This included, for example, consolidating industrial centres as well as establishing links between these centres and their costumer/supply markets, eventually constituting an important element in the formation of fully integrated markets (for example, Great Britain, in early industrialisation). In this sense, a widely held view still persists that the politically driven public investment in the railways jeopardised the economic development and the industrialisation of Spain (see Nadal 1975; Tortella 1994; Herranz-Locán 2006).

In terms of the overall development of the railways in Spain, these different political and economic sets of rationales, as well as the existence of public and private financing, led to the emergence of highly fragmented and incompatible sets of infrastructures across the country. More generally, the development of the railways in Spain illustrates the tensions, contradictions and disparaging political and economic strategies that operated at the national and subnational level. Furthermore, these tensions shaped the competing nation-building projects that operated across Spain at that time. Indeed, the highly fragmented nature of the national society in social, economic and political terms (Storm 2004), and the highly uneven level of development (Nairn 1974) across the territory of Spain, contributed to the development of divergent political strategies (Breuilly 1993) and visions for the future of Spain at the end of the nineteenth century.

Looking at the more recent past, Bel (2010) argues that contemporary railway policies in Spain regarding construction of the High Speed Train (1984–86) have followed principles similar to those of the 1860s. Indeed, one of the key objectives of such a set of policies has been to prioritise the railway interconnectivity of regional capital cities with Madrid (for example, the Seville–Madrid line was the first high speed railway link). However, while in the nineteenth century the overarching aim was to make Madrid politically visible both within and outside Spain, the development of the HST project in the late twentieth century involves a much more complex intersecting set of political and economic objectives that operate not only on the national, but also on the subnational and European levels. Indeed, while the nineteenth-century railways reflected a policy that exacerbated diverging political and economic struggles articulated at the national and subnational levels, contemporary railway policy has reflected a convergence of policy objectives dominant at the subnational, national and European level, where dominant elites operating on these different institutional levels have negotiated the implementation of their agendas within intersecting policy networks. The new political-administrative landscape after the death of Franco (1975), and the subsequent integration of Spain in the European Community (EC, 1986), brought about the possibility of building new alliances within the framework of competences and powers of different government levels in the struggle to shape, define and adapt such policies to local requirements.

In relation to the Basque Country, the increasing tendency in both Spain and Europe in the late 1980s and throughout the 1990s to encourage local governments to become "proactive" in policy initiatives (Pike, Pose and Tomaney 2006) opened up the institutional space and gave political legitimacy to the impetus of the Basque government to mobilise its resources (for example, fiscal autonomy and a strong local economy) and to shape national and EU policy. Indeed, the agreement to build the Y-shaped high speed train link in the Basque Country (the Basque Y) should be interpreted as an outcome of the active engagement of the dominant Basque political elite and its vision for the future of the Basque Country with different economic and political agendas within both Spain and Europe. These tendencies could be associated with broader economic and political changes across Europe that might be described as a transition from Fordism to Post-Fordism, while the crisis of Fordism and the specific Spanish version of semi-peripheral Fordism could be seen as leading to the transformation of the Spanish economy into a semi-peripheral and vulnerable Post-Fordist economy.

## The Crisis of Fordism

The crisis of Fordism is usually associated with over-accumulation and declining rates of profit combined with stronger trade unions and a changing consumer culture in which demands increasingly moved towards customised products and services (Arestis and Paliginis 1995; Kumar 1995; Jessop 1999). More specifically, due to growing state protectionism[1] and the dominant corporatist model of regulation (particularly strong in the UK but also across Europe) unions continued strengthening their position in relation to national capital and, as a result, wage increases went beyond increases in productivity, while profits were falling. This occurred within

1. The increasing external costs covered by the state (such as investment in technology, R&D, environmental hazards, social security triggered by the crisis, and so on) led to a rise in inflation while, simultaneously, the wages of the state's administrative employees continued to increase in tandem with inflation rates (O'Connor 2004).

a broader crisis-prone economic environment characterised by growing inflation, the end of the Bretton Woods Agreement and the oil crisis. Business responded almost immediately by cutting costs by either partly internationalising production or relocating to less developed countries, which was largely enabled by the rapid development of information technologies (Mouleart, Swyngedouw and Wilson 1988; Swyngedouw 1992; Harvey 2003). Within this context, the social consensus based on industrial and sectoral agreements negotiated in a process of national bargaining among the main stakeholders was broken and the power of the trade unions, in particular, was curtailed. For example, individualised agreements limited to specific companies were encouraged, which in turn led to the creation of core workers with relatively stable and gradually rising incomes, and peripheral workers who were unskilled or semi-skilled and subject to temporary contracts at the mercy of external demand. Other aspects of this adjustment included what Jessop (1994, 2002) calls a shift from Fordism to Post-Fordism from the perspective of the state as a tendential transition from a Keynesian welfare national state (KWNS) towards a new regime of accumulation which he calls a Schumpeterian workfare post-national regime (SWPR),[2] where the emphasis is on supply-side initiatives (for example, lifelong learning, re-skilling and creating the conditions for attracting investment to specific geographical areas).

### *Two Responses to the Crisis of 1970s: From Autocratic Statist Peripheral Fordism towards a Neo-Liberal-Statist Strategy*

The crisis in Spain in the 1970s could be seen as a multi-layered economic, political and social crisis. Initially, then, the specific articulation of Atlantic Fordism within the context of semi-peripheral, relatively underdeveloped and autocratic Spain also coincided with the large-scale political and social change that took place in the mid-1970s. There were two different responses to this crisis. First, the Franco government continued state intervention and (almost unconditional) direct financial support for the key industrial players (Cobanera 2002).[3] While such measures ensured

2. The distinction between KWNS and SWPR assumes that the state legitimises itself mostly within the economic domain and thus there is an implicit link between legitimacy and solidarity, which are defined in economic terms. National identities, however, remain important sources of group solidarity and can also play a significant role in the legitimisation of the existence and functioning of the state.

3. This continued under the newly formed centre-right party Union Centro Democrático (UCD) in the post-Franco period.

relatively low levels of unemployment, high inflation provoked growing social tensions, strikes and street demonstrations. Those were brutally suppressed by the police and the military and, in the Basque Country, this also included the declaration of a state of emergency and the introduction of martial law (see chapter 3).

After the political collapse of the UCD (Unidad Centro Democrático, The Union of the Democratic Centre) and the absolute majority of the PSOE following the 1982 general election, the new government adopted a strategy that included macro-economic stability (control of inflation and income policy), liberalisation of the economy (including labour reforms) and privatisation of state-owned companies (Martín Urriza 1996) with the declared broader aim of fully integrating Spain into global markets (Etxezarreta 1991; Holman 1996). However, unemployment grew significantly—tempered by a new political climate with broad social and political consensus for restraint from economic demands (Martinez Alier and Roca 1987). It was broadly accepted that the economic transition would be painful and that the political transition should take priority. However, the PSOE interpretation of the post-Franco economic crisis focused primarily on labour costs[4] and labour market rigidity as the main causes of the crisis (Ferreiro and Serrano 2001). This interpretation was closely aligned to a very broad understanding of the general crisis of Atlantic Fordism as well as to a neo-liberal policy reform as a dominant strategy for its resolution. For example, the first PSOE government lacked any industrial, technological or regional policy (Segura 1989, 1992; Gómez Uranga 1991; Banyuls and Recio 2012). Nevertheless, some priorities were set and the state offered support in the consolidation and internationalisation of the financial sector as well as offering support for foreign investment (Holman 1996). Further, this interpretation of the economic crisis also failed to consider the specific nature of Fordism in Spain and the important institutional and historical factors that co-shaped the crisis. Consequently, the post-Franco economic reforms initiated by the PSOE, but also supported

4. While low labour costs were initially seen as a response to the economic crisis, later labour market reforms, in 1977, 1984 and 1997 respectively, envisaged a much broader agenda in which low labour costs were considered to be the main competitive advantage of the Spanish economy. Spanish labour market reforms therefore generated the conditions for the under-development of training infrastructure and would lack any commitment to a high-skill and high-productivity strategy. Furthermore, the availability of a temporary workforce deterred employers from investing in far-reaching changes to organisational aspects of their businesses and instead encouraged using temporary workers as ad hoc responses to changes in demand (Blyton and Martinez Lucio 1995: 273–274).

by other major political parties and at least initially by the trade unions, rested in a belief that the poorly run public sector and state-owned companies had to be substantially exposed to competition in order to improve their performance. More generally, state retreat, the promotion of flexible labour markets, the increased role of the market more broadly and the projected foreign investments were expected to create the conditions for innovation (chapter 4) and growth.

In contrast to the neo-liberal strategy adopted by the central state in the post-Franco period, the newly established autonomous communities, and especially the Basque Country, negotiated strategies with key stakeholders (political parties, regional interest groups, regional development agencies and so on) and also involved the local provincial authorities directly in developing their own responses to the crisis. Hence, the development of industrial policy, support for restructuring, technology transfer and reconversion of the industrial base were areas of major concern for the Basque government (but similar policies were established in all autonomous communities). Further, the development of industrial policies was the outcome of intensive communication between tightly knit interpersonal networks of leading members of the ruling PNV and representatives of Basque industry, most strongly represented by the cooperative movement (Moso and Olazaran 2002: 62–63).

There are two pertinent issues about decentralisation in Spain: first, the extent to which can one discuss the autonomous communities as independent sites of regulation, given that their powers are mainly in the area of industrial and regional policy, infrastructural development and planning (accumulation) and less so in the area of social security, labour market and macro-economic policies (regulation) (Lovering 2001). And, second, the extent to which the economies of agglomeration (Storper and Walker 1989) (for example, industrial clusters) derive from local specificities (Keating 1998) and/or from uneven development (Harvey 1982) and, a fortiori, whether these advantages could survive over the medium- or long-term (Morgan 2004: 190).

Overall, then, the crisis of Fordism cannot be understood purely in relation to the national scale and this raises the question of the territorialisation of Post-Fordism. More specifically, the de-regulation of financial markets on an international scale (Hirst 1997) made it ever harder to control the movement of capital across national borders and further reduced the ability of states to control the supply of money (Mouleart, Swyngedouw and Wilson 1988). Further, MNCs were increasingly looking to raise capital on the international financial markets rather than internally, which in turn led to a gradual de-coupling of the links between banks and industry on the national scale. In this sense, the changing role of the state could be seen to reflect a relative de-territorialisation of economic relations. This entails the establishment and stabilisation of new forms of territorialisation that may well involve changes in the relative power of different territorial scales and lead to new scalar relationships and interdependencies. These changes often lead to both an upward (supranational) and downward (subnational) shift in state activities.

### *Post-Fordism, Spatial Restructuring and the Changing Role of the State*

"Region" became a fashionable word in European, academic and policy debates in the 1990s and the early 2000s. Regions, it has been argued, have become a focal point where different forms of political, economic and social functional (re)territorialisation and the creation of local economies of agglomeration[5] are taking place (Keating 1998) within a context of the restructuring of the state (Jessop 2002). However, some commentators relate this to "endogenous growth" and the capabilities of local regions to promote new innovation systems. The region (in such approaches) is assumed to be a new site of competitiveness, the latter being purely or mainly attributed to endogenous regional characteristics and regional level supply-side initiatives. Both of these, it is argued, illustrate a shift in the regulation of scale from the national level to the level of the locality (for example, Porter 1990; OECD 1996, quoted in Morgan 2004). This interpretation has been linked to a discourse that has been particularly influential among governments and policymakers and which argues that regions are better prepared to "spot and solve" issues of an increasingly challenging international economy. Further, this interpretation of regionalisation has strong affinities with the definitions of region in EU policy documents, while debates on regionalisation closely inform the EU economic and social agenda and its strategies (associated with a diverse set of concerns and objectives related to economic efficiency, market integration and reducing economic disparities) (Amin and Tomaney 2002; MacLeod

5. The new vertical disintegration/ flexible hierarchy refers to the rise of SMEs, which are functionally different, organisationally independent and collectively organised in spatial clusters. Other practices that facilitate the creation of agglomerations are new management strategies such as "just-in-time stock inventory system" and "on the spot control components and products," which contribute to the development of product differentiation and the adjustment to changes in market circumstances.

2001; Jones 2001). Moreover, this rationale has filtered into the strategies and discourses of regional movements and governments alike (Giordano and Roller 2002; Bourne 2003). This approach makes six interrelated, but analytically distinct, assumptions about the region, which has led to it being criticised on different levels.

First, commentators who draw on the work of Massey (1984), interpret this tendency of agglomeration as resulting primarily from the diverse spatial strategies deployed by MNCs in a context of increasingly free global movement of capital, products and resources. Regions are thus understood as new sites of global competition and uneven development (Harvey 1982; Brenner 1998) where there could be both winners and losers, while regions and localities are seen as a part of broader political and economic interdependencies (Harvey 1989; Peck and Tickell 1995). Second, in contrast to the optimistic view about the growing powers of the region, some commentators argue that new regional powers are just an extension of state policies and strategies of intervention (Jones 1998). Third, it has been argued that localities do not constitute a significant scale of regulation and therefore strategies initiated on the local level could only be expected to have limited impact on both competitiveness and broader social relations. This is because localities have not acquired significant powers in crucial areas such as the regulation and organisation of labour markets as well as macro-economic policy (Lovering 1999). Furthermore, the suggestion that empowering localities is the culmination of struggles to give voice to regional identities is overly exaggerated and would be more accurately interpreted as an aspect of a neo-liberal model of globalisation (Lovering 2001). Fourth, some commentators have argued that it is justifiable to focus on the region as a plausible scale of regulation and economic strategy generation. However, in contrast to approaches that define competitive advantage rather narrowly and mainly in relation to the available economic resources, these commentators (Amin and Thrift 1995; Storper 1997) attribute such advantages to a broad set of regionally based social, political, economic and cultural resources and institutions. Fifth, by shifting the focus away from the state and towards the region, this approach neglects other emerging (and potentially as or even more significant players) such as the city for example (Brenner 1999, 2004; Sassen 1999). Sixth, the use of the notions of region, in particular, but also scale and space, is all too often treated as ontologically pre-given (Jonas 1994). That is, the use of such terms is uncritical and fetishized (Collinge 2005; Jessop 2008) and does not raise questions such as why is it that a particular place, locality or region has become strategically significant (Jones 1997, quoted in MacLeod and Goodwin 1999: 706).

While these criticisms are a welcome correction to what could be seen as an overemphasis on the local and regional scale, they are also somewhat misplaced as they tend to draw on approaches (such as the early versions of the RA) that are implicitly state-centred and therefore inappropriate as a base for launching such criticism, given the (rather abstract) conceptual tools at their disposal, their aims and explanatory scope (Jessop 1995; MacLeod and Goodwin 1999). Some attempts to address these shortcomings have been made through the development of a richer, less abstract, and less state-centred conceptual framework through notions such as, for example, spatio-temporal fixes (Jessop 2001; Harvey 1982), modes of social regulation (Peck and Tickell 1995), local dependencies (Cox and Mair 1991) and glocalisation (Swyngedouw 1997, 2004). However, notions such as "institutional thickness," "urban regime" and a "local mode of regulation" should themselves be a subject of enquiry and may require further elaboration and explanation.[6]

In this sense, different spatial metaphors such as "region," "regionalisation," "rescaling" and so forth have political, economic, ideological, normative and rhetorical aspects that could stand for different sets of relationships and be employed in different strategies across Europe. For example, in Spain debates about the meaning and powers of regions have been mainly associated with a process of political devolution in which the main concerns were sovereignty and the territorial integrity of the state. In contrast, the larger body of academic work as well as EU policy documents on regionalisation is mainly concerned with the competitiveness and sustainability of regions. In the case of EU regulations and initiatives, like the Open Method of Coordination (OMC) for example, regions are imagined as disembedded spatial units to which administrative rationality is externally applied without consideration of their specificities and as a result they are often ineffective (Wim Kok Report 2004). Therefore, more broadly, regions could be seen as social constructs constituted through

6. There are also limits to how far processes can be meaningfully generalised without becoming trivial or misleading. As such, the abstract understanding of the processes involved in Post-Fordist restructuring cannot substitute for exploring the specific ways in which they get combined in concrete contexts, and where they could find different expression given the histories, relationships and institutions present in different states, regions and localities (MacLeod and Godwin 1999).

> historically contingent practices and discourses in which actors produce any given meaning to more or less bounded material and symbolic worlds . . . Similarly, "regions" are based at times on collective social classifications/identifications, but more often on multiple practices in which the hegemonic narratives of a specific regional entity and identity are produced, within a broader spatial division of labour. Regions, their boundaries, symbols and institutions are hence not results of autonomous and evolutionary processes but expressions of a perpetual struggle over the meaning associated with space, representation, democracy and welfare (Paasi 2002: 805).

For my purposes here, geographical scale will be understood as constituted and shaped by, as well as constitutive of and shaping, social, political and economic processes and relationships; they are only temporarily fixed, and are porous and contestable (rather than being ontologically pre-given) (Delaney and Leitner 1997: 93; Cox and Mair 1991).

## Politics of Scale

While these commentators acknowledge the significance of the regional and local scale, they further argue that supranational levels are at least as important as their national and subnational counterparts. Even more broadly, it is suggested that scale has been relativized: there is no single scale that is dominant and hierarchies are not necessarily simply nested but could also be tangled and that, additionally, scales are not just being reordered but new ones are constantly being developed (Jessop 2000). In this sense, globalisation is an ongoing "multicentric, multiscalar, multitemporal, multiform and multicausal process" (Jessop 2001: 1). Thus defined, globalisation requires a top down, bottom up, horizontal, and transversal analysis, where the meaning of borders and boundaries is destabilised and becomes much more flexible. Moreover, contrary to some (increasingly discredited) accounts, globalisation by no means entails the withering of the state but is associated instead with changes in its form and functions (for accounts of these changes, see, for example, Held 1988; Hirst and Thompson 1996; Shaw 2000; Jessop 2001). Alongside the rescaling of old and new functions, there is also a shift in the relative significance of different modes of governance in response to an ever-increasing complexity in the interconnected global environment.

Rescaling also implies a complexification of the relationships between nation and state, and even more broadly between territoriality, sovereignty, citizenship and legitimacy (Paasi 2001). The latter processes, however, do not entail the end of nations, states and nation-states, all of which are still alive and well.

According to Smith (1991), a key defining feature of a nation is a shared territory or claim on a common homeland; likewise, Gellner (1983), Hobsbawm (1990) and Giddens (1985) suggest that the ultimate goal of the nation is national "self-determination" (or other forms of political autonomy) within the territorial boundaries of a nation-state. While there are many examples of nations without states and states that do not comprise one nation, it is usually assumed that the nation-building project can only be fully complete with the establishment of a sovereign national state. It could be argued however that the "territorial trap" underlying this assumption (Agnew 1993) is to a large extent undermined by processes of global restructuring and the associated redefinition of the role of the state. Thus, full sovereignty is not currently necessary for the recognition and protection of the cultural, social, economic and political institutions of national groups. Nevertheless, the struggle for independence -including in some cases an armed struggle—has not disappeared. Indeed, non-programmatic ethnic politics sometimes seem to be mutating into national politics in the forms of national separatism, civic nationalism (Keating 1996) and national xenophobia (Hobsbawm 1996).

We are witnessing the emergence of intricate and convoluted links and interdependencies between (a) old and new forms of sovereignty and legitimisation and (b) identity and solidarity. A key role in this sense is being played here by the process of EU integration through the redefinition of inter-state relations and physical space, particularly through the role played by Euro-regions (Perkmann and Sum 2002) and the protection of minority rights. In the case of Europe this reorganisation is as much highly visible as it is complex and incomplete. The European institutional space is populated by a multiplicity of national, supranational and subnational units which open up a space for regions, nation-states, nations without states, strategic alliances, cross-border cooperation, and so on. However, in this *multi-complex European terrain* (Dillon and Reid 2000), it is still unclear which, if any, scale is dominant. This indeterminacy allows for the proliferation of economic, political, and cultural strategies, which in turn further complicate and serve to further rearticulate new scales, temporalities, and competing economic and political projects (Jessop 2002). Indeed, the debate over the idea of Europe has become closely associated with research into issues of post-nationality, post-sovereignty and post-identity (for example, Keating 2001, 2003). These are well reflected in the preamble to the proposed European Constitution, which sees the European space not as sovereign but as a democratic space in which no single unit holds all power.

Nevertheless, it could be argued that the national state remains the most stable territorial entity, largely keeps the monopoly of violence (Weber 1978; Giddens 1985), is strongly associated with political identity (both institutionally within an international system of states and as the ultimate goal of a national project) and remains the key expression of territorialised sovereignty (Jessop 2008). Given the complex political and economic interdependence across many scales, sovereignty in the sense of the capacity to take autonomous decisions affecting residents (especially those most relevant to the principle of subsidiarity) does not require full political independence. However, a claim on full territorial (state) sovereignty remains the ultimate goal for national ideologies. Consequently, the EU is mostly an association of nation-states, which are defined as sovereign territorial units. Recognising the existence of nations without states opens up an ambiguous space, as such nations, like the Basque Country, must be defined institutionally and discursively in such a way as to not challenge existing states. In other words, any coupling between territoriality and sovereignty could only be limited. The lack of alternative institutions and language to refer to and associate with such units does not allow for any form of territorialisation (in legal terms) of such nations, as this automatically makes them indistinct from nation-states and would allow them to demand such treatment. As a result, notions such as "region," "globalisation" and "rescaling" are useful starting points for analysis but they need to be opened up and further discussed within the complexities of specific contexts.

In relation to Spain, Börzel (2002) and Muñoz (1999) have argued from somewhat different perspectives that the development of the EU as a new power centre is rearticulating the main opposition in Basque-Spanish politics, especially given the significance of regions *of and for governance* in the European context. With the changing forms and functions of the state in economic and political arrangements, regions have several advantages in this regard – especially because of their closeness to their immediate surrounding when it comes to dynamic politico-economic adjustments and resource allocation. Thus, while Börzel argues that regions best implement policies and resources organised in a supranational level, Muñoz claims that they ensure the liberty and diversity of European citizenship. The Basque Country could be discussed as an example of a highly politicised, cultural and economic space, the boundaries of which are, at present, being redrawn and legitimised through a number of different institutional domains (Börzel 2002; Muñoz 1999). These would include the Basque Autonomous Community within the Spanish state and the extensive Basque business and diaspora networks (Totoricaguena 2004), yet it is the European institutional base, and specifically regional governance, which plays a central role here. The combination of these institutional changes opens up new possibilities for both national sovereignty and identity-building. This is reflected in the changing imaginings of the Basque nation. This imagining has traditionally been articulated through the opposition to Spain (Zallo 2001), and has more recently been redefining itself in relation to the European project.

## Reforming Spain and the Sovereignty of Regions

The imagining of both Spain and the Basque Country are embedded in specific processes of administrative, political and economic realignments; they are path-dependent and are articulated through competing and/or compatible discourses of modernisation and Europeanisation, competitiveness, historical justice, national self-determination, sovereignty, and so on. In this sense, the creation of the Basque Autonomous Community,[7] while justified historically through the claim on "historical nationalities"[8] and the restoration of political rights sanctioned by the legitimate government of the Second Republic in Spain, only emerged after deliberations on the actual shape of the territory and was subsequently created as a legal and administrative entity, sanctioned by the

7. As encompassing Araba, Gipuzkoa and Bizkaia, in particular, in contrast to other feasible alternative territorial configurations, for example including Navarre, but excluding Araba, and so on, which were discussed during the negotiation of the settlement and that could just as easily be justified historically.

8. Autonomous community and region are often used interchangeably in Spanish media and political discourses. However, in Spain, the two notions have a different symbolic and political status. Whereas some autonomous communities are identified as "historical nationalities" as a result of historical and cultural specificities ("*el hecho diferencial*"), others are identified as "regions." The autonomous communities identified as "regions" are defined in terms of geography (the Balearic and Canary Islands), socio-economic features (Andalucía) and historical prerogatives (Foral law, Navarre). Depending on their categorisation, there is a slow and a fast track to gain full political autonomy. The so-called historical nationalities, the Basque Country, Catalonia, Galicia and, later, Andalucía, followed the fast track. This means immediate devolution of powers whereas with the slow track it takes a longer period to obtain competencies. This specific system of devolution of institutional competencies is commonly known as asymmetrical federalism.

Spanish Constitution and its Charter of Rights. While this process was supported by the "historical nations" and the PSOE, it was at least initially strongly opposed by the Spanish political right, the Alianza Popular (Popular Alliance, AP), and the military, who would have preferred to keep the territorial divisions that existed under Franco. In fact, shortly after an autonomous community status was granted to the Basque Country and Catalonia (following the procedural aspect of asymmetrical devolution) a coup d'état took place (in 1981). It was unsuccessful and, soon after the restoration of democratic rule, the pace and dynamics, although not the direction, of the devolution process changed with the Organic Law for the Synchronisation of the Autonomy Process (Ley Orgánica de Armonización del Proceso Autonómico, LOAPA): a controversial law adopted in July 1982 that was introduced in order to slow down the devolution process and to standardise the level and degree of devolution among all ACs. This made devolution appear more like an administrative restructuring rather than "national disintegration" and was thus deemed to be more acceptable politically to the central government and the Spanish national elite.

One unintended consequence of the political crisis and the devolution process was that it facilitated new routes for economic restructuring that were neither debated as economic reforms nor available before the new policy was implemented. Thus, while the crisis facing Spain after the death of Franco was both economic and political, its articulation was mostly political. Hence, what started as a political articulation of the crisis was transformed into an economic and administrative reform, which in turn offered possibilities for the political and economic restructuring of the Spanish state towards a Post-Fordist mode of regulation where competencies and responsibilities are delegated from the centre downwards to regions and localities. This process was reinforced by Spain's integration into the EU because powers were also delegated upwards.

In addition to this administrative and legal restructuring, the post-Franco period also brought about new political and economic actors, coalitions, interests, strategies and ideologies. Specifically, in the Basque Country, the PNV, the newly emerging political leader governing the AC, was initially faced with the daunting task of creating entirely new administrative, economic and social institutions as well as territorialising the imagining of the Basque Country, while also deconstructing the coalitions and routines embedded into the previous institutional framework (see chapter 4). The political, economic and cultural elites shaping the ideas, priorities and strategies developed by the PNV have become a dominant force in the Basque Country. This coalition is centred on the cooperative ethos in the relations between labour and capital that are dominant in Gipuzkoa, and primarily represents the interests of SMEs integrated in the cooperative movement (although such cooperation has been intermittently broken, especially in the light of the current crisis and, to be sure, it is not the case in the non-cooperative sectors). However, this coalition has also avoided antagonising big capital, mainly located in Bilbao. The latter was faced with different sets of plausible options following the economic crisis and the uncertainties associated with the process of devolution (Beltza 1976a). As such, between a possible exit and the different futures for Bilbao, big capital has provisionally sided with the PNV-led moderate nationalist mission. Further, the PNV has also succeeded in developing tactical coalitions with both the PP and the PSOE on the local and provincial level, while forming a relatively stable (though not conflict free) strategic coalition with the PSOE on issues concerning regional, national and EU policies and projects. Two such examples are what can be called the growth coalition (Amin and Thrift 1995) in the urban area of Bilbao and the common regional agenda in supporting the Y shape of the HST (both in coalition with key stakeholders such as the Bilbao Chamber of Commerce and the Port of Bilbao) (see chapters 4, 5 and 6). However, while the PNV has been relatively successful in economic restructuring, it has been less successful in making any substantial advances in its negotiation with central government towards developing an alternative regulatory model (Jenson 1991, quoted in MacLeod and Goodwin 1999: 718) for the relations between Spain and the Basque Country.[9] The latter is one of the main declared aims on the political agenda and an important aspect legitimising its other aims and policies. These efforts, however, have more recently been undermined with, on the one hand, the global financial crisis leading to a process of re-centralising state powers and, on the other, the permanent ETA ceasefire (2010) leading to the inclusion of its political wing, Sortu, into the mainstream political process, and thus opening up some new uncertainties as to the future direction and shape of relations with the Spanish state.

---

9. For example, the "Agreement of Coexistence" that proposed a "free association" between the Basque Country and the Spanish state, launched by the Basque Autonomous Community president, Juan José Ibarretxe, in 2002.

## Implications for the Basque Nation- and State-Building Projects

During the post-Franco transition in Spain, the BAC has acquired control over some institutions and policy domains that have given its political elite substantial control over its territory. These are, for example, an independent Basque police force (the Ertzaintza), the capacity of the Basque authorities to levy taxes, a largely independent education system and a national media (Euskal Irrati Telebista, EITB). In this sense, it has been argued, the BAC has acquired state-like institutions which are also instrumental in terms of nation-building (Martinez-Herrera 2002). While the moderate nationalist PNV has effectively used the available resources in advancing its own national vision for the Basque Country, this process has been uneven and has been challenged by processes within and outside the Basque Country. These included, first, the specificities in the institutional make-up of the BAC. This is in relation to the confederate nature of the BAC in which it is the provincial councils of Araba, Bizkaia and Gipuzkoa that have the power to levy taxes rather than the Basque government itself. In addition, the existence of a government-like structure in each of the provinces means that the Basque government often needs to negotiate policies, especially where the ruling coalition is not dominant on the provincial level. Thus, for example, while the statewide Spanish conservative political party, the PP, has been in control of the Provincial Council of Araba, the Basque nationalist party, the PNV, has been hitherto dominant in the government of the BAC.

Second, historically the three provinces of the BAC have differed substantially in terms of their labour-capital relations and composition. It is only under the PNV-led government that a serious attempt has been made to coordinate these different sets of conflicts and interests from the perspective of a consolidated Basque national perspective centred on the territory of the BAC (see chapter 2).

Third, industrial restructuring and economic reform in the Basque Country needs to be understood within the context of the process of decentralisation in Spain. The latter, as I have argued earlier, cannot be narrowly defined as a political and administrative process but is instead closely interdependent with broader processes of the Post-Fordist restructuring of the semi-peripheral Spanish economy and with its full integration into the European and global economy. It is therefore important to note that the BAC acquired decision-making powers over industrial, territorial and infrastructural developments at a time when the central Spanish government –first, under the Spanish socialist party (the PSOE) and later, the Spanish conservative party (the PP)—took a neo-liberal turn in its macro-economic policies (see also chapters 3 and 4).

Fourth, the political and economic restructuring of Spain and the simultaneous institutionalisation of the BAC took place against tendencies of economic, political and cultural transformations at the EU level as well as broader processes of globalisation. This included not only a rescaling process of state power (Brenner 1999) downwards (chapter 4) but also upwards. In other words, nation and state institution-building in the Basque Country have coincided with the rescaling of state power upwards in the areas of policy agenda setting (European Commission), macro-economic regulation (European Bank) and accumulation strategies such as policies of innovation and technology as well as the development of transport infrastructural projects (see chapters 3 and chapter 5). These processes have challenged the reproduction of national identities and it has therefore become increasingly difficult for nation-states to act as guardians of national ideologies. Furthermore, according to Paasi, these processes will not only erode "the narratives of a homogenous national [identity]," but also of a "regional "we," both being expressions of a belief in the (causal) power of spatiality in determining identities" (2002: 144).

The debates surrounding the negotiation of the Y-shaped HST railway infrastructure in the Basque Country are located at the intersection of such contested political imaginings, alternative territorialisations and negotiated solutions operating on different scales. As a result, the Basque Y could be linked, first, to debates about the economic and political place of Bilbao within Spain and the Basque Autonomous Community; second, to its role in the consolidation of a national project around the provinces making up the BAC; third, as a contributing factor towards the consolidation of an integrated urban regional space (van Houtum and Lagendijk 2001; Meijers and Romein 2003); and fourth, in relation to improving inter-urban and transnational connectivity (Albrechts and Coppens 2003). Broadly speaking, these processes have also developed in parallel to major changes in the organisation of the transport industry and transport policy in both Spain and Europe, which have moved towards favouring intermodality: a specialisation of different modes of transport and selectively narrowing down what constitutes notions of public (universal) and private (competitiveness, efficiency) policies. Such a shift in priorities has also led to prioritising two groups of travellers: those who are mobile and who are well integrated into the global economy, and those who are immobile and are constrained to social and economic opportunities that are available within their localities.

The following chapters will expand further on the discussion about the debates around the high-speed train project on the national, subnational and the supranational levels. It will be argued that these debates are associated with two dominant social and economic imaginings in Spain and in the Basque Country and that these alternatives represent two different yet complementary strategies. First, from the perspective of the Spanish government, the HST project is mainly a means to connect the major Spanish cities, and vital for the economy of Spanish regions such as the tourist area of the Mediterranean coast. Second, for the Basque government, the focus is on engendering internal cohesion within the BAC by connecting the capital cities of the three Basque provinces and linking the BAC to key Spanish and European cities.

While dominant, this imagined future for the Basque Country is contested on the regional level. Consequently, for some Basque authors (Etxebarria Kerexeta and Franco Ibarzabal 2003), this scheme undermines the type of connectivity that was typical for old industrial regions. As one of these regions, it is argued that the Basque Country needs a different type of infrastructure which would support economic activities that revolve around an extended network of SMEs. The latter networks would mostly benefit, they argue, from a more organically integrated space, which also requires a transport system that prioritises short distance travel and transportation over the connection to a HST network. The Basque Y is further contested on the grounds of environmental sustainability as well as in terms of a much broader political imagining about what a Basque national plan should look like.

Focusing on a regulation approach, we have seen how economic geography and political economy have influenced the Spanish transition from what was argued to be semi-peripheral Fordism to what could be seen as a semi-peripheral form of Post-Fordism. It looks at Fordism as a broad characterisation of a complex international hegemonic system (guaranteed by the *pax Americana)*, involving a high degree of historical and country specific variations and, therefore, a variety of plausible and actual strategies and tactics to overcome the economic (as well as political and social) crisis, often developed through a process of trial and error (rather than proceeding as if it were following the eternal laws of capitalism) (Jessop 1992).

This contrasts with the academic literature, especially debates around *new regionalism*, which argues that in the context of Post-Fordist restructuring and the restructuring of the state, regions and localities have emerged as the new centres of power and thus also as the champions of advancing democracy, industrial districts (Piore and Sabel 1984), regional innovative regions and innovation milieus (Cook, Gómez Uranga and Etxebarria 1998; Cook 2002; Cook et. al. 2004). Further, the process of rescaling is neither obvious in terms of its meaning nor predetermined in terms of dominant scales and their configuration. Far from being objectively given, scales are "processes that are performed, limited, symbolised and institutionalised through numerous practices and discourses that are not inevitably bound to a specific scale" (Paasi 2002: 805).

Within this context, the restructuring in Spain and the Basque Country should be seen as a complex path-dependent, socially, economically, and politically embedded process where multiple emerging agents, strategies and tactics operate on different scales and are shaped by and co-shape the institutional ensembles within which they operate. These complex processes will be elaborated below.

In the next chapter we will see how Spain and the Basque Country are interesting cases for economic restructuring, state- and nation-building. This is because Spain is unusual compared to other Western European countries in that it was peripheral to the major conflicts in Europe from the start of the twentieth century on. Further, Spain is a former empire which was already in decline before the industrial revolution and thus had a different experience of industrialisation and state- and nation-building compared to other European countries. Francoist Spain, although partially integrated into the global markets soon after the Second World War, developed its own form of a social-economic model in which a liberal market economy coexisted with a highly centralised, bureaucratic and oppressive state, as well as a poorly developed welfare system which could be referred to as a quasi-KWNS. The notion of semi-peripheral Fordism introduced above will be further developed in chapter 2 through a more detailed analysis of the specificities of Spain and the Basque Country.

# 2

# Building (a) Spain: Post-empire, Late Development and "Failed" Nation-state (1850–1931)

The questions of nation- and state-building, and the closely associated issue of economic development, have been widely discussed in the academic literature (Poulantzas 1978; Holman 1996). Within the context of Spain such debates have been shaped by academic and political preoccupations with the presence of powerful centripetal and centrifugal processes in the country (Núñez Seixas 2001; Muro and Quiroga 2004). The focus on the experience of ongoing political, economic and cultural tensions between central government, regions and localities, as well as the difficulties in building an imagined national community bounded by a sense of solidarity (Poulantzas 1978), has led many commentators to describe the Spanish national mission as a "failed state-led national project" (Storm 2004; Balfour and Quiroga 2007). Scholarly research on Spain has been focused on developing an understanding of the processes that led to this "failure," while the dominant explanations have tended to identify the failed attempts of building sustainable liberal political and economic institutions and underdevelopment as the main causes (Nadal 1975; Romero 1996; Romero and Smith 2010). The two twentieth-century dictatorships in Spain (those of Primo de Rivera, 1923–1931, and of Franco, 1939–1975) and the Spanish Civil War (1936–1939) are thus seen as a direct consequence of the struggles over the liberalisation of Spain and the unsuccessful attempts to resolve intercultural and interregional tensions. The violence and trauma of this past has led to the moral imperative to learn "historical lesson"and has stimulated interest in broader questions such as what makes solidarity possible, how to prevent the rise of authoritarianism, and how to build a tolerant, inclusive and stable national community in Spain.

These approaches tend to build on comparisons with more advanced European super powers of the time (for example Great Britain, France, and so on) when asking why Spain struggled to achieve a comparable political and economic status (Thomson 2010). Such comparisons tend to build on the assumption that such processes have occurred in a rather unproblematic way in more developed countries, and that political, economic and cultural experiences should be contained, expressed and shaped by the "nation-state" (Agnew 1994). However, this particular reading of the history of Spanish nation-building as an exceptional history is not entirely accurate because similar processes have been experienced elsewhere (Weber 1976; Breuilly 1993). Furthermore, adopting such a perspective tends to normalise the Spanish nation-building project and treats alternative ideologies as somehow deviant. It also tends to build on a broader assumption that tensions and contradictions among different social groups are unnatural and therefore need to be examined as such. As argued earlier, this book takes a different approach. It aims to understand the Basque nation- and state-building process by problematizing the Spanish national project, and by treating tensions within the country as an outcome of necessarily contradictory class, ideological, economic and political interests and struggles. Furthermore, the book analyses these processes within different contexts and over time and examines how they are updated in concrete institutional and spatial configurations. In what follows, I will first outline three key approaches developed within economic history and nationalism studies in order to trace the development and territorial expressions of nation- and state-formation in Spain during the nineteenth and early twentieth centuries. I will then critically engage with these approaches, and will look at land reform in Spain, changes in mining laws and tariffs, public transport development and railway policy. I will examine these processes within the context of the decline of the Spanish empire and the consolidation of other European imperial powers (Elliot 1989, 1992; Ringrose 1996; Irigoin and Grafe 2008).

## The Problem of (Under)development and Nation (state)-building in Spain

Economic historians have for a long time debated the origins of Spain's "underdevelopment" that persisted throughout nineteenth century and the first half of the twentieth century. Drawing on the pioneering work of Vinces Vives, two main approaches to the question have emerged. On one side of the debate are scholars such as de la Escosura (1988) and Ringrose (1996) who have sought to dismantle the thesis of the persistent backwardness attributed to eighteenth- and nineteenth-century Spain. Accordingly, in contrast to arguments that explain nineteenth-century Spain as a succession of failures, stagnation and calamities, these authors suggest that Spain followed a path of economic expansion from the early eighteenth century onwards. Such arguments rest on their analysis of the evolution of trade and commercial activities carried out in Spain for much of the eighteenth and nineteenth centuries. These analyses have shed new light onto the actual economic consequences for Spain deriving from key historical junctures such as the Spanish Disaster of 1898. For example, the repatriation of capital from the remaining colonies, ongoing export activities of key agricultural sectors (for example, citruses) and Spain's non-involvement in the First World War contributed to a steady economic growth. Nevertheless, while such studies have been able to detect upward trends of growth, they have been less successful in explaining the development of political and social contradictions and tensions (for example, the collapse of the Restoration regime and the Primo de Rivera dictatorship) characteristic of much of the nineteenth- and twentieth-century Spain, and the impact they had on the building of a modern nation-state.

In contrast to these approaches, scholars such as Nadal (1975) and Tortella Casares (2000) have focused their analysis on deciphering the problems of long-term underdevelopment in Spain by looking at industrial consolidation. While both authors argue that Spain suffered from long-term economic and social paralysis, they approach the topic from rather different angles. Thus, Tortella Casares, from a Schumpeterian perspective, explores the conditions or lack thereof of entrepreneurial activity and innovation capacity in nineteenth-century Spain. Nadal, meanwhile, stresses the inability and/or willingness of the state to implement the right policy initiatives that could have supported and/or complemented the process of industrialisation. Nevertheless, there seems to be a general consensus among authors adopting such an approach about the negative impact that subsequent liberal reforms had on the development of a modern capitalist economy in Spain. More specifically, in their analysis of nineteenth-century land reforms, Malefakis (1970), Carr (1982) and Tamames (1986) shed light on why such policies might have failed to transform agriculture into an instrument of capitalist modernisation. According to these authors, these land reforms had at least three negative consequences. First, they led to the concentration of land in the hands of a small number of owners, thereby contributing to the consolidation of their political power. This landowning elite continued to have enormous influence on the political system well into the twentieth century. Second, most of the landowning elite (both the traditional oligarchy and the new property classes) contributed little to increasing returns and productivity levels from the work on the land. Third, these land reforms led to increasing inequality and class antagonism, which manifested themselves differently across Spain. While short-term violent outbursts organised by anarcho-syndicalism reflected the structural conditions of the rural peasantry in south and south-western Spain, geographically localised civil wars, informed by conservative and reactionary ideologies such as Carlism, erupted in the Basque Country, Navarre and parts of Catalonia (Blinkhorn 1975; Esdaile 2000). Therefore, the land reform had an impact on the process of industrialisation as it created conditions unfavourable for generating enough surplus value that could then be reinvested in other productive activities. The land reform also strengthened the power of the unproductive classes, thereby also contributing to intensifying social conflict and class antagonism.

In search for an answer to the question of (under)development and the problem of industrial consolidation, these authors also examine transport infrastructure policy and the development of the railways in Spain and ask why it was that they failed to contribute to the industrialisation of Spain (Nadal 1975; Tortella Casares 2000; Bel 2010). There are three key factors that they identify. First, the state took little interest in railway development until the mid-nineteenth century. Up until then, foreign capital was the main investor in the sector. However, foreign capital was primarily concerned with maximising return on investment and had little interest in the long-term economic sustainability of the sector, let alone in the strategic role it could play in integrating markets and reducing the costs for newly emerging industries. Second, given that the availability of state funds was scarce and institutional support absent, local entrepreneurs and councils were the other stakeholders that contributed to the development of railways. Their aim in doing so was to support local development and economic integration within regions. Finally, while the state got involved in railway development at a later stage, it lacked a clear strategic vision for the future of the sector and failed to offer preferential treatment to national industries that could support its development. In his recent work on transport policy in key sectors such as railways, motorways and airways spanning a period of over a hundred years Bel (2012) reiterates this thesis. Similar to Nadal (1975), Bel maintains that Spain's underdevelopment could also be due to the incompetence of its administrations as well as to an overemphasis on the part of key representatives of the Spanish state on transforming Madrid into the political and economic centre of the country (an old ambition of the Bourbon royal house).

The latter perspectives have led to developing a nuanced analysis of the origins of (under)development in Spain, and have also shed light on the interdependencies and co-evolution of local, regional and national institutions, the incompatible objectives of different interest groups, as well as the divergent access to state, private, local and foreign investment of different economic players. These approaches, however, tend to be overly state-centric in favouring top-down analysis. The priority is to explain why *a national* economy failed to emerge and why a *national economic strategy* did not guarantee opportunities for wealth creation and for a more equitable wealth distribution. The state is defined as a key agent of change, while underdevelopment, conflict and resistance to change tend to be interpreted as a missed opportunity (Nadal 1975; Bel 2012) that is a direct consequence of the inadequacies of state policy and the ineffective use of state power.

A state-centric approach has also been used by political scientists and students of nationalism in Spain, many of whom argue that the political system has failed to support and foster inclusive politics, which in turn contributed to the radicalisation of politics and to fostering peripheral nationalisms (Balfour 2001; Storm 2004; Romero and Smith 2010). Specifically, this analysis focuses on examining the struggles towards developing a liberal political culture and institutions (Junco 1996; Burdiel 1998; Esdaile 2000). And the key obstacles to achieving this objective are traced to the role of the military (Boyd 1979; Jensen 2000), the development of a national discourse that prioritised the "regional" as the site of "national" identification (Nuñez Seixas 2001) and the inability of the state to institutionalise a national culture (Boyd 1997). Indeed, according to Romero (1996) the failures of the liberal state could be summed up in the following way: first, the lack of an identity programme; second, institutional weakness in shaping national culture (for example, through the education system); and third, the exclusionary character of successive political system throughout the nineteenth century, including that of the most stable of all periods, the Restoration regime.

In the following three sections, I will draw on the contribution of these literatures to discuss questions of under- and uneven development, industrialisation and regionalisation as well as the challenges to a Spanish-centred nation- and state-building. I will critically engage with the "failed" industrialisation thesis and with the definition of the state as an agent of change. Building on work in political economy (Poulantzas 1978; Jessop 1990), I will define the state as a site of social relations as well as the condensation of the myriad of interests and antagonistic projects existing within a society. Furthermore, I will argue that the "inability" of the state to deliver change and the "failures" of "ill informed" policy developments are better understood in relation to already existing and newly emerging contradictory relations and antagonistic interests. Specifically, I will argue that the development of a (national) transport policy should be interpreted in relation to the consequences of other liberal reforms (for example, land reform, mining law and lowering tariffs), which created the circumstances for localised forms of industrial capitalism in conjunction with local entrepreneurs, regional institutions and foreign investors.

### *Uneven Development, Industrialisation and the Spanish State: Diverging Strategies*

Industrial development in Spain took off relatively early (1830–1840), although it remained for a long time geographically limited and highly dependent on foreign capital and international markets. Two economic sectors, iron and cotton, located in the urban areas of Bilbao and Barcelona respectively (although the Basque iron industry was inextricably linked to the extraction activity in an earlier phase), were the main driving force of industrial economic growth. Industrial activities in Spain occupied a relatively low position in the European supply chain, and the value produced constituted a small part of Spain's GDP until relatively late into the twentieth century. By the late nineteenth century, Spain had lost control over Cuba and its remaining colonies; the possibility of economic and political dominance internationally had been challenged by two major imperial powers (Great Britain and France, which not surprisingly became the main investors in the country); and hence, Spain entered into a major struggle to redefine itself politically, economically and culturally.

Somewhat counterintuitively, the loss of the remaining Spanish colonies did not negatively affect the Spanish economy. Indeed, Spain benefitted from the repatriation of capital that followed the "independence" of Cuba, Puerto Rico and the Philippines. Moreover, the agricultural sector continued to have access to its major European markets, which contributed positively to the overall economic performance of the country during that time (de la Escosura 1988). However, while economic and industrial growth are useful indicators that can help us refute the myth of the alleged "catastrophic" consequences of the loss of colonies for the Spanish economy, it tells us little about the struggles of coordinating and developing an entirely new economic (as well as political) system "confined" to the boundaries of the Iberian Peninsula. Indeed, in a period where Spain was struggling to redefine itself as a postcolonial project, a Spanish national project was struggling to emerge.

On the one hand, Catalan mercantile and industrial success had been inextricably linked to its influence in the Mediterranean area and, later, to the fate of the Latin American colonies and its trade in raw materials with the United States. It could be argued that it was a combination of factors in the early nineteenth-century –local entrepreneurship, newly established links with the former colonies (after the War of Succession, 1701–1714) and existing overseas trading arrangements– that made the development of the textile industry in Catalonia possible. Thus, after the loss of colonies, the Catalan political and economic elite found themselves needing to reassess their competitive position in international markets (dominated by Great Britain and France) (Harrison 1974) and to face the prospect of reorienting their economic activities towards supplying a new, protected and yet-to-emerge national market. From this perspective, perhaps, it is not difficult to understand why the development of Catalan nationalism sought, in the first place, to contribute to the political and economic development of Spain. From the very early conception of Catalan nationalism, the two goals of the Catalan political elite (inextricably linked to the interests of the industrial bourgeoisie) were to fight for regional autonomy (unlike early Basque nationalism) and to advocate the need to modernise Spain (Payne 1971). While cultural legitimacy has constituted the basis of Catalan nationalism (that is, language and cultural homogeneity cut across class cleavages) (Conversi 2002), class antagonism has tended to disrupt the hegemonic nationalist agenda at different historical junctures. For example, hostilities between the industrial bourgeoisie and workers" organisations, dominated primarily by anarcho-syndicalist unionism, escalated to violent confrontations during the economic downturn at the end of the First World War (1918–1923) (Gerald 1990). This was followed by the dictatorship of Primo de Rivera (1923–1930), which was widely supported by the Catalan industrial bourgeoisie (Harrison 1976; Medrano 1994; Graham 2004).

The industrialisation of the Basque Country had a very different history to that of Catalonia. It was associated with foreign investment in the mining sector of the Basque Country and was thus linked to the interests of the European superpowers of the time. Throughout the nineteenth century, the exploitation of underground reaches in Spain had been handed over to foreign capital (for example, Rio Tinto in southern Spain). A series of liberal reforms throughout the nineteenth century, such as those introduced following the Glorious Revolution in Spain (1868–1874), led to the introduction of legislation favouring privatisation and market competition as instruments of economic development (for example, the 1869 Mining Law). However, the pace and manner in which these policies were introduced (including land reform, see below) have been widely criticised as the reasons for Spain's "failed industrialisation" (Nadal 1975; Sanchez Albornoz 1985; Casares Tortella 2000). Indeed, these reforms consistently put foreign capital in an advantageous position, which in turn made it more difficult for the state to coordinate a truly nationally orientated political and economic project. Moreover, it is often argued that the interests of foreign capital were dominated by the objective of attaining short-term speculative gains as well as supporting the further advancement of economic sectors situated higher up the value chain, thereby extending the economic (and political) dominance of European imperial powers (Baeza 1945; Arrighi 1985). Indeed, at the end of the nineteenth century Spain's exports consisted mainly of minerals, 23 percent of all exports, and agricultural products, while finished industrial products only accounted for 1 percent of exports. Only a small proportion of the extracted iron ore was retained for processing and domestic use, while most of the country's needs for complex manufactured products were met through imports from Great Britain and other European countries. In this sense, the main role that Spain played during the industrial revolution was as a supplier of raw materials (Martin 1990: 32).

As noted earlier, an analysis centred on the role of the state in relation to its legislating capacity, policy development and economic strategy has been central to understanding the nature of Spain's (under)development and its failed national project (Nadal 1975; Romero 1996; Ross 2000; Bel 2012). These debates have shed light onto understanding how changes in legislation crucial for articulating a "national economy" (for example, land, public infrastructures and mining) failed to achieve the aimed for results. Indeed, many nineteenth-century liberal reforms and policy initiatives benefitted the interests of foreign rather than national capital, while also reinforcing the existing social, economic and political status quo.

For example, one such fundamental process was the often controversial issue of land disentitlement in Spain (for instance, the laws of 1836 and 1855) (Carr 1980). The privatisation of municipal land (the law of

1855) that the fragile Basque feudal socio-economic structure depended on (Carr 1982) led to fierce resistance and was a key factor in the outbreak of violent uprisings known as the Carlist Wars (1832–1839, 1846–1849 and 1872–1876) (Esdaile 2000). However, an important consequence of the massive sale of publicly owned land was increasing levels of concentrating landownership and land commodification in the Basque Country, which contributed to the development of utilitarian and commercially orientated practices of land exploitation. This had profound effects on the social, economic and political organisation of the region. In short, it led to the growing concentration of power in the hands of a small land holding minority, who used it to influence local institutions to their own advantage (Beltza 1976). Initially, this elite consisted of a group of entrepreneurs actively involved in the development of the extraction industry in Bizkaia (Montero 2005) and subsequently transformed into a national steel and iron monopoly capitalist class (Medrano 1995). It was this elite which established the firm foundations of the financial sector in Spain (Harrison 1983).

This process was helped by a constellation of other factors such as the "fortuitous" discovery of easy-to-extract iron ore (close to the surface) in the proximity of the estuary of the Nervion River in Bilbao, and the development of new metal processing methods in Great Britain (such as the Bessemer process). This conjuncture created the conditions for the profitable exploitation of mineral sites in Bizkaia and benefitted both Basque and British capital. For British capital, the extraction sector in Bizkaia was a source of profits and a cheap source of raw material to feed the British manufacturing sector, while for Basque capital the extraction industry paved the way for the development of manufacturing in the region. The competitive as well as cooperative nature of their relationship included trade, investment projects and exchanges of know-how.

Furthermore, both Basque and British ventures benefitted enormously from successive reforms that led to the introduction of lower tariffs and to the synchronisation of a customs duty within the borders of Spain. Consequently, up until the elimination of the *fueros* –the charters of rights predating the modern Spanish state which regulated regional administrative and fiscal powers—following the end of the third Carlist War in 1876, economic activities in the Basque Country were "constrained" by commercial tariffs situated both at the maritime border of Spain's Cantabrian Sea, as well as at the interior natural border marked by the Ebro River, that is, around the Basque Country. At the same time, these commercial tariffs were deemed an obstacle to creating a truly integrated market economy, since they constrained the free movement of capital and goods within the national borders of Spain. Thus, the liberal triumph over the traditionalist camp (namely, the Carlists), intent on defending the archaic social and political structure of its feudal societies (Suárez 1988), marked a renewed impetus towards further political and economic homogenisation. Although it should be noted that the Basque provinces retained their provincial authorities and their ability to levy local taxes. These transformations also contributed to creating favourable conditions for the development of a thriving capitalist economy which attracted involvement from local landowners, British industrialists and the Basque provincial authorities. These dynamic stakeholders actively contributed to the development of railways, mining and manufacturing in the region. Up until the development and consolidation of the manufacturing sector in the late nineteenth century, this bloc retained an interest in steering and shaping the state's overall economic policy along liberal market principles. However, once Basque capitalists completed the transition from extraction to manufacturing, they heavily lobbied the state to turn to protectionism and secure a monopoly position within the Spanish national market.

The consequences of these rapid transformations in the Basque Country in the period 1850–1890 were formidable. Unlike in Catalonia, large businesses in Bizkaia expanded in scale, wealth and power. They had excess capital and needed new markets in which to invest their profits. As a result they developed their own financial institutions and entered into new areas of production and commerce. These investments required access to larger markets, beyond the borders of Bizkaia and the neighbouring Basque provinces, and led in turn to the development of strong links with the central government in Madrid (González 2003). Socially, immigration, uncontrolled urban expansion and poor working conditions led to urban unrest, conflict and labour mobilisation threatening the socio-economic organisation of the Basque feudal system.

Against this background, it is perhaps not surprising that Basque nationalism emerged as a political ideology fiercely opposed to the development of capitalist society. Unlike its Catalan counterpart, Basque nationalism did not seek the modernisation and transformation of Spain for the sake of its national constituency, but instead expressed a longing for the preservation of its idyllic rural past (Galfarsoro 2001). Basque nationalism did not develop in an alliance with big industrial capital, but drew its support from small merchants, workshop entrepreneurs and the disenfranchised rural population. In its initial conception, Basque nationalism was inward-looking, fiercely traditionalist (influenced by earlier ideological movements such as Carlism) and exclusive, defined along ethnic, linguistic and religious lines (namely, those aligned with being Catholic and Basque-speaking) (Conversi 2002; Corcuera 2004). This early definition of the Basque nation excluded the majority of upper class capitalists as well as the urban, mostly migrant, working classes who, at the turn of the twentieth century, opted to embrace other secular ideologies to represent their own interests. Socialism and communism, then, as well as alternative forms of social organisation such as trade unionism, competed with the more traditional Christian conservative values represented by Basque nationalism. In its conception, and in contrast to the nineteenth-century pro-autonomy Catalan nationalism, Basque nationalism defended an "exit" option and separatism became a key policy of its political manifesto.

Although Basque nationalism originated in Bizkaia, it soon spread to the neighbouring province of Gipuzkoa, where it found its natural support. To understand this evolution, it is important to first of all highlight the specificity of geographical conditions in Gipuzkoa. The area largely consists of a hilly, mountainous terrain with towns and villages clustered in valleys and along riverbanks. As a result of these geographical characteristics, industrial and rural activities could coexist. As a result, workers maintained a blend of industrial and rural connections that created the conditions, absent in the urban metropolis of Bilbao, for the reproduction of existing social relations. Moreover, in contrast to the big manufacturing industry of Bizkaia, SMEs with fewer than twenty employees were the norm in Gipuzkoa. By 1900, there were 285 such industrial sites located in forty-five towns in the province. However, concentration was low and only Tolosa, Eibar, Errenteria (Rentería) and Bergara possessed more than twenty factories each (Gómez Uranga 2003). Thus, the workforce of Gipuzkoa was significantly different from that of Bizkaia and especially the big industrial centre of Bilbao.

Specifically, the profile of the workforce in Gipuzkoa was more homogenous and it was mostly recruited locally. Local workers tended to work in small workshops and/or become self-employed. They were skilled labourers (for example, artisans) and white-collar employees, and were generally better qualified than workers in Bizkaia. This led to the development of a more "peaceful and cooperative" form of trade unionism represented by SOV (Basque Workers" Solidarity, Solidaridad Obrera Vasca), which was organised along Catholic and Basque nationalist principles. In contrast, then, to the conflictive nature of industrial relations in Bilbao, which were dominated by the Spanish trade union UGT (General Union of Workers, Unión General de Trabajadores), labour-capital relations in Gipuzkoa were, in principle, corporatist and relied more on achieving negotiated settlements. Meanwhile, the provinces of Araba and Navarre remained predominantly rural, and while Basque nationalism had some impact in these areas, Carlism remained the core ideological substratum as the basis of the social, institutional and political life there.

While economic and social processes in Catalonia and the Basque Country were very different, the nationalist movements and ideas there co-evolved and shaped each other. Early Basque nationalism was influenced by the development of Catalan and other European nationalist movements. Indeed, by the nineteenth century, romantic nationalist movements were emerging across the whole of Europe (Hobsbawm 1990). The literary phase of Basque nationalism was more limited (compared to its Catalan counterpart) and the political party founded in 1895 by Sabino Arana, the PNV, only had a limited political impact up to the 1920s. I argued above that separatism was at the core of the political programme of Basque nationalism. However, after the premature death of Sabino Arana in 1903, the expansion of the PNV's electoral constituency and the renewal of its membership, the party underwent an internal split which, according to Mees et al. (2001), has remained until the present day. By the early 1900s, the party was divided between those in support of autonomy of the kind, they argued, the Basque provinces had enjoyed under the Old Regime and those who unreservedly defended independence (Watson 2003). Later on, the consolidation of a more moderate position within the PNV was to some extent influenced by the guarantees offered by the Spanish Republican government (1931–1936) for the introduction of an autonomy system for the Basque Country. The PNV was thus mobilised and actively participated in Spanish politics and on the eve of the Spanish Civil war (1936–1939) sided with the Republican cause.

So far, I have tried to underline the significance of regionalism and uneven development in Spain. It has been argued that Spain's postcolonial project (which evolved throughout the nineteenth century and gained momentum when the country lost its remaining colonial enclaves of Cuba, Puerto Rico and Philippines) pursued political, economic and cultural integration within its territorial boundaries on the Iberian Peninsula. However, the transition towards a modern capitalist society was constrained in several ways. Spain's consolidation as a modern nation-state was constrained by the international dominance of new imperial powers. Nineteenth-century liberal reforms and the twin ideological and policy mechanisms central for social and economic revolutionary change, private property and market reforms, tended to primarily benefit foreign investment capital. The manner and pace with which such policies were implemented by the state reinforced, antagonised and exacerbated local political, economic and cultural interests and elites inherited from the old regime. It has therefore been suggested that many of the state-led reforms contributed to local development, while they made it more difficult to achieve a nationally coordinated economic and political system. The mining law of 1869, land reform and public transport policies contributed to the flourishing of economic *centres*, at the *fringes* of the political centre of Madrid. In the following sections I will discuss in more detail these processes. I will focus on the two most contested policy reform areas of subsequent governments during nineteenth- and early twentieth-century Spain: land reform and public transport policy.

### *Land Reform, Regionalism and National Politics in Spain*

As in other countries (Esping-Anderson 1990), land reform and the process of agricultural restructuring in Spain were central to the consolidation of a modern industrial capitalist system. As discussed earlier, although industrialisation took off relatively early in Spain, agriculture dominated the economy until the mid-twentieth century. Moreover, this shaped the socio-economic and political structure of Spain in significant ways. By 1914, 40 percent of the national income was generated by the agricultural sector, while 60 percent of the labour force was employed by this same sector. In contrast, manufacturing and mining employed only 18.5 percent of the working population (Shubert 2000). This pattern remained largely unchanged well into the mid-twentieth century and, as late as the 1950s, agriculture still constituted the main economic activity in Spain. Indeed, it was only in the 1960s that the GDP generated by the industrial sector overtook that of agriculture (Guillen 2001).

Spain had been a maritime military empire whose wealth very much depended on a system of exploitation and military expansion as well as the control of overseas commercial routes (Elliot 1989). This political economic structure was costly and the military effort to retain the empire led inevitably to the bankruptcy of the state. In addition, the decline of the empire also led to the loss of income (namely, the bullion cargo from the Americas), the loss of control over commercial routes and, eventually, the loss of supremacy over international markets. Against this background, the main goal of introducing changes to the landownership structure was to transform agriculture into a dynamic source of wealth that would also support the industrialisation of Spain and would lead to building a competitive modern economy. However, as suggested earlier, the agrarian reform failed to achieve these objectives and led to socio-political conflicts.

Malefakis's insightful work on the topic (Malefakis 1970) provides a nuanced and highly sensitive vantage point to understanding the complexities and intricacies of this restructuring. He argues that one of the key defining features of the use of agricultural land was that it remained highly fragmented and that there was a high level of diversity of land tenure across Spain. The dominant land holdings in Spain were either too small or too large, favouring different types of economic and political elites and activities. Whereas large holdings were concentrated in south and south-western Spain, small and medium size holdings were mostly located in the central and northern parts of the country. This suggests that most of the agrarian practices in the latter two areas were only suitable for subsistence production and could not therefore produce any excess capital through which to support industrialisation. Moreover, the development of commercially orientated agriculture in northern Spain (for example, in the Basque Country) was also curtailed because land in the more mountainous areas was often held as common property. The land was subjected to strict local legislation by which its uses were orientated to sustain the needs of the whole community (Beltza 1976). These obstacles to capital accumulation did not apply to large land holdings. However, many such holdings were left unproductive either because they belonged to the Church, which did not pay taxes on them and was disincentivised from selling them (Callahan 1984), or belonged to absentee landowning elites, whose main interests and investments were linked to commercial activities and colonial endeavours.

In the nineteenth century, two important land reforms were implemented by Juan Mendizábal and, later Pascual Madoz, which led to the disentitlement of the Church (1836) and the privatisation of most municipal lands (1855) (Carr 1980). The objective of these reforms was to divide up the large estates owned by the Church, to redistribute the land among the more productive classes, such as peasants (sharecroppers and small owners) and the emerging bourgeoisie, and to create independent, medium-size farm units in southern Spain that would be similar to the tenure prevalent in Navarre, Araba and parts of Catalonia.

However, without government support through loans and low interest credits, it was the local merchants, middle-class professionals, wealthy landowners, politicians and urban financiers who were able to purchase land at relatively low prices. Hence, these reforms had mixed results. For example, as discussed earlier, the privatisation of the land in the Basque Country led to the concentration of land ownership in the hands of few families and the development of a dynamic capitalist economy in the region (Montero 2005). In contrast, the distribution of land in south and south-western Spain tended to either reinforce the tenure of the unproductive large estates or it fell into the hands of a new rentier class unconcerned with putting the land to productive uses. According to Malefakis (1970) and Tamames (1986), agricultural practices on the big holdings of south-western Spain were characterised by a high level of absenteeism among the landowning elites. This trend continued after the reforms, and the revenues obtained from this were usually invested in commercial and financial activities rather than productive endeavours. Moreover, for most of the new owners, the purchase of land was neither about subsistence nor about capital accumulation, but was instead motivated by the desire to gain social status. Thus, the bourgeoisie who purchased municipal and Church land acted as leaseholders to small producers rather than investing and developing economies of scale. It is, perhaps, worth noting that the land reforms did little to improve the living standards of the majority of peasants. On the contrary, the privatisation and concentration of land (particularly in south-western Spain) left many people destitute and the number of landless peasants increased significantly. The predominance of such socio-economic conditions among the peasantry in south-western Spain could explain, to an extent, why the peasants found it difficult to mobilise and organise themselves into a political movement. In contrast to the urban industrial centres, where trade unionism and other forms of organised mass politics could thrive, the predominance of the agrarian sector itself and the persistence of big estates (which often reproduced quasi feudal relations), made the emergence of organised and effective political mobilisation difficult. This was further exacerbated by the fact that it was mainly single cycle crops that were cultivated. In other words, day labourers (43.5 percent of the peasantry) were locked into seasonal cycles of mono-cultures (for example, that of wheat) with one harvest per year (usually harvested in June, July and August). In these circumstances, if crops were lost (due to strike action for example), everybody lost out – losing a whole year's income. In this context, it is not surprising that the most predominant form of peasant organisation in Spain was anarcho-syndicalism: short-lived mobilisation characterised by violent outbursts (Ross 2000).[1]

The context within which the land reform took place helps to identify some of the causes of the difficult path towards the industrialisation of Spain. We can further extend this analysis by taking a closer look at how the economic and status struggles surrounding the agricultural reform might also shed light onto the political process. As a result, throughout the nineteenth century, conservative-liberal forces and the military had been crucial to the political stability of Spain's timid parliamentary systems (Boyd 1979). At the turn of the nineteenth century, the most stable of the parliamentary systems implanted in Spain, the Restoration regime (1876–1923), rested on the power of the landed oligarchy and provided effective representation to the interests of the military and the Church. Antonio Cánovas del Castillo was the main ideologue of this renewed liberal system, which rested on a bicameral system dominated by two political parties: the conservatives (led by Cánovas del Castillo himself) and the liberals (led by Práxedes Mateo Sagasta). However, the liberal democratic credentials of this system were very limited. Parliamentary legitimacy rested on restricted suffrage and an appeal to divine authority. The peaceful political alternation (known as the *turno pacífico*) only included the conservative and liberal parties, while its successful reproduction depended on rigging the elections. This process was organised in each area by local "bosses" or "brokers." The stability and capacity of the modern state was, then, partly determined by the existing strong ties between the local landed oligarchy (who had the capacity and the opportunity to control the outcomes of local elections) and the central government, through a system known as *caciquismo* or bossism (Giner 1982; Gellner 1986; Shubert 1990; Ross 2000). This form of politics was more dominant in rural areas in central and southern Spain than in industrial and urban centres. It is worth noting that the localities were politically strong and very important in terms of organising national politics. Moreover, given the size and significance of the countryside in Spain, landed proprietors were better positioned to articulate political demands.

---

1. In contrast to the problems faced by agrarian workers, that is, putting at risk their short term existence, industrial workers had probably much less to lose. In fact, industrial action could only result in the suspension of the labour process, which could be retrieved to some extent in the market – whereas wages would be suspended for the time the mobilisation lasted. In this case, strikes would generate less money for the industrialists and some losses for workers, but also overall social gains as well.

This they achieved partly through their capacity to effectively mobilise the critical mass needed to sustain the constitutional monarchy devised by Cánovas del Castillo. However, the legitimacy of the system encountered numerous challenges. This was due to demands for broadening the political inclusion criteria (for example, progressive political parties, unions and nationalist parties), but also as a consequence of its inability to meet the numerous and contradictory demands made by different political and economic elites. The final blow to the system was the loss of the remaining colonies. This engulfed the nationally orientated intellectual and political intelligentsia (for example, Joaquín Costa, Ramiro de Maeztu, and so on) in search of a moral and political renewal of the Spanish "nation" as the answer to the inability of the state to articulate a political, economic and cultural national project (Balfour and Quiroga 2007). This led to the emergence of potent ideologies, such as Regeneracionismo, which, it could be argued, established the basis of proto-fascism in Spain.

So far it has been argued that exploring the processes surrounding the agricultural restructuring in Spain allows us to understand the problems concerning a shift from an imperial economic structure based on exploitation and military expansion to a modern capitalist industrial system. However, land reforms achieved mixed results, and the Spanish economy continued to be dominated by an inefficient agricultural sector. Development was uneven and mostly localised within relatively close economic systems which were integrated into international (rather than national) economic circuits. Drawing on this analysis, I argued that an emphasis on land reform allows me to develop a bottom up approach to understanding the cleavages, political alliances and socio-economic forces that shaped and guided the direction of state policy. However, it has been also suggested that a focus on policy development and implementation offers insights into the role of the state to carry out such reforms. Following on the work of Germa Bel (2010), I will now look at the role of the state in the development of public transport policy and its impact on economic development and regionalism in Spain.

### *Uneven Development, Public Transport Policy and Regionalism*

Practices and processes related to railway development in Spain were not immune to the intense centrifugal and centripetal tendencies of the country's uneven economic and political development. In many ways they reflected and reinforced political and economic strategies at national and regional levels in different ways.

In this sense, during the nineteenth and early twentieth century, railways fulfilled two main functions. First, a political one orientated towards the consolidation of the city of Madrid as an administrative as well as political centre (Bel 2010). Second, railways also fulfilled an important social and economic role by broadly supporting the development of local and regional economies across Spain (Novo López 2005; Alcaide González 2005; Ormaechea 2012). During this period the more complex function that railways could play in terms of their capacity to articulate the national territory was only secondary and understated, in the sense that the projection of railway development nationally was aimed at prioritising the connection between the capital city of Madrid and the main provincial capitals. In the meantime, regional railways were part of local economies, thus reinforcing the social, economic and political integration at regional and local levels. In contrast to these tendencies, as I will argue in the following chapter, the economic significance of railways grew under Franco and the global developmental agenda adopted during his regime. The economic significance of railways was then seriously challenged by the consolidation of road transport and the growing use of cars. Consequently, by developing an historical approach to the interrelationships among the context, logics, institutions, main stakeholders and economic structures of the different periods in which the railways evolved, I intend to shed light on the tensions and complementarities of nation-building processes at the national and subnational levels in the nineteenth- and twentieth-century Spain.

The first railway projects in Spain date back to early 1830s, following the construction of railway systems in England in the early 1820s. However, early railway ventures were few, scattered across different localities, heavily dependent on private initiative, funding and technical expertise, and only some of those planned were completed. It is noteworthy that early in the 1830s the government of the province of Bizkaia (which could count on its own resources, thanks to its tax collection competences) initiated a project to build a railway track between Bilbao and Burgos. Although that project was never completed due to lack of funding (since Burgos council could not or was not willing to pay its share), it illustrates the significant role local authorities eventually came to play regarding the design and implementation of railway projects directed to support social and economic integration. However, interestingly, one could argue that such integration was aimed at fulfilling the need of particular urban and industrial centres as well as the interests of venture capitalists, rather than developing a national consolidation strategy on a regional level.

As in other regions of Spain, railway development in the Basque Country was closely linked to the complex organisational needs associated with the specificities of local economies. Indeed, the mining industry, which began its consolidation circa 1840 in the areas surrounding Bilbao, demanded the introduction of an efficient and rational transport infrastructure via which to link the pits to the ports (for example, the Orconera railway fulfilled such a role) (González Portilla et al. 1995). While the specificities of the mining sector heavily influenced the beginnings of railway development, the rationale for railway development also included spatial organisation and the integration of markets. Railways were thus instrumental in articulating interregional markets (such as Bilbao–La Robla, León and Tutera [Tudela], Navarre–Bilbao) as well as linking labour markets with the extraction industry, and later the industrial centre of Bilbao. One such scheme, financed by the provincial authority of Bizkaia, was the Triano railway (1865), which consisted of a 15km stretch narrow gauge railway connecting the various municipalities along the left bank of the Nervion River, the port and the mining centres of Somorrostro (González 2003).

Nevertheless, as argued before, there was a generally low rate and number of railway projects between 1830 and 1855 due to political and economic instability and the lack of interest shown by national governments. The 1850s marked a new era for railway development in Spain with the introduction of the 1855 Railway Law. This piece of legislation reflected the interest of the national government for getting involved, for the first time, in the construction of railways. This new legal arrangement established the conditions for acquiring railway concessions and stated that the private sector would play a key role. The new regulatory framework also allowed for the establishment of private-public partnerships concerning the planning, construction and exploitation of infrastructures. This was often the case in the development of local railways. Second, for the first time the Spanish government allocated part of the state budget towards building national railways. This was complemented with the establishment of favourable conditions for foreign investment: lengthy periods of exploitation rights; generous tax breaks; and repatriation rights for profits made from the investment in and exploitation of the railways. Undoubtedly, the passing of this legislation marked the beginning of a new era for railway development which was reflected in the large number of projects and companies between 1855 and the early 1900s. However, it also created important contradictory dynamics at national and regional levels.

As mentioned earlier, the national railway strategy followed a clear political agenda (Bel 2010). Specifically, the aim was to elevate the political and economic status of Madrid. According to Herranz (2005), then, the railways adopted a radial layout privileging the centre. Bel argues (2010) that this decision did not improve connections between the main centres of production and consumption and therefore limited the effect that railway infrastructure had on economic development in Spain. Additionally, implementation of this railway development strategy led to two immediate problems. The question of under-population and its uneven distribution rendered the exploitation of passenger railways unprofitable (Tamames 1986: 10–22). But in addition to the problem of the "lack of people," the absence of a plan to promote sectoral and market integration resulted in low volumes of freight being transported by the railway system as a whole (Olaizola 2006). Consequently, the national railway system in Spain, unlike in other European countries, failed to help business expand and reduce costs (Nadal 1975). It is also important to note that the width of the national railway infrastructure was different from that of local railway infrastructures, reflecting the different motivations for its development. For example, while the Spanish state aimed at developing new railway connections within the main provincial capitals of Spain as well as with key European capitals, a Spanish track width was adopted in order to act as an obstacle to any potential military invasion from abroad. The existence of multiple track widths made the integration of already existing infrastructure into a larger national network difficult.

As already suggested, the development of railway systems in Spain, and in particular the Basque Country and Catalonia, was closely linked to the process of local economic development. Basque railway development responded to the needs of commercial interests (for example, Bilbao–Tutera) and was aimed at linking industrial hotspots situated along the Cantabrian coast. Thus, the spatial development of railways during this period of economic and social expansion tended to cut across interprovincial areas (such as Bilbao–Donostia-San Sebastián, 1906), interregional boundaries (like Bilbao–Santander; Bilbao–Tutera; or Donostia-San Sebastián–Hendaia [Hendaye]) as well as intra-provincial boundaries (for example, Bilbao–Lezama). Moreover, and unlike the current situation, in which nation-building plays an important role in the infrastructure development of the Basque Country, in the late nineteenth century it was local concerns and interests, both private and public, which dominated decision-making.

In effect, provincial as well as municipal authorities became great promoters of the railways. They entered into private-public partnerships together with local stakeholder associations and contributed land and funding. Nevertheless, railways were primarily a private capital affair. The 1855 legislation set concessions and licences as the basis for railway development. The effect of this legislation was felt in the numbers of companies and associations that formed the basis for railway development. This in turn had important consequences for the diversity of techniques, technologies and track widths used. The large number of associations and partnerships implicated in railway development meant that levels of investment, expertise and objectives also varied between different projects (Bel 2010). Furthermore, the railway system in the Basque Country was very much affected by the mountainous and hilly terrain there, and by the fact that many of these railways were narrowly conceived to satisfy the problems of integration and connectivity of the extraction sector and their overseas markets. Hence, many of these railways used cheaper technologies, were built with a narrower gauge and operated on a single track basis (like the railway network operated by the Railway Company of Northern Spain, Ferrocarril del Norte, created in 1858). The legal framework also encouraged competition between providers, and thus implicitly encouraged fragmentation while making cooperation between companies less likely. This, inevitably, affected the quality of services, which were irregular and uncomfortable (for example, journeys would be affected by time spent adjusting rolling stock to different railway networks).

Nevertheless, the development of railways did contribute to the social and economic development of regions, and its effects were more strongly felt in the industrialising North. Thus, for example, the railway services of the Bilbao metropolitan area, promoted by the Provincial Council of Bizkaia, served to transport workers from adjacent villages to the industrialising centre of the city. The development of railways along the Nervion River, moreover, was instrumental for the spatial integration of an expanding industrialising city, which required the development of service to accommodate labour to the production centres of the iron and metal sectors situated at the banks of the river (González Portilla et. al. 1995). The railways also provided the wealthier social strata with new leisure opportunities by providing easy access to coastal areas. Although railway development in Spain was fragmented and poorly coordinated, the regional railways provided some degree of municipal, provincial and interprovincial integration of markets and economic sectors. The significance and success of that localised logic of transport development is reflected in the fact that between 1882 and 1905, overall intra-regional passengers transport amounted to 47 million individuals, whereas the amount of freight transported during the same period reached 11 million tonnes (Novo López 2005: 153).

Over time, the initial competitive nature of railway development in Spain gave way to concentration of ownership and control. Gradually, local (Basque and Catalan) capital was entirely absorbed by foreign investors. Three big companies remained in control of the provincial and regional railway networks: M.Z.A. (the Madrid–Zaragoza–Alicante Company), the North Company (the Railway Company of Northern Spain), and the Andalucian Network Company. However, this concentration of capital did not mean improved productivity, higher efficiency and increasing returns. For the reasons already discussed earlier (namely, an uneven quality of service and a lack of social and economic integration), these companies entered into a spiral of losses and debt that crippled the expansion of the entire railway network, as well as preventing further investments in improving tracks and renovating the rolling stock (Carr 1982).

It is widely acknowledged that the exploitation of railways was never profitable. Although monopoly positions tended to develop within the sector, competition between different companies persisted well into the 1920s. However, the near collapse of the sector led to the first attempt at nationalisation during Primo de Rivera's dictatorship (1923–1930). Nevertheless, their full nationalisation was only fully completed under Franco. The aftermath of the Spanish Civil War led to an economic crisis, lack of resources and the destruction of major communication infrastructures. Hence, in a way, the civil war accelerated the need for the nationalisation of hitherto privately run railway companies.

To sum up, the development of railway infrastructure in nineteenth-century Spain did not achieve territorial integration (at the national level) and did not play any significant social or economic role (except regionally). On the one hand, the increasing centralisation of authority and power within an emerging modern state since the mid-eighteenth century and throughout the nineteenth century provided weak and general guidance and planning direction for railway developments. The (re)organisation of the subnational level, according to a provincial map that attempted to mirror the French *département* system (1833) (García Álvarez 2002), provided some direction to local initiatives. However, these were not centralised even on the local level. This was because there were no centralised authorities with a vision for the direction any potential development might take, that is, they lacked financial resources and a clear political project defining the physical and ideological borders of an economic and political space. For example, Basque "federal" government was truly achieved after the transition in the 1970s when it gradually developed a consistent nation building project. Hence, the stakeholders, local entrepreneurs as well as administration followed the logics of individually configured projects. Although locally developed railway networks were highly "disorganised," they were better at achieving a degree of social and economic integration than those operating on the national level.

Consequently, two broad logics operated that shaped the development of railway networks in Spain: a political logic behind the efforts of the national government to transform the political status of the capital city of Madrid; and a social and economic logic that responded to the investment requirements of a nascent urbanised capitalist sector, although unevenly distributed across regions. The legal framework introduced in 1855 set the basis for private initiative in the development of railways and most public funding was only made available for building a series of networks that would put Madrid on the political map of Spain and Europe. As a result, funding, technology and expertise depended on the development of private initiatives. The investment structure was, then, based primarily on private concession and licences, characterised by fragmented exploitation and ownership, and reflected the interests in local and foreign investors.

The dominance of private investment as the main driving force behind railway construction, and the existence of different interests regarding its function and role, led to a high level of fragmentation (an issue which resurfaced with plans to develop a High Speed Train infrastructure in Spain, discussed in chapter 5). Further, the private nature of railway exploitation became inefficient and unprofitable. Their downturn and bankruptcy preceded the First World War, but it was only after the Spanish Civil War that all railway networks were nationalised. According to Harrison (1995), the public rescue of the railway industries was welcomed by the railway companies themselves. Following on from this development, a vertically integrated state public company emerged, known as Renfe (Red Nacional de Ferrocarriles, the National Railway Network), which in contrast to previous years, aimed to promote the railways as a universal service (Campos 2008). However, and given that this coincided with the economic autarky period, investment continued to be low, which affected the structure, the rolling stock equipment and the overall quality of service (World Bank 1963). Like other European countries, then, railways started to decline in importance in the face of competition from other modes of transport. However, transport infrastructure, and in particular railways, emerged as key policy target after the transition, following Spanish economic reforms and EU membership, which will be further discussed in chapters 4 and 5.

The process of state- and nation-formation in Spain took place against broader political and economic developments taking place from the late eighteenth century through to the nineteenth and early twentieth centuries. This periodisation coincides with the consolidation of a modern capitalist system parallel to the emergence of a novel ideological configuration (Billig 1995) as well as the container of institutional violence and power (Weber 1978; Giddens 1985) characteristic of the European social, political and economic context (Anderson 1991) which is the modern nation state. In other words, the nation-state is seen as a historical product rather than a normative configuration; as a formation that is associated with key economic and political processes within the European context; and as a specific spatial configuration that is associated with a particular understanding of territory, that is, as a container of homogenous political, economic and cultural experiences (Gellner 1983). However, and given its uneven nature (Nair 1974), nation- and state-formation is subject to contestation (Breuilly 1993) and struggles for reconfiguring political, economic and social processes within alternative territorial configurations (namely, at the local, regional and national levels) (Keating 1996).

Specifically, it was argued that the demise of the Spanish empire and, particularly, the loss of links with Latin America reduced its access to markets and resources. These changes slowed down the industrialisation of Spain and also led to a highly uneven distribution of economic activities across the country. Furthermore, there was also an institutional shift that coincided with the demise of the Spanish empire. The centre had to coordinate very diverse outward looking economic and social networks as well as the interests of the rural elites that came to play an increasingly important role within mainland Spain. In this sense, the process of *decolonisation* affected political and economic developments within Spain; and it could explain, to an extent, the diverging geography of external links developed by different Spanish regions and the ambivalent attitude adopted by the subsequent Spanish nation-building ideologies towards the former empire.

As well as occupying a semi-peripheral position in relation to core capitalist economies (Holman 1996, 2004), Spain was also a latecomer to nation-state-building. As I will argue in later chapters, Spain never achieved the degree of national integration that is usually associated with other Western European countries (in particular France and, to some extent, Great Britain). The initial steps of railway-building and industrialisation were supported by foreign capital and railways began to develop in 1850s through local and private initiatives at the local level. These circumstances, together with the highly fragmented social fabric and highly divergent economic priorities, resources, networks and interests, made it hard to create an integrated national market and to initiate the industrialisation of Spain (Nadal 1975).

It was only with Franco, through military dictatorship, oppression and the establishment of an authoritarian regime, that some degree of ideological and territorial unification was achieved. This was in sharp contrast to the failed eighteenth- and nineteenth-century attempts to achieve this through negotiations and a political process. The civil war and its end constituted a major juncture in the reorganisation of Spain. Franco's unifying national project was built through violence and oppression, yet it constituted the first consistent attempt to build a modern Spanish nation-state. It was only under General Franco that the modern Spanish nation and the modern Spanish nation-state, with a consolidated Spanish national identity, integrated Spanish economy, administrative apparatus and social institutions, was finally and truly born.

# 3

# Towards the Consolidation of the Nation and State Project: Francoism (1939–1975)

Chapter 2 shed light on the irreconcilability as well as exacerbation of centripetal and centrifugal economic and political forces for much of the nineteenth and early twentieth centuries. Drawing on the empirical findings of economic historians (for example, as regards land reform and transport policy) and critically engaging with debates surrounding the question of (under) development and "failed" industrialisation in Spain, the chapter sought to unravel the mechanisms that led to diverging spatial configurations of political and economic processes at local, regional, national and international scales. Further, and following on from this, the broader objective was to seek alternative explanations of the struggles to consolidate a *Spanish* nation and state project at the historical juncture, on the one hand, of the decline of a multi-territorial empire (Elliot 1992) and, on the other, the consolidation of new European imperial powers.

This chapter continues to explore processes of nation- and state-building in Spain, and the main focus is on Franco's dictatorship. In general, the chapter traces and analyses the institutional, ideological, political and economic dimensions of Franco's regime, and his success, albeit temporarily, at consolidating a nationalising and centralising political economic model. Largely following the regulation approach (Lipietz 1987; Jessop 1992; Arestis and Paliginis 1995; Holman 1996, 2004; López and Rodríguez 2010), and drawing on the concept of "institutional fix" (Peck and Tickell 1992), chapter 3 will seek to identify the social and institutional ensemble as well as the set of social norms that underpinned a more stable and durable social compromise "achieved" between labour and capital and amongst diverse capitalist interests for the first time within Spain (González 2003). This compromise operated at, as well as contributed to the formation of, the national scale as the site of social, political and economic (re)production. However, accumulation (the nexus between production-distribution-consumption) remained highly uneven throughout the forty years of dictatorship. Nevertheless, one of the main objectives of this chapter will be to interpret and explain the conditions leading towards the development of a nationally articulated political, economic and cultural sphere.

Within such an approach, Franco's Spain has been broadly defined as a case of "delayed Fordism" (Peck and Tickell 1995), peripheral Fordism (Lipietz 1987; Arestis and Paliginis 1995) and semi-peripheral Fordism (Holman 1996; 2004; López and Rodríguez 2010). Franco's dictatorship instituted a combined export economy, in which a gradually increasing middle-class segment participated in the consumption of durable goods produced under a protected economy (Carr 1982: 746–749); wages paired to productivity gains and Fordist methods of production formed, to a degree, the basis of industrialisation (for example, in the car manufacturing sector and white goods), and its capacity to export part of its production; and public infrastructure development formed part of the economic strategy of the regime's industrial development programme. I will therefore argue that Franco's political economic model is best defined as one of semi-peripheral Fordism. Within this context, it should be noted, railways initially played a vital role in the distribution of passengers and freight throughout Spain. In fact, nationalisation of the sector (1942) was carried out on the premise that railways should provide a universal service. However, under Franco's regime, the structure and design of the railway network accomplished by the early twentieth century (Bel 2012) did not enjoy significant modifications. According to Campos (2006), one should assess the significance of railways in terms of how the industries that formed the sector contributed to employment, productive activities (such as equipment and rolling stock) and the energy sector. Thus, the focus on development and territorial articulation were but of secondary importance under Franco's regime.

In addition, and similarly to the previous chapter, this chapter will explore the significance of the state under Franco's regime, and will discuss the characteristics of the Francoist state as an interventionist state. In other words, I will explore the significance of the state in relation to its contribution to rapid industrialisation (namely, from the late 1950s onwards) and economic growth in Spain. Nevertheless, this analysis will not be limited to its institutional configuration, normative framework and policy development, but will also acknowledge the specific balance of social forces instituted within the institutional ensemble of the state: importantly, and during the period of industrialisation, the conglomeration and representation of big industrial and financial capital, state bureaucracy and multinational capital, while labour politics remained restrained and secondary (Roldan, Muñoz and Serrano 1977; Maravall 1982; Lopez III 1990; Holman 1996).

Generally, it was within, firstly, a fascist and repressive state (Richards 1998) and, later on, within a reformed "benign" authoritarian state (Linz 1970, 2011), that Franco's regime developed a series of social, normative and institutional complexes that shaped and moulded the new political economy and cultural imaginary characteristic of the dictatorship. In the longer term, however, the regime could not respond to the contradictions generated by its economic model (like technological obsolescence, uncompetitiveness, deficit, unemployment and inflation), which, coupled with the consolidation of democratic movements (for example, primarily labour, but also nationalist movements), led to the political and economic transformations of the 1970s (namely, the adoption of parliamentary democracy and further efforts towards integrating in the world economy via the EC).

Therefore, my analysis of Franco's regime will be developed in relation to two distinctive periods. The first can be defined as the autarky period, characterised by violence and suppression, and (in part) economic nationalism (Richards 1998) following the Italian fascist model. It consisted of "the regulation by the state of a "capitalist" economy cut-off, as far as possible, from the world market" (Carr 1980: 155). This period was also shaped by the fact that Spain did not participate in the Second World War and towards the end of the war and immediately afterwards, following the Allied victory, Spain was subjected to an international economic and political boycott on account of its tacit support for the Axis powers. The second period is marked by the reintegration of Spain into the international community following its admission to the UN; the adoption of radical economic reforms; and the partial internationalisation of the Spanish economy. Furthermore, in this chapter I will also discuss the nature of Spanish nationalism under Franco's regime. This was based, I suggest, on the identification of an internal (rather than external) national enemy, which was broadly associated with the anti-Francoist forces during the civil war (Richards 1996; Romero Salvadó 1999). Some of the latter enemies, however, such as the Basque provinces of Bizkaia and Gipuzkoa, were given a "special status" as "enemy provinces." In this sense, the "Basques" became the enemy within and constituted an important part of the Spanish nation-building ideology under Franco, and to some extent after his death (especially as developed by the Post-Franco Spanish political right). I thus follow Aretxaga (1999) in arguing that Basque national ideologies, and especially their radical forms most visibly represented by the terrorism of ETA, have become an integral part of the Spanish national project, both within the Franco and post-Franco periods. Suspicion, distrust, fear and threat of violence (for example, class politics), as well as territorial fragmentation (such as the "rural versus urban" dichotomy which played an important role in the ideological constitution of Franco's nationalism, by which the urban symbolised the centre of conflict and transgression in the form of identity and class politics with a profound sense of anti-clericalism), were exclusively associated with the *enemy within.* The *enemy within* became, then, a key constitutive block in building a Spanish national identity and an important aspect in constructing a consolidated modern Spanish national state.

## Franco's Regime: Towards the Consolidation of the National Integration, 1940–1955

Franco's national movement (Movimiento Nacional) won the Spanish Civil War and the newly established regime came to be governed by a "grand coalition" that comprised diverse groups (the landed oligarchy, financial and industrial elites and the military, among others) with different and often conflicting interests, although political legitimacy was firmly based on the charismatic leadership of Franco, whose authority, he claimed, derived from "God and History" (Balfour 2000). During the autarky period, which lasted from the end of the civil war (1939) until approximately the mid-1950s, the dominant faction of the regime was a "reactionary and traditionalist" land-owners' coalition, who eventually, according to Harrison (1995), together with the financial elites, managed to stop the aims of the Falangists' (members of the official state party, the Falange) goals to implement land reforms and to carry out a series of nationalisation programmes, including nationalisation of the banks. Broadly, the devastation that the Spanish Civil War brought upon social, political and economic life was dealt with by the newly established regime in two ways. First, it used institutionalised repression in order to eliminate ideological opposition, stabilise the regime and guarantee acquiescence and obedience from the labour force. This was achieved with the introduction of the Law of Political Responsibilities in 1939, with a retroactive character back to 1934. Moreover, it also involved control of the media, the support of the Church and the backing of the military. This led to imprisonments, executions and the exile of hundreds of people. Second, the new political economic policies of the regime aimed at creating import substitution industries, supporting national industry and making state intervention and control a key feature of the organisation and direction of the economy. Indeed, the form of the state (Jessop 1990) in Spain under Franco's regime could be defined as highly centralist, highly bureaucratic, governed extensively by a techno-administrative elite who controlled all decision-making and who only rarely referred to the Francoist "parliament" (the Cortes) and then again, primarily using the parliament as a consultative body. It is worthwhile noting here that planning and decision-making took place largely at the level of the central government and "decentralisation" took place only administratively and, to a very limited degree. More specifically, all aspects related to trade, credit circulation, the prices of consumer goods and wages, and general aspects of industrial development such as spatial distribution, expansion, and so on, were controlled by and through the central government. This concentration of power, which continued to characterise organisation within the Spanish state after the death of Franco (see chapter 4), created a culture of favours where knowing someone well placed in the regime's power hierarchies was the best way to secure benefits through state funding and through state regulated routes (Cabrera and del Rey 2007). Therefore, for several authors (Grugel and Rees 1997) the best way to describe the dynamics of this alliance is as a regime based on family and friendship ties. In other words, the power levers of the regime were effectively controlled by a few families, among which jobs and other compensatory arrangements were distributed. As a consequence, members affiliated to the regime filled most of the high profile public positions, including jobs in different ministries, official trade unions, and so forth.

The territorial expression of this highly centralised state was based on a provincial structure that was first introduced in 1833 following the French *département* system (García Álvarez 2002), when "centralisation" began to establish itself as a key policy objective of a centralising state. Regions under Franco did not exist in their current form, and powers and boundaries at the subnational scale were reconfigured differently. Provinces under Franco were mere administrative appendices of the state and the presence of the state was heavily felt through the roles performed by Civil Governors – central state representatives at the provincial level. In contrast to this highly centralist model, urban corporations were established in major economic and political cities, such as Bilbao, Madrid and Barcelona as part of the government structure (Font et al. 1999).

As already suggested, the institutional design of the Spanish national economy was closely influenced by Mussolini's fascist conception of the state and this shaped, for example, the development of the INI (National Institute of Industry, Instituto Nacional de Industria) (1942), which was in charge of investment and industrial development, and the development of the Labour Charter of 1938 (Liebermann 1995). The Labour Charter was the basis for the development of the vertical syndicate. The vertical syndicate was aimed at developing a conflict-free institutional space to deal with labour related issues. It claimed to represent workers' interests and facilitate coordination between workers and employers. Generally, the Labour Charter regulated all aspects of economic life and industrial relations, including income policy (Fishman 1982; Balfour 1989). Further, in a context where social protection was underdeveloped (mostly in fragmentary ways and dependant on charity), the Labour Charter made permanent jobs compulsory. In return, the regime expected a cooperative and trouble-free labour force, while strikes were forbidden on the grounds that they amounted to political treason. Moreover, both workers and employers were liable to be charged with insurrection were they to alter or change the principles issued in the Labour Charter (Broncano 2003: 459). This level of centralisation, in all aspects related to social and economic control (including industrial relations), has been used as the basis to reject the notion that Franco's regime could ever be defined as a corporatist state (Giner and Sevilla 1984; Martinez-Alier and Roca 1987). Nevertheless, it has been convincingly argued that the labour reform of 1958, on the basis of which new institutional practices allowed a more "real" as well as autonomous participation of the labour forces in the economic management of the labour process generally, contributed to the emergence of a corporatist organisation of the economy as a whole (Fowerarker 1987).

As argued above, Franco's regime aimed to create the conditions for the development of a Spanish national industry based on the Fascist Italian model of industrial restructuring. In many ways, one can argue that the early period of Franco's regime was dominated by a fascist ideology that was reflected in the type of economic nationalism that it aimed to develop, first after the civil war, then in the Second World War and, later, during the period of international and economic isolation. Although Spain remained "neutral" during the Second World War, Franco's regime openly supported Hitler and Spain's neutrality was largely due to the disastrous economic consequences of the Spanish Civil War.

From on the outset, after the civil war, in the 1940s, the Spanish economy suffered from supply shortages, a low demand market and lack of financial resources. Faced with strong economic and social restrictions, Franco's initiatives were to introduce new legislation for import-substitution as well as conditions for industrial (re)development. Thus, on 24 November 1939, the Law of Regulation and Defence of National Industry was passed. It aimed to "create a prosperous national economy, freed of dependence on the external forces, able to re-evaluate national primary sources" (Lieberman 1995: 30). The law stressed that those Spanish industries receiving government financial support would only use domestically produced components and raw materials in their production process. Further, the law envisaged incentives for private initiative while the state's role was to develop a set of guarantees. Though Spain lacked a financial system that could adequately support large business as well as long-term projects, the five main Spanish banks became central investors and shareholders in many Spanish public companies.

It is within this context that a new law was passed on 25 September 1941, to establish a state holding company, the INI, modelled on the fascist *Instituto per la Riconstruzione Industriale*, to facilitate credit and channel investment to companies of strategic national importance (Harrison 1995; García Delgado 1986; Schwartz and González 1987). Generally, then, the INI was intended as an instrument for reindustrialising the country instrument as well as for enhancing its military capability. However, the main objective of the INI remained that of spreading and developing industrialisation in Spain. The investment priorities of the INI were diverse, however, and included the generation of electrical power with the creation of ENDESA (the National Electricity Board, Empresa Nacional de Electricidad, S.A.), which also became one of its highest priorities.

In addition, nationalisation of the railway industries took place also around this time (1942), with the aim of rescuing the debt crippled private operators in Spain. As already suggested, the railway companies had been near to collapse due to many reasons, including insufficient resources, heightened competition, fragmentation of the railway network and political conflict. The nationalised companies were grouped in a state public holding, known as Renfe (National Network of Spanish Railways, Red Nacional de Ferrocarriles). Renfe assumed the control and management of the sector on a monopoly basis, which ultimately lasted for sixty-five years. In a similar way to the INI, Renfe was established as a vertically integrated government monopoly, and both institutions were only accountable to the appropriate ministries. It is worth noting here, as mentioned, that in contrast to the pre-Franco period, with the nationalisation of the railways they were defined as a universal mode of transport (1947). Until the 1950s, this guaranteed the supremacy of railways financially and legally (for example, they enjoyed protection from competition from other modes of transport) (Campos 2006, 2008). However, pressures from industrialisation and the more flexible and cheaper nature of road transport led to the decline of railways as the main means of passenger and freight transport in Spain in the 1960s and 1970s (Bel 2012).

Interestingly, Renfe only took charge of and serviced the standard width track network (1.688 mm), while up until the mid-1960s the narrow gauge railway network operated under private companies. These companies, however, were later integrated under another state-owned company, known as FEVE (Narrow Gauge Railways, Ferrocarriles de Vía Estrecha), which was established in 1965 (Campos 2006). FEVE operated along the provincial regions of the Cantabrian coast where, as discussed in chapter 2, an industrial capitalist economy emerged linked, initially, to the extraction economy and, later, to the iron and metal industry. The development of the railways in these industrial and mountainous areas suffered from lower investment and fragmentation in its planning and execution stages. The railway network adapted narrow specificities, and as result diverse width tracks were implemented at different stages of the track. The concern for integration (regionally, nationally and internationally) and the need to overcome the spatial limitations of this mode of transport, however, would only surface in the post-Franco period when operating powers were transferred to regional governments (such as the Basque Country, Catalonia, and so on), and new instruments of planning and financing were made available at the regional, national and EU level (see chapters 4 and 5).

Nevertheless, and as suggested earlier, the emphasis on railways during Franco's regime was more centred on their contribution to employment, production activities and the energy sector (Campos 2006). The railway network was not modified (keeping the radial structure it acquired in the nineteenth century) and investment for maintenance of the network and the rolling stock replacement was severely limited. Ultimately, and in a similar way to other European countries, the railway service fell into crisis and disrepute by the 1970s.

The regime's dream of developing an endogenous national economy freed from foreign dependence became impractical and, for example, already by the early 1950s, major industries (such as automobile manufacturing) were being developed in combination with foreign licences and investment. This was also the case for the rolling stock and equipment companies operating under the protection of Renfe (Babcock and Wilcox, US capital, were invited as minority partners to invest in the firms of La Maquinista Terrestre y Marítima, Ateinsa, Macosa and CAF) (Guillen 2001: 103). Other industries supported by the INI, mostly associated with the military, fuel-oil derivatives as well as extraction activities enjoyed foreign (predominantly American) incentives. Thus, paradoxically, the INI became a public organisation of mixed public and private capital companies whose power was concentrated and subjected to strict state control.

The economic experiment of the autarky period proved to be a disaster from the perspective of achieving rapid industrialisation and a sound national economy. While "national industrialisation" was central in the autarky period, the regime provided too much help to the agrarian sector (with subsidies, irrigation plans, and so forth) and industrialisation did not consolidate fast enough. Therefore, on the one hand, Spain continued to depend on foreign capital goods and expertise, which created a deficit in the balance of payments. And on the other, the increasingly depressed agrarian market gradually displaced workers to only steadily expanding industrial urban areas (Preston 1990). Inflation and unemployment led to the first wave of (illegal) strikes in the early 1950s.

Franco's regime pushed for a reshuffle in the government and set the path for Spain's political and economic opening-up. On the eve of the Allied victory in 1945, this began with a series of reforms that sought to change the image of the regime as fascist. All paraphernalia and public rituals based on fascist symbolism were, accordingly, to be eliminated, while the regime rebranded itself as a Catholic and organic democracy (Balfour 2000). However, and most importantly, the growing tensions between the US and the Soviet Union, and the bipolar world that derived from these tensions, turned Spain into a strategic asset for US foreign policy as a bulwark against communism. Following on these international events, a Spanish diplomatic comeback was staged with the signing of two important accords in 1953. One of these, the Pact of Madrid, was signed between the US and Spain. As a result, Spain obtained important economic aid, similar to that of the Marshall Plan, in exchange for allowing the US to build military bases on Spanish territory. The second accord was signed between the Vatican and Spain, which confirmed the regime's confessional character and the privileged place of the Catholic Church in Spanish political and social life, in return for the Vatican's international endorsement. Finally, in 1955, Spain was readmitted in the UN.

## The (Re)integration of Spain into the International Economy, 1959–1973

During the earlier period of Franco's regime, the economy in Spain suffered from a constrained market, lack of raw materials and capital goods, as well as an inadequate supply of electrical power to feed industrialisation, which depended on basic and mature industries. In this context, however, the Iron Curtain offered Franco the perfect opportunity to promote Spain as the last anti-Communist bastion in Europe and, thus, gain international recognition and access to such badly needed American money.

US economic aid has to be interpreted within a broader political and economic context too; that of the US political and economic dominance after the Second World War in terms of establishing a new economic model, dominating a new international financial structure, establishing the dollar as the dominant international currency and the development of international institutions closely linked to the geopolitical and economic interests of the US (Hirst 1997). As such, the relatively conflict-free territory of the US was able to emerge as a politically stable country with a highly competitive international economy. However, it might be argued that the success and continuation of US political and economic hegemony became intrinsically linked to the rebuilding of Western European political and economic infrastructure (Keyder 1985). US influence was disseminated through the institutional operations of the IMF (International Monetary Fund) and the WB (World Bank), which designed a series of economic policies that served as the basis for the economic reforms of various countries, including Spain (Tayfur 2003). This created the background for the implementation of the Stabilisation Plan of 1959.

This economic policy arrived at a time of social and economic turmoil in Spain. Another government reshuffle in 1957 led to the appointment of a new cabinet under the leadership of neo-liberal technocrats linked to the Opus Dei religious order. This was crucial for two key reasons. First, this elite group was instrumental in translating the market-orientated reforms proposed by the IMF and the WB. The Stabilisation Plan thus became an agenda for liberalising the Spanish economy. Second, the spectacular economic growth of the 1960s turned into the new legitimating discourse of Franco's regime. Some key changes were: the devaluation of the peseta and deficit control and the opening Spain's borders to foreign investment. While such measures did not produce immediate results, Spain was to experience the expansion and consolidation of its industrial base and the flourishing of the tourist sector for a decade during the 1960s. It was, however, the arrival of remittances from Spaniards working abroad and revenues from tourism that kept the balance of payments in check. Generally, the growth outlook improved and the Spanish growth rate in the 1960s was kept at an average level of 7 percent (Harrison 1995: 144). Meanwhile, productivity levels in the steel and electricity production industries grew 21 percent and 30 percent more, respectively, in 1961 alone (Lieberman 1995: 64). And for the first time, agriculture ceded predominance to the secondary and tertiary sectors. As a result, the active population in rural areas decreased to 35.7 percent in 1964 and two years later it had plummeted to 16.3 percent (ibid.: 59).

In contrast to what this impressive growth figure might suggest, there were certain flaws in the new Spanish model that were of central importance for shaping the unfolding of the economic and political crisis of the 1970s. First, the state-controlled industrialisation process continued to partly rely on protectionism; and, in general, a lack of competitiveness deterred innovation (García Delgado et al. 2005); but also, this benefited the investment strategy of a number of foreign companies (particularly from the US) that enjoyed access to the cheap Spanish labour market within a context in which trade unionism was actively supressed by the state. Spain therefore allowed privileged access to its cheap labour market for specific companies, while excluding others. These selected companies also enjoyed protection when it came to selling their final products on the Spanish market, and some of them were also given additional privileges for products re-exported back to the country of origin, normally intermediary goods (such as car parts), making the production of final goods back home much cheaper (Lipietz 1982). These developments coincided with a series of policies that were aimed at liberalising trade and encouraging foreign investment. This included, for example, the removal of import quotas, while foreigners were allowed to make up to 50 percent investment in any company without prior government approval. Additionally, and most importantly, the right to repatriate profits was granted. It was mainly US investors and companies that benefited from these measures. US investment in Spain grew from 27.82 percent in 1961 to 48.3 percent in 1964 (Poulantzas 1976: 28). Overall, the strategies of these big international companies, concerned with looking for emerging markets in which they could sell their products and employ cheap labour, also deterred Spain from advancements in technological innovation. Third, economic changes required a level of political adjustment in terms of looking for more dynamic forms of economic and social management. Such changes opened up the possibility for labour to grow stronger while the overall organisation of the political system remained undemocratic. The latter created tensions within the regime. Fourth, industrialisation reinforced the uneven development of Spain. While industrialisation was conceived on a "national" scale, its spatial articulation was centred on key urban regions such as the metropolitan area of Bilbao, as well as the industrial belt of Barcelona, Madrid, and, to some extent, Valencia. Despite the attempts of the regime, drawing on the French indicative system, to ameliorate the spatial impact of the industrial expansion in Spain by developing 4-year plans for 1964–67, 1968–1971 and 1972–74 (Harrison 1995: 145), support for the "regionalisation of industry," urban expansion and demographic and industrial concentration remained focused on a limited number of urban areas at the expense of their increasingly impoverished rural counterparts. Moreover, the existing regressive tax system meant that while real wages increased linked to the pace of industrial expansion, the gains of such growth failed to be evenly distributed across regions, sectors and within the class system (Carr 1982: 748–749).

As a rule, Franco's regime maintained a strict protectionism that deterred the "efficient" restructuring of industry as a whole and exposed its weakness to, initially, the growing industrial competitiveness of newly industrialising economies (like Taiwan and South Korea) and, later, to the competitive economies of Northern European countries (such as West Germany). Nevertheless, industrial expansion was successful to some extent in the light of an economic upswing in Western countries under the hegemonic political and economic umbrella of the US, which also included the development of key mechanisms towards future European market integration with the establishment of the Treaty of Rome in 1957. In the main, Spanish industry continued to be largely dominated by the labour intensive sectors and protectionist policies tended to favour exports from traditional, semi-skilled and low labour cost sectors, thereby hindering Spain's opportunity to move up in the international division of labour and commodity chain. Moreover, Spanish industry continued to depend on foreign licences and capital goods and also to rely heavily on energy imports. Roughly, the Spanish economy was dominated by big industrial sectors (steel, mining, shipping, the automotive industry, construction and banking) and state monopolies (like tobacco, oil, chemicals, communications and transport). Furthermore, Franco's regime introduced laws to stop the proliferation of companies with fewer than a hundred employees and medium and large size enterprises only accounted for 1.3 percent of all companies (Wright 1977: 103). Moreover, these macro-economic imbalances had in addition a concrete geographical expression. Thus, for example, as argued previously, nationally big industrial centres were located in the Basque provinces, Madrid and Barcelona. Within the Basque Country, big industry was primarily concentrated in the metropolitan area of Bilbao, while SMEs were predominately located in the countryside of Bizkaia and, more generally, the province of Gipuzkoa.

In sum, Segura (1992: 57–73) discusses the problems regarding the Spanish economy and industrial accumulation during the period of Franco's regime in the following way. First, Spanish industry was severely affected by market constraints during the autarky period. In this sense, the specificities of Spanish industry were shaped by the particular characteristics of the Spanish internal demand. Isolationism during the autarky period prevented the development of modern labour and capital markets. Industry grew only in specific sectors that additionally lacked and were simultaneously dependant on better foreign technology such as capital goods. The lack of large companies, only 1.3 percent of the total number of firms in Spain, prevented the development of economies of scale that, together with poorly developed markets, kept incomes low. In addition, the allocation of production was guaranteed in the market regardless of prices and costs, while inflationist financing mechanisms were used to compensate for the lack of internal savings. Nonetheless, big industrialists and industrial sites (dependant on foreign capital) continued benefiting from government support, while the SMEs were left on their own and without almost any government backing. Furthermore, the development of new infrastructure such as transport and communications, as well as technology and education, were seriously underfunded. Thus, for example, Spanish public expenditure was only 15 percent in 1945 (compared to, for example, 52 percent in France; 44 percent in West Germany; 36 percent in Great Britain; and 31 percent in the United States) and rose to only 20 percent in 1973 (compared to, for the same period, 50 percent in France; 36 percent in West Germany; 50 percent in Great Britain; and 34 percent in the United States). In this sense, Spain could be described as an example of (at best) a semi-peripheral, Fordist economy.

### *Corporatism and the Consolidation of the Labour Movement*

As argued above, Spanish industry was dominated by the large private manufacturing industry and state monopolies and geographically concentrated, a situation which also relied on low labour costs and protectionism in order to stay competitive. Since its inception, the vertical syndicate played a pivotal role in regulating, as well as suppressing, wages, thus playing a key part in the formation and preservation of low cost labour markets. It could be argued, though, that the vertical syndicate, given its ideological role as a guarantor of "social harmony," also functioned as an effective institution for social control. However, with increasing economic liberalisation, the expansion and diversification of industrial activity, following the technology, expertise and interests of foreign capital, a more effective coordination of workers and employers became necessary.

While some authors claim that the state under Franco's regime did not really deploy a corporatist strategy (Martinez-Alier and Roca 1987) as part of its overall control over the economy, this interpretation could be contested. Accordingly, as suggested earlier, and contrary to this view, Fowerarker (1987) argues convincingly that the necessary legal and institutional changes (1958), which coincided with the introduction of the Stabilisation Plan (1959), opened up real avenues for the contribution and participation of the labour force in the control applied on the economy. These arrangements offered some possibility for flexibility in relations between employers and workers.

The possibility of such flexible arrangements and more effective coordination underpinning workers' and employers' relations became increasingly necessary, and this was for at least two key reasons. First, efficiency and productivity gains (such as innovation in the forces of production, training, new working methods, and so on) were only to be achieved with a more willing participation of the labour force in the changes to the labour process. Second, the rigid labour market imposed by the regime (for example, it retained control over the definition of job profiles, salary ranges for specific types of jobs, salary and occupational mobility, and so forth) impeded, on the one hand, the development of a more flexible and geographically mobile labour force, and, on the other, an occupational mobility based on incentives and professional development (López Novo 1995). As a result, the arrival of foreign investment and the beginning of industrial expansion required that the government, although reluctantly, had to pass a law to make the coordination of industrial relations more flexible. The passing of the Law on Collective Bargaining in 1958 opened up, albeit still under strong state control, different avenues of collective bargaining where workers and employers had some leverage to negotiate pay, working conditions and jobs. Broadly speaking, the law provided two different bargaining models: one that was applied at the level of industry and administrative territorial units, and another that applied at the company level. It is worthwhile noting here, however, that with the passing of this law the bargaining process between labour and employers was moved to the newly created institutional structure, the *working committees*, at the shop floor level. This was important for two reasons. It provided workers with a degree of freedom to choose their own representatives. And this created the institutional conditions for clandestine workers from different trade unions to integrate and be able to use the institutional structure of the state for their own activities. As a result, the *working committee* soon turned into a consolidated platform for labour mobilisation across major industrial urban areas of Spain (Balfour 1989).

The organisational strength achieved by the labour movement soon translated into gains related to increased salaries and better working conditions. Moreover, in big companies and especially those dominated by international capital, a more direct bargaining approach with freely elected labour representatives was preferred to handling industrial negotiations within the bureaucratically instituted vertical syndicates. This contributed further to legitimating the labour movement (López Novo 1995). However, overall, the intermediation of industrial relations was heavily dependent on the state and irresolvable disputes between workers and employers had to be resolved through state intervention. In other words, the state was heavily invested in the pace, extent and degree of industrial expansion as well as its capacity to contribute to a sustainable economic development.

Often, pay and working condition disputes ended up with the state granting pay rises above what companies wished. One could argue that this was a tactic used to prevent strikes and social unrest. However, with an ever stronger labour movement, rising inflation and a looming economic crisis, mass mobilisation became a central organisational strategy of the labour movement. The state, employers and the labour force entered into a spiral of tension that eventually triggered state repression. This was aimed at eliminating freely elected workers' leaders as well as supporters by force, imprisonment and dismissal. While hitherto labour organisation was largely committed to the interests of its members and collaborated with employers (Fowerarker 1987; Fishman 1982, 1990), labour mobilisation turned into a political advocate of individual and collective rights (Harman 1988). Strikes thus became a symbol not only of economic demands and workers' interests but also a political protest calling for political amnesty for incarcerated activists, legalisation of trade unions, free associations, free speech, and so on. Confrontation and tensions between labour and the state, coupled with peripheral nationalism and student conflict, turned Spain into the country with the third most pronounced labour conflict in Europe, after Great Britain and Italy. At the height of the labour protest, the number of strikes could be counted in their hundreds, and in 1973 alone, 80 million hours were lost due to strike actions (Broncano 2003: 457).

Although on 8 April 1976 the regime issued a new law of industrial relations, it was clear that the regime could neither control the social conflict nor could it find a political solution to the economic crisis and the rift that had been created with these social movements. Further, within the so-called "reformists" group of the regime, it became clearer that political and economic reform would require the collaboration of the labour force. "The truth was this; if we wanted to reduce salaries below the average level of inflation, it was necessary to concede political and trade union freedom among other things. If we wanted to guarantee to neo-capitalism that the market model of the economy continued, we had to accept reforms" (Areilza, quoted in, Harman 1988: 318). Therefore the need to guarantee the model of economic accumulation triggered the need to reassess the politico-institutional ensemble that had hitherto sustained Franco's dictatorship.

### *Industrial Expansion and Basque Nationalism: The Birth of ETA*

The above section has discussed key structural changes that acted as important catalysts when it came to endowing the labour force with new institutional powers to "intervene" and demand new economic and political changes. Labour organisation penetrated state structures and used the available resources as well as existing institutional links to create platforms of resistance and mobilisation. These mobilisation strategies were most successful in large companies where foreign capital was dominant and had acquiesced to working with the newly developed *working committees,* in the first place (Balfour 1989). However, Franco suppressed any opposition violently, relying on the military and the police as well as the judicial apparatus (Hartman 1998).

The creation of ETA coincided with Spain's gradual integration into the international financial institutions and the processes of industrial expansion, which stabilised Franco's regime,[1] and at a time when the strategy of the PNV-led Basque government-in-exile, which focused on mobilising diplomatic pressure through international organisations, grew increasingly irrelevant. Gradually, the exiled PNV leadership adopted a more passive strategy consisting of waiting for the international environment to change, while ETA members, who belonged to a younger generation of nationalists and thus lacked direct experience of the civil war,[2] adopted a more radical stance. ETA's approach consisted of directly challenging both the Spanish authorities and the political strategy of the PNV government-in-exile.

ETA's evolution, from a student-led cultural group in the 1950s to an armed separatist organisation in the late 1960s, within a period of about fifteen years, was marked by increasing social unrest and industrial protests which were suppressed violently by the regime. The rise and subsequent evolution of ETA has been widely discussed and linked to the historical context (Letamendia 1994); framed as a cultural response to rapid social and economic change in the Basque Country and Spain (Zulaika 2006); in relation to the lack of a cultural gravitas (language) that could draw together different elements of society into a national project (Conversi 1990); as the product of clandestine operations and secrecy vis-a-vis the lack of institutional forums where political dialogue and competing national projects could evolve and eventually consolidate as an alternative to ETA (Llera, Mata and Cynthia 1995; Medrano 1995); and, in relation to wider transnational dynamics characterised by the development and consolidation of nationalist and independence movements worldwide (Watson 2003).

Extending the above arguments, it could also be argued that the gestation of ETA's subsequent violent strategy could be interpreted in relation to Franco's violent inauguration of his unitary Spanish nation-state project

1. This period also witnessed a relaxing of the restrictive cultural policies of the Spanish state and some Basque cultural productions were released (Lamikiz 2002).

2. In its formative years (1951–1959) ETA was constituted by university students who wanted to study the Basque language, culture and history. In contrast to the PNV, however, this group believed that independence rather than an indeterminate solution such as "autonomy" should be their goal. During this period their intellectual resources drew on the then popular existentialism and global national liberation struggles. The group started to attract more public attention and in the mid-1950s the PNV and ETA (at that time called EGIN) activists met and formed a single group called EGI (Domestic Basque Youth, Eusko Gaztedi del Interior) (Letamendia 1994).

(Richards 1998; Graham 2004; Watson 2007). This included the foundation of Franco's regime on a triumphalist discourse based on the celebration of the "winning camp" in the Spanish Civil War (in other words, the Spanish nationalist movement) over the "defeated" (that is, republicans, communists, and regional nationalist movements). This legitimating discourse was subsequently institutionalised within the new state project under Franco's regime.

As argued before, the suppression of class and alternative national (including Spanish national) projects were at the heart of the institutional and ideological make-up of Franco's regime (examples being the Law of Political Responsibilities, the Labour Charter passed in 1938, and the vertical syndicate). Indeed, the intensification of class struggles, identity politics and religious and regional cleavages (Payne 1984; Graham 1999; Nuñez Seixas 2001), played out before and during the civil war, were widely blamed for the increasing lack of economic, social and political cohesion in Spain. The tensions derived from the "inability" to develop a political, economic and social programme that could articulate a "successful" Spanish national project, within a context with equally strong contending national building programmes (based on conservative, fascist, communist, anarcho-syndicalist, republican, or regionalist alternatives), were finally "successfully" overcome by a Catholic and fascist-led Spanish nation-building project that instituted the form of a unitary nation-state in its cultural, economic and political shape, as a hegemonic project. While this interpretation, highlighting ideological fragmentation and institutional failures as explanations for the rise and consolidation of Franco's dictatorship, has prevailed in academic circles (O'Donnell, Schmitter and Whitehead 1986), as discussed in chapter 2, wider contextual factors and processes also played an important role in preventing the establishment of an hegemonic bloc prior to the rise of Spanish fascism. These contextual factors included uneven development, the coexistence of feudal and liberal market forms of economic and social organisation well into the twentieth century, the long period of imperial decay, the marginalisation of Spain from new forms of imperial expansion (Blinkhorn 1980; Balfour 1997), the need to establish a hegemonic national project within the boundaries of Spain and the dominance of Europe as a new centre of political and economic power (Carr 1980) and the continuing limitation of representative politics unwilling to adapt to twentieth-century mass politics (Romero 1996; Balfour 2001).

The material conception of the new Spanish nation-state under Franco was shaped by the above contradictory dynamics, and crystallised as a national state based on the exclusion of large parts of the population (Graham 2004), which also had a particular form of territorial expression. For example, the legal charters (of autonomy) granted to the Basque Country, Catalonia and Galicia by the Second Republic were abolished by Franco on the grounds that they promoted separatism and threatened Spanish territorial unity (seen as the "destiny" of the nation). In contrast to the "regional" character of contemporary Spain, as suggested before, a new administrative structure was adopted based on the provincial structure introduced in 1833 and the development of urban corporations, such as the Administrative Corporation of Bilbao (ACGB) established in 1947. Moreover, and in practical terms, this also meant the abolition of *foral* rights in the provinces of Gipuzkoa and Bizkaia. The other two Basque provinces, Araba and Navarre, maintained their rights. This was because during the civil war they had sided with Franco's national movement (the *nacionales*), and were therefore considered loyal regions. Hence, the two Basque provinces of Bizkaia and Gipuzkoa occupied a special place in the sense that they became some of the legitimating enemies within Spain (Aretxaga 1999), becoming the only provinces in Spain to be declared "traitors" of the state, soon after the end of the civil war. As a result of this, according to Watson (2003: 308–309),

> To compound the sense of defeat and loss within Hegoalde [the "southern" Basque Country, that is, within Spain], the new Francoist state officially branded Bizkaia and Gipuzkoa as "traitor" provinces. Without doubt, this stigmatization carried with it a cultural or ethnic dimension and served to legitimise the state terror imposed on the inhabitants of the two provinces. To a certain extent, these inhabitants were terrorised for being Basque, just as the decision to bomb Gernika in 1937 had been ideological (rather than tactical). Franco's regime continued to distinguish Bizkaia and Gipuzkoa from the rest of the country throughout its existence, imposing, for example, twelve "states of exception" (periods of martial law) between 1956 and 1975.

As a direct result of this legislation, large waves of members belonging and/or in danger of being accused of belonging to the "republican camp" that fought against the national movement, including the PNV leadership, left Spain. Franco's nationalist project aimed to unify Spain by eliminating all cultural and political symbols of alternative national projects, and by imposing Castilian as the only language for all Spanish citizens. In a similar way to all other nation-building projects, Franco's Spanish nation-building project found its components of national identity in essentialising and idealising traditional culture, in this case, by promoting particular representations of the Castilian rural world and Catholicism as part of the conception of Spanish identity (Boyd 1997), as well as by promoting the myth of the Spanish empire as the foundational myth of Spain (Blinkhorn 1980; Balfour 1997; Kamen 2008). Such cultural policies were developed in tandem with policies that excluded the use of minority languages from public life. The use of the Basque language in particular, as well as any cultural expressions[3] that could be associated with Basque culture, cultural institutions such as schools and universities and other institutional representations including archbishoprics and regional hearing courts were also outlawed (in contrast to other areas such as Catalonia for example, where such institutions were allowed to operate) (Crespo el al. 1981).

Therefore, while Catalonia as such was granted a degree of territorial representation, the Basque Country would only enjoy such institutional and territorial recognition after the collapse of the regime and the decentralisation of Spain that recognised, for the first time, the Basque Autonomous Community (BAC), which was constituted by the three provinces of Bizkaia, Gipuzkoa and Araba. However, at this point, it is necessary to note that while Bizkaia and Gipuzkoa were officially recognised as traitors, paradoxically, Bilbao, where the big steel and iron industry was located as well as the headquarters of important banking sectors such as the Banco Bilbao and Banco Vizcaya, remained a privileged city. Indeed, Bilbao was one of Spain's most important cities. And it was only after the collapse of the regime and the crisis of the heavy industry that Bilbao ceased to be a privileged city (and became even of secondary and perhaps tertiary importance in Spain) and its future more uncertain (see chapter 4). Hence, during Franco's regime, it was the inland areas of the Basque provinces with their high concentration of SMEs and corporatist capital-labour relations that lost out during that time.[4] In this sense, for example, during the late Franco regime and early post Franco period (1970–1980), public funded initiatives in the Basque Country, promoted by the INI, only constituted

3. The Basque language and expression of culture were strictly limited to the private realm of the family and friends. The refusal of the Catholic Church in the Basque provinces at the local level to side with the regime also helped to maintain and reproduce the Basque language and culture in this period through church-related activities.

4. These were also the type of capital-labour relations that would later constitute the social and economic bases of the PNV-led Basque government.

a mere 3 percent of all the investment capital promoted in the region (Gómez Uranga 2003: 38). Further, Moso and Olazaran (2002) point out that none of Spain's ninety-two public state sponsored Research Council Centres were located in the Basque Country and, generally speaking, R&D expenditure remained lower in the Basque Country in comparison to the Spanish average.[5] Further, within this same period, the few research centres that were actually developed in the Basque provinces were associated with the work of SMEs in the manufacturing sector, and therefore their focus was more applied than experimental. The technology policy developed by the newly established Basque government after 1980, and in association with the leading employer in the BAC , the Mondragon Cooperative, aimed to address the immediate needs of SMEs, and particularly the needs of companies that were linked to the cooperative manufacturing base (Moso and Olazaran 2002: 63–64). However, it should be mentioned that the post-Franco period opened up a new chapter for the Basque provinces in which the newly established Basque government had a say in the development of policies not exclusively within the territory of the BAC, but also within Spain more generally. Thus, in addition to the powers that it acquired in relation to restructuring the economic base located within the Basque provinces, the Basque government also took part in the development of policies led by the central Spanish government for the statewide restructuring of big industry, particularly in cases where such companies operated in the BAC.

In general, social conflict has been avoided within the cooperative movement partly due to its unique ownership structure that ensures shared ownership of the companies among all the workers. This leads to the conclusion that there is coupling among social, economic and political connections at territorial and sectorial levels, which is also linked to specific types of labour organisations. These couplings are of course provisional only and relationships among different political and economic interests are necessarily contradictory, while relationships among different stakeholders are often relations of conflict. The latter are related to further specificities of the BAC. While the new labour institutions and labour market reforms had a national reach, labour loyalty was split in the Basque Country. For example, the statewide trade unions UGT and

5. In the BAC it was 0.069% of GDP in 1977 and 0.063% of GDP in 1979, in contrast to the significantly higher Spanish average of 0.30% in 1977 and 0.42% in 1981 (Moso and Olazaran 2002: 63).

CCOO (Workers' Committees, Comisiones Obreras), did enjoy representation in the three Basque provinces (Gipuzkoa, Bizkaia and Araba), but they only played a secondary role, while the local Basque nationalist ELA[6] emerged as the main trade union in all three territories.[7] Furthermore, the landscape of labour organisation in the Basque Country is also characterised by a more fragmented and competitive system of labour representation (Unanue 2002).

In many ways, social and labour struggles became an integral part of ETA's meaning, identity, aims and objectives. Throughout the 1960s and 1970s ETA experienced several internal splits and redefinitions of its objectives, ranging from cultural and national goals through to the protection of workers' rights and the broader anti-capitalist struggle. During the 1970s, out of the two prominent factions within ETA, ETA political-military and ETA military, it was the latter that continued the armed struggle, while ETA politico-military integrated into the Spanish political system when its members renounced armed struggle and formed the EE (Basque Left, Euskadiko Ezkerra) political party. Initially, then, ETA drew support primarily from industrial workers demanding better social conditions, a struggle which also became associated with a struggle for liberation from Franco's regime. After the split, however, ETA focused primarily on issues of Basque sovereignty and its socialist ideals were reduced to only a secondary priority (Letamendia 1994). From the mid-1990s onwards, then, ETA's support, which was hitherto socially broader among the working classes in the Basque Country, became mostly reliant on the support of those workers who had a stronger nationalist outlook and who also tended to be more closely associated with the SMEs predominant in the inland areas of Bizkaia and Gipuzkoa.

The restructuring of ETA was further related to changes in the broader political landscape in the Basque Country. Thus, the post Franco transition saw the reestablishment of the PNV as well as the emergence of new Basque nationalist political movements such as KAS (Patriotic Socialist Coordinating Council, Koordinadora Abertzale Sozialista) and HB

---

6. The SOV trade union that was discussed earlier was later transformed into ELA. This change largely related to the secularisation of the trade union.

7. Electoral results in 2006 showed that ELA had 40.7% of representatives in the BAC, followed way behind by the statewide trade unions CCOO and UGT, with only half of the representatives in contrast to ELA. In "ELA se mantiene como primera fuerza sindical del País Vasco, con el 40% de la representación," *El Diario Vasco*, 8 February 2007.

(Popular Unity, Herri Batasuna), both of which were related to the split in the radical nationalist movement and its participation in the democratic political process. More specifically, KAS set up an agenda of a democratic transition to Basque independence, in which the Basque Country included Navarre, the three Basque provinces of Gipuzkoa, Araba and Bizkaia and the three French Basque provinces of the Atlantic Pyrenees *département*. The KAS "alternative" was largely endorsed by the newly created (1978) Basque political party HB. Both KAS and HB were subsequently outlawed (2003) and ceased to participate within the legitimate political process until the regional (autonomous) elections of October 2012, when in a new coalition, Bildu (which includes the political parties of EA, Alternatiba and Sortu), it obtained 20 percent of the vote and twenty-one of the seventy-five seats in the parliament of the BAC. The legalisation of HB (currently termed Sortu, Create), follows the process of ETA's permanent ceasefire (announced in 2010) and changes within its political strategy which has abandoned a traditional anti-systemic stance, endorsed the political process route to independence and shifted towards a more social-democratic strategy rather than socialism (Beltza 2012; Letamendia 2013; Whitfield 2014).

## Crisis of State Legitimacy and Political and Economic Downturn, 1975–1982

The 1970s were characterised by a major international economic crisis. This serious economic downturn was symbolised by the oil crisis of 1973 and the collapse of the Bretton Woods agreements. The Spanish economic model of industrial expansion was crippled by the soaring prices of energy imports and a continued dependency on foreign investment as well as technology imports. Inflation and a continuing negative balance of payments were threatening living standards and jobs in the principle industrial centres of Spain, primarily located in the Basque Country, Catalonia, Madrid and Valencia. As a result, labour and regional cleavages became major political issues that the regime had to deal with. As a result, the need for economic reforms and desperate industrial restructuring as well as the inability of state institutions and the administration to unite and organise diverse interest groups also coincided with an internal political crisis regarding the question of the future direction of the dictatorship.

In other words, the solution to the political and economic crisis had to include some kind of transformation into a new political order (that of parliamentary democracy), aimed at the refounding of a new state based on a new constitutive power endowed with renewed legitimacy (Ruipérez 2002) to carry out political and economic reforms (further, it could be argued that this new constitutive power aimed also to displace or, at least, minimise the organised power of labour while at the same time the state would regain control over the political and economic initiative).

In this respect, after Franco's death in 1975 the "birth" of a Spanish parliament based on universal suffrage followed the self-dissolution of the regime's parliamentary institution after the approval of the Law for Political Reform in September 1976. This inaugurated a new social contract between that segment of the Spanish population that had been hitherto excluded from politics and state institutions (since Franco's legitimacy only depended on "God and History" at the expense of the citizens). The inclusion and constitutive character of this act was further reinforced when the new parliament headed by Adolfo Suárez, a former minister in the Francoist regime, called for a referendum to ratify the new law on 15 December 1976, which was then followed by the first general elections since the Second Republic, on 15 June 1977. These crucial steps became important for two reasons. First, it was the "Spanish people" who were the new source of power and legitimacy of the new state (and not the labour movement). Second, the parliament and the decisions taken by and/or on behalf of the parliament by the newly legalised and elected political parties became the new consensus on which political and economic decisions could be enforced. However, it could be argued that the real test as well as consolidation of this newly inaugurated constitutive power was the development and approval of the Spanish Constitution in 1978. Its approval symbolised the consensus and the union of different political and social sensitivities in society, including, but not exclusively, that of the labour movement (Escribano Collado 1985).

To be sure, not only was there a case to be made regarding the relationship between the evolution and consolidation of the labour movement and the crisis of Franco's state, but the process through which a new political consensus could be built had to integrate the views and demands of the political opposition (represented by the POSE and PCE, and mainly Catalan nationalism), and representatives of the labour movement. Thus, the adoption of the Constitution (prior discussion on which excluded Basque nationalist parties), but also the Moncloa Pacts (1977), could be interpreted as political efforts to translate the political demands of the labour movement into practical results, which was a precondition for the Spanish government to be able to implement the industrial and economic reforms that would mostly have an impact precisely on those same labour movement (Bermeo 1994). In this sense, the constitutional text could in part be read as an attempt at reconciling the demands of different political and economic interests in Spain. These included, for example, the recognition of employers and trade unions; the right of workers to strike; the right to work; the right to freely join a trade union; the right to collective labour bargaining between workers and employers' representatives; and the binding force of the agreements. The transition from an authoritarian dictatorship to a parliamentary democracy might, then, be explained in relation to the need of the state to seek new legitimating instances to overcome the political and economic crisis of the 1970s. While the political and economic aspects of the post-Franco period will be discussed in the following two chapters, it is worth mentioning here a couple of key changes that had an impact on the political, institutional and territorial as well as economic dimension of the Basque Country. As such, the political changes in Spain began soon after Franco's death in 1975. These changes led to a process of profound political restructuring that radically redefined the centralised state structure on which Franco's regime was based, including the territorial expression of state power. It has already been suggested that the implementation of a parliamentary democracy and a constitutional settlement aimed at finding new legitimating sources and bringing together key social and economic forces within a new institutional arrangement to facilitate the necessary economic restructuring. This inaugurated a period of "politics of consensus" (Pérez-Díaz 1993) which redefined, institutionalised as well as legitimised the parameters and "rules of engagement" that would guide the labour and industrial reforms throughout 1980s and 1990s.

Moreover, though, the constitutional settlement extended towards integrating and dealing with the question of "regionalism." The Constitution strived to strike a compromise that included addressing the cultural, linguistic and the political aspirations of regionalisms while, simultaneously, it drew the parameters of regionalisation; partly, it could be argued, as a response to the need to search for alternative mechanisms of decision-making and economic control (García de Enterría 1976), but also as way to having to avoid facing problems (Le Galès and Lequesne 1998) such as industrial restructuring, unemployment and budget cuts that affected regional areas like the Basque Country greatly. However, this "compromise" was ambiguous and at times contradictory, which has led some authors to suggest that the Constitution should be treated as a flexible and an open-ended document (Colomer 1998; Colino 2009; Keating and Wilson 2009). Therefore, as far as cultural and territorial recognition is concerned, for example, the Constitution aimed to achieve a balance between a unitary vision of the nation-state, on the one hand, and the recognition of existing "nationalities" within the territorial boundaries of Spain, on the other. This included recognising minority languages as co-official for the first time, although this was limited to those geographical areas where the language was spoken. In contrast, however, in its Article 3 the Spanish Constitution clearly gave a special status to the Spanish nation because it established the duty of all Spanish citizens to know and speak the Spanish language. Further, Article 8 of the Constitution made a provision for the use of military force in the event of any attempted secession, giving the military a central role as a guardian of the territorial integrity of the Spanish state.

The new Spanish Constitution, as a result, met with different reactions by sections of the Basque society, with only 35 percent of those who voted in the referendum to ratify it backing it. The two major Basque political parties representing the nationalist vote, the PNV and HB (KAS was a nationalist political movement that did not take part in the elections), adopted a very different stance in relation to the Constitution. While the PNV was, from the outset of the transition, actively engaged in the political process, defending a broad autonomy for the Basque Country, HB refused to participate in almost any of the political institutions defined within the Spanish Constitution.

The farthest reaching changes established within the new Spanish Constitution were related to the process of decentralisation in Spain and were mostly associated with the creation of seventeen autonomous communities (ACs). Although the initial aim of this process was in part to accommodate the claims made by regionally based (mainly Basque and Catalan and to a lesser extent Galician) minority nationalities, the process of devolution was a key mechanism for delegating state powers that extended to other parts of Spain, mostly on administrative grounds. More specifically, the Basque AC obtained exclusive juridical and administrative powers over issues related to health, education, culture (including its own TV station), industrial policy, innovation, a regional police, infrastructures as well as, and perhaps most importantly, a special fiscal status,[8]

8. Such competences are not exclusively given to the Basque Country, and the Autonomous Community of Navarre has a similar arrangement.

which allowed the BAC to collect taxes within its own territory (Gómez Uranga and Etxebarria 2000). Nevertheless, the special powers given to the BAC should not be overstated. These issues are discussed further in the next chapter and, for now, I would like to simply stress that devolution in Spain was as much a political as an economic process.

As I have demonstrated, key political, economic, institutional and cultural dimensions underpinned Franco's nation and state project. In doing so, I drew broadly on the theoretical contribution of the regulation approach to discuss and advance further the debate on the question of uneven development in Spain, but also to unravel the contradictions associated with its normative, social and institutional temporary compromise as well as the paradoxes intrinsic to its industry based economic growth model. This was helpful in order to identify the diverse set of coalitions and contradictions operating at different scales within Spain, even at the time of a firmly established nation(al) state political economic project. In the case of the Basque provinces, and in a similar way to the situation during the pre-Franco period, Franco's regime of regulation and accumulation also contributed to the fragmentation of interests and allegiances there. This fragmentation ran within and across class, regional and identity lines, in which large capital and the organised labour movement, along (clandestine) syndicalist principles and strategies, coexisted in Bilbao, although this was not the case for Gipuzkoa and the rest of Bizkaia. The latter continued to be dominated by small businesses for whom the main markets were local, while conflicts with workers were mainly resolved through negotiations within the type of business structures organised along cooperative lines. Consequently, identity and class in the Basque provinces continued to be played out in a complex way and according to particular locations. Moreover, and despite the repressive nature of the regime, the private and clandestine spaces offered by clubs, family, local churches, and so on (Heiberg 1989) provided the institutional spaces that would allow for the continued reproduction of a Basque national and identity-oriented vision, which was later to be condensed mostly visibly in the radical organisation ETA.

However, while the process and direction of accumulation contributed to the ongoing uneven development in Spain, Franco's regime succeeded in establishing the longest and, perhaps, most durable social, normative and institutional compromise nationally since the late nineteenth century in Spain. Not only did it succeed in establishing the parameters of and possibilities for a politico-institutional space delimiting, to a degree, the boundaries for a new cultural imaginary and political action (which was crystallised within the later constitutional order), but it also laid the foundations for a more stable capitalist state which, partially reformed, constituted the basis for the politico-economic model underpinning the post-Franco period.

Now I turn to a closer examination of the interplay of the different legacies and the changes that took place after the death of Franco and the establishment of the dominance of the Christian democratic nationalist party, the PNV, in the Basque Country. I will argue that, despite the significant political restructuring that took place with the institutionalisation of the so-called State of Autonomies (the new state model envisaged by the Spanish Constitution), the new democratic regime in Spain is characterised by a parliamentary system with a strong government, a predominantly national economy and the dominance of the state as a broker in policy and agenda setting in supranational forums, such as the EU (Heywood 1998).

Nevertheless, and while the process of devolution has been generally accepted as legitimate (Colino 2008), it has also been at the centre of academic and political debate in relation to questions about the fitness of the structure to address questions of social and economic uneven development in Spain. These debates have also been framed around concerns about social solidarity and territorial cohesion, developed by the Spanish centre-left and centre-right parties.

My contention in subsequent chapters is that the "transition" from dictatorship to parliamentary democracy should not be narrowly interpreted as a political restructuring in search for a new political and social compromise defined along cultural and identity politics (although such a discourse is clearly predominant in academic literature). But, more broadly, the "transition" should be interpreted as a political economic reform carried out in response to pressures of global economic restructuring and, in particular, EU integration. More specifically, I will argue that the political economic reforms undertaken following the death of Franco sought to address the need for a new "institutional fix" (Peck and Tickell 1992) able to accommodate a new regime of accumulation centred around the growing significance of urban centres associated with new economic growth models based on the development of urban regeneration projects and transport infrastructure policies (Swyngedouw, Mouleart and Rodríguez 2002; Rodíguez, Moulear and Swyngedouw 2003; González 2006; Logan and Molotch 2007; Harvey 2006). It is within this context that the emergence of the region (as a set of institutional and political competences, cultural imaginaries and political and economic stakeholders) should also be interpreted as an actor in the process underpinning the new mode of accumulation (for example, via the planning, execution, and distribution of resources), but also as the site of struggles and tensions over different national projects articulated through the legacy of different political alliances, the economic sector and associated labour-capital articulations.

# 4

# Modernisation and Institutional Change within the Context of Post-Fordist Restructuring

The crisis of Atlantic Fordism (Lipietz 1987; Agglieta 1979; Jessop 1992; 1994) had many ramifications for the political and economic "transition" in Spain. The crisis of semi-peripheral Fordism in Spain (Holman 1996; López and Rodríguez 2010), unlike in other parts of Europe, coincided with the major political reforms towards democratisation that followed Franco's death. It was the latter events however, rather than the economic crisis and the broader economic restructuring in the country, which took precedence in the imagining and analysis of restructuring in Spain. Thus "the transition in Spain" has widely been discussed and interpreted as a mainly national, internal to the country, political crisis that was "successfully" overcome due to the abilities, skills and willingness of the reformist political elite of Franco's regime, under the leadership of Adolfo Suárez as well as due to the political moderation exercised by the political opposition (such as the Spanish Communist Party, Partido Comunista de España, PCE) (Gunther 1992). In general, approaches to the Spanish transition tend to offer actor-centred explanations, emphasise the role played by political culture (namely, the new norms, values and principles informing the actions and strategies of political actors such as the notion of democracy "as the only game in town"), the building of consensus politics (Pérez Díaz 1993; Encarnación1997) and the continuities and discontinuities in, primarily, formal political institutions (Linz and Stepan 1996). Importantly here, the "successful" end of the political restructuring was also seen as legitimising the Spanish state as a nation-state and therefore making any claim for further devolution problematic. The political reforms were deemed to have then been followed by a "realisation" of the need for an economic reform, while EU membership has been widely interpreted as the final step on the road towards "normalisation" in Spain (Moreno 2001; Royo and Christopher 2003; Closa and Heywood 2004).

In this chapter, I argue that the post-Franco "transition" needs to be discussed in the context of a whole set of political and economic changes, such as the crisis of Fordism and the ongoing political and economic restructuring of Europe, which were simultaneously occurring on the global, European, national and local levels. Thus, more specifically, Spain was faced with a crisis of the economic model based on industrialisation and the institutions regulating it. This crisis was articulated through a crisis of the Spanish centralised and interventionist model of state, and was unfolding simultaneously with a crisis of the political and economic institutions regulating advanced Fordist economies more generally (García de Enterría 1972; Jessop 1993, 1997).

Addressing these series of crises implied a need to construct an alternative model which, however, required a mandate for implementing substantial economic and administrative changes and for consolidating a "new" institutional ensemble with the ability to redraw the balance of interests and the rearticulate conflicts between different social groups. This would appear to have been a very difficult task at a time when Spain was also faced with a crisis of legitimacy of the existing elites and institutions after the death of Franco. However, it was also the case that a broad spectrum of players was willing to work towards a "democratic" solution (Fraser 1976; Holman 1996), forming highly unlikely and improbable alliances among often contradictory and antagonistic political, but also economic and social, interests and visions for the future. These included coalitions on the national and regional levels between, for example, the PSOE, former Francoist Ministers, Spanish financial institutions, large foreign investors in Spain, on the one hand, and small businesses, labour organisations, formerly illegal nationalist parties on the other (Beltza 1976a), and could be described as a process designed to construct a new hegemonic bloc and a new hegemonic project (Gramsci 1971).

Importantly, the transition in Spain also coincided with a couple of other significant developments both within the EU and in Spain. Thus, the post-Franco transition occurred when the European Community (EC) was trying to overcome a period of "sclerosis," "crisis" and "stagnation"[1] and developed a policy agenda to boost transport infrastructures, and in

---

1. These notions were all very prominent in the EC as well as in political and economic analyses that questioned the overall future of the EC and the European project. The ERT became a powerful player in shaping the direction of this change, dominated by the idea of Europe as a common market.

particular, as a part of an industrial policy for employment, growth and technology development. This agenda was supported by the president of the European Commission (between 1985 and 1995), Jacque Delors, and was actively promoted by the growing strength of the European Round Table of Industrialists (ERT) (Apeldroon 2002), voicing the opinion of large European businesses. This new European project envisaged continuing market integration and, most importantly, the acceleration of the European Monetary Union (EMU). Both objectives became guiding political and economic priorities as part of Spain's EC membership in 1986. In addition, this was a period when important breakthroughs took place between France and Spain regarding the handling of ETA. Under Franco's regime, France allowed ETA members to reside there as refugees; this policy changed in the late 1980s when an agreement between France and Spain was reached to extradite ETA refugees to Spain (Woodworth 2001). Further, while economic reforms tend to be discussed in the academic literature and in public discourses as a *Spanish* problem, their negative social and economic consequences were most acute in the Basque Country and Catalonia, the geographical areas of Spain where the industrial base of the country was concentrated. For example, two of the three provinces in the Basque Country, Bizkaia and Gipuzkoa, had occupied first and second position, respectively, in terms of income per capita in Spain in 1960s and early 1970s. However, from the mid-1970s onwards they had substantively dropped from that position. Thus, according to Cabrera and del Rey (2007: 140), in the period between 1975 and 1985 unemployment in Bizkaia and Gipuzkoa rose from 2.1 percent to 23.5 percent, while for the same period Gipuzkoa and Bizkaia fell from first and second to seventh and sixteenth in the country, respectively, in terms of production, and from third and first to eleventh and fourteenth, respectively, in terms of income.

The Spanish industrial crisis of the 1980s and early 1990s had, then, a very strong regional dimension. As a consequence, the restructuring of the Spanish economy was closely associated with the search for a more competitive economic strategy. Some of the features of the new model included: the development of "national champions"; the concentration of the financial sector; the privatisation of public sector companies; withdrawing state support for the mature manufacturing sector; the adoption of a new democratic political system along corporate lines, including the process of devolution and the creation of intermediate governments (the autonomous communities); and the integration of trade unions and business representatives into the social and economic policy process. Furthermore, the direction and speed of the "Spanish transition" was influenced by the acceleration of the process of EC integration and the reorientation of key industrial and monetary policies alongside the new EC priority projects.

The interdependencies of these often contradictory processes could be observed in relation to the debates surrounding the construction of high-speed train (HST) links in Spain. The HST project became an important aspect of a Spanish "modernisation" agenda during the early period of the post-Franco era and has been on the political agenda ever since.[2] It was one, among many, flagship projects supported by the Spanish government that also included organising major sporting and cultural events such as the Olympic Games in Barcelona (1992) and the universal exhibition that Seville hosted in 1992.[3] However, unlike other flagship projects that were mainly aimed at raising Spain's international profile, the significance of the HST was more than symbolic as it was much more closely linked to broader political and economic reforms in Spain. Therefore, debates around the construction and route of the HST were closely linked to the restructuring of key economic areas and urban regeneration and development projects. In addition, the preparation and implementation of such a project also involved intensive international cooperation, the involvement of central and regional governments and an investment and technology transfer from multinationals.

## Institutional and Economic Legacies

The tendency in the literature on Spanish nation- and state-building after 1975 has been to operate with the image of consensus (del Aguila and Montoro 1984; Desfor 1998) in order to refer to the transition as a successful stepping stone towards the consolidation of the Spanish democratic (nation) state (Carr and Fusi 1981; Preston 1986). As such, the notion of consensus became the foundation on which the "necessarily left"

2. However, the extent to which the project was seen as one of the major central and autonomous government priorities changed over time as did the emphasis on different aspects of its significance. These changes will be discussed in the next three chapters.

3. 1992 also marked the 500-year anniversary of the "discovery" of Latin America and in this sense the modernisation agenda was closely linked to the reimagining of the Spanish nation as a former empire (as opposed to a former fascist dictatorship).

"transition" in Spain[4] could be built. As suggested before, the aim of the consensus was to secure "stable conditions" that would eventually help the ruling PSOE (which came to power in 1982) carry out the necessary socio-economic reforms before and after Spain joined the EC (Bermeo 1994). For some authors (Petras 1990), meanwhile, it was also a means of guaranteeing the construction of a new power block under the auspices of PSOE,[5] which would ultimately guarantee the continuation and legitimisation of old political and economic elites that might have been (in one way or another) closely related to the previous regime. This was the case, for example, in relation to personal networks between the PSOE government and representatives of major baking sectors such as the Banco Bilbao and Banco Vizcaya, which together prioritised a policy that sought to facilitate the concentration and internationalisation of the banking sector (leading ultimately to the merger of the Banco Bilbao and Banco Vizcaya into one bank, the BBV, Banco Bilbao Vizcaya) (Holman 1989; 1996).

The strong political dimension of this consensus –namely to avoid a perceived and/or real threat to the "Spanish democracy"—led to the (re) establishment of a collective bargaining system. The aim of this was to win the support of the trade union leadership and their participation in the political process, and thus prevent mobilisation as a strategy for achieving economic and political gains when negotiating issues such as wage increases, welfare provision and general working conditions (Fowerarker 1987). More specifically, this consensus was based on a series of bipartite and/or tripartite agreements, known as the Moncloa Pacts, which sought to involve, in principle, the government, trade unions and business representatives. However, the level of participation and contribution on the part of trade unions was not always straightforward.

In general terms, the scope and extent of these "social pacts" consisted of a series of labour policy reforms (1977, 1980, 1984, 1985, 1986 and 1997), which on the one hand sought to contain salary increases with the objective of controlling inflation and, on the other, tackle labour rigidities

4. It could only be carried out by the Socialist Party as it had no links with the Franco regime, although the economic reforms insofar as they were implemented in this early period were clearly neo-liberal; and as opposed to the "necessarily right" post-Communist transition in Eastern Europe, for example.

5. Specifically, Petras (1990: 193) lists the myriad of interests that came together under the PSOE umbrella, including banking, real estate and speculative groups; corporate executives and lawyers who were auxiliaries of multinational corporations; and highly placed state technocrats and executives who managed state enterprises and financial institutions.

as a structural legacy associated with the organisation of the labour market under the highly bureaucratic vertical syndicate. In fact, the PSOE's interpretation of the post-Franco economic crisis focused primarily on labour costs and labour market rigidities as a way of controlling inflation and dealing with the economic crisis in general (Ferreiro and Serrano 2001).

Although the PSOE government seemed to acknowledge that the most adequate way of addressing the link between wage determination, productivity and inflation was by consolidating a new institutional framework for cooperation and the resolution of often diverging capital and labour interests, the Moncloa Pacts failed to deliver in terms of their institutional purposes and outcomes. Thus, for example, the first of these agreements, the Pact of 1977, which established "social consensus" (*concertación social*) as the basis for the new industrial-relations framework, was conceived outside parliament. It was, in fact, signed by the two main political parties at the time, the UCD and the PSOE, behind "closed doors" and therefore it did not include either the contribution of trade unions or business associations such as the CEOE (Confederación Española de Organizaciones Empresariales, the Spanish Confederation of Employers' Organisations) (Martinez Alier and Roca 1987: 75). Further, the Interconfederal Master Agreement (AMI) (1980), which aimed to address procedural issues regarding collective bargaining, was only signed by UGT and the CEOE, while CCOO abstained from any participation. CCOO called for a general strike in 1985 against the government's proposed pension policy, but UGT decided not to back it up. Thus, the 1980s witnessed a growing political fragmentation among the labour movement as well as an increasing decline in trade union membership. Such fragmentation became more accentuated by the reorganisation of labour representation at the regional level (for example, ELA and LAB in the Basque case) and, according to Heywood, by 1994, only about 10 percent of salaried workers belonged to any of the statewide or regional trade unions (1995: 250). Furthermore, although such pacts have been very weakly institutionalised (Heywood 1998), they have served as the basis on which to gradually introduce labour reforms consisting of reducing employment insurance, introducing temporary contracts and making it easier to "hire and fire" (Koch 2005)

Eventually, the Moncloa Pacts and subsequent agreements between the government, unions and businesses representatives, met strong opposition from the main statewide trade unions, leading to general strikes between 1988 and 2003. According to Koch, it was precisely in response to trade union resistance that the government went on to impose reforms by decree law, which consistently favoured the interests of business (for example, the introduction of fixed terms contracts and legalisation of employment agencies). Indeed, the ability to issue decree laws has been associated with, first, the design of the Spanish Constitution that was aimed at ensuring legal protection for a strong state and the power of the executive over parliament (Heywood 1995: 247); and second, with an electoral regime that prioritises the dominance of a bi-party parliament system (Petras 1990; Colomer 2007) in which an absolute majority would also guarantee support for introducing exceptional measures (Article 86 of the Constitution) whenever the governing party deems this necessary. This solution has been implemented whenever trade unions and business associations have failed to reach a consensual agreement.

Generally, the introduction of these labour reforms contributed to a significant drop in labour protection and the development of a dual labour market (Blyton and Martinez Lucio 1995). While the aim of such reforms had been to achieve a more competitive labour market, it has been suggested that unintended consequences have included the underdevelopment of training infrastructures as well as the lack of commitment to a high-skilled and high-productivity strategy from businesses and government alike (Gómez Uranga 1991; Martinez Lucio 1995).

Therefore, while this consensus opened up a "time window" during which the PSOE could carry out major reforms, the substance of these reforms, according to some authors (Navarro 1989, 1997; Gillespie 1990, 1993; Albarracín et al. 1993; McVeigh 1999; Prieto del Campo 2005), followed a clear neo-liberal agenda. In this sense, these authors have interpreted the Moncloa Pacts as circumstantial agreements that led to the introduction of neo-liberal economic reforms[6] and were in effect related to policies of industrial restructuring; these included closing down companies and downsizing as well as privatising public sector companies (such as oil, telecommunications, tobacco and transport). In this context, according to Chari (1998), key INI companies such as Seat, Enasa, MTM-Ateinsa (see chapter 5), SKF-Española, Astican and Transatlantica were sold in

6. Interestingly, Spain represented a paradox because, when the PSOE came to power in 1982, it did so in a political and economic context in which Conservative parties governed in most of Western Europe. However, as noted before, this did not prevent the PSOE from leading industrial restructuring and introducing important changes in the legislation of the labour market. Moreover, these political and economic changes were also accompanied by internal ideological debates that led to the assumption that the market was an important and constitutive element of the economy.

very advantageous conditions to foreign companies such as Volkswagen, Fiat, GEC-Alstom and Ercros. Furthermore, Petras has observed that the industrial plants established in Spain were dependant on semi-skilled workers (1990: 191).[7] Indeed, industrial restructuring in Spain involved opening up the borders to import foreign technology, which in turn has displaced local technology and accumulated know-how (for example, in the case of the HST, see chapter 4).

Furthermore, these reforms also involved lying off more than 100,000 workers, investing in modernising the companies and then selling them off to foreign companies for a fraction of what the state had invested refurbishing them. This included a series of agreements whereby the Spanish state agreed to share subsequent investments to update and improve the companies over the years. Furthermore, while the industry and banking sectors had hitherto cooperated closely, under the new economic reforms the latter opted to stop supporting the Spanish industrial structure and instead pursued a strategy of expansion and growth (in order to compete in the international market), thus initiating the first mergers among the principal banks of Spain, led by the aforementioned BBV.

Nevertheless, I would argue that the novelty of these neo-liberal reforms, in contrast to the above accounts, should not be overly exaggerated given that their introduction was not that dissimilar from measures adopted by other European countries with strong neo-liberal agendas. Yet in contrast to all other European countries, these reforms were taking place within the context of a large-scale political restructuring in which entirely new political subjects, processes of negotiation and institutions were being established. Further, these political and economic reforms were also taking place within the context of legacies left by the previous regime, which was characterised by a paternalistic bureaucratic system (McVeigh 1999), a (quasi) top-down, highly centralist but corporatist state (Fowerarker 1987), and one that was dominated by a small number of very large com-

7. This might explain, to some extent, why the Spanish government has prioritised bringing down the rigid barriers of the Spanish labour market. One way of explaining this, for example, is by looking at the human resources policy of multinational companies located in Spain. Depending on the type of production facilities built in Spain, if we assume that these facilities do not integrate high levels of innovation and technology, then one could argue that the production facilities owned by multinationals in Spain favour and promote a low-level skills labour force. In this context, it can be concluded that the notion of a "cheap labour force" could constitute an advantageous position for the Spanish economy. This, in turn, would mean putting an emphasis on hire-and-fire laws, with the associated subsequent fragmentation of the labour force and the loss of its capacity for organisation and mobilisation.

panies organised under public state holdings (in collaboration with foreign investment) with strong political links (Lopez III 1990; Cabrera and del Rey 2007). In terms of economic development, this system severely hindered any possibilities for international expansion, while its reproduction was also dependent on tight political control over the labour market that, in the absence of welfare provision, made labour redundancy nearly impossible except in the case of proven illegal political and trade union affiliation. The labour market was controlled through vertical syndicates and was based on a belief in the possibility of a harmonious coexistence and resolution of capital-labour conflicts. However, social demands were met with a mixture of repression and politically motivated wage increases. These arrangements privileged in part large businesses and pushed up wage levels above productivity levels in sectors where foreign capital was present, while damaging SMEs. This eventually undermined Spain's competitive advantage, based initially on lower labour costs, and did not offer a viable alternative as there were no mechanisms that might encourage innovation and diversification (see chapter 3).

In addition, further controls over market prices secured the allocation of goods in a protected national market, weakly developed due to a limited domestic purchasing power (Segura 1992). Thus, as a result of these institutional practices, Segura argues, Spanish industry became dominated by what he calls a "macro-cephalic" industry of labour and energy intensive, technologically mature sectors, predominantly steel, shipbuilding and textiles. The latter existed side by side with SMEs, which were highly dependent on the main industrial centres, and to which favours of political protection were not extended (ibid.: 57). At the beginning of the transition, then, the economic crisis affected not only big industrial companies dependant and/or in direct relation to the state but also small companies found themselves unprepared to compete internationally (Pastor 1992; Navarro Arancegui et al. 1994).[8] Particularly affected were manufacturing companies of intermediate size, such as the automotive industry (an important basis of which can be found in the Basque Country), which had to quickly adapt to an environment that required rapid development of technological capacity, innovation, design, quality, after-sale service, and so on. It is within this context, in which both large and small businesses

8. The authors base their conclusion on an assessment grounded in the notion of competitiveness that looked at exports, sales, cyclical disparities between different countries, the capacity to supply the internal and international markets and control over prices and costs.

were equally unprepared for the internationalisation of the Spanish economy, and one in need of substantial reform, that the government opted for a radical industrial restructuring that included privatisation and the closing down of companies as well as the belief that external investment and technology transfer ought to be important constitutive aspects of such reform (Etxezarreta 1991). Indeed, Spain became one of the primary recipients of FDI in the EU in the late 1980s and 1990s (Navarro 1990; Mangen 2001).

In summary, the Spanish government concentrated on developing rather short- and medium-term solutions by aiming at attracting international capital through labour reforms that would guarantee low labour costs while simultaneously reducing taxes on capital and businesses (Share 1988: 51). Moreover, the government set out to bring declining industries into shape, first by heavily investing in them and then selling them on for a fraction of their price to foreign capital. The PSOE government lacked any long-term industrial policy and instead opted to develop favourable conditions to attract FDI. At the same time, the Spanish government adapted the legal system to create a framework that would allow banks to merge and grow, and subsequently compete in the international market (Holman 1996). Nevertheless, as a result of this, the government did manage to lower inflation and achieve macro-economic stability. However, and following the increasing dualisation of the labour market and the fragmentation of the labour force, it failed to address growing structural problems, especially job stability and equal opportunities for women and young people.

## The "State of Autonomies" as a Multi-layered Strategy for Economic Restructuring

Within this context there were two interrelated aspects of the emerging Spanish government strategy: European integration and administrative decentralisation in Spain. Initially, this strategy was clearly oriented towards further integration into the EC, which was a trade-off between the implementation of EC requirements for liberal reforms in exchange for generous provision of funds for infrastructural, agricultural and regional development. More specifically, Spain's agreement to implement EC policies on competitiveness (such as the removal of industrial subsidies and lifting all market protections) as well as convergence regulations towards a monetary union (like limitation of public expenditure) –in other words,

Spain's commitment to further political and economic integration—has been associated with two key developments. First, the development of a compensatory mechanism, such as the Cohesion Fund, as a means to contain and redress the negative social consequences of state withdrawal from key sectors such as industry, fisheries and agriculture (Pastor 1992; Heywood 1995, 1998; Murphy 1999). And second, the process of decentralisation, which has traditionally been associated with the devolution of "historical rights" (in other words, autonomy) (Aja 1999; Viñuela 2000; Moreno 2001; Börzel 2002; Nuñez Seixas 2005), should also be associated with an emerging economic rationale that was consolidating across advanced Western economies in response to the crisis of economic management at the national level (Jessop 2002). More specifically, the ACs were created at the same time as the flexibilisation of the economies of Western Europe (Piore and Sabel 1984; Storper 1995), and this was accompanied by the belief that, within the context of Post-Fordist economies, smaller subnational (as opposed to national) units have superior institutional and organisational capacity (Morgan 1997; Cooke, Gómez Uranga and Etxeberria 1998) and are better able to drive and promote economic competitiveness (Keating 1998). The view that "small is beautiful" was further linked to the notion of "endogenous growth" as well as the capabilities of regions to promote new innovation systems and to articulate supply-side initiatives (Morgan 2004). Consequently, regional and local governments became heavily involved in the development, planning and delivery of key local industrial initiatives (Arboníes and Moso 2002; Porter 2002).

The focus on regions and localities as driving forces of economic change and innovation as well as effective units of governance became highly influential among national and regional governments as well as policymakers across Europe (Giordano and Roller 2002; Bourne 2003). The European regions also occupied a central place in the economic and social agendas of the EU as well as in debates around economic efficiency, market integration and social cohesion (MacLeod 2001; Jones 2001). The EU became instrumental in financing regional projects across Europe (Rodríguez and Martínez 2003; González 2004 2005) and, as suggested earlier, Spain became a net beneficiary from the Structural and Cohesion Funds that were key driving forces of this process (Amin and Tomaney 1995; Heywood 1995). As a result, the political reform that took place in Spain, with its strong focus on institutionalising a politics of "consensus" (for example, through the Spanish parliament, Constitution, and "social pacts"), was intimately related to addressing the political as well as the economic crisis of early 1970s. The process of decentralisation, in addition to its political rationale, also had an economic dimension where responsibility for the painful reforms was shared equally by the central and newly established AC governments (Cobanera 2002).[9] This also had an administrative and institutional aspect as the transition exposed the weaknesses and unsuitability of Franco's institutional framework within the new more open political and economic climate. The old institutional arrangement was further challenged by pressure from EC institutions, restricting significantly the ability of central government to intervene directly into the economy.

### *State of Autonomies*

The process of devolution in Spain modified the centralist and unitary nature of the Spanish state that prevailed under Franco's regime. This process triggered a new territorial configuration where regions emerged as new political players in the new democratic political landscape.

The new Spanish Constitution (1978) provided for the establishment of regional governments as well as local charters (that is, statutes). This constitutional agreement transformed the territorial distribution of powers in Spain as well as the mechanisms of decision-making. Furthermore, new inter-governmental relations and political alliances between state-wide and regional political parties were established within Spain partly as a result of these changes (Aja 1999, 2000; Roller 2004; Colomer 1999, 2007). In this sense, one of the most far-reaching changes established under the new Spanish Constitution was the devolution process. As I have pointed out, devolution was linked to the creation of seventeen ACs, commonly known as the State of Autonomies. Although the initial aims of this process were to ensure the accommodation of the claims made by regionally based minority nationalities, mainly in the Basque Country and Catalonia,

---

9. Thus, according to Article 18/30 of the Basque Autonomous Statute, the Basque government received powers that would enable it to participate in the industrial restructuring of companies located in the BAC. The participation of the Basque government, however, was made possible upon the condition that those companies located in the BAC made up at least 10% of the total employment in the state sector. The Basque government would mediate between the expressed needs of the companies and the central state. Further, its competencies would include direct funding of companies as well as developing its own industrial policies and shaping and having leverage in shaping the implementation of policies of the Spanish government (Cobanera 2002: 55–56).

and to a lesser extent in Galicia, the process of devolution extended to other parts of Spain mostly on administrative grounds.

More specifically, the 1978 Spanish Constitution (SP) established a twin-track process for devolution that gave special privileges to the governments of the "historical nationalities" of the Basque Country, Catalonia and Galicia.[10] These ACs, in contrast to other ACs, gained immediate access to powers. The competences and powers of the ACs are included in the Article 148 of the Constitution. Some of the juridical and administrative powers include health, education, culture, industry, infrastructures and innovation. In the case of the BAC and also the AC of Navarre, these ACs obtained a special fiscal status (known as the *cupo* or quota). This basically means that the BAC and Navarre can levy taxes in their territories and in return, they have to give back an agreed part of these taxes to the central government in exchange for the services that these ACs cannot provide themselves (Gómez Uranga and Etxebarria 2000). However, this power should not be overestimated since the state has retained ample control over finance as well as distribution of resources (Maíz, Caamaño and Azpitarte 2010). Article 149 of the Constitution includes all the rest of the powers that belong to the state. These powers include: control over borders, macro-economic policies, international relations, the military, and so forth.

This process was constituted on the basis of a series of political negotiations with key political players during the transition (Agranoff 1994), and while most ACs were granted limited powers, Andalucía was granted a special provision. However, after an attempted coup d'état in 1981, the government introduced the Organic Law for the Synchronisation of the Autonomy Process (LOAPA): a controversial law adopted in July 1982, which was introduced in order to slow down the devolution process and to standardise the degree of devolution among all the ACs. This new drive for synchronisation subsequently led to a new agreement in 1992 between the two main statewide political parties, the PSOE and the PP, which paved the way for devolving a substantial number of political competencies, including education, to the level of the ACs.

The emergence of these new ACs reconstituted the organisation of regional power in a couple of different ways. First, they created an entirely new institutional layer overarching the re-established historical provin-

---

10. The division between the competencies given to the "historical nationalities" and other ACs has mostly disappeared and at present all ACs enjoy a similar degree of autonomy.

cial councils (for example, in Bizkaia, Gipuzkoa and Araba), and second, the city-based institutional frameworks (metropolitan corporations) were dismantled, while many of their powers were transferred to the provincial governments and the respective ACs (Baena del Alcazar 1994; Heywood 1995; García Álvarez 2002). This change reduced the power of cities within Spain's administrative structure, yet simultaneously, due to the growing significance of global financial capital cities, they also became central nodes of the new Post-Fordist restructuring strategy as well as sites of intensive policy intervention (Jessop and Sum 2000; Rodríguez, Martínez, Guenaga 2001; Rodríguez, Swyngedouw and Mouleart 2003; Brenner 2004). However, it should be noted that different Spanish cities were very differently affected by these contradictory tendencies. Madrid and Barcelona, for example, continued to be significant players in Spain (despite their reduced administrative powers) and also emerged as major European urban areas. In contrast, the significance of Bilbao, now located on the periphery of both national and European circuits, declined. Consequently, the city of Bilbao came to occupy only a secondary role in Spain during the Post-Franco period when compared to Madrid and Barcelona, while it remained peripheral on the European level. These different fates of the cities can be explained to some extent by the growing geopolitical and economic significance of the Mediterranean as opposed to the Atlantic-centred geopolitical and economic relations in Europe and in Spain, in particular.

The paradox of the simultaneous decline and growth of power of urban areas in Spain is paralleled by a similar paradox of the growing power of regions and the continuous high level of centralisation in Spain (Heywood 1995, 1998; Chari and Heywood 2009). This paradox is especially visible in the debates concerning the administrative structure in Spain, which has been described as having a quasi-federal structure (Aja 1999, 2004; Romero González 2002, 2005), or as an American model of dual federalism in which the emphasis is on the separation of the central-state and regional powers (Börzel 2002: 93). Indeed, there is, to a degree, a separation between the central and regional powers, but federal-like institutional structures such as the Senate, as I will point out, are of secondary importance and they do not have any political weight in Spain.

Indeed, Moreno (2001) argues that the centralising tendency of the government should also be taken into consideration. In this sense, Heywood (1998: 105–109) argues that, constitutionally, the Spanish executive continues to enjoy a great concentration of power which allows plenty of room for formulating and implementing policies. Thus, in spite of the devolution of powers to the ACs, the Spanish government in general and particularly the Ministry of Economy -comprising the treasury and the site for formulating and elaborating the state budget, fiscal policy and foreign trade and investment policy—remain very powerful. Further, the overwhelming policymaking and legislative powers belong to the central government. In addition, in cases where legislative powers are given to both the regional and central government (for example, as regards environmental protection, economic development, health and welfare), it is the latter that develops the basic laws and these are subsequently elaborated and adapted within the ACs. In contrast, municipalities, for example, only serve a basic function such as that of delivering services and, in cases of larger municipalities, also that of delivering social services (Font et al. 1999).

### *The Senate*

Other authors have looked specifically at the low-profile role that the Senate plays among the Spanish political institutions (Aja 1999; Börzel 2001; Romero González 2002; Roller 2004). Ideally, the Senate should be able to articulate regional problems, that is, it should be able to deal with matters affecting the competences and rights of the ACs. What this means is that although regional governments, in particular, and regional political parties do exercise influence on the national government (agreements between statewide parties and their regional counterparts are not uncommon in parliament, especially when the government wants to pass a bill or build support for the annual budget), the Senate does not work as a space where the voice of the ACs can be heard. This lack of regional representativeness in government has prevented any real discussion on common regional issues and, in this sense, a more integrated approach at the inter-regional and national policy level is missing in Spain. Furthermore, this institutional framework has rather facilitated a more "confrontational" relationship at different government levels, where issues of competencies (who can do what) and budgetary distribution (how much each AC should pay and receive from the national budget, this also prompting many discussions regarding "solidarity" among the regions) have taken precedence when dealing with regional problems and have been heavily mediated by, mostly, the Constitutional Court.

The changing balance between centre and regions was also paralleled by continuities between the Franco and post-Franco eras in the organisational structure and key personnel of major institutions such as the Crown and the military as well as in the administrative and the financial systems. This, according to Navarro (1997) and Prieto del Campo (2005), demonstrates that the reform initiative as well as its implementation was mainly carried out by the same politico-economic elites that had supported Franco's regime. These elites had to respond to pressures from different socio-economic players (mainly an already constituted and organised industrial workforce) as well as the awareness that the economic challenges to be faced in the future (the internationalisation of the economy and further internationalisation of the division of labour) required a new institutional adaptation based on democratic legitimisation (Jessop 1990). Furthermore, this was the criteria by which Spain could secure NATO and EU membership.

Successful post-industrial restructuring therefore depends not only on the powers of administrative competencies within the Spanish state but also on developments within the EU, the balance of power within the AC itself as well as the structural advantages that particular scales have within Post-Fordist restructuring. In this sense, it could be argued that within this ambiguous position of diverging objectives, perspectives and strategies, the rhetoric of further decentralisation is both political and "pragmatic." It is political because it can only lead to independence given the level of the decentralisation already in place, but it is also "pragmatic" given the inadequacy of the existing institutional frameworks to deal with the restructuring and internationalisation of the economy. Thus, one possible alternative could be the aggregation of a more effective intermediate institutional level, which might, on the one hand, put some restrictions on the powers of the ACs, and, on the other, enhance "cooperation" and "consensus building" as the principles of institutional practice within this new supra-territorial forum (Romero 2004) (as opposed to, for example, further decentralisation as a mechanism of coordination). Indeed, it is the latter, namely further decentralisation, which is primarily taking place, given that the solution preferred by the ACs, particularly the BAC and Catalonia, is the development of bi-lateral relations with central government and direct participation within EU institutions. As a consequence, while efforts were made to strengthen and coordinate interregional dialogue and interests, for example, by developing the *Conferencias Sectoriales* and later, the *Conferencia de Presidentes,* established under José Luis Rodríguez Zapatero's government upon winning the elections in 2004, the ACs have sought to negotiate inter-institutional arrangements outside the Spanish institutional framework and primarily within the institutional arrangements available within the EU. Börzel (2002) predicts that EU integration will increase cooperation among the different territorial governments within Spain. Others, however, suggest that new radical sovereignty alternatives (Keating 2001) within the EU, such as the somewhat controversial *New Political Pact for Coexistence,* also known as the Ibarretxe Plan, published in September 2002 by the PNV president of the BAC (Bourne 2003: 407; Keating and Bray 2006), and more recent calls for self-determination by the government in Catalonia may emerge within a post-national European context.

In this context, the options available to specific cities and regions, for example, always depend on their particular environments and cannot be generalised. The latter can be well illustrated by the substantial differences that developed after 1975 between what otherwise seem very similar cases, the ACs of Catalonia and the Basque Country and their major urban areas of Barcelona and Bilbao, respectively. Accordingly, in contrast to Catalonia, for example, the Basque Country faces a much more complicated future, particularly in terms of deciding where its competitive advantages are. This can be illustrated by their position as regions within Spain and the EU and in relation to the place that their key cities, Barcelona and Bilbao, occupy within those two contexts, but also within their own ACs. Catalonia as an AC is dominated by Barcelona, which is a major European hub as well as one of the two major cities within Spain. In contrast, Bilbao is only of semi-peripheral significance within Spain and is periph eral within the EU as a whole. Further, Bilbao's place is contested within the Basque Country itself (in contrast to Barcelona in Catalonia) and it is not accepted as the country's clear economic, political-administrative and cultural centre. Furthermore, the three Basque provinces are very heterogeneous. This does not suggest that governments are totally determined by external conditions but, rather, indicates the changing structural constraints within which they operate. And while reflexivity and active governance (for example, in the case of the Bilbao-Ría 2000 consortium) are certainly becoming far more important in the current stage of capitalist development, these are still operating within strategically selective structural contexts (Jessop 2004).

### *Industrial Crisis and the (Re)Imagining of the Basque Country*

As argued above, the Spanish industrial crisis had a very distinct geographical dimension insofar as many of the affected industrial areas were located in the Basque Country and Catalonia. Indeed, Basque governing institutions as such only started to emerge in the post-Franco era (Gómez Uranga and Etxebarria 2000). If they existed prior to that time, it was only on the provincial level (namely, that of Bizkaia, Gipuzkoa, Araba and Navarre, although the configuration of the BAC consisted only of the first three of these provinces). As a result, it has been suggested, all-too-common references to the "Basque Country" and the "Basque economy" need to be treated cautiously. While the three provinces certainly were of central economic significance within Spain from the time of the empire, through early industrialisation, to the Franco and post-Franco periods, in some authors' opinions it seems that they were only very loosely institutionally connected (Crespo et al. 1981) on a supra-regional level or, if they were, these links were similar to those among other (neighbouring) regions within Spain. In contrast to this view, Agirreazkuenaga (2011) convincingly demonstrates the long term effect that political and juridical institutions had on the perception of a sense of Basque nationhood. This was primarily among the Basque elite where a strong sense of identity emerged through participation in quasi-state institution building in the period following the decline of the Spanish Empire through to the dawn of industrialisation in the Basque provinces.

So we must distinguish between the Basque economy and institutions before and after 1983, as it was only after 1983 that economic and political institutions that encompassed the three Basque provinces were established. This allows us to examine the post-1983 period as one of institution-building and state and nation formation (Martínez Herrera 2002) rather than assuming their existence and therefore looking at their restructuring and evolution in response also to Post-Fordist challenges. The direction of the economic restructuring within the three Basque provinces cannot be separated from other factors. These include: first, the political dominance of the moderate Basque nationalist political party, the PNV (Mees et al. 2001) and its strong links with a particular economic elite that dominates all three provinces, although it is especially powerful in Bizkaia and Gipuzkoa; second, the association of a substantial part of the cultural elites in the Basque Country with a Basque national project in general (although using different imaginings from those of the dominant political-economic elite); third, the different yet equally attractive options available to Bilbao (and Bizkaia) in terms of possible directions for its economic restructuring. For example, Bilbao could either develop as a centre of the Cantabrian economic zone (one that could possibly even be extended to an

Atlantic economic zone at a later stage) (González 2003) or alternatively as a part of the Basque economy, state and national project. Thus the economic restructuring of the Basque economy also means the imagining of a Basque economy within the territorial boundaries of the three (rather than four or five, including Navarre in Spain and/or Zuberoa (Soule), Lapurdi (Labourd) and Lower Navarre in France) Basque provinces, as well as the creation (rather than restructuring) of supra-regional political and economic institutions and physical infrastructures, the HST being central among the latter; and fourth, Spanish EU membership was crucial in the sense that the interpretation of the Basque economy and, subsequently, the development of a series of conceptual tools with which to guide the Basque governing institutions in their intervention in the Basque economy were the result of engaging with a broader set of policy strategies developed in the national and European context. This included the elaboration of key policy documents such as *Euskadi Siglo XXI* (Twenty-first century Basque Country); short and medium term economic policies (1989–1992; 1994–1997); and urban restructuring plans such as "Gipuzkoa 2000" and "Alava 2000" (Franco 2004: 301). However, the most important and undoubtedly the most far-reaching consequences were associated with the regeneration of the Bilbao Metropolitan Area.

The establishment of a Basque autonomous government and institutions coincided with the industrial crisis and the subsequent economic restructuring. The industrial crisis in the Basque Country was marked by a high sectoral specialisation concentrated in industries that were vulnerable and ill-prepared for international competition. Further, the productive environment consisted of, on the one hand, large manufacturing sectors and, on the other, of SMEs that were dependant on a limited and declining number of large firms. Furthermore, the fragile industrial infrastructure in the Basque Country suffered from a poor provision of services such as marketing and design, as well as low levels of R&D and the lack of a clear strategy for product diversification (Etxebarria Kerexeta and Franco Ibarzabal 2003: 2).

Accordingly, the new Basque authorities were immediately faced with taking some of the responsibility as well as the blame for large job losses as well as the broader negative consequences of the reforms. More specifically, the Basque government had to deal with a number of strikes as well as mediate between the interests of the workers and industrial capital, both of which formed its electoral base. This was a new situation for both the Basque Country and Spain, where central government and the autonomous authorities were both held responsible for the crisis and also led to the rebuilding of new coalitions and loosely defined associations. These included, for example, those between the ruling moderate nationalist PNV, the dominant economic elite associated with the ruling party, the central Spanish government (governed by PSOE), industrial workers and ETA (with a nationalist and Marxist programme), where economic interests and national aspirations were intertwined in complex and contradictory ways. The tensions and processes of renegotiating responsibilities at that time are well illustrated by the reminiscences of a former member of the Basque government who recalls how, initially, in the absence of a stable institutional order (for example, regional government) as well as the capacity for coercive enforcement (that is, the Ertzaintza, the Basque regional police force), government making (in other words, regulation) was at hoc, in response to immediate problems, and often carried out in highly unpredictable political (as well as personal) situations.

> So that you get an idea of the situation, a couple of weeks into the government, we had a very important strike including the kidnapping of the four or five of us who had started to work on transport issues, by four hundred lorries in Vitoria, Lakua [the location of the Basque government] . . . when we had neither a government or the Ertzaintza or anything . . . [the situation] forced [us] to create the Hiring and Loading Law, among many difficulties, but it was an attempt to plan.[11]

Moreover, in a period when the distribution of state competencies were neither clear nor sufficiently stabilised at an inter-institutional level, the legislation process was marred by tensions and conflicts over the redefinition of boundaries of authority. The struggles for institutional competences included "fighting for" as well as "taking the initiative" for developing and prioritising a "national strategy." In this sense, government decisions began to be framed in relation to possible economic alternatives that the Basque government could pursue. These included the redrawing of economic boundaries and identifying a new "economic growth" strategy.

> [I]t became very controversial in the sense that it was held to be interventionist . . . within the Port of Bilbao over which we did not hold any competencies. But we lived under lots of pressure and we knew that the Port of Bilbao was one of the few sources of wealth at the time . . . it has to be remembered that we were in a very deep economic crisis, we were

11. AA, former member of and advisor to the Basque government.

> in a very delicate situation, a negative GDP . . . and the Port of Bilbao was one of the few available resources. We didn't have any competencies over it, we didn't have any say on what was going on there but we tried to save that. The big infrastructural projects of the port were at a standstill (it was not working properly and labour conflicts were constant), the necessary infrastructures [to access] the port were missing . . . it was a chaotic situation.[12]

It could be argued that the growth in strength and the weakening of ETA coincided to a large extent with the beginning and end of the industrial crisis in the Basque Country as well as the creation and strengthening of the institutional infrastructure of the Basque Autonomous Community.

The early stages of the political and economic restructuring of Spain coincided with the release of highly influential reports such as the "Blue Banana" (Brunet 1989). These reports showed a series of maps that claimed to identify areas of economic growth (for example, the "banana shape" geographical zone that included a large area from London to Milan) and decline in Europe. These reports became powerful reference points for members of the newly formed Basque government and it was in relation to them that it began to actively promote interregional alliances among those areas within the Atlantic Arc that were affected by economic decline. Consequently, the imagining, evocation and, to an extent, the institutionalisation of the Atlantic Arc became associated with a regional (rather than national) strategy that pursued the social and economic recovery of areas in decline within the boundaries of the EU. It was argued that the Atlantic Arc, in contrast to the "Blue Banana" and the "Mediterranean Axis," required extra support as part of the EU's "convergence strategy" (Amin and Tomaney 2002). It is worth noting here, however, that policy development emerged within the context of policy trends as well as strategies established in wider national (for example, the modernisation of the Spanish railways) and supranational forums (such as convergence/cohesion).

> It's an old story; a pact was made with the central government regarding the Basque Y in 1987, when [José] Barrionuevo was Minister of Transport and Public Works . . . the government coalition between the PSOE and the PNV was in a critical condition and the nationalist branch [of the coalition] promoted the "Europe 93" plan. The context [the background of the policy] was to get ahead of ourselves in two areas: first, the

12. Ibid.

> "Cecchini" report, which addressed the cost of the new Europe . . . we were scared of the living conditions in Euskadi . . . we were convinced that if robust actions and radical solutions were not taken immediately, we would have ended up as an absolute peripheral region isolated from European developments. It was the time of the "Blue Banana" discourse, the great growth from London to Milan and anything else outside of that schema disappeared. It was a major concern and we needed both physical connectivity and, let's call it, convergence with Europe. The plan was born in this context and it put forward intelligent and physical structures of connectivity, such as the social network platform (a competitive characteristic of the country).[13]

While the need to "borrow" and/or "import" policy might be related to issues of state capacity in the sense that national states can both deploy a wider range of resources, expertise and know-how and have access to forums outside the jurisdiction of regional governments, like the Council of Europe, it should also be noted that the national government (for example, the Treasury) enjoys constitutional protection in terms of policy-setting, budget development and overall steering of the economy. Generally, policy development with a focus on infrastructural projects seeking to facilitate "connectivity" fits well with a strategy of Post-Fordist restructuring where supply-side initiatives (such as the creation of attractive conditions for capital to "settle" as well as to facilitate its movement) (Jessop 1993) substitutes demand incentive management mechanisms.

> Second, the "Single Market" had been planned to come into effect on 1 January 1993. Therefore, [the aim was] to prepare the country for that new stage. It was then that [the project to] upgrade our country emerged, while at the same time [our country could develop] as a platform for connectivity and integration with the rest of Europe, economically, socially and politically. [It was the context] where new ideas emerged, [such as] the planning of the high speed trains as a solution; clearly the railway made a comeback . . . [in this sense] it has to be remembered that railways had been neglected for fifteen years.[14]

The free movement of people, capital and information across state borders within Europe had for a long time been high on the priority agenda of key players and elites within the EU. As a result, discourses of integration

13. Ibid.

14. Ibid.

led to the development of economically viable industrial solutions that also had the objective of overcoming regional socio-economic imbalances, encouraging and introducing innovations, as well as the development of transport infrastructures across Europe. Subsequently, these processes led to the development of a new perspective of European spatial intervention. Specifically, issues of transport and mobility came to play a central role in taking decisions over interventions and in developing a unified European space, while the notions of "connectivity," "peripherality," "sustainability," "mobility" and "policentricity" underpinned the agenda for economic and social integration of the EU (Jensen and Richardson 2007) (see also chapter 5). Further, Jensen and Richardson argue that these discursive practices look "upon the European Union territory within a single overarching rationality of making "one space," made possible by seamless networks enabling frictionless mobility" (ibid.: 10).

In this sense, social and economic mobility were to coexist alongside strategies of growth as a means of encouraging a balanced distribution of people, capital and information across the EU space. This led ultimately to the development of a series of infrastructure projects around transport and communication known as TEN (Transport European Networks). This consisted of a series of projects in relation to roads, airports and railways (such as the HST) that included liberalising the abovementioned sectors on the principles of competitiveness (Urry 2007). This also rested, ultimately, on the belief that economic competitiveness could be associated with the circulation of vital resources such as human capital.

Therefore, within a context of economic reform and industrial restructuring, the emergence of powerful discourses identifying the existence of European areas of economic growth as opposed to areas of social and economic decline shaped the Basque government's vision for its future. The elaboration of the Basque government's policy agenda in the late 1980s was preceded by the development of a powerful discourse on the central role that building "connections" with areas of economic growth would have on the BAC's competitiveness. The notions of "connectivity" and "access" to European economic networks and areas of economic and social growth became central concerns when assessing the level of social development and economic capacity of regions (Gómez Uranga and Etxebarria 1993). Consequently, as the Spanish economic and industrial crisis deepened, so the territorial area formed by the BAC became identified as suffering from "disconnectiveness" or in "danger of not being connected" to the poles of growth. In other words, the Basque government raised concerns regarding "the peripheral" location of the BAC based on the belief that it was becoming marginalised from the political and economic centres of both Europe and Spain.

Further, there was a real fear that the Basque Country might "end up as an absolute peripheral region isolated from the European development [areas]."[15] As a result, the Basque government promoted an infrastructure plan called "Europe 93" (1989)[16] and negotiated with the central government the inclusion of all three provinces of the BAC into the high-speed train network (also known as the Basque Y). In this sense, the Basque government elaborated arguments concerning the BAC's privileged location at the crossroads between France and Spain (Agirre 1989). These arguments were central to the elaboration of issues of competitiveness in policy documents such as "Europe 93." Moreover, the idea that the Basque Country held such an advantaged geographical location as the corridor between Spain and Europe became one of the fundaments on which the Basque government built its case for the inclusion of the BAC into the European and national HST networks. In many ways, this notion of accessibility and "lack of access" has largely featured in EU policy documents in relation to economic competitiveness, particularly affecting peripheral regions in Europe. Equally, this concept has been explored within regional studies which consider "accessibility" crucial for the spatial distribution of economic activity (Holl 2007). This, however, as I will argue later in this chapter, can be linked to the EU aim of social and economic cohesion, where the objective of convergence became central after the further enlargement of the EU following the incorporation of Portugal (1986), Greece (1981), Spain (1986) and Ireland (1973) (Arestis and Palegini 1995; Amin and Tomaney 2002).

I will also contend later that, after Spain's EC incorporation in 1986, the Basque government acquired a presence in international institutions. At that time, Basque government representatives built and argued a case for

---

15. Ibid.

16. Subsequent transport infrastructure policy documents include *Euskadi XXI: Plan interinstitucional de infraestructuras y revitalización de áreas desfavorecidas* (Gobierno Vasco and Diputaciones Forales 1996) and *Avance del plan territorial sectorial de la red ferroviaria* (Gobierno Vasco 1997). See also Franco Ibarzabal (2004).

the inclusion of the Basque Y into the EU infrastructure priority projects. This included promoting the project by building on alliances with various Europe-wide regional associations such as the Association of European Trans-Border Regions;[17] and within the recently established Atlantic Arc Commission.[18] In many ways, this international lobbying activity was very important in making sure that the Basque Y was included in the European Essen priority projects (1994). This also reflects trends and practices within the EU whereby local and regional governments had to be perceived as being proactive or, in other words, entrepreneurial in promoting as well as contributing to creating competitive conditions within their respective economic spaces (Jessop 1997: 25; Jessop and Ngai-Ling 2000). The Basque government was successful, and this highly unlikely project was indeed included among the European Essen priority projects.

It has been argued that the integration and coordination of transport within EU policy initiatives transformed the EU into a key agent of the European "Single Market" plan (Ross 1998). As such, the revitalisation of areas in decline became associated with EU regional policies that aimed to counterbalance the rising dominance of so-called growth areas such as the Mediterranean corridor, the Ebro River area and the Metropolitan area of Madrid, in Spain. This local and regional focus on competitiveness and growth was complemented by wider policies on infrastructure development (mainly concerning transport) which included roads and railways. The rhetoric and visions of "growth" and competitiveness also became part of the Spanish railway policy agenda. In other words, the process of identifying "emerging areas of economic development" became the rationale as well as the justification for adopting and implementing particular projects and was an important principle guiding the political and economic strategy of the national government. Therefore, once the Madrid–Seville HST was completed, the government initiated the second stage of the Spanish HST network by developing the Madrid–Barcelona–French border HST railway system.

It could be argued that the development of regional and infrastructural policy programmes (nationally) is an important background against which to interpret Spain's decision to drop the use of "direct intervention"

---

17. "El País Vasco formará próximamente parte de la Asociación de Regiones Fronterizas Europeas," *El Diario Vasco*, 3 November 1989.

18. "El Consejo de Aquitania y el Gobierno Vasco crean una comisión del 'eje Atlántico,'" *El Diario Vasco*, 3 September 1989.

(for example, subsidies) as a mechanism to deal with the pressing demands of the industrial crisis. Indeed, Spain's "European solution" (Ross 1998) to the industrial crisis could be closely associated with being able to secure EC funding. This required the adoptions of industrial reforms such as downsizing and the closing down of unprofitable factories, privatizing public sector companies, labour market reforms and limiting public expenditure. In contrast, the Basque government pursued its own, more interventionist (given the scope of its powers) policy agenda that including developing an industrial policy focused on the specific problems of the industrial infrastructure in the BAC.

More specifically, the efforts made to address the industrial recovery in the BAC have included the implementation of a broad range of instruments that have been deployed at different levels such as firms, sectors and territorial areas. These instruments have consisted of different programmes and policies centred on aspects related to employment, technology and infrastructures. For example, the Basque government set up regional agencies such as SPRI (Sociedad para la Reconversión Industrial, the Basque Business Development Agency), which first developed a series of loans to help case-by-case problems (1981–1984), rather than a sectorial agenda. Subsequently, it evolved and became responsible for promoting technology innovation (1987–1992), company projects, enterprise creation (1994) and, later, internationalisation programmes. Other more sector orientated plans were the Plan Marco General de Actuación de Politica Industrial (General Framework Plan for Industrial Policy Action, 1991–1995) linked to steel-making companies. Other such sector-orientated plans developed by the Basque government included the clusters policy (1991–2002) based on consultancy work offered by Michael Porter and its notion of competitiveness (Arboníes and Moso 2002; Porter 2002; Ahedo 2006).

In addition, the Basque government also developed strategies that were negotiated with key stakeholders (like political parties and interest groups) and in which the local authorities (provincial governments and town councils) were also directly involved. Thus the development of industrial policy, support with restructuring, technology transfer and reconversion of the industrial base were areas of major concern for the Basque government (although similar strategies, with varying levels of success, were adopted in other ACs). Further, the Basque government's industrial policies were the outcome of intensive communication between tight-knit interpersonal networks among leading members of the ruling PNV and representatives of Basque industry, most strongly represented by the cooperative movement (Moso and Olazaran 2002: 62–3). These tight-knit interpersonal relations extended to the national level, which acted as the gatekeeper to relevant institutions of policy and decision-making at the EU level. This was crucial to opening up possibilities for the BAC to secure EC funding for its industrial recovery plans.

> This could take years. First of all we did not have the power to present it as a government initiative. So, there were some kind of "steal" agreements and the like, and with [José Claudio] Aranzadi, the former Industry Minister [of the Spanish government], I reached an agreement with him and he said "I will do something, being the Industry Minister, I will drop your proposal in Brussels but I will neither defend it nor pass any comment on it. I don't believe in this but you can find as many ways as you like, talk to whoever you need to talk to in order to defend it." He therefore presented the proposal and we spoke to the Competition commissioner and several others and as a result, our proposal was revised. It took them two years to reach a conclusion which was that the proposal could not be implemented in some cases. So what we did was to present the document along the European argument lines but what the document did not obtain was an approving settlement [*lo que no había era una resolución aprobatoria*].[19]

The difficulty here was that the BAC political and economic leadership had to necessarily operate in relation to specific historical legacies, while the European and national industrial policy strategies sought to adjust to global and international industrial competitiveness (European Commission 1993).

When we did the 3R here, industrial recovery, it was a time when nobody in Europe believed in industrial policy. [The main arguments had it] that industrial policy didn't exist. [However,] we wanted to pursue an active intervention because the country and the companies were falling apart. But Europe didn't allow us any public intervention. Neither did Spain. So we resorted to something else: the EU had developed the White Book on Industrial Policy. This book was finished a year before we started the debate and nobody had taken any decisions based on the findings and advice set out by the White Book. Such advice consisted of helping certain companies in crisis, but those companies in crisis with which the EU could compete against Japan and the US (as a continent not as a country)...

19. AA, former member of and adviser to the Basque government.

those companies also had to make up 10 percent of all EU employment. So what we did was where the text said Europe, "for us is Euskadi," where the text said interesting industries for Europe, for us were "interesting industries for Euskadi." We adapted the text with all the EU preambles and recommendations and we prepared a case. The problem was that the EU had to approve it.[20]

Despite such lobbying, however, the Basque government was unsuccessful in securing EC funds for its "industrial recovery" plan. For while the Basque government tried to develop a plan for industrial intervention, the EU and Spain had moved towards a neo-liberal agenda in which industry could not be directly supported. However, there was a difference between strategies in Spain and the EU. While Spain adopted EU policies to be able to draw on EU funding (and indeed successfully so), the EU had a more complicated agenda where it supported some industries and companies which were significant as a whole for Europe rather than just for individual countries (Apeldroon 2002).[21] In this sense, during the time that it took Brussels to decide whether or not to grant funds to the Basque government's industrial recovery plan, the Basque government went through a series of difficult negotiations with trade unions in order to settle the redundancy of no less than 22,000 employees. In fact, as a result of massive redundancies, in the mid-1980s unemployment rates in the BAC reached around 20 percent.

However, it is within this context that Spain managed to attract and successfully negotiate the Cohesion Fund. This was exclusively available to the poorest countries in Europe (Ireland, Greece, Portugal and Spain) (Murphy 1999) and Spain became one of its net beneficiaries. In other words, the Spanish government's compromise to advance further in the European integration process was "compensated" initially by successfully

20. Ibid.

21. Initially, the EC had an agenda to protect European strategic sectors against global competition. That is, during the time when Spain undertook to restructure its industrial base, the EU was concerned with developing "European national champions" that could compete against the US and Japan. Moreover, since such competition was unravelling in the technological gap between the EU and non-EU industries, EC strategy at the time tended to favour a type of industrial policy based on technological cooperation (for example, in the case of Airbus) and developing trans-European (infrastructure) networks. Therefore Spanish adoption of EU regulation (such as labour market flexibility and disincentives towards industrial intervention) was aimed at encouraging other sectors that incidentally happened to be sanctioned, not only by policy orientations (that is, regional cohesion) but also available funding in the EC (TENs, Structural and Cohesion Funds in the areas of infrastructures and, in particular, transport infrastructure).

accessing and acquiring Structural Funds and, later, playing a major role in settling the Cohesion Fund, after which Spain agreed to the proposed EU expansion and membership of the Eastern European countries, in particular Poland (Ross 1998; Granell 2001).

Spanish regions qualified for three out of five priority objectives, which were: Objective 1 (regions where GDP was less than 75 percent of the EU average), Objective 2 (areas of industrial decline), and Objective 5b (rural areas in need of economic diversification) (Heywood 1995: 153). Structural Funds were allocated according to a Community Support Framework (CSF) and then in turn developed for each priority area of the European Commission. The Spanish regions under the Objective 1 programme were Andalucía, Extremadura, Castile and León, Castile La Mancha, Asturias, Galicia, Valencia, the Canary Islands and Murcia, and they obtained approximately 300 million pounds (over 500 million dollars) for the period 1989–1993. Indeed, the money amounted to 27 percent of the total budget approved by the Commission.[22] As a result, the Spanish commitment to public investment in roads, railways, ports, airports and hydraulic engineering between 1986 and 1989 increased by 128 percent (ibid.: 227). The Structural Funds covered, to large extent, infrastructure projects, as is evident in the table 4.1.

**Table 4.1. Community Support Framework (CSF) ñ Breakdown by categories (%)**

| | Portugal | Spain | Ireland | Greece |
|---|---|---|---|---|
| *Infrastructure* | 27.3 | 53.1 | 17.1 | 31.3 |
| Investment aid | 17.0 | 9.9 | 26.5 | 7.0 |
| Agriculture | 11.9 | 14.0 | 24.5 | 13.0 |
| Manpower | 28.0 | 22.7 | 31.2 | 12.7 |
| Regional programmes | 15.6 | (a) | (b) | 34.5 |
| Others | 0.2 | 0.3 | 0.6 | 0.4 |
| TOTAL | 100 | 100 | 100 | 100 |

Source: European Economy, 1991a. Note: (a) Included in other categories
Adapted from Arestis and Paliginis (1995: 279).

22. "Landaburu: No descarto financiar infraestructuras en el País Vasco," El Diario Vasco, 21 September 1989.

From 1994–1999 Spain again became the major beneficiary, receiving 26.3 million ecu (approximately 31 million dollars) (Heywood 1995:154). Generally, the funds from which Spain benefited enormously had a significant impact on constructing and upgrading Spanish transport infrastructure projects. The importance of the funds and their impact on the Spanish transport infrastructure policy developments are well illustrated by the series of road-building programmes carried out at the turn of the century. Thus, while the Spanish motorway network consisted of 1,933 km in 1980, this increased to over 9,000 km by 2000. Further, an additional 1,400 km of dual carriageway were also built over the same period of time (Holl 2007: 286).[23] Equally significant has been investment in the HST. Since the development of a series of HST projects in Spain, 1,780 km of the railway infrastructure were built by early 2000s, while it increased to about 3,100 km by 2015 (Adif 2015). While transport infrastructure policies have been high on the EU policy agenda, there are significant differences between the types of infrastructures supported. Thus support for building road transport infrastructure is usually associated with poorer areas and sustainability priorities. In contrast, the very expensive and long-term oriented HST infrastructure is mainly about linking affluent key urban areas and is associated with competitiveness. While it could be expected that Spain has benefited enormously from EU support for improving and extending its road network, it is somewhat surprising that it has been also one of the main beneficiaries in building a HST infrastructure. These issues will be further discussed in chapter 5.

It is precisely in this context, in the late 1980s, that the Basque and Spanish governments negotiated a series of agreements by which the central government would undertake to invest in infrastructures in the Basque Country, including the Basque Y. The agreements, however, as I have already noted above, took place in difficult circumstances. In addition to the state withdrawal from industrial policy, by the time the Spanish "areas of industrial decline" (Objective 2) underwent a process of restructuring and regeneration, the EC's investment policy for such zones had already shifted to programmes related to employment and productivity, the environment and R&D activities. The EC was, then, now more reluc-

---

23. This, according to a key informant [EC], makes Spain, comparatively, the fourth best country equipped with motorways in the world behind the US, China and Germany.

tant to channel any funds into transport infrastructure projects[24] in the Basque Country.

Several initiatives, such as a report commissioned from Louvain University[25] which identified the factors that affected the Basque industrial structure negatively, seemed to have helped towards changing the opinions held within the EC concerning funding for Basque infrastructural projects. In fact, shortly after the study conducted by Louvain University was made public, Brussels announced that construction of the Bilbao underground and several other road plans included in the "Europe 93" plan would indeed be financed by the EC.[26] But in many ways, and most importantly, it was the development of new coalitions within the new Spanish democratic state -such as that formed between the PNV and the Basque branch of the statewide PSOE, the PSE (Basque Socialist Party), between 1986 and 1991—that was decisive in the Basque government's quest to implement and gain recognition for its major plans such as "Europe 93" and the Basque HST. Indeed, two of the key government positions within the Basque government (Transport and Public Works and Finance) were occupied by members of the PSOE-PSE (Bourne 2001). In this sense, Bourne argues that the PSOE-PSE was very influential in securing the first ERDP map that acknowledged the need for financial support for the traditional industrial area situated on the left bank of the Nervion River in Bilbao. It was designated as an Objective 1 area (ibid.: 12), hence subject to Structural Funds and the recipient of important EC investment money for the city regeneration plans that would largely rest on regenerat ing former industrial land and developing important transport infrastructure projects, such as the Bilbao underground (Rodríguez 2002; González 2003; 2005). Incidentally, while the Louvain University report offered a full assessment of the state of Basque industry, the study also expressed the need for the Basque Country to be connected to other European areas of

---

24. "En Bruselas se cuestionan la conveniencia de financiar infraestructuras en el Plan de Reconversión Vasco," *El Diario Vasco*, 6 September 1989.

25. "CE: informe encargado por la Comisión recomienda inversiones en infraestructuras en el País Vasco," *El Diario Vasco*, 22 November 1989. Among the factors, the problems affecting the Basque industrial structure identified in the report were: the small dimension of companies; the lack of cooperation between subsectors in the areas of metal transformation, machine-tools and automotive components; weak productivity in low value added activities; poor development of marketing, design and advertisement; low profit margins and a high dependency on credits; low R&D, etc.

26. "La Comunidad Europea financiara proyectos de infraestructura en el País Vasco," *El Diario Vasco*, 23 November 1989.

growth, and following on this it pointed out the importance of the city of Bilbao within the European "scale of cities."

Bilbao, among the different cities and towns situated along the Atlantic coast (including the two other provincial capital cities, Donostia-San Sebastián and Vitoria-Gasteiz, in the BAC) and other settlements within inland areas of northern Spain such as Pamplona-Iruñea (Navarre) and La Rioja, became regarded as a metropolitan area of major importance in Spain. One of the major strategies, then, as a solution to the Basque industrial crisis, coincided with a European shift, within the context of integration and increasing internationalisation of capital, towards the development of urban areas and a strong regional policy. In this sense, Gómez Uranga and Etxebarria (1993) refer to the study carried out by RECLUS in 1989, centred around the classification of different metropolitan agglomerations according to some sixteen indicators, which concluded that centres made up of industrial towns in crisis such as Bilbao occupied a very low position among other European metropolitan cities due to their lack of internal as well as external communication infrastructures. This can illustrate, in some ways, how the solution of the "industrial crises" that hit the Basque industrial structure in general, since it rested on the heavy industry (steel, iron and shipbuilding, mainly in Bizkaia-Bilbao) and the intermediate manufacturing production of SMEs (mainly in the inland towns of Gipuzkoa; and to a lesser extent in Araba), was articulated through policies of urban regeneration rather than comprehensive industrial plans. There seems to have been a division of labour and different priorities among the coalition partners in the Basque government. The Christian democratic nationalist party, the PNV, focused mainly on putting the Basque Country on the map of the Europe of regions and peoples, while the PSOE-PSE was predominantly concerned with the regeneration of Bilbao, for which it was lobbying both nationally (using its links with the ruling PSOE in Madrid) as well as on the European level. Thus the Basque government sought to pursue a combination of regional- and city-centred strategies on the national and international levels, both of which aimed to build links and create shorter distances between the Basque Country, Spain and Europe.

## The EC, the Convergence Plan and Transport Infrastructures

Internationally, the late 1980s and early 1990s witnessed the acceleration of market integration (as a result of the collapse of communism), a number of budgetary arrangements for various programmes (including infrastructures) and the inauguration of the INTERREG programme (with EU emphasis on Euro-regions in order to encourage regions to collaborate with one another on common problems so as to foster a more cohesive European market). As suggested above, programmes and policies regarding infrastructures, and particularly transport infrastructure, became very important in the context of Spanish industrial restructuring and EC membership.

Some authors note that (transport) infrastructure programmes were linked to the creation of the European Single Market and the more than successful lobbying activity of the industrial sector through the European Round Table of Industrialists (ERT) (Apeldroon 2002; Peters 2003). In particular, Peters refers to the ERT's 1984 report "Missing Links – Upgrading Europe's Trans-border Ground Transport Infrastructure: A Report for the Roundtable of European Industrialists," which in her opinion "outlined three specific proposals for a "channel link between England and France," a Scanlink plan for road and rail connections in Scandinavia, and a trans-European network of high-speed trains" (ibid.: 328). Further, Apeldoorn (2002) suggests that the ERT played a key role in promoting (transport) infrastructure programmes on the European integration agenda from 1983–1988. Yet its involvement was neither straightforward or (to use some of the favourite policy jargon within the EU) a "cooperating and coordinated" effort but, rather, the outcome of contested and conflicting interests, visions and strategies. In fact, Apeldoorn identifies two main contending factions at this stage: a neo-mercantilist approach and a neo-liberal approach. The former defended an agenda of market integration (similar to the aspirations of the business leaders within the neo-liberal approach, Apeldroon notes) but, contrary to the latter, the neo-mercantilist faction further suggested that a European Single Market could create economies of scale and thus help European businesses grow enough to be able to compete against US and Japanese firms. In other words, European market expansion, according to this approach, should be accompanied by protectionist measures to secure the dominance of home-bred European businesses. In addition to tariff removals, the ERT also proposed five key areas of action, one of which was, importantly, the development of infrastructure programmes (ibid. 2002: 114–132). In this context, the new European Commission chaired by Jacques Delors took the ERT idea seriously and five months later he produced his famous White Paper on Growth, Employment and Competitiveness (1993), which developed a conception which, according to Ross, "revolved around major public work projects under an overarching EU regulatory umbrella [and] having economic growth and employment objectives" (1998: 198) as well as advocating the completion of the Single Market by 1992.

This explains why several authors highlight the immense influence that industry, embodied by the ERT, had on key Commission groups (Doherty and Hoedeman 1994; Richardson 1997). These authors also note that transport policies thus conceived cannot and have never been unable to fulfil the EU's environmental policy requirements, nor have they been able to satisfy any financial, viability and profitability criteria (Ross 1998). I will argue in chapter 5 that financial issues and risk-taking problems (which are, to some extent, related to the former) dominated the progress and development of European (transport) infrastructure programmes in the 1990s and 2000s.

Generally speaking, according to Apeldoorn (2002), the neo-mercantilist approach did not succeed because the removal of internal tariffs was not accompanied by the setting up of any external barriers, thus allowing the penetration of US and Japanese firms; and also because the collapse of the Berlin Wall facilitated the rise of neo-liberalism as well as opening up the possibilities of new markets in Central and Eastern Europe. Nonetheless, infrastructure projects remained valid as an element of European industrial policy and there was a further push towards an internal market integration project. Furthermore, in the run up to the passing of the Maastricht Treaty in 1992, the ERT published four more reports on infrastructures (Apeldroon 2002: 143) which supported the development of Trans-European Network (TEN) projects and which were finally formalised in the Maastricht Treaty itself (Title XV, Articles 154–156). In fact, the proposals the ERT put forward in the early 1980s were later materialised into a list of fourteen TEN priority projects adopted at the Essen Summit in 1994 by the Christophersen Commission Group. Thus, according to Peters, "not only did the 1994 EU list end up including the Channel tunnel and the Oeresund [also spelled Øresund in Danish, Öresund in Swedish] road-rail bridge as individual priority projects, but both were also integrated into a network of high-speed rail links that picked up most of the connections originally proposed by ERT 10 years earlier" (Peters 2003: 329).

In addition to the ERT lobbying for the development of trans-European infrastructure networks, internal pressure also pushed for the adoption of the missing links. Although the EC, at that time, had taken important steps towards further integration (mainly through the promotion of the single market, transport infrastructure projects and measures towards the flexibilisation of the labour market), other initiatives such as common defence and foreign cooperation (that could suggest, partially, advancement towards a "European state") could not be introduced within an integration agenda. In this scenario and trying to keep a sense of union alive and evolving, the missing links, given their cross-border nature, provided a truly pan-European policy scheme (Ross 1998; Apeldoorn 2002; Peters 2003). In fact, given that the reality of developing the TENs has been riddled with problems related to financing and profitability concerns, as I will argue later, they nevertheless remained under the coordination responsibilities of what later became the EU Commission.

Therefore, the development of the TENs was not only closely linked to the creation of the European Single Market, under the active involvement of the ERT but, as noted above, internal pressures also facilitated the creation and adoption of trans-European networks. These were initially formalised in the Maastricht Treaty and approved at the Essen Summit in 1994. Finally, they were approved and it is in this sense that the development of a Trans-European Transport infrastructure map, in particular, preceded the establishment of the EU. Furthermore, national governments were also interested in seeing these projects through. In particular, France's EC Presidency agenda in 1989[27] sought to put forward discussions over a future trans-European network schema. In this sense, Apeldoorn (2002) notes that French national interests were very close to those expressed by the neo-mercantilist faction within the ERT and that in the 1980s this shaped the process of market integration. In other words, France agreed with the idea of domestic market development as grounds on which to nurture the consolidation and expansion of transnational corporations (TNCs) in order to be able to compete against global competition in the future. But moreover, given France's interventionist tradition, it would have been keen on developing an industrial scheme that would support France's strategic sectors. I will argue that France's interest in promoting the TENs is related to the fact that a large number of them are high-speed trains. That is, France saw in the development of the TENs a way to promote its home-grown high-speed train technology and thus provide its national railway industry (Alstom) with further European

27. "Barrionuevo defiende ante la CE la conexión del TAV por Irún," *El Diario Vasco*, 17 October 1989.

markets. In particular, as I argue later, Alstom benefited from the Spanish public tender to produce the Spanish high-speed train because, as some observers noted at the time, only European railway technology would have been allowed to operate in Europe (Suárez 1989), as opposed to Japanese competition, for example. Two other factors also influenced the awarding of the public tender to Alstom. First, Alstom agreed to lead the restructuring of the Spanish railway industry and produce 70 percent of high-speed trains in Spain. Second, it has been observed that Spain and France might have developed a series of bilateral agreements concerning ETA members living in France, who hitherto had been residing there with more or less tacit French approval (Woodworth 2001). According to these interpretations, then, the awarding of the tender to Alstom would have been the result of a series of political agreements that might have also included the extradition of ETA members by France to the Spanish authorities.[28]

As I have suggested so far, a transport infrastructure programme was regarded by the ERT and the EC members as an essential pillar of European integration alongside the achievement of the internal market. However, the restructuring of the transport sector also became a question of synchronising regulations (in the case of railways, restructuring the public railway companies), in addition to "bringing existing networks up to EU standards" (Peters 2003: 320). In this sense, though, until the mid-1980s EC member states resisted the introduction of a Common European Transport Policy. In fact, the opposition of member states reached breaking point in 1985 when the European Constitutional Court warned that the lack of a common European transport policy breached one of the principles stated in the Treaty of Rome. As regards the stepping stones of the Community towards a single Transport market, it was not until 1988 when the EC declared free movement and competitiveness as well as transport infrastructure projects to be part of the development of the internal market that the conditions emerged to start developing a common transport policy. I will address the stages and development of the EU transport liberalisation process in the next chapter.

---

28. José Barrionuevo was quoted saying "If ETA members were coming in the French TGV, I would sign the purchase immediately" [*Si en el TAV francés vinieran los miembros de ETA, firmaría la compra*], *Cinco Días*, 25 November 1988, quoted in AHTaren Aurkako Asanblada (2000). Note that the awarding of the public tender to produce the Spanish high-speed train to Alstom was made public on the 23 December 1988.

As far as transport investment is concerned, the TEN's budget was created specifically to finance its priority projects. According to Peters (2003: 320), 60 percent of that budget covers the nine high-speed rail projects among the fourteen TEN priority projects.[29] Thus Peters suggests that, given that transport infrastructures were linked to the creation of the internal market, transport spending became a kind of compensatory formula for the countries perceived as "less well positioned" or "less prepared" to compete within the future single market. For them, transport investment was a kind of "competitive policy" in the sense that it compensated and at the same time tried to improve the "competitive" chances of less "able" European member states. So it seems plausible that the structural and, later, Cohesion Funds became mechanisms of redistribution under the disguise of enabling supply-side restructuring and readaptation. It is in this sense that, as suggested earlier, transport infrastructure projects became further linked to the notion of the "accessibility" as well as "connectivity" of peripheral areas to areas of economic and social activity. In particular, under Maastricht Treaty Title XV, TENs aim at "promoting the interconnection and the inter-operability of national networks as well as access to such networks . . . in particular of the need to link island, landlocked and peripheral regions with the central regions of the Community" (Article 154). Further, the TEN became linked to the regional policy through Article 155: "the EU would support specific projects of common interest [which are backed] by member states . . . the Community would be able to provide a financial contribution through the Cohesion Fund . . . to specific projects . . . in the area of transport infrastructure" (See further discussion in Ross 1998: 186–187).

The macro-economic disparities within the EU and the introduction of even more varied institutional regulatory frameworks (Jessop 2008) were further complicated by the acceptance of new member states which were also facing economic problems that differed from most of the old member states. These different processes made it necessary to develop new institutional mechanisms that would be better suited to these conditions. One example is the creation and administration of the "Structural Funds"

29. However, not all transport infrastructure projects were part of the TEN, nor were they related to high-speed trains. In particular, most transport spending under the Cohesion and ERDF funds was aimed at building roads. Specifically, two-thirds of all investments went on roads and highways. Spain and the countries designated as "poorest member states of the EU" (Greece, Ireland and Portugal) continued enjoying TEN-related priority investments in the period 1993–1999 (Peters 2003: 320).

that were aimed at assisting the convergence of member states' economies. However, the funds available especially after the 1988–1993 reform were insufficient to improve the productive capabilities of peripheral economies (Arestis and Paliginis 1995: 263).

Convergence policy mostly addresses one of the two key EU priorities: sustainability and competitiveness. These seem to be the notions around which a new "structure of coherence" (Harvey 1982) is organised in order to address problems as well as strategies and tactics in order to create the necessary conditions for an emerging new round of mode of accumulation. In this context, the OMC (also referred to as soft law[30]) and spatial planning have emerged as mechanisms to encourage the adaptation as well as transformation of national, regional and local policies, practices and procedures (Jessop 2008). However, as suggested in Kok's report (2004), the tendency towards an overly managerial approach on the EU level reveals an inability to address the broader political, historical and social embeddedness of these processes. Thus, as will be discussed in the following chapters, the process of building the HST infrastructure has been continuously negotiated and adapted (changing over time) to strategic priorities of different stakeholders. While these negotiations are adapted in terms of rhetorics and substance to the different objectives set by the EU, they are also embedded into a specific institutional framework, historical legacies, economic interests and national projects in Spain and the Basque Country.

In other words, the link between transport and poorer areas became a powerful notion that underpinned the orientation and objectives of EU funding mechanisms such as the ERDF and Cohesion Fund. This is rather ironic because many have claimed that the development of infrastructures tends to favour and tends to be more important for central rather than peripheral areas. And in cases when it connects peripheral areas it tends to favour more centrally positioned urban areas rather than regions as a whole (Peters 2003).

Therefore, the formula of "people and regions *travelling* from poverty to richness" has been questioned by many commentators and other EU documents and has been challenged by other approaches such as the

30. The Open Method of Coordination, also so-called "soft law," refers to an informally agreed set of mechanisms put in place to try to influence states to comply with EU regulation, without having to use punitive law enforcement. These mechanisms include guidelines, benchmarking, peer pressure, timetabling, and so on.

European Spatial Development Perspective (ESDP). Thus, for example, perspectives on agglomeration strategies, which seek to prevent the over-concentration of resources into small number of locations,[31] that is, by promoting the development of policentricity, have rejected general claims that support the argument that TENs can contribute to social and economic cohesion. In particular, Peters refers to a document adopted (but not published) by the European Commission in 1999 which recognises that "a large part of the EU transport investments are concentrated on high-speed railway lines connecting major conurbations and that cities close to high-speed stops will profit most from these investments" (2003: 327). In this respect, in the opinion of some of my informants the high-speed train is proving to have the same sucking effect in favour of the biggest metropolitan urban areas as the highways have.[32] In this sense, Peters's conclusion is very relevant because according to her, behind the EU investments in transport infrastructure lies the objective "to improve conditions for business and trade between the most powerful, most competitive urban agglomerations in Europe" (ibid.: 331).

Nevertheless, as I argued above, the Spanish government's involvement in the development of the Cohesion Fund was crucial. In particular, the former Spanish prime minister, Felipe González, played a pivotal role in the creation of the Cohesion Fund in exchange for Spanish support for the EU enlargement in 1992 (Viñas 2001). I also suggested that Spain became the most important recipient of the Cohesion Fund –no wonder that it became the second best EU member state in implementing single market directives– and also received just over a quarter of all Structural Funds for the periods 1988–1991 and 1993–1999 (Heywood 1995).

All of this suggests that the division of EU guidance and competencies reveals a myriad of ways of interpreting and conceiving transport infrastructure development – although Peters (2003) suggests that ultimately a businesslike approach prevails and the main urban areas are those getting most from it. In this sense, Apeldoorn (2002) argues that transport infrastructure was conceived as part of a European industrial policy which

31. Peters (2003) argues that the strategy based on fostering other agglomeration centres is due to the influence of the French spatial planning agency DATAR, which produced a series of maps claiming to represent the concentration of areas of economic growth, against more marginal areas, and as such, it identified the London–Milan corridor as the central area of economic and social importance.

32. AJ, member of Ecologists in Action; and AB, journalist and railway specialist.

would accompany the creation of the single market development. Further, regional policy guidelines developed an approach that linked the notions of transport and poverty. In other words, transport became like a silver bullet to target the "ills" of peripheral and marginalised areas within the future of the new European Single Market space. Consequently, the Structural and Cohesion Funds covered to a significant extent transport infrastructure projects and although TEN programmes largely promote high-speed trains, the bulk of all Structural and Cohesion budgets went to the construction of roads and highways. Hence, the distribution of this money, partially, became a way to compensate poorer countries in a far worse location to compete within the European common market.

However, it has been argued that transport infrastructure cannot be invoked to explain and cure more marginal areas of the EU. It seems unlikely that TENs, especially the HST, will shift road traffic to the railways and, in any case, EU transport infrastructure investments already benefit central rather than peripheral areas. This is because the most competitive urban agglomerations in Europe benefit most from investments in transport infrastructure. In subsequent chapters I will maintain that Spain's railway strategy and, overall, transport and urban strategies, have clearly "enabled"/benefited the development/expansion of the two main metropolitan areas, Madrid and Barcelona, and especially their connection to Seville and Valencia. In particular, the Spanish government's priority, after the completion of the Seville–Madrid link, was the development of the Madrid–Barcelona–Valencia–Madrid triangle, something that did not change significantly in the shift from PSOE (1982–1996) to PP (1996–2004) governments. In this sense, I argue that public transport infrastructure investment and industrial restructuring (privatisation and liberalisation) were key economic strategies pursued by the Spanish government under the PSOE leadership.

Interestingly, however, the Basque government could also draw on Structural and Cohesion Funds by claiming "peripheral status" as part of the Atlantic Arc and relative isolation from major EU circuits of the global economy. Hence the Basque City, which will be discussed in chapter 7, can be seen as a region (NUTS II) within the EU, an autonomous community within Spain and imagined homeland for the Basque nation, as well as a competitive polycentric urban area/urban region (in this sense, as opposed to Bilbao alone fulfilling that criteria). Thus, while it might seem that the Basque government advances apparently contradictory arguments, it also appears that the Basque government can build different types of coalitions (for example, that of the PNV-PSOE) and reconcile apparently contradictory arguments (namely, being peripheral / the Basque City). This can be read as a form of strategic adaptation and also as an example of the Basque Country's indeterminate position in terms of economic competitive advantage and future. As a result, unlike Catalonia, where Barcelona dominates the autonomous community and is the undisputed leader as well as a central city within Spain *and* a major European hub, the Basque Country has an indeterminate direction of economic development and competitive strategy (for example, Bilbao has equally attractive prospects whether as part of the Basque Country project or as a major urban area of northern Spain or even the Atlantic Arc). The different narratives as well as strategies of Basqueness can, then, be linked politically. However, this can only be done provisionally as significant competencies are distributed amongst the three provincial councils, and also there are different and often competing definitions of spatial and institutional boundaries that overlap within the same territorial space. I will explore this in chapter 5 but, for the moment, I want to emphasise that this early period (comprising the mid-1980s and early 1990s) was marked by the success of the Basque government's strategy, within the PNV-PSOE coalition, to (a) secure structural funding, (b) to develop an intensive international networking activity to promote the Atlantic Arc on the grounds of the peripheral position of the regions situated along the arc, and (c) to introduce the Basque Y into Spanish railway development plans and into trans-European networks.

The cases of Spain and the Basque Country show that EU transport infrastructure policy frameworks and political and economic strategies had different objectives and depended on the stages of EU development. Equally, the debates on transport infrastructure and, in particular, the HST, were also evolving differently within Spain and the Basque Country and the focus of debates changed over time, with the project acquiring different meanings in each period on the national, subnational and supranational level. For example, the EU transport agenda was dominated by economic concerns over industrial protection as well as support for home-bred European firms. Politically, EU institutions found in transport infrastructure a way to bridge the gap between poorer and richer spaces within the union. In other words, as suggested earlier, funding of transport infrastructure projects became a way to compensate/distribute money to poorer regions on the grounds that they could develop a better competitive chance once the single European market was established. Likewise, while the Spanish government was developing transport infrastructure projects as a way of supporting a new strategy of economic growth, links to the EU and access to EU funds, the main concern for the Basque Country was economic development and industrial restructuring together with developing broader links with the EU on the one hand and, on the other, social cohesion within the project of state- and nation-building. This contrasts with Spain, where transport infrastructure was purely dominated by an economic rationale and the HST was discussed through the vocabulary of modernisation. Later chapters will argue that in the Basque government case, the economic aspect has disappeared and its justification remains mostly around issues of "cohesion" and "connectivity."

Changes in Spain after the death of Franco were mainly a period of transition in which a predominantly political crisis was followed by an economic restructuring. Such an interpretation of the transition implies that economic restructuring can be seen as a set of processes that were, first, independent from the process of the political transition and, second, that there was a temporal sequence in the unfolding of separate sets of political and economic changes. The political crisis is mainly assumed to have originated from the "unhealed scars" of the civil war and Franco's autocratic regime that suppressed its political opponents. In this sense, the recovery and the transition to a democratic political system (which is seen as the last stage in the long process of the Spanish nation-state formation) is usually associated with the "reinstatement" of justice by granting autonomy to the "historic nations" as well as the legal re-establishment of trade unions and political parties. In this sense, joining the EC was seen as an important part of the "completion" of the political transition in Spain as well as the motivation for undertaking economic reforms, a prerequisite for EC membership.

However, as I argued in chapter 1, the political and economic aspects of the transition in Spain need to be situated within broader processes of global economic and political restructuring and the crisis of Atlantic Fordism. In this respect, the Spanish transition primarily was a transition from Fordism to Post-Fordism. More specifically, devolution in Spain cannot be narrowly defined as just a political and administrative process but is closely interdependent with both the Post-Fordist restructuring of the relatively peripheral Spanish economy (including its internal restructuring and the creation of a Basque economy), and its full integration into the European and global economy and political institutions.

Institutional restructuring and the political and economic implications of the creation of the State of Autonomies in Spain. The latter involved the establishment of the seventeen autonomous communities (ACs), the dismantling of urban corporations and the creation of a weak Senate. In this sense, although Spain is often considered a quasi-federal state in the sense that the central and regional powers remain to an extent separate, the government remains the centre of policymaking, bilateral relations prevail in relations between central government and the ACs and political negotiations within central government are established at the level of political party coalitions and alliances that often include regional parties. Further, the process of devolution in Spain needs to be discussed within the context of ongoing restructuring in the EC.

EC integration and access to EC funds were key aspects of Spanish government strategy for an economic restructuring. Access to these funds, however, was tied to requirements for adopting EU legislation, expectations for a far-reaching administrative reform as well as adopting neo-liberal policies. While the latter were introduced under pressure from the EC, they were also dominant in international policy and business circles, and were also believed by successive Spanish governments to be the right way to restructure the capitalist system in Spain. Second, the changes introduced were discussed in relation to normatively charged discourses associated with the need for (as well as the benefit of) "modernisation" and market development, privatisation and liberalisation as the only mechanisms to achieve it. In short, the need for reform and Post-Fordist adaptation and restructuring of the economy was met by consolidating a liberal market economy on the national level, which was the only available option and was discussed through a discourse of "modernisation."

While access to EC funds was crucial for both the Spanish government and the autonomous communities in regard to economic and political restructuring, their strategies in this regard were very different. Accordingly, national and autonomous governments were integrated differently within the EC institutions and pursued different strategies of restructuring that ranged from almost total withdrawal from intervention in the case of central government (where intervention was mainly based on the development of partnerships) to the moderate pursuit of a state interventionist industrial policy agenda in the case of Basque government. This is consistent with a process of institutional restructuring within Spain in which central government was increasingly adopting a steering role in the channelling of EC funds among different priorities, while the ACs took over designing, planning and implantation.[33] However, institutional restructuring in Spain cannot be reduced to the elaboration of a hierarchical institutional model as it was significantly complicated by the multi-layered relations that developed between national and autonomous authorities, the EC, regions, cities and businesses.[34]

In contrast, in chapter 3 I discussed Franco's regime as a form of semi-peripheral Fordism. Franco's regime differed from other Fordist States in terms of its institutional structure and the role of the state in the process of wage bargaining, managing social consumption and aggregate demand. More specifically, Spain lacked a consolidated institutional bargaining framework and that one of the outcomes of this was that Spanish industrial relations were managed through so-called vertical syndicates, which in turn were effectively a part of the bureaucracy of the state and controlled by the government. The lack of an appropriate institutional structure for collective bargaining meant that wage rises did not always follow productivity gains but were used as a political tool to counterbalance workers' demands (primarily within industries where foreign capital was dominant). Further, I also argued that Franco's regime was characterised by a weak welfare provision combined with an authoritarian regime, which can be described as a quasi-Keynesian welfare national state (KWNS). In this sense, the neo-liberal reforms which took place in Spain cannot be associated with measures as painful as in other parts of Europe where the welfare state was strong (for example, in Eastern Europe), while it also dif-

---

33. In this context, according to Keating, "like the unions, the employer's organisation found it difficult to gain access to the process of policy formulation under the Socialist administration, dominated increasingly after the mid-1980s by the drive for competitiveness within Europe" (1993: 340). Following Keating's analysis, it could be argued that, given that the Spanish employer's organisation (the CEOE) lacked direct "access" to the Spanish government, strong territorial autonomies in Spain would drive towards intra-regional strategies, while the Spanish government focused on national strategies for those specific industries the EC considered competitive European-wise.

34. Talking about Structural Funds is just as important for the political and economic elites of a regional area that is in charge of implementing and developing projects. Thus, for example, the small and medium automotive and machine tool industry in the Basque Country has found in internationalisation its most prominent strategic adaptation; in contrast to, for example, Madrid or Barcelona, where there are headquarters of multinationals companies and therefore a strategy based on internationalisation is less likely. Moreover, tertiarisation and the secondary sector require different types of strategies as is evident from the emergence of entrepreneurial cities (Jessop 2000) and, for example, the "clustering" of regional economic activity, both of which are dependent on different types of investments and the capacity to attract different types of capital.

fered from other Western European countries in the sense that state support of public services could remain relatively low (Navarro 2004), simply because such a provision has never been extensive.

The socio-political agreements known as the Moncloa Pacts formed the basis of a weakly institutionalised collective bargaining system in Spain. However, they opened up a time-frame in which the PSOE could initiate a series of key reforms. Although the PSOE defines itself as a social democratic party, the reforms that it undertook, such as the reduction of fiscal deficit, privatisation, control of inflation and salary increases, were profoundly neo-liberal in nature. The latter reforms had a direct impact on reducing labour security as well as the fragmentation of the labour movement. In this chapter I also suggested that, in addition to adopting neo-liberal macro-economic policies, the Spanish government abandoned its hitherto planned industrial policy, while also giving more powers to the banks (Pèrez 1997). The PSOE government, then, adopted a legal and institutional framework which allowed banks to restructure, grow and become internationally competitive. In this sense, the post-Franco restructuring led by the Spanish national government is defined best as a state led neo-liberal strategy.

In addition, the prevailing EC liberalisation agenda was strongly influenced by the ERT (Round Table of Industrialists), which also put transport reform at the forefront of EC policy-making "by calling for a more activist European regulatory dimension for industry and for transport infrastructure upgrading" (Ross 1998: 49). In a way, transport infrastructure projects were considered viable instruments to assess the effectiveness of regional cohesion policies and therefore, as noted earlier, a whole set of funding was put in place such as, partially, the Cohesion Fund and, specifically, the TENs. In this sense, the Basque government put the "Europe 93" plan at the centre of its development strategy with the "aim of enhancing our role as a strategic axis of connection with Europe and within the Spanish state."[35] Indeed, the need to connect the Basque Country to the main economic and political centres became a powerful motto of Basque political and economic elites.

The post-Franco transition in Spain was led by the centre-left PSOE, which prioritised the flexibilisation of the labour market, industrial restructuring and the development of supply-side initiatives (namely, infrastruc-

35. Advertisement spot for "Europe 93" in *El Diario Vasco*, 31 October 1989.

tures), the consequences of which were the privatisation of (often still profitable) industries and the reorganisation of unprofitable industries that had been previously supported through INI (Navarro 1997), including the railway industries and the public railway company Renfe. From the political viewpoint, the establishment of the State of Autonomies created the regional government level, against the opposition of the Spanish right, which became a new player within the new electoral game; although as Heywood (1995) and Börzel (2001) point out, there is no significant representation in the Senate for a more interregional and national articulation of problems. As a result, Spanish policy and budgetary distribution has been mediated and dominated by the Constitutional Court and unilateral bargaining (Montoro 2005).

# 5

# Economic Restructuring, Institutional Reform and the Return of the Railways

I argued in the previous chapter that the Post-Franco transition and subsequent EU entry marked two very important moments in the recent history of Spain. With the transition, Spain became a fully democratic state which brought far-reaching political reforms such as the constitution of the State of Autonomies (which radically transformed the centralist and unitary nature of Spain by institutionally setting up a new regional government layer) as well as important economic reforms and industrial restructuring. Chapter 4 mainly focused on the early stages of the post-Franco restructuring in Spain when political and administrative reforms were at the top of the government agenda, although I argued that economic restructuring should be interpreted as intrinsic to the very process of the "transition." In this chapter I will continue discussing the nature and direction of economic restructuring, but I will focus on the debates surrounding the question of transport infrastructure development. More specifically, I will argue that the restructuring of railways and the development of the HST project, in particular, from the mid-1980s onwards, need to be understood in relation to several factors and processes: first, the industrial restructuring process in Spain. This included the development of commercial partnerships with MNCs with the aim of achieving a more efficient and technologically competitive sector for equipment and rolling stock development (Guillen 2001). Hence, railway policy had a clear sectoral and economic logic. This concern, the recovery of the railway industry (as argued in chapter 4), was taken up at the supranational level as a European industrial policy strategy; second, the shift from an industry-based economic growth model to a model based on urban regeneration was important for two reasons. On the one hand, public transport infrastructure development was crucial in relation to regeneration projects for post-industrial cities such as Bilbao (for example, as regards its underground and tram systems) (Rodríguez and Martínez 2003; Siemiatycki 2005). In addition, railways were associated with a rationale of spatial articulation and territorial planning. This was further linked to a) questions of nation-building at the national level (Bel 2012), but also, as I argue in this book, at the regional level too, and b) the promotion of a European (high-speed) railway network in order to enhance the connectivity between major European cities. This lent support, to a large degree, to the transportation of passengers/workers employed in the emerging sectors associated with the transformation of cities: finance, cultural industries, and so forth. This was further linked to EU *integration*, and it is not surprising that it emerged at a time when the Single European Act came into effect (1987) and the creation of a Single Market (1992) was looming already on the horizon; third, the issue of public transport infrastructure development needs to be contextualised also in relation to funding availability as well as the reconfiguration of the institutional framework encompassing the development and implementation of such projects. Therefore, the evolution of public transport infrastructure development policies at the EU (for example, TENs) and national (for example, the first management contract, 1984–1986, Primer contrato programa; PEIT 2005–2020) level were crucial because they involved the creation of financing instruments and budgetary arrangements (such as the Structural Funds). This in itself constituted an important source of money to boost employment and economic indicators at the regional level (although such policies involved restructuring and downsizing the state railway company Renfe). Moreover, transport infrastructure development was closely linked to the decentralisation process in Spain and the devolution of regional powers related to planning and infrastructure development, similar institutional trends upwards at the EU level as well as the creation of systems of governance for transport policy development and implementation (such as transport consortiums and private-public partnerships).

The new political system in Spain, characterised by a structure of bilateral relations between national and regional units (in the absence of intermediary structures to articulate interregional interests), provided the new scenario for developing inter-party alliances between regional branches of statewide parties and specifically regional parties. Accordingly, the political coalition formed by the PNV and the Basque regional branch of the PSOE, the PSE (at the time when the statewide PSOE was in government and implementing all the key reforms) was also crucial for implementing transport infrastructure policies in the BAC. In this sense, questions about the significance and feasibility of the HST have been framed by debates about the role that railways and transport infrastructure more generally should have in relation to modernisation and economic development (Bel 2012), their contribution to R&D and industrial renovation (Guillen 2001), connectivity and cohesion (Gómez Uranga and Etxebarria 1993) and competitiveness (Campos 2008). These debates are a useful entry point into the ongoing negotiation and renegotiation in the strategies of different players such as central and autonomous governments, transport authorities and consortiums, multinationals, infrastructure developers, railway operators and the infrastructure related production and service industries (see discussion below).

As I argued in chapter 4, Spain was allowed access to EC structural and later also to Cohesion Funds in exchange for its commitment to privatisation and liberalisation strategies, the adoption of EEC guidelines to restrain from direct intervention in the economy and subsidizing industrial policy in the future (Etxezarreta 1991). More specifically, and concerning the restructuring of the transport sector, this meant steps towards the privatisation of the state-owned railway company, Renfe. This move involved the separation of rail-track operation (Renfe operadora), on the one hand, and infrastructure development and maintenance, Adif (Railway Infrastructure Administrator, Administrador de Infraestructuras Ferroviarias), on the other. However, the privatisation and liberalisation of these state-owned companies only took place with the 2005 railway law, introduced by the new PSOE government led by Zapatero in 2004 (Barea, Dizy and Ruiz 2007).

While in the early 1980s (as discussed in chapter 4) the newly established Basque government was mostly concerned with the process of consolidating as well as legitimating its politico-institutional apparatus, the late 1980s was characterised by a growing confidence and a focus on developing a long-term economic and social vision for the future of the Basque Country. In a similar way to the Spanish central government and the EC, the government of the BAC also emphasised the significance transport infrastructure had for social cohesion and competitiveness. Within this context, the Atlantic Arc discourse played an important role for supporting claims concerning questions regarding the peripheral status of the Basque Country (not simply the capital cities of the Basque Country) with regard to other major European urban areas (Wise 2000b). I will argue that one of the main successes of this strategy was the incorporation of the HST, but, in particular the Y layout, in Spanish national transport infrastructure policy (PEIT 2005) and EU transport infrastructure policy (Essen 1994), which put forward a railway infrastructure plan to develop a railway network linking the three capital cities of the BAC (Donostia-San Sebastián, Bilbao and Vitoria-Gasteiz). Broadly, I will argue that the strategies of the Basque government could be discussed in relation to the development of city- and region-centred approaches in which city and region could be linked to different forms of Post-Fordist adaptation, although this argument is developed in more detail in chapter 7.

## The Return of Railways to the Political Agenda: Tendencies and Debates

The return of rail as a mode of transport can be associated to several factors and processes. Importantly here was the landmark established by the Shinkansen high-speed train (1964), developed to provide an exclusive passenger service between the highly populated and urbanised areas of Tokyo and Osaka in Japan. This was followed by the launch of the French high speed train connection between Paris and Lyon (1981), which was the result of a successful collaboration between the private French multinational company Alstom and the state-run company SNCF. This private-public partnership resulted in important technological innovations applied to the infrastructure, operation and the rolling stock equipment required by this new mode of transport. These developments were very important for two reasons. First, the technological changes led to less oil dependency regarding fuel-powered locomotives in the context of an international oil and energy crisis (1973). Second, the new technology opened up the possibility of recovering rail transport from the brink of extinction in most European countries by offering a fast and efficient service that would recover a sustainable demand and, also, because it offered incentives towards the development of higher added value products capable of transforming the sector into an international competitive business. All these prospects were welcomed, especially, if we also take into consideration that European countries were undergoing one of the worst economic crisis since the 1930s. In other words, the rail sector promised to make a positive impact regarding creating employment (particularly linked to high added value activities and highly skilled labour) and to boost demand for the service, with a positive impact on economic growth. All this did not escape the attention of the EC as well as interested parties and stakeholders, which at a time of European stagnation in the 1980s, needed to search for an innovative solution to aid European economic recovery. Indeed, the subsequent direction of such policy objectives as well as the availability of resources was necessarily shaped and moulded according to the establishment of specific political alliances regionally, nationally and internationally (for example, the PNV-PSOE coalition; the creation of the Atlantic Arc political and institutional space; and the emergence of pressure groups protesting against HST projects like the environmental groups AHT gelditu! Elkarlana [Stop the HST! Cooperation] and Ekologistak martxan [Ecologists in Action]); inter-government relations (like those between Spain and France); the dominance of powerful economic interests (like the ERT; MNCs, such as Alstom; and construction companies); institutional configurations and funding mechanisms (for example, the EU, and specifically the Essen Treaty and TENs); together with economic trends (like de-industrialisation) and economic narratives (such as "cohesion," "networks," and so on). My analysis of the development of the HST project in Spain, the EU and the Basque Country (chapters 5, 6 and 7) will involve examining the articulation as well as the unfolding of these social forces at different scales and the impact in the direction of this transport infrastructure project at the regional, national and international level.

As has already been stated (chapters 1 and 4), my framework of analysis for interpreting these changes draws broadly on the contribution of methods stemming from the regulation approach. In this sense, I will suggest that the return of rail should also be associated with a general shift towards supply-side initiatives as the basis of a new round of Post-Fordist economic restructuring in Europe. This means an emphasis on creating the "right conditions" as the basis for economic stimuli: for example, by providing incentives of relocation and investment associated to, say, the availability of technology parks, flexible labour markets, re-skilling programmes, corporate tax deductions, fiscal holidays, public-private partnership arrangements, start-ups, connectivity and networking infrastructures, and so forth (Jessop 2002). Thus, the more specific set of literatures and debates concerning transport infrastructures and, more particularly, the HST, will resonate with some of these questions and will also address the concerns of the various stakeholders involved with such projects.

Specifically, in order to trace the debates, policy developments and rationales underpinning the evolution and the unfolding of the HST train projects in Spain, the EU and the Basque Country, I will draw on three key set of literatures. First, my analysis of Spanish railway policy and the development of the HST will examine debates related to the ongoing industrial restructuring process in the 1980s and the impact of EC membership in the direction of industrial reform. This will be the basis on which I will approach the emergence of inter-government collaboration between Spain and France concerning the "U-Turn" in railway policy (from a policy of modernisation or upgrading the existing network track to the development of the HST rail service between Seville and Madrid) and the elaboration of public tenders on the basis of which the Spanish government hoped to develop future partnership agreements between the national rolling stock industries and MNCs to boost its national railway sector. Related to the ongoing process of industrial restructuring in Spain, I will examine transport infrastructure policy in Spain and the HST in relation to the development of urban regeneration projects of key cities (for example, Madrid, Barcelona and Bilbao). Moreover, drawing on literature that assesses the benefits of the HST for economic development (Gutierrez, González and Gómez 1996; de Rus and Inglada 1997; Vickerman 1997; Givoni 2006; Bell 2012), I will contend that there needs to be a critical assessment of policy claims about the alleged polyvalent character of the HST (the policy objective was to use the infrastructure for both passengers and freight transport); the capacity to integrate and articulate the national territory; and the spillover effects in terms of investment and relocation of economic activities to secondary and tertiary cities. For, as Bell convincingly argues (2012), studies about the HST effect have shown time and time again that such projects "should only be carried out in relations that connect very populated metropolitan areas with important problems of road traffic congestion and deficient air connections" (ibid.: 103). Furthermore, drawing on key informants and secondary data, I will argue that the consequence of the Spanish national HST policy has been the consolidation, politically and economically, of the capital city in Spain, Madrid, since it has managed to enjoy and retain most of the investments, while at the same time keeping its economic activities. Not only that, it has also managed to boost its international standing as well as its status as the nation's capital city.

Second, I will approach critically literatures concerned with questions of spatial planning, territorial integration and connectivity (Gómez Uranga and Etxebarria 1993; Williams 1996; Cooke, Gómez Uranga and Etxebarria 1997; Ross 1998; Gómez Uranga 2003) to understand how stories of "connectivity," "missing links," "cohesion" and "peripherality" have formed potent economic narratives (produced and reproduced in policy circles and academic forums alike), underpinning claims in policy documents and political discourses that attempt to build strong cases in favour of transport infrastructures, including the HST railway network, as mechanisms of economic development (Wise 2000a; Van Houtum and Lagendijk 2001; Amin and Tomaney 2002; Peters 2003; Esteban et al.

2009). Furthermore, I will suggest that the use of such concepts has created conflicting spatial storylines regarding the appropriate scale as well as the type of (railway) transport infrastructure projects that should be prioritised (for example, urban centred, underground, trams; interprovincial and regionally focused, HST, and so on). Moreover, I will contend that these stories and projects are necessarily associated with different visions of nation-building, different economic models (such as regional-industrial; urban-financial/cultural industries) (Etxebarria Kerexeta and Franco Ibarzabal 2003), different political and economic alliances, conflicts and tensions, institutional support and funding mechanisms (O'Connor 2001: 106; González 2003). Additionally, this perspective develops a very narrow understanding of economic processes and, therefore, fails to address the social, institutional and normative conditions underlying them (Peck and Tickell 1992; Amin 1994; Amin and Thrift 1995). I will address some of these questions in relation to the Basque Country and the EU.

Third, I have suggested that the Post-Fordist restructuring of Spain's semi-peripheral Fordist model was driven by a state led neo-liberal strategy (Albarracín 1994; Jessop 2002), which in Spain –ironically, in a European and transatlantic context dominated by a shift to right-wing politics— was driven by the centre-left political party, the PSOE (Share 1988; Petras 1993). At the heart of its key policies were industrial restructuring (involving the dismantling of INI) and the flexibilisation of the labour market. However, the pace and degree of privatisation and liberalisation was not consistent (Brenner and Theodore 2002) across companies and sectors (Pérez 1997, 1999), and while the rolling stock and equipment industries were soon subjected to a policy of mergers and absorptions by MNCs, the state monopoly company, Renfe, remained publicly owned until the mid-2000s. In other words, control over the infrastructure and services remained in the hands of the state. However, I will argue that despite setbacks, pressures and various turns, the process of privatisation and liberalisation initiated at the EU (the EC directive 91/4-40) and national levels (marginal changes in 1990) constituted the background to understanding the direction of railway policy generally, and, more specifically, the relationship between the restructuring of the public company, Renfe, and the development of the HST. In other words, the introduction and development of the HST concept paralleled changes in the legal and political definition of what the railways are for. While in Franco's time railways were defined as a universal service, under the PSOE government in democratic Spain the notion of providing rail services would gradually change to one defined narrowly in terms of profitability, efficiency and performativity. Moreover, it can be argued further that the macro-stability criteria (EMU) imposed by the EU, which required tighter budgetary as well as debt and deficit controls, meant a closer scrutiny over debt and deficit levels across the state controlled companies. Thus, principles of market optimisation and deficit control were gradually embedded into the restructuring process of Renfe. Drawing on some of the literature that explores the evolution of these changes (de Rus and Inglada 1997; Obermauer 2001; Cantos and Maudos 2001; Barea, Dizy and Ruiz 2007; Gómez-Ibañez and de Rus 2006; Campos 2006, 2008), I will explore how the conception of operation and maintenance hitherto based on a universal approach to railways has changed in relation to a more commercially orientated conception embodied in the development of the HST. I will discuss some of these debates in relation to Spain and the EU.

## Railway Infrastructures: In Search of Integration and Modernisation in the Spanish Economic and Political Agenda

In a comment to the specialised journal on railways in Spain, *Vía Libre*, the former prime minister of Spain, Felipe González, celebrated the inauguration of the new high-speed link between Seville and Madrid as a significant stepping stone in recovering the railway as the basis for progress.[1] The paradox, however, is that the railways in Spain, in contrast to other European countries, did not play a significant role in the process of industrialisation due to the different economic and political conditions related to the particular legacy of underdevelopment in Spain. It can be argued that it was only in the post-Franco period that railways came to play a significant role, initially as a flagship project demonstrating to the rest of the world the return of Spain as a major European power, and also in terms of strengthening the social and economic potential of cities (in particular). Indeed, transport infrastructural projects constitute an important aspect of urban regeneration plans (González 2003).

### *The PTF and the Seville–Madrid Connection: Topography, Modernisation and the Vision of a Progressive Spain in Europe*

The HST was preceded by the development of the Railway Transport Policy (Plan de Transporte Ferroviario, PTF) in the mid-1980s. Initially,

1. "Un futuro de nuevas realizaciones," *Vía Libre* 339 (April 1992).

the aim of this railway policy was to address problems and shortcomings related to the main national railway network operated by Renfe.[2] Specifically, the policy sought to address issues such electrification, signalling and communication, and old equipment.

The document preview was launched in December 1986 and it was finally approved on 30 April 1987 by the Spanish cabinet. The PTF time horizon expanded from 1986 to 2000 and some observers regarded it as the most revolutionary railway policy that had been approved "in the last century."[3] In particular, the former Transport, Tourism and Communication Minister, Abel Caballeros, claimed that the PTF was the first comprehensive *national* railway policy of the new Spanish democratic state.[4] In this sense, the minister stated that the policy's objective was to ensure levels of general demand as well as, and to a large extent, improving the general standard of railway services, including the investment in and acquisition of new rolling stock. He further claimed that one of the underlying concerns of the PTF was to guarantee the future of the Spanish railway system,[5] given that, similarly to trends in most EC countries, not only had road and air transport overwhelmingly replaced the railway as a mode of transport, but also they had threatened to substitute it for good. Generally, the objective of the PTF[6] was to upgrade and improve mainly the (conventional) railway system (exploited by Renfe[7]), by following a schema that prioritised a north–south axis and the connection between

2. The structure of the national railway system is of a radial shape in which the main arteries of the rail network radiate out from Madrid to the principal production and consumption centres towards the peripheral areas of the country. The RENFE network consists of broad-gauge lines (1.672 metres), but alongside RENFE there were also a small number of narrower gauge lines, the most extensive being the 1-metre gauge.

3. "Aprobado el proyecto ferroviario más importante del siglo: El PTF diseña el ferrocarril español del año 2000," *Vía Libre* 280 (May 1987), 8–10.

4. Ibid.

5. "El nuevo futuro del ferrocarril necesita el apoyo de la gran familia ferroviaria," *Vía Libre* 281 (June 1987), 7–9.

6. "Aprobado el proyecto ferroviario más importante del siglo: El PTF diseña el ferrocarril español del año 2000," *Vía Libre* 280 (May 1987), 8–10.

7. As opposed to, for example, FEVE, the company that exploited the 1-metre gauge railways in Spain. In northern Spain there is an extensive system of 1-metre gauge railways operated by FEVE (Ferrocarriles Españoles de Vía Estrecha, Spanish Narrow Gauge Railways) and Eusko Tren (Eusko Trenbideak, Basque Railways). Altogether they form a network that runs 650 km along the entire length of Spain's north coast. The main train lines exploited by Eusko Tren are situated in Bizkaia and Gipuzkoa. As far as the railway network exploited by Renfe, also referred to as the "conventional railway," it is 1.67 m wide.

Seville and Madrid; and Madrid and the Mediterranean coast, particularly the triangle formed by Madrid–Barcelona–Valencia–Madrid. Figure 5.1. illustrates this.

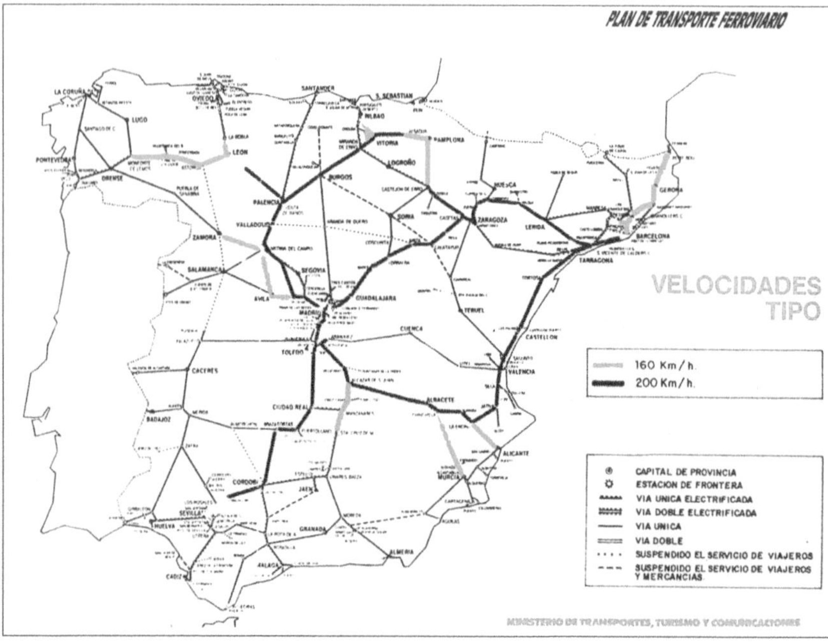


**Figure 5.1.** This is a map that illustrates the improvements the central government had envisaged within the new railway policy before the HST took centre stage. This map illustrates the importance of the connections between Seville–Madrid; Madrid–Barcelona; Barcelona–Valencia; and Valencia–Madrid. This is what eventually would take precedence in subsequent central government plans. Source: *Vía Libre* 274 (November 1986), 8–10.

All in all, although initially the aims behind the policy draft were to modernise the (conventional) railway system, the HST soon became the star project and was linked to the new connection between Seville and Madrid, which consisted of an alternative railway link to that of Despeñaperros (Jaén) via Brazatortas (Ciudad Real)–Cordoba. Moreover, the HST was expected to be ready and functioning in the new Madrid–Seville railway connection by 1992, the year in which other major events such as the Universal Exhibition in Seville, Expo 92, and the Olympic Games in Barcelona were going to be held.

As has been suggested, the PTF aimed, generally, at modernising the Spanish railway system by upgrading and improving the existing network in all its aspects, including increasing speed limits, carrying on further electrification work and investing in new rolling stock, as well as identifying areas of increasing mobility, economic activity and demand (Rivas 1997), such as the triangle formed by Madrid–Barcelona–Valencia–Madrid in the Mediterranean area, and solving bottlenecks. Regarding the latter, in the case of the Madrid–Seville link, the need to "overcome the topography" (overcome the particularly challenging and mainly but not exclusively mountainous terrains) became a powerful discourse underpinning the arguments justifying a new HST between the two cities. Topography and landscape have featured heavily in the Spanish literature as a way to address a series of "national problems" (Swyngedouw 1997). In the case of railways, too, the existence of topographical difficulties has often been used to address the lack of territorial integration, technological development and, more broadly, late-development (Nadal 1975).

Consequently, the Spanish railway network had particular areas of difficult access such as, for example, Bizkaia (the Orduña Pass), the Pajares mountain pass, which communicates Asturias with the central plateau, as well as the Despeñaperros gorge corridor.

> Despeñaperros is a natural corridor between the Castilian plateau and the Guadalquivir Valley. This was the site where the first railway between the centre of the Peninsula and Andalucía was built. In the same way as the railway system of northern Spain, the railway between the centre of the Peninsula and Andalucía was a narrow-gauge railway. There had always existed a project to tackle this problem but there have always been difficulties to find the money to carry it out. The alternative projects sought to avoid the natural passageway of Despeñaperros. One such alternative envisaged an alternative route from Madrid to Cordoba through Ciudad Real.[8]

According to AB, a journalist and railway specialist, the Despeñaperros narrow gorge is a natural corridor and, in this sense, it has always been a key nodal point of railway (as well as road) communications between Andalucía and Castile-La Mancha, or at least, between Andalucía and the rest of Spain. In fact, the single railway track line that crosses through it was the first centre–south railway link ever constructed. Given the topography of the gorge, the train reached the border of the Castilian plateau in

8. AB, journalist and railway specialist.

a double line, stretched into a single narrow gauge track inside the gorge and came out of the other side in a double electrified railway-line.

AB argued that several projects had been drawn up before (1979), including building a new track along the existing one. However, given the topographical conditions of the area, an alternative route to the Despeñaperros corridor altogether was considered the best available option. However, it was not until 1987 that the Spanish government agreed to undertake the project. As AB explains:

> Since by the 1980s France and Japan had already experimented with speed limits of up to 270 km/h, we decided to build a 250 km/h high-speed train between Seville and Madrid. Thus, the new project aimed at solving the bottleneck problem created by the single and narrow gauge rail-line that existed in the natural Despeñaperros corridor. Initially, a 160 km/h train was planned for the Seville–Madrid connection. However, we started to receive funds from the EU after Spain joined. Furthermore, a new government led by the Felipe González-Alfonso Guerra "couple" was formed. They *came across* with the new alternative railway line to that of Despeñaperros. They did not invent it. In contrast to previous years, however, they found themselves with greater purchasing power and a new emerging European Transport Policy [emphasis added].

The development and successful implementation of high-speed trains elsewhere, particularly in France, had opened up the possibility of using the HST in Spain, and specifically in the new connection between Seville and Madrid; thereby simultaneously symbolizing modernisation while also building domestic territorial integrity. Generally, the issue of increasing speed limits was at first not related to high-speed technology. Speed increases, from 140km/h or even 70km/h in some stretches to 160 km/h and 200km/h, were intended to benefit and spread throughout the railway network. This seemed a quite plausible as well as affordable endeavour since these increases required introducing improvements in the railway network and it further allowed the adaptation of *Spanish* rolling stock technology. The new railway connection between Seville and Madrid, then, was not an exception. In fact, initially the project envisaged introducing speed limits of up to 160km/h.

In addition, it was Spanish EU membership and the subsequent access to EU funding which made introducing the HST possible. In this context, the Spanish government developed plans to introduce changes in the railway link between Castile-La Mancha and Andalucía through Despeñaperros that had already been there before. Further, the government's decision to develop a new railway connection between Madrid and Seville with the HST took place at a time when the powerful political tandem composed by Felipe González (prime minister and leader of the PSOE) and Alfonso Guerra (deputy-PM) began to gain prominence in the Spanish political landscape. In this respect, it is worth noting that key leaders (including Felipe González) as well as core members of the PSOE (including Manuel Chaves himself, President of the AC of Andalucía) were from Andalucía.[9] In this sense, it seems safe to argue that the Spanish government picked "a problem" as much as "a project" that had already existed before and, additionally, it opted to introduce the new high-speed technology at a time when Spain started to attract EU funding. In this context, the HST and "the problem" of Despeñaperros were brought together on the grounds that the railway link that connected central and southern Spain was already more than a century old (built in 1886) and, from the onset, projects had always been limited by the difficult topographical conditions of the area and lack of appropriate technology and resources to tackle it (Rivas 1997: 10).[10] Furthermore, this was also a time when the government was promoting the Olympic Games in Barcelona and the Universal Exhibition of Seville, in 1992. Hence, the high-speed connection between Seville and Madrid was expected to coincide with the inauguration of the Universal Exhibition. Moreover, the latter can be also interpreted as further evidence of Spain's ability to access EU funding and investment efforts channelled into a series of urban development programmes, as was the case in Barcelona and Seville, but also other old industrial cities such as Bilbao.

In many ways, as regards the development of the new railway infrastructure between Seville and Madrid avoiding the Despeñaperros corridor, the specialised media at the time applauded "the political decision" to undertake development of the new high-speed connection between Seville and Madrid. Furthermore, it expressed surprise, but nonetheless delight, at the fact that barely some months had passed since the government had set out to develop the project and the names of the companies that would undertake the works were made public in the official Spanish state bul-

9. Andalucia (Seville is the capital), with approximately eight million inhabitants and one of the most populated ACs, became a traditional PSOE political stronghold. The core members of the PSOE became part of a faction (the "dons") who prioritised a centralised Spain, as a political project, in contrast to a Spain where regions had important powers.

10. "Nuevo material ferroviario español," *Vía Libre* 285 (October 1987), 9–17.

letin. In fact, work on the new railway infrastructure began in July 1987, only a couple of months after the official state bulletin had made public the winners of the public tender to construct the new railway connection on the 14 April 1987 (Ruiz del Árbol 1987: 10).

However, as far as the HST is concerned, I will argue that the cabinet decision to introduce and acquire the high-speed technology has to be interpreted, in addition to the significance of Spanish EC membership, in the light of Spain's economic and industrial reforms throughout the 1980s as well as conflicts and tensions with the French government over the "status" of ETA members living in France. Further, one should take into consideration wider EC trends regarding the development of a European Single Market, EC (transport) infrastructures, including the development of a trans-European high-speed railway network, and EC transport policy development and aspects concerning, in general, the liberalisation of the railway sector. In this sense, the introduction of the HST itself altered and further (re)defined substantially the actual priorities and aims of the Spanish Railway Policy preview (PTF). Accordingly, this meant, for example, moving from an alleged "general modernisation of the railway system" to targeting specific projects such as the Seville–Madrid connection (eventually, this project alone received all the available funds originally budgeted to improve the entire railway network for the 1986–1991 legislation), and later expanding the concept of the high-speed technology as well as fast trains[11] to other specific links and railway network areas such as the Madrid–Barcelona–French border connection and the Mediterranean area.

11. The Spanish government developed a distinction between "*Alta velocidad*" (high speed trains, or the HST) and "*velocidad alta*" (fast trains). With such a distinction, the government intended to differentiate between high-speed technology proper (trains that can reach speed limits of up to 250 km/h and more) and trains that can reach speed limits of up to 200/220 km/h. For example, the railway network formed between the cities of Madrid–Barcelona–Valencia–Madrid was upgraded for fast trains that can run 200/220 km/h, while the Madrid–Barcelona railway link is a HST connection proper. It might be argued that the introduction of such a distinction was a way of trying to "convince" the increasing number of ACs and cities alike that demanded access to "high-speed trains" that fast trains were going to be extended across the entire network. But further, one could also argue that the notions of the HST and fast trains can, subsequently, be interpreted within broader EU tendencies to rationalise railway services by transforming the railways in general into a specialised mode of transport. In this sense, it is not surprising that during the 1980s, almost 1,000 kms of railway lines were closed down in Spain. In fact, I will argue in the next chapter that, in the late 1980s and early 1990s, a wave seeking to liberalise and privatise the transport sector favoured the specialisation of different modes of transport in general, including railways, according to the competitive advantage of each one of them.

I suggested earlier (chapter 4) that Spain's EC membership coincided with a period in which business associations, such as the ERT, and a number of EC members alike, such as France, favoured EC market integration as well as the protection of EC industry (Apeldroon 2002). In this context, the ERT defended the development of (transport) infrastructure projects as a means to advance the economic, industrial and technological advantage of the EC. Thus, the idea of building a trans-European (transport) infrastructure network was grounded on the assumption that it would advance the development of a single market a step further, and in the case of the high-speed railway network project, it could be argued that the development and subsequent expansion of European technology and industry (for example, to China and India) were also at stake. In this sense, France's EC Presidency in 1989,[12] for example, took steps forward to set the conditions to agree on a schema for the future European high-speed railway network. And this was finally materialised at the Essen Summit in 1994.[13] In addition, this was a period in which the development of an EC transport policy was taken a step further under the presidency of Delors. In the next chapter I will deal more in detail with EC transport policy and aspects concerning the privatisation, (re)regulation/liberalisation and synchronisation of the railway sector and its implication in the government priorities, debates and arguments underpinning the HST in comparison to the period in which it was initially conceived.

Nevertheless, it must be noted, the EC had a more complicated agenda where its stand in favour of protectionism was mediated by the distinction between those industries and companies deemed to be significant as a whole rather than for individual countries, hence its stand in favour of protectionism. It is against this background that the extent, scope and options of the Spanish industrial restructuring have to be contextualised.

As I argued, Spain underwent a profound industrial crisis during the early-to-late 1980s, and industrial restructuring took its toll in former industrial cities such as, for example, Bilbao, and also other areas of the newly formed BAC such as Debagoiena (High Deba) and Donostialdea

---

12. It seems fair to argue that Frances's interest in supporting the development of a European high speed railway network was rooted in the fact that the French company, Alstom, became one of the most important European companies regarding the development of high-speed technology.

13. In general, the Essen projects were a series of fourteen priority transport infrastructure projects, nine of which belong to the European high-speed railway network.

(the area in and around Donostia-San Sebastián) in Gipuzkoa and Elorrio in Bizkaia. In this context, Spain complied with EC regulation and opted not to support a (re)industrialisation programme, in return for EC funding support. Moreover, in the case of the BAC, for example, the Basque government's efforts to pursue an industrial policy in an attempt to rescue "Basque industry" (in order to abate increasing social unrest –together with the increasing violence of ETA– and thus try to stabilise and legitimise the new government and its institutions) clashed with EC industrial strategies of supporting key EC sectors and companies. As such, the Basque government mainly limited itself to the development of an industrial policy focused on addressing issues concerning SMEs and their competitiveness.

In the case of Spain and the HST, as I will elaborate further below, the central government's privatisation strategy was based on a favourable context in which the EC encouraged partnerships between EC companies as a legitimate form of industrial "intervention" under EC regulation (Internal Market White Paper 1988; McVeigh 1999). I will thus argue that the idea to introduce the high-speed technology provided the Spanish government with the opportunity to carry out industrial reforms within a number of public industries related to the railway sector, including rolling stock producers (MTM-Ateinsa). Without doubt, the development of a high-speed connection between Seville and Madrid offered the government the possibility to foster cooperation between local and "European" companies to produce the high-speed train as well as to build the appropriate infrastructure and the superstructure required by the HST (Ruiz del Árbol 1987: 10–12); and hence, in addition, to set the conditions to import foreign technology which, it was believed, could create the necessary conditions in which to introduce more technologically advanced economic activities (Holman 1996).

In this context, the tender awarded to Alstom to produce the HST, amidst criticisms that the tendering was tinted with political manoeuvring (Suárez 1989: 5–6), meant that Alstom would carry out the restructuring of the Spanish public rolling stock companies. But, in addition to the economic consequences of such a deal, I will also argue that this included the decision to change the width of the Spanish railway gauge.[14]

---

14. The Spanish (conventional) railway gauge width measures 1.67 m in contrast to its European counterpart, which measures 1.435m.

In what follows, I will address the significance of inter-governmental encounters between France and Spain, the political and economic implications of the French HST acquisition (including efforts to build a trans-European high-speed railway network) and the subsequent disputes and tensions both within Spanish central government as well as between central government and Renfe. Further, I will suggest that the idea of introducing the HST, specifically, given its association with European corridors and funding, paved the way for the ACs to increase their demands to have a HST in their regions on the grounds that it was essential to build high-speed railway links with Europe (as was the case of Basque government, Navarre, Aragón, Catalonia, and so on).

### *The High Speed Train and Spanish Railway Industrial Restructuring*

The decision to introduce the HST triggered a number of concerns regarding the capabilities of the Spanish fixed installations as well as rolling stock companies to produce and deliver the HST. Those concerns led to the need to assess and reflect on the conditions of the Spanish railway sector in general in order to face up to the challenges of what it seems where initially the Spanish government's aspirations to produce a *Spanish* HST. Thus, for example, by mid-1987, Renfe had conducted a series of meetings with several European railway administrations in order to study how and what was being produced regarding electrification and communication and safety. Renfe concluded that Spanish manufacturers were not yet capable of meeting the technological standards regarding fixed installations required by the HST[15] technology. Equally, however, as far as the production of the rolling stock was concerned, Julian Ruiz, former President of Cemafe (*Asociación Nacional de Constructores Españoles de Material Rodante*, the National Association of Spanish Rolling Stock Producers), acknowledged that the situation of the Spanish rolling stock companies was not generally very good. In particular, for example, he revealed that the degree and extent of automation involving highly skilled tasks was not very extensive, generally, within the sector (Ruiz del Árbol 1988a: 20). Moreover, he suggested that it would be necessary to import some technology, as in the case of power control mechanisms, where the number of electronic components was very high (Ruiz del Árbol 1988a: 21). In other words, Spain was

15. "Instalaciones: Un aspecto prioritario," *Vía Libre* 289 (February 1988).

very dependent on the import of electronic components involved in the production of the HST.[16]

As a result, the Spanish government sought to promote partnerships between Spanish and multinational companies with the aim of facilitating the import, acquisition and learning of new technology that Spanish manufactures would then have to apply in order to produce the HST. Nevertheless, on the other hand, the Spanish government was counting on the fact that the Spanish railway track width as well as the direct current that feeds the Spanish trains[17] was different in order to create a technology adapted to the Spanish railway system and therefore, its own technology. In effect, to adapt, for example, the HST already produced in France would involve changing at least 60 percent of the existing technology. At the same time, it was believed that the different Spanish track widths put Spanish companies in a more advantageous position, for example, concerning the production of bogies more suited to the Spanish railway system (Ruiz del Árbol 1988a: 20). In this context, Renfe called for an international public tender to award the concession to produce the HST and all-powerful locomotives, with the announcement of the winning tender to be made public on the 21 October 1988.

## *The HST and Track Width in Spain*

In many ways, at the beginning, the main government representatives such as the Minister of Transport, Abel Caballeros himself, and the former President of Renfe, Julian Valverde, were very reluctant when it came to the idea of changing the Spanish railway track width.

> The issue of the European railway gauge width and the possibility of its introduction in Spain cannot be considered a real problem. First, this kind of problem is already technically solved. The change from one width to another takes very few minutes. Hence, within a journey that takes more than six hours, say from Madrid to Paris, the loss of time as a result of that operation can be regarded as insignificant. . . . Second, the economic cost resulting from the introduction of a new railway gauge width would be enormous. It would go far beyond affordability because it would imply changing the entire network, since we could not afford to have two net-

16. "En espera de la decisión y de los pedidos," *Vía Libre* 299 (December 1988).

17. For example, the French is 1.5 kV in contrast to the Spanish, which is 3kV. See "Alstom solo comprará Ateinsa y Maquinista si gana los dos concursos," *Vía Libre* 292 (May 1988).

works with different gauge widths. Third, international traffic is less than 10%. Therefore, it is not convenient to invest in a project where transport amounts to less than 10%. Fourth, it would take us up to twenty years to bring the change into the entire railway network and thus, it could provoke the collapse of the railway since the change would only be able to take place on double track railway stretches by working on one track at a time, thereby provoking the collapse of the entire railway network.[18]

The government of Catalonia had demanded the introduction of the international track width in the cross-border railway connection with France and for this to be extended as far as Barcelona (the Catalan government had even approached the French government to request that it extended the French high-speed railway network to the border, Port Bo) (Ruiz del Árbol 1988b). Yet many coincided[19] with Abel Caballeros when he argued that changing the railway track width at the cross-border sections did not make sense, because in their view, linking Madrid and Paris was not a commercially viable option.[20] In such journeys people would usually travel at night and if so, Caballeros argued, the time spent making adjustments to the Spanish trains at the border crossing before continuing on with the journey into France was insignificant. Moreover, international railway traffic constituted a little bit less than 10 percent. In a similar way, Valverde was quoted as saying that: "if there was money available to change the Spanish railway track width for the European one and someone asked me what I would do with that money, I can assure you that I would never carry out such a change because there are many things yet to be done. The percentage of international traffic is not very significant."[21]

It can, therefore, be concluded that it was against this background that Caballeros and others initially argued in favour of a *Spanish* high-speed *network*, meaning that the development of the HST technology should serve two purposes. First, by developing already existing technology and fitting it to the specific requirements of the Spanish railway system, such

18. Interview with Abel Caballeros in "El nuevo futuro del ferrocarril necesita el apoyo de la gran familia ferroviaria," *Vía Libre* 281 (June 1987), 7–8.

19. See, for example, "Antonio Monfort: Es posible una variante a 250 km/h entre Zaragoza y Barcelona," *Vía Libre* 289 (February 1988).

20. The argument rested on the notion that if the HST had been created and designed as a type of train that could compete with air travel in distances between 400 and 700 km, then clearly the distance between Madrid and Paris exceeded that.

21. "Congreso de los diputados: El PTF a debate," *Vía Libre* 291 (April 1988), 6.

as the track width, it was possible to create a Spanish product and, at the same time, lay down the conditions to restructure and revitalise the railway industrial sector. Second, the development of a Spanish high-speed network should serve as part of the modernisation plan for the railway system as well as an alternative to railway connections previously constrained by topographical obstacles such as Despeñaperros, between Andalucía and the Centre (thus, integrating the South and the Centre), and Guadarrama, between Madrid and the northern part of the country, thus completing a south–north corridor towards the French border to the west, as well as improving the connections from Zaragoza to Barcelona, and the French border to the East.[22] Moreover, many coincided with Caballeros when he argued that changing the track width would be hugely expensive and difficult to introduce as well as to run simultaneously along with the (conventional) Spanish railway network.

In this respect, the Minister of Transport argued that one of the underlying concerns of the PTF should be to guarantee the future of the Spanish railway system, meaning dealing with issues regarding demand, access as well as improvement of the entire Spanish railway network.[23] Thus, he further distanced himself from other countries where the HST had been exclusively built with a view to connecting specific locations as well as servicing a particular type of demand, as was the case of the Paris–Lyon train line.[24]

Therefore, initially, the government did not foresee changing the track width, on the grounds that it was expensive and impractical, and it preferred instead to develop a HST that would adjust to the existing Spanish railway network. Moreover, as I have contended, the introduction of the international track width seemed to be a rather negative move against the Spanish industrial railway sector, in general, and thus, the idea behind

---

22. "Antonio Monfort: Es posible una variante a 250 km/h entre Zaragoza y Barcelona" and "Gonzalo Martín Baranda: Pronto habrá un TALGO a 200 km/h," *Vía Libre* 289 (February 1988).

23. "El nuevo futuro del ferrocarril necesita el apoyo de la gran familia ferroviaria," *Vía Libre* 281 (June 1987), 7–9.

24. The Paris–Lyon HST is a straight rail connection conceived as an airplane, without any stops and a fast connection that serves a particular type of traveller: the white male business person (while women tend to use local transport more). In general, the concept of the HST was born with the aim of competing with air travel and revitalising the railway industry. Further, the HST became the perfect solution to the surplus of nuclear power production in France, and an alternative to transport based on fuel consumption amidst the oil crisis of the 1970s (interview with AB, journalist and railway specialist).

keeping the Spanish track width can be further associated with the aim to promote the national railway industry as well as the development of an indigenous technology (although some observers also pointed that it would be difficult to export an entirely Spanish product to other countries).

In many ways, the new Spanish high-speed railway connection between Seville and Madrid was in line with European trends based on the development of (transport) infrastructure projects as well as in the idea of fostering cooperation between European companies in the development of technological projects. In this context, the Spanish government encouraged partnerships between Spanish and foreign manufacturers of electrification and communication and safety measures as well as producers of high-speed trains. As far as partnerships regarding electrification and communication and safety, a Spanish-French alliance with three industrial groups seemed to be the dominant option: 1) Abengoa, Spi, Semi, Gresa and Cobra with Spi-Batignolles, 2) Vimac and Elecnor with CGE-Alstom, and 3) Radiotrónica with Alstom, Jeaumont-Schneider and Compagnie de Signaux. Other alliances also included: a Spanish-British alternative, Dimetronic and Westinghouse; and Dragados y Construcciones with Alcatel and General Electric Company.[25]

As far as the HST is concerned, Renfe had secured an important budget to acquire high-speed trains as well as all-powerful locomotives. The money to invest in the railways in general, together with the acquisition of rolling stock material, was stipulated in a series of contracts between Renfe and the Spanish government which became known as *contratos programa* (management contracts). As such, Renfe was responsible for starting the process of tendering, the announcement of which, as I mentioned earlier, was expected in October 1988. This tender became very important for two reasons. First, Renfe had the budget to place a big order of rolling stock material for the first time in many years. Although the Spanish railway sector was not technologically very prepared, as has been noted, the government expected that Spanish rolling stock producers in collaboration with multinationals would benefit from the planned investments to acquire the HST. Thus, acquiring the HST was a way of simultaneously acquiring the know-how that the Spanish producers would be able to combine with their own knowledge of the Spanish railway idiosyncrasies to produce a Spanish HST as well as introducing reforms that would make them more com-

25. "Instalaciones: Un aspecto prioritario," *Vía Libre* 289 (February 1988), 21–22.

petitive in the international context. In this sense, among the conditions Renfe drafted so that companies could participate in the tendering process was that the train should be produced in Spain as well as the requirement to explain how *they saw* that the HST could be adapted to the Spanish track width and overhead power cables.[26] It does not, then, seem too far-fetched to argue that the Spanish government was expecting that, by getting involved in the adaptation of a foreign HST to the Spanish railway system, it could claim "a new" Spanish technological product.

Second, Renfe had to choose between different technology producers and thus, I will argue in what follows, the process in general became tinted by political and economic struggles as well as pressures within the Spanish government, between the Spanish government and Renfe, and between the Spanish government and major European contenders, specifically, Alstom.

### *The HST: A New Spanish Industrial Product?*

Five major contenders entered the Spanish public tender to produce the high-speed train: Alstom (France), the ICI (a German consortium led by Siemens), Mitsubishi (Japan), ETR 450 (Italy) and possibly Talgo (Spain) (Suárez et al. 1988). In terms of experience, Alstom and Mitsubishi were the strongest candidates and to a lesser extent the ICI, since it lacked any commercial experience. However, both the Italian and the Japanese contenders expressed some doubt as to their chances of winning the tender. On the one hand, the Spanish government wanted the winner of the tender to buy and be in charge of restructuring the INI companies, Maquinista and Ateinsa. In this sense, soon after the tender was made public the Spanish government entered into negotiations with different candidates.[27] From the very beginning, however, it was clear that the European producers were in a better position to win the tender. Indeed, the Mitsubishi representative pointed out that since Spain was an EEC member it was unlikely that a non-EEC company would stand any serious chance of win-

26. "25 Ramas y 70 locomotoras para Alta Velocidad a Concurso," *Vía Libre* 289 (February 1988), 16.

27. In this context, the Italian contenders and the government did not reach any agreement and thus the Italians concluded that not only their chances of winning the tender were very slim but also, in their view, it became more apparent that the winners would come from among those candidates that would lead the restructuring of the INI. See "Italia se presenta a los dos concursos," *Vía Libre* 292 (May 1988).

ning the tender.[28] Further, the European producers were also differently positioned in terms of their chances of winning the tender:

> In Europe there are two railway powers: Germany and France. Behind them, come Great Britain and Italy. Within the EU-15, Spain is situated far behind those options. If we take into consideration Eastern European countries, a different situation emerges. There are many railways in Eastern Europe because roads have not been exclusively developed. Now, then, the French developed their own railway based on their own technology, which is the TGV. Naturally, they will try to push for more high-speed train lines that incorporate their technology as the European choice. And how best to achieve that than by supporting a common policy?[29]

In this sense there were important political aspects to the choice that the Spanish government could make that were not restricted to its internal political and economic rationality, but also had an important European dimension. That is, the tender was about selecting a European HST technology. In this context, the French and the German producers were the strongest candidates with the best chance of winning the tender. However, both the German and French contenders had to agree to carry out the restructuring of the Spanish national rolling stock companies, Ateinsa and Maquinista.[30] Yet as far as Alstom was concerned, it claimed that it would only agree to buy Ateinsa and Maquinista as long as it won the tender to produce the HST and the all-powerful locomotives. Further, Alstom was reluctant to introduce changes or alter in any way its own product, the TGV (as would have been the case had the Spanish government not decided to introduce changes in the Spanish track width) and, hence, I will argue, not only did Spain not succeed in producing a Spanish HST but the Germans and, particularly, the French dominated the production and delivery of the HST, thereby confirming Alstom's ambition to make the TGV the principle technology associated with the European high-speed railway network. In this context, the following two main alliances were created: on the one hand, Krauss Mafei [ICE]-Boveri-Siemens together with the Spanish company Talgo, that is, a Spanish-German alliance; and

28. "Clave en lo político," *Vía Libre* 294 (July 1988), 25.

29. AB, journalist and railway specialist.

30. "Alstom solo compra Ateinsa y Maquinista si gana los dos concursos," *Vía Libre* 292 (May 1988); "Finalizada la negociación alemana con el INI," *Vía Libre* 297 (October 1988).

on the other, Alstom together with the Spanish company CAF (actually based in the Basque Country),[31] that is, a Spanish-French alliance.

During this time, a Spanish cabinet reshuffle took place during the summer of 1988, as a result of which Abel Caballeros was replaced by José Barrionuevo as Minister of Transport. That substitution proved crucial since it meant a change in the government's heart and mind towards the introduction of the international track width. Not only had the government warmed to the idea of introducing the international track width in border connections but it also decided to extend it further to the rest of the corridors where it had planned to increase speed limits over 200 km/h. Moreover, the Spanish government had participated in meetings to design a European high-speed railway network, hence, under the new minister, the south–north corridor towards the French border to the west, as well as the connections from Zaragoza to Barcelona and the French border to the east, were defined along the new European high-speed railway corridors. Therefore, it was argued, Spain could not afford to keep its own track width within a wider European railway network (Ruiz del Árbol 1988b: 19).

In this context, on the day when the announcement of the winner for the production of the rolling stock was due, 21 October 1988, the president of Renfe publicly postponed it. Just hours before, the government spokesperson had asked Renfe to produce a report in order to assess the feasibility of changing the Spanish railway track width for the international standard one, which at the same time would affect the conditions of the development of the HST technology. Interestingly, the government, in the form of the new Minister of Transport, Barrionuevo, had not informed the president of Renfe, still at that time Valverde, of the government's wishes to explore the costs and consequences of introducing the international track width (Graiño 1988). Furthermore, some argued that the relationship between Renfe and the Ministry of Transport had gradually become tense. In fact, after the president of Renfe had repeatedly claimed that changing the Spanish track width was unfeasible and he personally would not by any means undertake such a task, and later that he "had been forced" to rectify his position once the government backed plans to carry out changes in the Spanish track width (Graiño 1988). Finally, The Spanish government announced its decision to introduce the international track width on 9 December 1988.

---

31. "CAF firma con Alstom el contrato para construir los trenes de alta velocidad," *Diario Vasco*, 31 October 1989.

During the time the Spanish government had put on hold the tendering process, pending Renfe's report on whether to introduce the international track width or not, the Spanish and French governments carried out a series of meetings which for some sealed the outcome of the process. According to Suárez and Ruiz del Árbol (1988), the Spanish government "had agreed" to offer the concession to produce the HST to the company which would also purchase the Spanish public rolling stock companies. As regards the other company, meanwhile, with a smaller order (the production of all-powerful locomotives) it would benefit from compensations outside the railway sector (specifically, in telecommunications, since this decision also came under the remit of the Ministry of Transport). Thus, on these conditions, Alstom, which agreed to lead the restructuring of the INI (Ateinsa and Maquinista), won the concession to produce the HST, while the German consortium would produce the all-powerful locomotives. The TGV thus stood out as the dominant European rolling stock technology.

As mentioned earlier (chapter 4), however, some observers have also seen in those meetings the realisation of a Spanish political agenda. During the Franco regime, many political activists and later ETA members used to find political refuge in France. This pattern continued well into the 1980s and even after Spain had embraced a democratic system. The fact that the French government continued to offer a safe haven for ETA members was openly challenged by the Spanish government (since it undermined the legitimacy of the Spanish democratic state). The Spanish government thus demanded more active collaboration between the two countries in handing over suspected ETA members living in France. At the same time, it was during this period that the (pro-Spanish government) paramilitary group GAL was created, which made several incursions into France killing and kidnapping ETA members in order to take back into Spain (Woodworth 2001). In the meantime, the Spanish government sought different ways to "induce" the extradition of ETA members, and it is in this context that some have suggested that part of the reasons why Alstom might have been awarded the concession to produce the HST is because of the fact that the French government had agreed to extradite ETA members living in France.

## The case of a HST for the Basque Country

The Basque government's pursuit of a HST connection has to be contextualised in the period in which the Spanish government took the decision to build a HST link between Seville and Madrid and, subsequently, to introduce the international track width in all high-speed railway lines. This decision, as noted, coincided on the one hand with the restructuring of the Spanish rolling stock sector and refusal of major HST technology providers (Alstom) to reform and adapt their own product to the general Spanish railway system requirements (including limited collaboration in technology transfers), and on the other, with the advancement of a European transport policy and the idea to develop a trans-European HST railway network (see further chapter 6).

In general, as suggested earlier on in this chapter, this period coincided with political devolution in Spain as well as with general economic reform and industrial restructuring. In this context, the Basque government and other institutions were set up and a string of competencies started to be transferred from central government to the BAC, although not without disagreements, tensions and political negotiations as well as judiciary mediation (all of which have generally accompanied the process of devolution down to the present). In this sense, for example, the Basque government came to operate the narrow gauge railway services (EuskoTren) in the BAC that had previously been run by FEVE. However, as I will elaborate later, the ownership and running of the national railway services remained, respectively, with the state and Renfe. In regard to the latter, I will later briefly address the distribution of competencies between different administrative levels.

During and particularly after the transition, that is, after stable conditions for political institutions were achieved, and when the scale of the economic and industrial crisis became a reality, the newly democratic institutional apparatus[32] had to deal with a large number of different and closely interconnected challenges. Thus, it has been argued, Spain underwent an economic crisis that particularly hit the industrial areas of the country. In this sense, Alcaide Inchausti's (2003) study of the general economic evolution of the Spanish regions shows that economic conditions in relation to the EC average fell more sharply in the Basque Country and, therefore, the crisis was felt more dramatically (in all its social dimension) than any other region of Spain.

The political and institutional negotiations to resolve the crisis as well as to stabilise and guarantee the ongoing process of institutional building in the BAC (amidst political violence, social unrest and economic crisis)

---

32. Territorially distributed between the central, regional and, in some cases, provincial and municipal levels.

were difficult, problematic but a most urgent priority. And such negotiations and outcomes were certainly conditioned by a number of factors such as Spanish EC membership, including Spain's commitment towards further EC integration, support for the EC's own agenda towards supporting a set of industrial sectors and the development of certain technology projects (related to transport, like Airbus, the HST and so on) (Apeldroon 2002), as well as access to EC's funding availability, which was set up on the principles that investing in transport infrastructure projects would facilitate the access of poorer regions to areas of economic wealth and therefore enhance a better cohesion between richer and poorer regions (Arestis and Paliginis 1995).

In what follows, I will first briefly address the distribution of competencies regarding transport and, in particular, railways and the context in which this took place. Then, I will move on to describing the circumstances and the context in which the idea of the Basque Y took shape and in this sense, I will refer to a series of infrastructure projects that the Basque government envisaged on the grounds that the Basque Country needed to be better connected. I will thus concentrate on the efforts of the Basque government to set up international lobbying activities that facilitated and promoted the formulation, creation and dissemination of the idea of an Atlantic Arc. Once the context of the HST is established I will turn to developing in more detail the negotiations that led to the introduction of the Basque HST in the national and EU plans.

## *The Framework and Context of Competencies*

After administrative decentralisation in Spain in the 1980s, a process of institutional building (government and provincial councils) took place in a context of harsh economic and industrial conditions. The process of decentralisation allowed the BAC to assume a set of competences which, together with the singular fiscal system (the *concierto económico*[33]),would

33. The Basque economic arrangement, the *concierto económico*, stipulates that "the Basque Country must contribute to general state expenses which correspond to powers which have not been assumed." The quota, then, a mechanism central to the economic arrangement, establishes "the transfer of revenues which correspond to non-assumed powers from the Basque Country to the state." But further, "as the Statute of Autonomy sets down, levying, management, liquidation, collection and inspection of all taxes except import-export duties are to be carried out within each historical territory by the respective provincial councils," which later must deliver "a part of the revenues collected (allowance) to the Basque government" (Uranga and Etxebarria 2000: 523).

enable them to develop and implement a range of policies in new diverse areas such as culture, education, health, and so on (Gómez Uranga and Etxebarria 2000). But perhaps more importantly, these competences also included managing as well as looking for ways to intervene within the Basque economy, which at that time meant, among other things, dealing with the industrial crisis. In this context, the Basque government developed a series of policies and projects including setting up aid programmes developed by the Basque Trade and Industry Department and channelled through the public agency SPRI, directed to providing financial support to improve aspects of the industrial fabric that, as many scholars and studies pointed out at the time,[34] had prompted Basque industry into such a deep crisis. In this sense, the Basque government developed a series of policies addressing the issues of technological change, innovation, the development of new products as well as efforts to identify, manage and coordinate the players (firms, research centres and universities) identified as the factors needed to improve the lack of competitiveness that allegedly marked the Basque industrial crisis (for a much more detailed analysis of the extent, scope, limits and consequences of the policies aiming to address issues of innovation, R&D, and so forth, see for example, Díez and García Artetxe 1990; Navarro 1992; SPRI 1992; Borja Álvarez 1996, 1998; Ahedo 2004; Cilleruelo Carrasco 2005; Goikoetxea Martínez 2007).[35]

Therefore, the BAC achieved a high level of judicial and managerial autonomy in the areas of innovation and industrial policies and, aside from the fields of education and health, infrastructure projects also became central in the management capacity of the BAC. In many ways, however, it has to be noted that the transfer of powers conferred in the Statute of Autonomy are limited in scope, in the sense that many key policy areas such as labour and macro-economic policy have remained within the competences of the central government's domain. Further, competences have often been only partially transferred and as regards a number of other fields, includ-

---

34. "CE: informe encargado por la Comisión recomienda inversiones en infraestructuras en el País Vasco," *El Diario Vasco,* 22 November 1989.

35. Indeed, a critical assessment of the results obtained by the series of policies on innovation developed by the Basque government seems to prevail. These authors suggest that investment has not been able to consolidate research activities in companies and one of their general concerns is that the money directed towards promoting research activities has been used instead to increment capacity and productivity, rather than research activities. Further concerns address the existing learning and training avenues in the Basque Country and conclude that, for the most part, there is still an important gap between the learning and training qualifications on offer and the labour market requirements.

ing the judiciary system, have not been transferred at all. Moreover, as Goikoetxea Martínez (2007) notes, the specificities of some competences are vague and too general, which makes their transfer all the more subject to political conflicts, interpretations and negotiations. This is generally the case regarding infrastructures, an area in which the ACs cannot develop their own infrastructure policies owing to their shared competence with the national agenda and, increasingly, dependence on European frameworks. In this sense, different modes of transport constitute, to a different degree, national and local priorities. More specifically, airports and ports are considered of strategic national importance and are thus remain within the competence of Spanish central government. Roads, in contrast, are clearly within the domain of ACs unless they are part of national corridors. In the case of railways, though, competences are similar to those of roads. However, railways are more complicated because of the state ownership, through Renfe or FEVE, of the entire rail infrastructure in Spain. In this sense, there are a myriad of entities that might be involved at any one point in the planning and management of infrastructures, but also the problems and tensions surrounding key aspects of competences, decision-taking and financing.

> First of all, we have a type of institutional framework that we might regard as confederal; in this sense, we need to see who holds the competences for each of the policies. So, internally, the competence regarding transport in general corresponds to the provincial councils [*diputaciones*], rather than the [Basque] government. The government has a main job, which is, to put it very simply, planning and management. But such planning is not one that you can impose from top to bottom disregarding everyone else; it has to be dynamic and consensual planning. And this is what it has to be considered first: anything you try to do from the government without taking into consideration the provincial councils and even the local councils themselves is bound to fail. Additionally, regarding certain modes of transport the competences are complicated, for example, in the case of railways. If a project exceeds the boundaries of the AC, it belongs to the central administration [the Spanish government]. First point, there is a problem. Secondly, there are railway companies within the BAC in which 100% of the powers should have been transferred but which keep causing problems [Renfe and FEVE]. Renfe and FEVE have discovered that railways have a market and a certain political presence in the Basque Country [of Spain, in Euskadi]. Paraphrasing [José] Bono [the Spanish Home Secretary], I heard him saying this morning on the radio that he would hand over Montjuit Castle [in Catalonia] if they promised that a

> Spanish flag would fly every day. It's something like that, a very strong presence . . . So, there is an attempt to gain back profitability and the railways of the Basque Country themselves. [In addition to the issue of competences] the Bizkaian Consortium of Transport was created, at a time when [people] believed in metropolitan consortiums and if you analyse the consortium, the number of competences it holds is preposterous; the consortium would become the sole transport authority in Bizkaia, and of each and every mode of transport. The consortium is in charge, among other things, of constructing the [Bilbao] underground [by sheer coincidence, because nothing like that had ever been done but both coincided at the same time]. With it, the big issue concerning financing emerged: whether it was up to the consortium to finance the infrastructure and the supra-structure and so on . . . as usual the provincial councils and the [Basque] government ended up paying for everything. In addition, the underground didn't make any sense unless it took advantage of other infrastructures such as Renfe and Eusko Tren. Another additional problem. So it becomes a complicated reality to put into practice. And the authorities have believed for years, which I think is a big mistake, that every other entity is excluded from taking decisions.[36]

In this sense, the Basque HST would fall within the category of the kind of infrastructure that, given its size and nature (namely that of a regional, national and European railway network), is beyond the competences of the BAC. However, it should be noted that the Basque government did receive the railway competences regarding the exploitation of narrow gauge railways within the BAC.

The Basque government was, then, given the right to operate railway services within the BAC, yet not the interregional services. In this sense, since, as suggested above, the HST falls within regional, national and EC frameworks, the HST was a project that in terms of design, implementation and exploitation corresponded almost exclusively to the central government (although technically regional governments have been able to participate in developing prospective as well as environmental impact reports; and although the EC adopted a consensual decision on the trans-European HST layout and established financial mechanisms and resources to finance it). The latter has been used in order to argue that the adoption of a HST project is only an extension of statewide transport policy strategies that do not correspond to Basque social and economic needs,

---

36. AA, former member of and adviser to the Basque government.

that is, of an "old industrial region" (Gómez Uranga and Etxebarria 1993, 1998; Etxebarria Kerexeta and Franco Ibarzabal 2003; Goikoetxea Martínez 2007). The latter has become an important aspect of the alternative to rhetorics of the "social train," which also builds on a different imagining of the Basque national project (further discussed in chapter 7).

In the next chapters I will address in more detail the arguments and debates surrounding the Basque HST regarding its economic (questions concerning what the HST does for the type of economic activity in which most of the people are involved in the BAC, including the activity developed by ports as well as implications for the primary and particularly secondary sector) regional (cohesion and articulation, from a networked and tangled socio-economic fabric towards a "diffused" urbanisation and tertiarisation of society) and territorial implications (questions about the nation). In this respect, I will argue that the HST raises issues regarding a more traditional nation-building link to the preservation of national capital (real economy) and the type of socio-economic spatial distribution against transnational capital that is not concerned with more traditional forms of links but instead emphasises cities and outer linkages.[37] The Basque Y, then, in addition to being a project that serves to articulate visions of the Basque Country and the nature of Basque economy and society, is also linked to promoting competing modes of restructuring centred on city and region. These could be associated with two different types of communication infrastructure: one that facilitates "the flow of information" and another that facilitates the "exchange of knowledge and know-how" (these will be further elaborated in chapter 7).

### *From the HST to the Basque Y*

I argued earlier in this chapter that the main focus of the PTF was to upgrade and improve mainly the (conventional) railway system (exploited by Renfe), by following a schema that prioritised a north–south axis and the connection between Madrid and the Mediterranean coast, particularly the triangle formed by Madrid–Barcelona–Valencia–Madrid (see figure 5.1).

37. Hence the regeneration plans for Bilbao with their particular emphasis on mobility and communication infrastructures together with globally recognisable emblematic buildings such as the Guggenheim Museum Bilbao, and the Baiona–Donostia-San Sebastián Euro City, where communication infrastructure projects take priority, are linked to projects that prioritise global capital.

However, in the case of the north–north-west connection, and in particular the case of Madrid–Valladolid–Burgos–Vitoria-Gasteiz–Altsasua–Donostia-San Sebastián–Irun, the PTS did not foresee either an immediate implementation of plans or any concrete plans at all. In fact, at the time of the PTF launch there were a number of uncertainties that surrounded the project. These were related to extending the HST link to northern Spain, and concerned when, if at all, such a link could be constructed, how such an extension would be funded, where the train would pass through and what would be the shape of the railway link.

In what figure 5.2 I produce a sketch of what the main (conventional) Spanish North–North-West railway network would have looked like before the PTF.

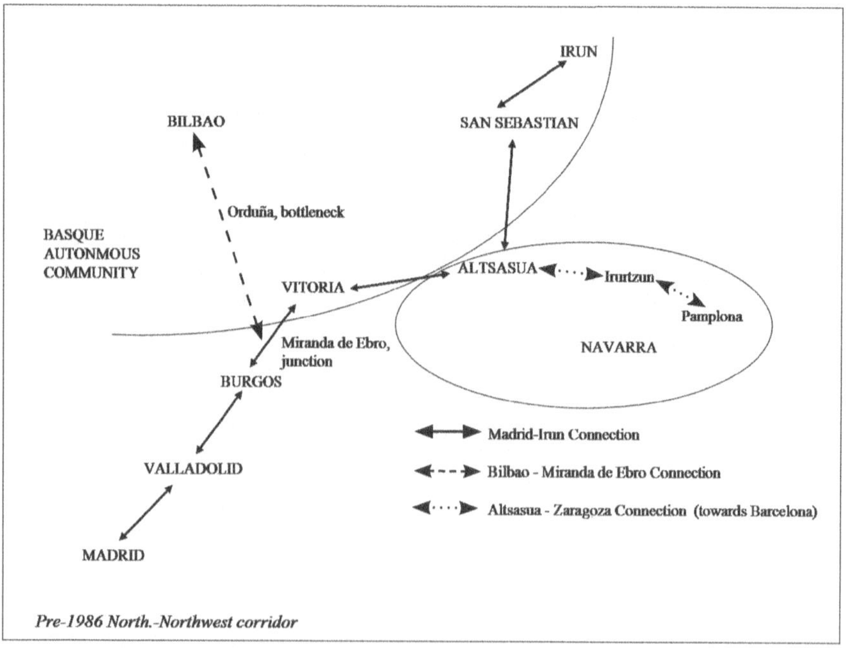


**Figure 5.2.** Sketch of the main (conventional Spanish north-south-west railway network would have looked like before the PTF.

In this railway network corridor the following can be highlighted: first, the Spanish (conventional) railway network (Renfe) does not link the main capital-cities (Bilbao–Vitoria-Gasteiz–Donostia-San Sebastián–Bilbao) of the BAC, as the Basque government would demand later. Second, the connection between Vitoria-Gasteiz and Donostia-San Sebastián goes through Altsasua, a town situated in the AC of Navarre, and thus outside the competencies of the BAC (although a part of the broader imagined Basque homeland). Third, to go from Bilbao to Vitoria-Gasteiz one has to go via Miranda de Ebro (the AC of Burgos). In sum, the capital cities in the Basque Country are only connected by railway through other ACs.

Consequently, the PTF did not envisage changes between the Vitoria-Gasteiz–Donostia-San Sebastián connection but the PTF, however, did suggest building two new connections at 160 km/h, one from Bilbao to Vitoria-Gasteiz and another from Irurtzun (Navarre) to Irun (Gipuzkoa).[38] The new connection from Bilbao to Vitoria-Gasteiz sought to overcome the Orduña Pass as well as to open up a new link from Bilbao towards the plateau and the Ebro Valley. The Irurtzun-Irun railway link would provide Navarre with a connection to the French border through Irun, situated in Gipuzkoa, in the BAC.

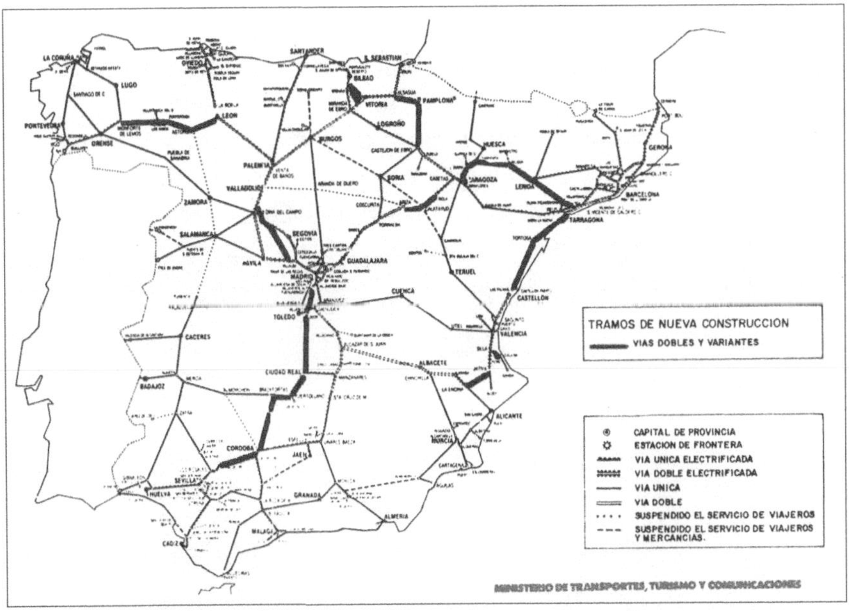


**Figure 5.3.** The new railway lines the central government had envisaged constructing are in red. One of them was the relief railway line between Bilbao and Vitoria-Gasteiz. Otherwise, the central government did not have any immediate plans to alter the Renfe railway layout as it existed at that time in the BAC. Source: *Vía Libre* 274 (November 1986), 8–10.

38. Sarriegi Eskisabel, "Euskal Herriko burdinbideetako," Zientzia.Net, 1 November 1991.

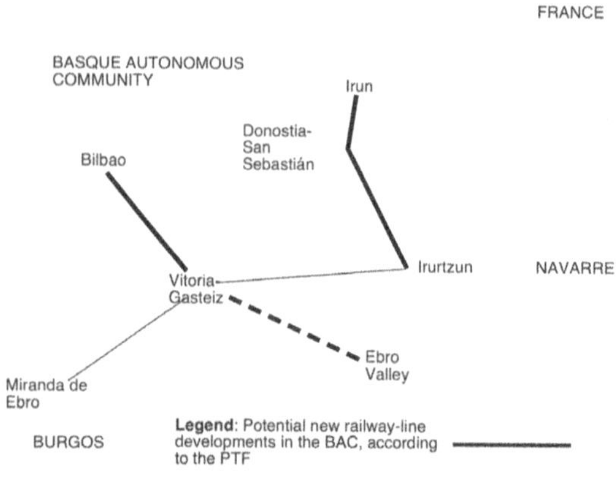


**Figure 5.4.** Potential new railway line developments in the BAC, according to the PTF. This is a closer reproduction of what the central government had initially planned to introduce in the BAC and the AC of Navarre.

However, neither of the proposed two new links addressed the issue of developing a railway connection among the three capital-cities of the BAC as well as the BAC and Navarre, or even developing a HST connection at all (from Madrid towards the North-West or in any way within the BAC). As far as the Basque government was concerned, these projects were insufficient and, as a result, it proposed the introduction of a project as well as the type of project it thought best suited the BAC: the Basque high-speed train, with a Y layout that would connect the three capitals of the Basque Country.

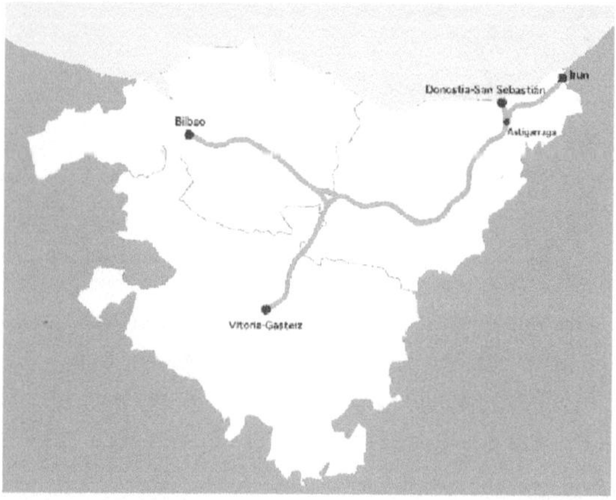


**Figure 5.5.** The Basque Y. Source: Basque government, www.euskalyvasca.com/es/home.html.

However, the Basque Y faced various challenges. First, the Spanish cabinet had agreed in December 1988 that the Madrid–Barcelona high-speed connection would follow the Seville–Madrid connection in order to complete the north–south axis that would form part of the European High-speed network. Second, the same cabinet had agreed that the upgrading and improving of railways making up the Madrid–Valencia–Barcelona–Madrid connection were also a priority. Thus, after the Seville–Madrid connection came to an end, the Minister of Public Works and Transport, José Borrell, pointed out that:

> Until 1992 there has been an absolute priority towards the new HST between Madrid and Seville based on the agreement approved by the cabinet in December 1988 . . . thus dedicating a big part of the existing budget towards completing this connection. This same agreement, which is still valid, establishes that from 1993 onwards the Madrid–Barcelona connection will have priority. And it is in relation to this being a priority that the current studies are being done so that works can start next year [1993] (quoted in Lozano 1992).

In addition, the Basque Y coincided in the early 1990s with a context in which the EU changed direction towards supporting "intermodality," the liberalisation of the transport sector across Europe and limiting public funding for the development of transport networks (discussed in chapter 6). The latter had immediate implications for the shaping of the HST project within Spain and in the Basque Country, in particular. Thus, in what follows, I shall elaborate further on the circumstances in which the Spanish government adopted 1) a Bilbao–Vitoria-Gasteiz–Donostia-San Sebastián–Bilbao high-speed connection, 2) a further high-speed connection to Madrid through Valladolid, and 3) a high-speed connection through the border town of Irun with France and the rest of Europe. In this sense, I will argue that the PNV-PSOE coalition became vital to the advancement of the HST project in the Basque Country from a "national," "regional" and even "European" perspective. Therefore, while the rhetoric and debates surrounding the HST, generally, were about modernisation and integration, in the case of the Basque HST project, I will show later, these centred on the notion of connectivity, the efforts of the Basque government to develop the Atlantic Arc and, at a later stage, also the creation of a closely consolidated national space within the borders of the BAC (discussed in chapter 7).

## The Basque Y and Its Way into the National and EU Essen Priority Projects

As suggested earlier, besides the active involvement of the Basque government in setting up internationally collaborative networks, Bourne (2001) argues that the coalition government in the BAC formed by the statewide PSOE political party and the PNV was very important when it came to ensuring that the Basque Y was included not only in the national Railway Policy document but also in the European high-speed network projects, including the TEN-T.

Therefore, the fact that the Public Works and Transport portfolio was in the hands of a PSOE member of the PNV-PSOE government coalition helped very much not only in advancing the infrastructure projects the Basque government had programmed to develop,[39] but also the HST project. In effect, during the period in which the Spanish government participated in negotiations to develop a series of trans-European network projects, which included HST railway connections, members of the PSOE in the Basque government coalition and the Spanish government itself defended the project,[40] although not without disagreements.

All in all, the HST was included in the EU plans and thus the Basque HST evolved from being a project intended to tighten up the northern part of Spain to becoming part of the European network, with the opportunity to access EU funds but also subject to the same principles of synchronisation, privatisation and liberalisation as the rest of the corridors that were part of the European high-speed corridors.

During this period, the Basque government became very active internationally by forming, creating and participating in numerous agreements and alliances[41] with cross-border regional entities in what can be described as an attempt to gain influence and power in aspects and issues identified as important in EC institutions. In doing so, the Basque government became successful putting forward its agenda surrounding infrastructure

39. "Ruiz de Alegría: Nadie cuestiona la validez del acuerdo en infraestructuras con Madrid," *El Diario Vasco*, 23 September 1989.

40. "Jáuregui afirma que antes de fin de año la CE aprobara que el TAV pase por la frontera de Irun," *El Diario Vasco*, 14 October 1989; "Barrionuevo pide a la CE dos salidas para el TAV: Irun y Port Bou," *El Diario Vasco*, 3 October 1989; "Barrionuevo defiende ante la CE la conexión del TAV por Irun," *El Diario Vasco*, 17 October 1989.

41. For an extensive discussion and coverage of the multiple agreements and interregional institutional collaboration, see Jáuregui et al. (1997).

projects and in particular the HST, at the same time that, together with the Aquitaine regional council (on the French side of the border), it came to form a strong partnership in support of developing a cross-border HST connection through Irun. In fact, it seems that it was this partnership[42] between both the Basque government and the Aquitaine regional council that led to the development shortly after of a more consolidated collaboration by setting up a permanent Atlantic Arc working group to work on common interest projects and, mainly, infrastructures.[43] Consequently, the Atlantic Arc,[44] in addition to being framed as a geographical area that would roughly include regional areas in a broad line from the North-East of Scotland, through the regions of the French West Atlantic coast and also incorporating the Spanish Cantabrian regions (including the BAC, and the ACs of Cantabria, Asturias and Galicia), and down to parts of western Andalucía as well as Portugal, became a loosely connected association consisting of heterogeneous interests that was a part of the Atlantic Arc Commission within the Conference of Peripheral Maritime Regions in 1989. In the words of AC, a member of the Atlantic Arc commission in the Basque government:

> Well, I think it's the appropriate question to ask. In the socio-economic sector and in the Basque government, we can talk about what the Euskadi area is; there is an expression which is the Atlantic Arc or the Atlantic Axis, which is very much used by the chambers of commerce, universities . . . and I believe that it represents more a philosophy rather than an entity. It is a philosophical notion in the sense that all sorts of exchanges are promoted. In this sense, if one talks from the chambers of commerce perspective, obviously, they will barely consider economic data; if one is talking about universities, the subsequent contacts in this geographic area through programmes strictly linked to, for example, an Erasmus programme or previously agreed programmes, etc. It is in this sense that

---

42. "Tavernier: no existirá el eje atlántico si no hay relaciones entre Aquitania y País Vasco," *El Diario Vasco*, 17 September 1989.

43. "El consejo de Aquitania y el Gobierno Vasco crean una comisión del 'eje Atlántico,'" *El Diario Vasco*, 3 September 1989; "Cooperación transfronteriza: el día 4 será firmado un acuerdo País Vasco-Aquitania," *El Diario Vasco*, 23 September 1989; "El País Vasco y Aquitania desarrollaran acciones conjuntas a nivel Europeo," *El Diario Vasco*, 29 September 1989.

44. The number of regions, the diverse countries they belonged to and the variety of entities and projects they lobbied for, which were often contradictory, or simply the diverse interests that only rarely united them at all, have led many to interpret the Atlantic Arc as a unifying symbol more than anything more concrete.

I want to insist on the Atlantic Arch as a philosophy in order to delimit an area.

The underlying incentive of the subnational entities forming the Commission of the Atlantic Arc was to develop a pressure group within EU institutions. AC continues:

The Atlantic Arc, of which we, the Basque government, talk about is a specific organisation formed, I think, by approximately thirty-four, I was going to say regions, but perhaps later I will explain why I haven't used [that term]. Let's call them sub-state entities, that encompass Ireland, the United Kingdom, the French Atlantic Seaboard, the Spanish Cantabrian coast, including the Andalucía Atlantic zone. Well, in this sense, this is an association of sub-state entities whose objective is to achieve a closer collaboration among those thirty-something entities to look for projects and lobbying activities before Brussels and state governments. Therefore, this Atlantic Arc, this particular physical expression, in terms of the association of these entities, is part, at the same time, of a bigger entity which is the Conference of Peripheral Maritime Regions. We always talk of members that are classified as sub-state entities.

It is worthwhile noting here that the "common interest" that brings these subnational entities together (with varying degrees of competences) is the perception that there is a "peripheral effect" that might have potentially fatal consequences for their prospects of economic growth. As AC concludes, "When someone wants to travel from La Coruña to Rennes, in the French region of Brittany, most likely she will have to do a couple of transfers because there aren't any direct flights. There are complicated communication problems with the centres of social and economic power."

In effect, the principle behind the Commission of the Atlantic Arc frequently addressed the fact that the regions forming the geographical area of the European Atlantic side were in a very disadvantaged position in regard to access and lack of connectivity concerning the centres of European economic and social activity (Bourne 2001). In this sense, particularly within Spain, according to the majority of Spanish North-West regions, this was the case due to the historical legacy of central government (including the new Railway Policy preview) to foster a radial shape transport infrastructure structure (Bel 2010) and its strategic priority, at that time, to first develop the southern connections and later move on to Mediterranean linkages,[45] while links to the North were of a very low priority. In this sense, promoting the idea and building a coalition around the notion of an Atlantic Arc played a pivotal role in organising common positions at the EC level in defence of a HST cross-border connection through Irun as a way of acquiring a means of transport to get closer to centres of economic advantage and as a counterbalance to the infrastructure investment projects carried out on the Mediterranean coast.[46] In this regard, some authors have suggested that the Atlantic Arc might be best approached as a unifying concept (Wise 2000), because of the variety of entities and projects for which they lobby for, rather than as a political and/or economic system.

Spanish transport policy envisaged a general modernisation and upgrading of the national railway network before the HST became the main priority project. Generally, railways and the HST were linked to a modernising and national agenda and thus also celebrated Spain joining the EC and its full integration into the international economic and political institutions. However, this modernising agenda was linked to an industrial policy agenda which sought to encourage the participation of foreign capital in Spain. The latter was expected to carry out the necessary restructuring, including issues related to technology and process innovation. The awarding of the public tender to build the HST was mediated by (1) an EC agenda to protect and promote European technology, (2) Spain's industrial restructuring policy and, (3) Spain's domestic policy agenda regarding ETA activists living in France. As far as the BAC is concerned, that although Spanish transport policy intended to upgrade the national railway network, plans to improve the national railways in the BAC were general and unlikely. In this context, the Basque government PNV-PSOE coalition played a crucial role not only when it came to introducing the HST into national (that is, statewide) railway plans but it was also important to promote, initially, connectivity to the main economic centres in Spain and Europe. What became known as the Basque Y rail track layout

45. It has to be said that there is some truth to those assertions: for example, in regard to the massive development of cheap flights, in Spain, most incoming international flights are located in airports along the Mediterranean coast; in the case of Catalonia, with multiple airlines to the main airport of Barcelona and other secondary –but increasingly expanding– ones such as Girona and Reus. In addition to Barcelona, Madrid is another major airport hub hosting various cheap international airline flights.

46. "High-Speed to the Spanish coast," Guardian.co.uk, 18 February 2008. At http://www.guardian.co.uk/travel/2008/feb/18/railtravel.spain.

was, at a later stage, also linked to ideas of internal integration within the BAC by connecting the capitals of its three provinces.

Further, the Basque government demand for the HST coincided with increasing involvement and support for interregional cooperation, where the strongest alliance was the cooperation promoted between Aquitaine and the BAC. The chapter has shown that this collaboration extended to other regions along the Atlantic Arc. Both the agreements with Aquitaine and the Atlantic Arc platform were actively promoted in order to extend pressure at the respective national and European levels, which finally led too to the inclusion of the Basque Y among other Essen priority projects in 1994.

More generally, and within the broader context of restructuring in Spain, the hugely expensive aspect of the changing the track width as a part of the modernisation of the railways in Spain demonstrated the high degree of symbolic power that the idea of being seamlessly linked to Europe had for the Spanish government. It was this connectivity to Europe that took priority over other objectives, including concerns over achieving internal territorial integration within Spain.

# 6

# Linking European Cities and Transport Liberalisation: Is There Space for the Basque Y?

This chapter focuses on changes at the EU level related to transport policy where there has been a shift from an agenda mainly linked to the objectives of cohesion and integration towards one that prioritises competitiveness and efficiency. This more recent policy orientation within the EU is (in contrast to earlier periods) informed by a stronger neo-liberal agenda. Indeed, as suggested in chapter 5, the introduction into force of the Single European Act (1993) and monetary union (1999–2002) inaugurated a phase within the EU in which Post-Fordist restructuring was marked by imposing fiscal-monetary discipline on a national level. Consequently, controls over fiscal deficit and debt became paramount to controlling and restraining the possibilities of economic restructuring and performance. Privatisation and liberalisation, twin mechanisms of the market discipline, were promoted further into more spheres which hitherto had been dominated by notions of public good and universal service. This requisite for integration was imposed particularly on southern semi-peripheral Fordist countries, where the pace of privatisation and liberalisation became unrelenting (Gill 1998; Bohle 2006). This certainly became the fate, albeit quite gradually, of Renfe.

More specifically, some of the most prominent features of this turn are reducing public expenditure, wide ranging privatisation of major publicly owned companies (the railways being a prime example), liberalisation and support for public-private partnerships in key sectors. Public investment was only encouraged as a supply-side intervention where it could be seen as a form of enabling accumulation through building capacity (O'Conner 2001) and improving possibilities for market penetration (Harvey 1982). Transport was one such area.

This change of priorities on the EU level also affected the structure of the debate and priorities within Spain and the Basque Country. Successive central governments in Spain privatised major state monopolies such as the railways and telecommunications, using a rationality and rhetoric of efficiency and value for money. The development of the railways was expected to facilitate intra-urban mobility and has been widely interpreted as a strategy within which priority is given to cities over regions and/or autonomous communities. Further, such a strategy was seen as leading to deepening the existing inequalities across Spain (Fernández Duran 2000; Sanz 2000), while also strengthening and deepening the links among cities. In chapter 7 I will discuss the strategy of Basque government as one of building the Basque City, but here it is worthwhile noting some of the ways in which such a strategy is compatible with (yet also different from) the broader EU and Spanish agenda.

In this chapter, I will look in more detail at the debates surrounding the priorities of different modes of rail transport, particularly the HST, and I will argue that there are contrasting (but not incompatible) strategies developed by the central Spanish government and the Basque government that also operate through different visions of social cohesion, competitiveness and priorities according to different social and economic objectives. More specifically, the HST had a very different rationality and fitted into strategic objectives that were differently defined by the Spanish and Basque governments. Indeed, the very persistence of the HST project in northern Spain and even more the specific form that it took in the BAC, as the Basque Y, both appeared unlikely outcomes. While the HST network that was developed in southern and eastern parts of Spain had a clearly defined economic rationality, the plans to extend it to the North did not satisfy such criteria. The HST link to the BAC was mostly supported by the PNV-led Basque government and therefore its implementation could to a large extent be seen as an expression of a specific vision for the building of a Basque national space within the borders of the BAC.

However, my main focus here remains the restructuring within the EU and its impact on Spain and the Basque Country. Accordingly I will relate these processes to the institutional relationship between the Spanish state and the BAC. In addition, this chapter will also look at some of the complex interdependencies between different institutional levels and the strategies employed in overcoming obstacles to the further development of the HST project.

## EU and Transport Policy

The early 1990s were dominated by the rhetoric and active implementation of neo-liberal policies across Europe. Such policies, however, were not uniform and differed both in terms of their scope and the shape they took across different countries and sectors (Peck and Tickell 2002; Brenner, Peck and Theodore 2010). These policies were mainly driven by the IMF, WTO and OECD, but were also to a large extent endorsed by the EU. In the case of transport policies, in particular, liberalisation meant an active support for privatisation with a special emphasis on railways, which were traditionally subsidized and maintained within the domain of national states. More specifically, according to the Treaty of Rome, one of the areas to be subjected to common policy was transport. However, after many unsuccessful attempts to engage EC members in developing and applying EC transport regulation, there were changes under Jacques Delors's leadership of the EC when member states finally committed to the free movement of goods, people and capital. The latter agreement set the conditions by which to begin developing an integrated EC Transport Policy. The elaboration of key transport documents (1988–1989) constituted the basis for the EC Transport Policy Document (1990), which came into force in January 1993, together with the Single European Act (Carballo 1990: 5–8).

In this chapter I argue that the railway policy reflected the economic tendency in Europe towards cutting back on public expenditure in preparation for the European single currency. Thus, one of the main aspects of railway policy was to regulate the role of states, in general, and their relationship with private capital regarding financing issues, in particular. I will further argue that the growing significance of issues related to finance also led to the rearticulation of the meaning of railways from a widely defined public good available to everyone, towards a narrowly defined and highly specialised form of transportation, the availability of which depended on efficiency and value for money. This tendency could also be detected in other sectors such as telecommunications and postal services (Geradin 2002; Bartle 2002; Levi-Faur 2003; Arocena 2004). The withdrawal of the state from its role as the main long-term investor in the development of railway infrastructures also meant that long-term risks had to be transferred to private capital. Such a transfer, however, needs time in order to develop the necessary institutional arrangements and to negotiate types of risk taken by different stakeholders, and thus led to debates and concerns on the part of different finance bodies and construction companies. Further, this change demonstrated the embeddedness of markets and more specifically the crucial role that could be played by the state in long-term projects where risks are difficult to predict and profit is not guaranteed. In addition, the particular case of the restructuring of the railways demonstrated that the neo-liberal agenda is far from homogenous. It took different shapes in different countries, while both governments and private capital expressed their own concerns and objections.

## *Global Financial Institutions and the Growing Significance of Private Capital*

On 18 and 19 January 1993, an OECD meeting was held in Paris in which representatives of EU member states, bank and industry, among them the Spanish construction company Dragados y Construcciones, met to discuss their views and concerns regarding the restrictions on public expenditure and the disinclination of national governments to get involved with the development of transport infrastructure (del Val 1993: 27). These concerns led to the need to find new formulas of financing that would make the funding of such projects attractive to private capital, especially the financial sector.

The participants in the conference called for state involvement in projects where the rate of return was uncertain. In the case of the HST, the network was identified as profitable and, therefore, in addition to a limited EU funding, generally, it had to be subject to private financing mechanisms as well as private administration.[1] One of the most interesting aspects discussed during the conference was the increasing complexity of infrastructural projects and therewith the ever-increasing delay of projects, which are, by their nature, already lengthy. Thus, the participants identified projects such as networks, that is, projects that require the involvement of more than one country for their completion, as notoriously difficult to deal with. In addition, members of the conference were also positive but, at the same time, concerned, with the need for increased transparency and public feedback regarding the development plans, which opened up the process to challenges, including legal complaints, and thus to even further delays. Participants also agreed that environmental assessment, in particular, could cause very lengthy delays. These concerns were

1. In contrast, as discussed earlier, states had to get completely involved, for example, in the cases of urban and intra-urban railway services, since according to EU regulation, those services were subject to the category of "public interest" and hence not subject to profit.

at the core of the reluctance of financial institutions to get involved with big infrastructural projects.

The participants in the conference made a couple of recommendations on how states could enhance the attractiveness to private capital of getting involved in big infrastructure projects. For example, they suggested that states should offer incentives in projects where the marginal returns are likely to be low. They also suggested that states should transfer operating rights to the companies in charge of building and administering a particular infrastructure project and, finally, the participants also suggested that states could take on private operators to administer infrastructure-related services by setting appropriate and competitive public tenders.

As a result, in the case of the railway sector, the EU Transport regulations framework seems to reflect the concerns and worries of the OECD participants. In other words, as suggested earlier, the EU set a number of procedures by which to establish a new relationship between the state and railway companies as well as the state and private capital. While states could only partially subsidize railway infrastructure development companies,[2] the "new imperative" to look for *additional funding* resources has enabled states to partially cover the costs in case of low returns; ensure that private railway operators administer railway networks identified as "non-public interest" concerns, such as the HST; and ensure a reasonable fare to railway operators in return for the use of the infrastructure. For example, the procedures and mechanisms associated with ensuring a reasonable fare are related to, first, dividing railway companies into railway operators and companies in charge of building and administering infrastructures. This split aimed to create a separate and clear division and accountability in terms of costs and benefits. In turn, the introduction of formal accounting procedures was viewed as the mechanism by which to ensure transparency and fairness in establishing fare charges for the use of railway infrastructure. For example, the International Railway Council noted that the price structure for HSTs was unclear due to the high level of fragmentation of rail operators and service providers that were also using different standards, languages and procedures for issuing tickets.

2. This reflects the new economic discourse to limit public expenditure and also reduce the large deficit some public companies, such as railways, have historically accumulated.

## *Spain and the EU Context*

In this context, the development of debates surrounding the HST in Spain moved away from discussions on progress, modernisation and technology acquisition towards the EU agenda of railway liberalisation and the predominance of a neo-liberal economic discourse emphasising the reduction of public expenditure and maximising efficiency and profitability. This stands in contrast to the 1980s, which were characterised by a positive attitude within the EC towards expenditure on (transport) infrastructures associated with concerns over growth and employment that were argued on the basis of a rhetoric of cohesion. However, it is worth distinguishing between, on the one hand, liberalisation of transport in general (which has remained an ongoing process) and, on the other, changing funding patterns justified through arguments based on cohesion, employment and growth towards sustainability and the knowledge economy (introduced in the Lisbon Strategy of 2000). In this sense, the agenda was framed by discussions about maximising public investment and, in the case of transport policy development, also became associated with defining a narrower role for railways within a broader understanding of coordinating different forms of transport, or *intermodality*.

The notion of intermodality expressed the view that different modes of transport had to specialise according to their competitive advantage in relation to other modes of transport. Thus, it was argued that roads were a universal mode of transport and air travel was most efficient for long distances. Railways were considered to be the most appropriate form of travel for congested cities, and they could both facilitate intra-urban connections (suburban trains within the metropolitan area) and also link cities located within middle-range distances of between 400 and 700 km. In the latter case, trains were seen as both potential competitors to air travel but also as an alternative that could help reduce the pressure on already saturated air traffic routes. In addition, railways were also increasingly assessed on the basis of their profitability: "They came to realise that certain railway passenger routes were profitable; one such case was the Barcelona–Madrid connection. It is then when transport became transport for passengers and not for goods."[3]

There were, then, different sets of justifications within which the building and restructuring of the railways was framed across Europe. These justi-

3. AD, member of the Barcelona Chamber of Commerce.

fications were related to the profitability of the HST, a perspective taken by the French government for example, where the HST was initially designed to compete against air travel, and which emphasises the importance of connections between highly significant urban areas. From another perspective, new railways could also be seen not only in terms of improving passenger travel but also promoting the transportation of goods. Such rail links, inter-city trains, were preferred in Germany for example, and they connect more widely dispersed networks of urban areas. In Spain, it was the latter approach that was preferred by the Barcelona Chamber of Commerce, where a combination of an expanding and improving capacity for both freight and passenger travel was seen as especially appropriate for the Port of Barcelona, and the connections that it might develop with other ports along the Mediterranean coastal line.

> [T]he central government believes more in the development of the Mediterranean Arc because the perception of its influence and expansion towards the Mediterranean is bigger . . . other projects include Algeciras [as a significant port for container traffic]. The port works as a hub, that is, it's a zone of distribution for goods. Containers are put on a train and then carried somewhere else. The Mediterranean [zone covers an increasingly more important trade area] and Algeciras is a main port for the arrival of cargo. That is why there are studies underway [Fermat] in relation to a possible railway connection between the Port of Algeciras and the cities of Valencia, Barcelona, Marseille, Lyon, up to the Ruhr and Antwerp basin.[4]

From this latter perspective, the railways are seen as an integral aspect of local economic development through promoting and enhancing trade routes. In this sense, it seems that the Catalan government has been more inclined towards the German model. As such, "France" and "Germany" appear as two reference points for how future railway transport is conceived, including its relationship to distinctive forms of social and economic organisation.

In addition to the notion of *intermodality*, I have argued that the emphasis on reducing public expenditure was accompanied by concerns with new financing arrangements that would replace state investment. In fact, a key aspect of EU transport policy development involved the budgetary regulation of public railway companies as well as discussion of the

4. AE, member of the Bilbao Chamber of Commerce.

appropriate role of the state in developing public-private partnerships. In other words, the EU railway policy attempted to create a framework in which the role and responsibilities of states were defined in cases where private capital was involved in infrastructural projects. For example, national governments would be allowed to cover the extra costs of unprofitable projects. Further, EU regulations concerned with railway ownership, operation and concession also established rules for calculating the price of the private use of railway infrastructure (Carballo 1990). Although the prevailing EU transport policy clearly centred on liberalisation, problems of long-term risk and the lack of investment interest on the part of private capital softened the EU stance on government involvement and allowed states and public railway companies to remain partially responsible for railway infrastructural projects. More specifically, states were allowed to continue subsidizing unprofitable railway projects, such as urban and intra-urban services for example, in cases where governments could prove that it was a matter of *public interest*. In contrast, the EU wanted to ensure that construction and management of profitable railway services and infrastructures were passed onto the private sector (while ownership ultimately remains in the hands of the state). To sum up, railway networks that were identified as profitable were to be developed and managed by private railway companies, while also being partially privately financed. Conversely, since railway infrastructural projects are so costly and returns are uncertain as well as long term, states had still to assume some of the risks where private financing could not otherwise be attracted.

In this context, the European HST network, which is both relatively new and expected to be highly profitable, was not defined as an area of *public interest* and thus, compared to other railway projects, was most open to the involvement of the private sector. Because governments were least expected to be involved in the HST infrastructure, the development of HST projects became one of the areas of strategic importance as far as EU liberalisation policy was concerned. The nature of such connections, middle-range distances and linking the main European cities, meant that the profile of the potential customer for HST services was that of young to middle-aged men working in the service and financial sectors. Therefore, the HST according to EU transport and railway policy was, in contrast to urban and intra-urban railways, discussed as a *profitable* domain rather than one where *public interest* is a priority.

The link between liberalisation on the one hand, and the identification of "public interest" and "non-public interest" in relation to distance of travel on the other, further implied a distinction between relationships mainly constrained within the locality and those that imply longer distance mobility. Further, the latter serves to redefine relations between different types of labour and capital as well as between labour and capital within individual states. These relations are mediated by national governments that are in a position to define priorities in serving the *public interest* and the form of support that specific cities would receive. Thus, in the case of Spain it was only the major urban areas, like Madrid, Barcelona, Valencia, Seville and Bilbao, which were identified. These are all cities of key national importance that also have the financial and administrative strength to develop and improve their rail and broader transport infrastructures.

As argued above, the liberalisation of the railways was initially primarily about the privatisation and restructuring of former state companies. This only happened slowly. In Spain, the restructuring was implemented in two stages where first the state company Renfe was split into the maintenance and development of railway infrastructure (GIF, later Adif) and the operation of trains (Renfe). Both remained in state ownership until 2005 when Renfe was privatised (Campos 2008). Campos argues that Renfe was further internally restructured, as a result of which some services remained under state support while other services were newly developed and expected to be run for profit. The HST became the most significant and rapidly expanding among those services and since the mid-1990s it was already, within the Spanish context, considered to be a profitable enterprise.

### *Differences in the Process of Privatisation*

In light of the new regulation introduced in the early 1990s and the concerns expressed by the private sector, the European Commission released a report exploring the extent and degree of restructuring railway companies themselves had achieved (del Val 1998: 4–8). Since the Commission identified "accountancy balance" as a mechanism to achieve better management efficiency and, subsequently, constitute the basis from which to calculate the canon private companies should pay in return for the use of the infrastructure, the separation of railway company operators and railway infrastructure company promoters became important from the EU point of view. However, it became apparent that such separation was diverse and did not always provide the expected results. In fact, the report classified the separation between railway company operators and infrastructure company promoters in three categories. In the first category, the report identified Sweden and Great Britain followed in the process by

Denmark, Finland, France, Portugal and the Netherlands. In their case, they opted for the separation of two juridically different entities. In this respect, Great Britain delegated the management and development of infrastructures to a private company, whereas all other countries created public companies. In the case of Benelux, public companies take charge of the maintenance as well as traffic control of the infrastructures. In the case of France and Finland, they have created different public companies that will finance the infrastructure while the real administration falls within the national public railway company in question. Austria, Germany, Italy and Spain compose the second category. These countries have opted for the diversification of services within the same integrated business unit. For example, in the case of Renfe in Spain, it deals separately with AVE (the Spanish acronym for the HST), regional and urban services. Lastly, there is the category composed by Greece, Ireland and Luxembourg, with smaller railway networks, which opted for a totally integrated railway company with different accountancy balances.

Just as the process of restructuring was diverse and unequal in its results according to EU standards, other aspects, such as reduction in deficit, also produced mixed and uneven results. Thus, the report noted that the financing situation of five railway companies was very grave in 1995. The companies the report identified were in Greece (CH), Portugal (CP), Spain (Renfe), Sweden (SJ/BV) and France (SNCF). Moreover, EU member states had had to intervene in order to reduce the debt and improve the finances. Basically, the Commission assessed the financial state of the railway companies against the 91/440/EC regulation although this regulation was not in place during the 1980s and hence the deficit of companies was a legacy of practices from the past.

Generally, it can be concluded from the report that the EU plays a steering role which oversees the regularisation and rationalisation of a developing new economic space. This process has clashed with national and economic interests from member states as well as a multiple ways of dealing, understanding and implementing EU regulations. Moreover, this development has been in many cases influenced by the economic and political legacies in which railway companies operated.

Likewise, in a 1996 report on the progress in developing the Essen priority projects,[5] a working group led by Neil Kinnock and composed

5. These are fourteen transport projects defined as priority projects by the EU in 1994. Ten of those are railway projects including the Barcelona–Portbou and Vitoria-Gasteiz–Dax lines.

of representatives of the transport ministers of member states and experts from the private sector, such as financiers, civil engineers and managers, concluded that there were several factors that prevented the development of the Trans-European transport networks. The report duly identified political and non-commercial aspects as factors that prevented the involvement of private capital in the development of the Essen projects. In particular, the report addressed difficulties in coordinating projects across different legal and administrative systems. In fact, the working group recommended that the European Commission appoint coordinators that would operate as mediators who would negotiate the legal and administrative differences across different countries. And this procedure was implemented in the 2000s under the tenure of Loyola de Palacio as EU Transport Commissioner.

In this context, states found themselves with a limited budget regarding transport infrastructures in general and railways in particular; and they were also obliged to rely on other sources such as private capital. It must be noted, however, that in contrast to other countries, Spain received substantial financial assistance from the EU to develop transport infrastructure (see chapter 4). The money came primarily from the Cohesion Fund and European Regional Development Fund (ERDF).[6] Overall, 85 percent of Spain's transport budget was constituted by EU funding that was received under different programmes (although not all of it could go to the HST. That is, the HST was allotted only a limited sum of money from the main EU funds, plus a specific budget to be used in the development of European Transport networks and special European bank credits).[7]

## *A Turn in the Conception of the HST*

As discussed in chapter 4, the development of various new EU funds, such as the Cohesion Fund, was partly aimed at cushioning the negative social and economic effects of the Single European Act that came into force in 1993. This was especially aimed at supporting poorer EU countries such as Spain. In the case of Spain, generally, the integration of mar-

6. For example, the EU contribution for 1997 was estimated to be about seven hundred million pounds (1.2 billion dollars) of which four hundred million (just under 700 million dollars) were channelled into transport. Regarding ERDF, the contribution was estimated at around 1.4 billion pounds (2.3 billion dollars) of which four hundred million were channelled into transport.

7. AF, former member of the EU Transport Directorate.

kets that came into force in January 1993 provoked the devaluation of the peseta and a general economic crisis that paved the way to less optimistic discourses about the EU by the right-wing political party, the PP (which subsequently won the general election in 1996).

In this context, I have suggested that member states developed policies that addressed the need of intermodality (Rivas 1993: 20). This required a shift from sectoral policy development, which would traditionally address the problems and needs of a particular mode of transport, to a more multi-sectoral perspective, which would consider the interdependencies of the existing modes of transport. I also argued that this coincided with the development of different EU policy programmes that aimed to intervene at different scales. These were policies with the objective of tackling economic disparities at the regional and urban level. Thus, while competitiveness and technology programmes were designed to be implemented on the regional level, policy plans, such as the ESDP, focused on the urban scale. The latter was measured in terms of functionality of metropolitan areas and the "effective management" of this scale was perceived as the key for its economic growth and success (Davoudi 2006).

Therefore, in mid-1993 (after the symbolically important year of 1992 for Spain, when the Olympic Games were held in Barcelona and the first Spanish HST service came into operation), the Spanish government published the Plan Director de Infraestructuras (Guiding Plan of Infrastructures, PDI) (MOPT 1994) (Ordóñez 1993c, 1993d). This reflected the trend towards refocusing on cities. Generally, the plan sought to distribute "efficiently" the government's budget into different modes of transport and, in the case of the railway sector, develop the most appropriate links at the urban and intra-urban levels regarding cities located at middle-range distances of about 400–700 Km. In the words of the then Minister of Public Works and Transport, José Borrell: "The PDI does not consider the closure of railway services as a result of a limited demand, however, as I have said earlier, the railway has to look for its specialisation within those territorial areas and type of services where it is economically and socially more useful. Following this premise, railway services will be cut down only as long as they can be substituted by other more efficient modes of transport" (quoted in Lozano 1993).

In contrast, then, to earlier conceptions of the HST, with the emphasis on modernisation, technology and economic development (see chapter 4), the central government's priority now shifted towards the implantation and development of links within a wider territorial conception that prioritised urban and inter-urban connections, rather than the HST on its own. In other words, the PDI guidelines had a strong urban focus and suggested that the main emphasis of the infrastructural development should be first within cities, and second between urban areas. These guidelines were gradually implemented in the 1990s and at present transport systems with a high degree of integration already exist within different urban areas across Spain. Indeed, Bilbao is a good example of such an integrated system (further discussed in chapter 7).

### *Who Needs a HST?*

As noted above, the extension of the HST to the BAC was an unlikely outcome given the lack of support for the project both internationally and within Spain, while attitudes within the Basque Country itself were at best dubious.[8] Further, the implementation of the project within the framework demanded by Basque government was even less likely given that economic justification for this particular shape of the line was even less forthcoming (chapter 5).

Thus, the viability of the link between Madrid and Bilbao could be justified as an extension towards a link with Paris, yet this was met with little enthusiasm on the part of the French government:

> In addition, France hasn't been much of a help. The project hasn't been France's priority, since the other side of the border is a depopulated area, deprived economically; and so on . . . there hasn't been any interest in developing anything. That is why networking is important, which is the case of the Atlantic Arc, regardless of all its difficulties. Similarly, the agreement between Bilbao and Bordeaux was an attempt to engage the latter into supporting the Basque Y and make things easier. However, as a result of several circumstances, ten years now since that agreement, we are still hoping that the project will go ahead [2004].[9]

A link to the BAC was, likewise, very low on the list of priorities for the Spanish government as successive governments were developing strat-

---

8. In the early 1990s, the Basque Y appeared for the first time in the European HST plans. However, from the very beginning, this project has been seen as inappropriate given the distances between the three cities involved and the benchmarks for efficiency, which could be achieved in medium-range distances between 400 and 700 km.

9. AA, former member of and adviser to the Basque government.

egies oriented to the Mediterranean area.[10] These were influenced by economic and political priorities.

In addition, the building of different stages of the HST is closely associated with Basque nationalist political claims, which can be interpreted in terms of the organisation of democratic accountability at a regional level.

> There are concepts that belong to the Spanish politics itself, that is, we must not forget that in the period when the PP was in Government [1996–2004], the Community of Valencia was hugely favoured in terms of new developments. The reasons were, on the one hand, the Community of Valencia was a PP stronghold and several government ministers came from there. On the other hand, it became an alternative to Catalonia at that time under the government of CiU [Convergencia i Unio, Convergence and Union, the Catalan equivalent of the Basque PNV, Christian democratic nationalists], as a result of the PP's crusade against nationalisms. In fact, the PP finished the N-3 dual carriageway, a free connection, something that Barcelona hasn't got [in order to reach Barcelona you have to use one of the toll roads]. It's a connection between Madrid and Valencia, connected directly. Big investments have been made in the port and into the logistic activities of Valencia and Sagunto Ports. Valencia rises as the counter power to Barcelona.[11]

As far as European support for the Basque Y is concerned, the preference of the EU was for Bilbao to be connected, yet not as a major European city, but rather as a centre that happens to be on a major European route connecting Lisbon–Madrid–Vitoria-Gasteiz–Dax. Since the proposed Basque Y scheme, which the central government finally approved (chapter 5), was expecting to go through the cities of Vitoria-Gasteiz and Donostia-San Sebastián, of some tertiary importance in Spain but of no particular socio-economic importance at the EU level, it was obvious that Bilbao could not be excluded of such project (see also figure 6.1): "I have already explained in some seminars: that the Lisbon–Paris corridor is more important, from an EU perspective, than the Basque HST per se. The Basque HST consists of just a link to the EU network [Bilbao]. To put it in a different way, the aim of the TENs is not that one can arrive from Vitoria

10. The Mediterranean area has been "measured" according to demographic expansion and capacity to attract FDI. I argued in chapter 1 that the Spanish government's economic restructuring was based, among other things, on offering support to the consolidation and internationalisation of the financial sector as well as support for foreign investment.

11. AE, member of the Bilbao Chamber of Commerce.

to San Sebastián in ten minutes. The whole corridor must be taken into account." Further, AF adds: "The Lisbon–Madrid–Vitoria–Irun–Dax corridor . . . the connections of San Sebastián and Bilbao are not necessary [to form the Madrid–Vitoria–Irun–Dax corridor] but it wouldn't have been logical to leave Bilbao out."[12]

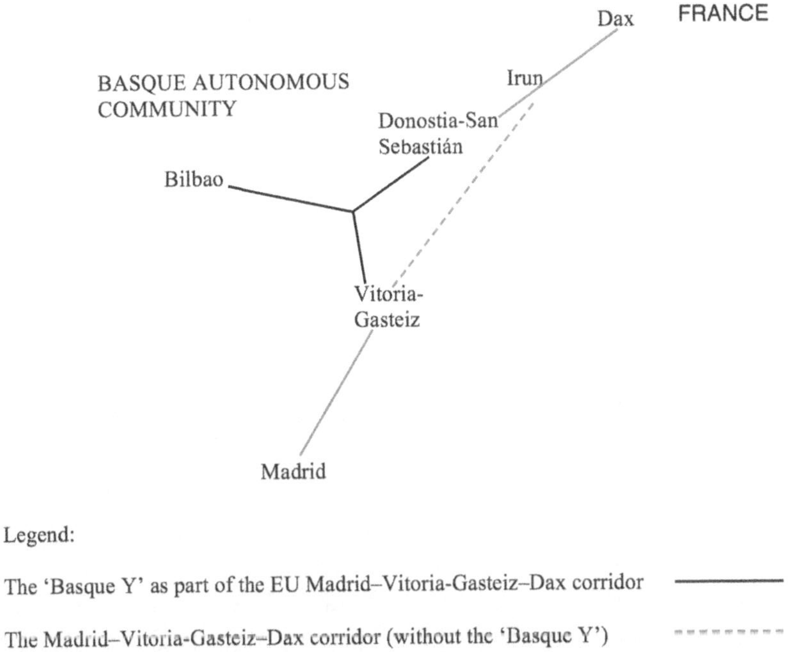


**Figure 6.1.** MISSING CAPTION

There is, then, little doubt as to how much importance the central government attached to the Basque HST, in its Y shape, in the late 1980s, at a time when the EC countries were deliberating on the future European high-speed network. The consequence of this was that the Basque HST became eligible for EU funding and somehow, as a result, the Basque government (led by the PNV who supported the Basque HST in its Y shape) obtained at the same time the support of the EC institutions:

> Among [the trans-European network projects] number 3 is the one which addresses the Madrid–Vitoria–Dax corridor . . . the Basque HST,

12. AF, former member of the EU Transport Directorate.

> from being a local and regional project, became a trans-European one, thus Europe and the Spanish institutions alike became responsible for its implementation . . . [that is] Europe acknowledges that there is an important link that enables the connection of the Peninsula, the Southern Europe, with Central Europe . . . the Vitoria–Dax link, concerning this corridor the [Spanish] state is only responsible for the Basque Y.[13]

The Basque government had to persuade other parties involved in the development of HST infrastructures (the EU and the Spanish government) of the viability of such a project under the logic of their own rationales. But in addition, the Basque Y project was also facing other possible contenders within the BAC, such as the less successful and short-lived L-shaped project. "The Bilbao [railway connection] becomes a branch line that links to the Trans-European network. The "L" means to change the Trans-European Network design and in addition, it's about money as well. If the project is about a Trans-European Network, the Basque Y [becomes an integral part of the] trans-European networks, therefore subject to Trans-European funds."[14]

This is why chapter 5 argued that the inclusion of the Basque Y among the priority projects had two important consequences. First, it created a lock-in effect in regard to the possibility of bringing forward other layouts, since they would have to agree with the Madrid–Vitoria-Gasteiz–Dax corridor, in other words, the EU number 3 priority project. Second, the conception of the Basque Y was linked to the idea of passenger transport as well as other associated notions such as the "underground of Europe." In other words, the EU's interest in building TENs evolved from "connecting Europe" in terms of transporting people and avoiding borders (missing links) and mostly linked to the notion of "cohesion" (discussed in chapters 4 and 5), to emphasising competitiveness and connection among cities, to which the "underground of Europe" notion refers. In addition, I discussed earlier how one of the EU requirements was that HST projects should be financed partly by private capital, as a condition of further access to EU funding. However, private capital became reluctant to participate is such projects and, from the mid-1990s onwards, transport also became mostly

13. AG, former Basque Minister of Transport and Public Works.

14. AE, member of the Bilbao Chamber of Commerce.

associated with freight connections,[15] which further differentiated long distance rail travel for goods and passengers. It is in this context that, from 1998 on, the Basque government proposed that freight transport should be central to the Basque Y.

Indeed, given increasing diversification regarding investment in different modes of transport, and in particular railways, and the shift towards urban areas and the development of integrated transport systems, fear of losing the opportunity to benefit from EU funding played a significant role in the attitude and increasing mobilisation on the part of the Basque government to support the Basque Y. In this context, the Basque government mobilised a host of political, social and other civic organisations, including universities, the Port of Bilbao and Chambers of Commerce, arguing that as a result of delays in the construction of the Basque Y, the Basque Country would lose the opportunity to benefit from EU funds and suffer from severe backwardness. "[T]he management of the project [was at stake] . . . we suggested managing the project, given the delays concerning the starting of works. "Give us the EU funding and we will be in charge of the project." But the EU won't be able to afford funding unless private capital also takes part in funding [the project]. Moreover, new members are joining the EU, so it's likely that the funding available would be even more limited."[16]

In this sense, from 1998 the Basque government proposed that freight transport should be central to the Basque Y. As a result, justifications for the construction of the Basque Y became intertwined with environmental arguments.[17] According to the Basque government, the new railway would connect the Port of Bilbao with major European railway lines. This in turn would guarantee that cargo traffic by train would remove lorries from the roads. In other words, the Basque Y would not only facilitate mobility among the Basque capitals, by reducing significantly travel times among the three capital cities, but it has been consistently argued by the Basque government that it will play a significant role in achieving envi-

15. For example, the *EU White Book on Transport* (European Commission 2001) puts the emphasis on "sustainability" and favours freight transport as an alternative to road transport.

16. AG, former Basque Minister of Transport and Public Works.

17. The EU developed extensive guidelines on environmental protection and sustainability, which partly informed the change of direction in EU transport policies.

ronment targets regarding reducing cargo traffic on the roads.[18] In this regard, at the same time, efforts have been made to develop a comprehensive logistics policy in order to coordinate efficiently different modes of transport involved within the freight transport sector.[19]

However, subsequent reports such as that of Van Miert (2003) showed that the Vitoria-Gasteiz–Dax corridor has consistently suffered from a lack of institutional coordination and support. Indeed, as suggested before, there was a lack of interest on the part of the Spanish and French governments when it came to developing the project, as a result of which, later, in 2003, Loyola de Palacio, EU Minister of Transport at the time, proposed removing the Vitoria-Gasteiz–Dax link from the list of Essen priority projects, and introduced a new "quick start" priority list:

> [L]ater there were many reports, for example, the first of those reports by the Commission concerning Trans-European networks, in 1995, outlined the progress of the different priority projects and concluded that there were many delays, including in the priority Dax–Vitoria project. [the Commission claimed that this project] didn't have a timetable and it lacked [a framework of] coordination by the two member states [involved in the project] . . . this went on like this until 2000–2001; the latest report by the Commission claimed that among the fourteen priority projects that didn't have a proper programme, [it] could be eliminated and [they could] move on to other projects . . . this decision was taken in 2003 because of all the priority projects adopted in 1994, only 20% had been completed. As a result of these delays, the "quick start" priority list was proposed, amidst wide controversy.[20]

Nevertheless, the Basque government continued to develop HST related policies and offered new justifications for building the HST, as well as linking the project to the changing discourses on competitiveness and cohesion adopted on the EU level and within Spain. This could be seen in two central documents published by Basque government in 1997: the Territorial Planning Guidelines (DOT, Directrices de ordenación del territorio) and the Railway PTS (Territorial Sectorial Plan), which also introduced for the first time the notion of the *polinuclei urban region*. The

18. AG, former Basque Minister of Transport and Public Works.

19. The Aquitaine-Euskadi Logistic Plataform (the PLAE) was conceived to this end. AI, member of the PLAE.

20. AH, member of the Assembly Against the HST.

latter was a key element of the ESDP (European Spatial Development Perspective) that emphasised the functionalities of urban areas across Europe (Davoudi 2002, 2006) and was introduced within the general framework of territorial planning of the BAC (Franco 2004: 410). This gave further legitimacy to the plans of Basque government to construct a HST in the BAC and also offered an early platform through which to develop the notion of the Basque City (discussed in chapter 6) as a Basque but also a European project.

> In 1997 the DOTs were passed, the Territorial Planning Guidelines . . . the Basque City. If you want, the official discourse until then supported the idea of the Madrid–Paris train passing through the Basque Country and, thus, attaining a position in the international axis . . . [the idea that] "we have always been a historical corridor" . . . The DOT already includes the Basque City, that [thing] about the polinucli system regarding the Basque capital cities . . . In my opinion, this belongs to European territorial planning . . . Europe is pushing for a more polarised system, if you will, all this discourse on globalisation . . . the region as the major urban scale . . . [the DOT] assumes all these schemas . . . you can see, there are new interpretations or new interests if you like, initially it was the Paris–Madrid connection and the corridor . . . this hasn't changed, one thing doesn't contradict the other . . . however, since then, since the passing of the DOTs, in 1997, as well as the crisis of the connection with the North [the French Basque Country] and Europe . . . that the three Basque capitals could be connected by a linked HST became the most important thing. This is how it says so: "the objective is to connect the three capitals with a HST," this [notion] was introduced in the DOTs . . . but the HST project had already been decided since 1988, this hasn't changed![21]

However, despite Basque government's earlier success in introducing the Basque Y within the Spanish Railway policy (1989) and later, within the Essen priority projects (1994), the Basque Y project entered a lethargic period during the early and mid-1990s. This was due to change of policy direction, first at the EU and then at the national level, with a stronger emphasis on urban transport system developments, further specialisation of different modes of transport (particularly railways) and a lack of private investment as well as diminishing EU funding, partly as a result of further EU integration.

21. Ibid.

## Institutional Support, Political Manoeuvring and the Construction of the Basque Y

Faced with EU's decreasing financial availability and ability, the Spanish central government renewed its interest in pursuing the development of the Basque Y. Until that time, Spanish HST links were entirely absent from the northern part of the country (see figure 6.2). Thus, in February 2004, the PP-led central government decided to call to public tender the construction of the Basque HST infrastructure.[22] However, the tender coincided with a terrorist attack in Madrid in March 2004 that prompted an unexpected turn in the forthcoming general elections. While the PP was expected to comfortably win these elections, the events that followed[23] tipped the balance towards the PSOE.

Although this change in government was felt, for example, in a new foreign policy direction,[24] other policy areas, such as transport, did not experience any substantial change. In fact, in January 2005, the new PSOE-led government carried out the privatisation of the state-owned railway company Renfe, which had started under the previous PP government. In addition, under the previous government, 80 percent of the Development Ministry budget had already been distributed among different projects, including the Basque HST. Thus, the Strategic Infrastructures and Transport Plan (PEIT) (2006), designed under the new government, introduced marginal changes to the transport policy (Infrastructure Policy, 2000–2007) that it had inherited from the previous government. The new policy was more of a continuation of the previous programme, because the PSOE government found itself in a situation in which it could only carry

22. This also coincided with the launch of a new campaign in support of the Basque Y by the Basque government. AH, member of the Assembly Against the HST.

23. After several bombs exploded on four commuter trains, killing 191 people and injuring over 1,000 more. The PP government's reaction , which sought to apportion blame for the attacks on ETA right up to the eve of election day itself, despite increasing evidence that they were actually perpetrated by Islamists, appeared to many to be a cynical attempt to withhold the truth of the investigation in order to secure victory on polling day. In other words, had it really been an ETA attack, this would have justified the PP's hard-line stance against the group and secured victory for the party in the elections. However, if the perpetrators were Islamists (as indeed they were), this could have been interpreted by the electorate as the price paid for Spanish support for the US intervention in Iraq, a deeply unpopular policy in Spanish society as a whole.

24. The new prime minister, José Luis Rodríguez Zapatero, immediately called for the return of Spanish soldiers from Iraq. Generally, the new government moved from a policy supportive of US foreign policy towards a more EU-centred perspective.

out projects that had already been agreed, more or less, under the previous administration.[25]

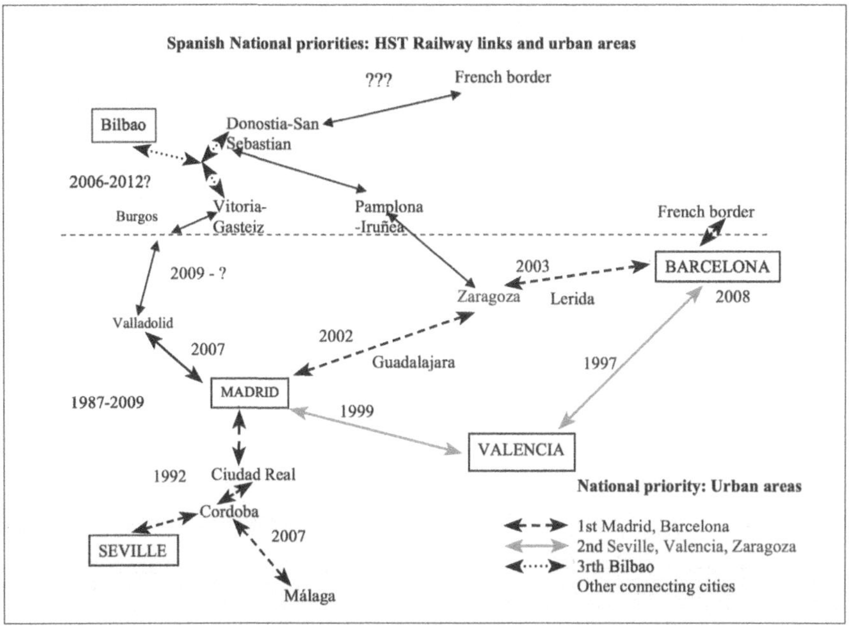


**Figure 6.2.** Between 1987 and 2009 the central government focused on the development of the Spanish high speed train (AVE) connecting the principal cities of Seville, Madrid, Zaragoza and Barcelona. Improvements were introduced in the railway links between Barcelona, Valencia and Madrid in order to increase speed limits of up to 220 km/h. Regarding the 'Basque Y', the works started in 2006 but its connections to Madrid (via Burgos and Valladolid) and the French border are not yet specified. Source: Based on the railway map produced by the Spanish Development Ministry, in December 2007.

On the 24 April 2006 the central and the Basque governments signed an agreement to construct the Basque Y. This agreement was important for two reasons. First, because the central government agreed to start the construction of the Basque HST; and second, because the central government transferred the necessary powers to the Basque government so that it could partly be involved in managing and building the Basque Y. The agreement thus included the provision that the Basque government would be exclusively in charge of building the infrastructure of the HST

25. AJ, member of Ecologists in Action.

in Gipuzkoa, while the central government (through the public railway company Adif) would undertake the construction of the infrastructure in Bizkaia and Araba. These powers extended to the compulsory purchase of land, which would allow the Basque government to actually carry out the necessary tests on the land and bring in the machinery to construct the infrastructure.[26] Both administrations agreed that the Basque Y should be developed as an infrastructure for the transport of goods and passengers.

From the perspective of the Basque government, this agreement was important for two reasons: first, according to the Basque Minister for Transport and Public Works, Nuria Lopez de Guereñu, "this is a very important infrastructure for the development of our country."[27] This could be interpreted in two ways. On the one hand, from an economic point of view, that this infrastructure would offer better connectivity to major growth centres and other important cities. On the other, that the infrastructure was a means to achieve further integration and cohesion,[28] by prioritising one type of scale, the city, as well as, in terms of markets, institutional development; and also functional cohesion at different institutional levels and among the three provinces.[29] Second, according to Lopez de Guereñu as well, "this is a step forward towards further self-government,"[30] in the sense that the agreement made it possible for the Basque government to participate in the construction of the Basque Y.

The Basque Statute of Autonomy, which defines the relationship between the BAC and central government, offers some financial flexibility in terms of structuring its investment decisions. As such, in the case of the financing arrangements for the HST, the above-mentioned agreement allowed the Basque government to begin construction works on the project and to finance these works through funds that would, at a

26. "Acuerdo entre los gobiernos central y vasco para construir la 'Y' vasca por 4.178 millones," Diariovasco.com, 24 April 2006.

27. Quoted in "Acuerdo entre los gobiernos central y vasco para construir la 'Y' vasca por 4.178 millones," Diariovasco.com, 24 April 2006.

28. AS, member of the transport committee of the Basque Ministry of Transport and Public Works.

29. AE, member of the Bilbao Chamber of Commerce, and AA, former member of and adviser to the Basque government.

30. Ibid.

later stage, be subtracted from the overall tax contribution that the BAC makes to the Spanish budget.[31]

Although the agreement signed with central government meant that the Basque government could use this financial mechanism, this capacity is important because it allows the Basque government to rely on its own budget. Therefore, this can eventually help central government to decide to move a project forward (a capacity that is unavailable to other ACs). This "financial flexibility" is often criticised and linked to issues of solidarity and cohesion in Spain. In other words, this is seen as an advantage that the BAC has over other ACs, which rely entirely on the central government budget in financing their own projects.[32] However, the case of the Basque Y shows that although the Basque government has some "financial flexibility," the implementation of this project was dependent on a combination of different factors and the involvement of many stakeholders on the EU, national and regional levels. In addition, the federal-like structure of Spain offers other layers of complexity that were important in the process of the HST negotiations (chapter 3).

The agreement between the central and regional authorities concerning the HST could also be related to the specificity of the electoral system in Spain where political support from smaller nationalist parties is often crucial for the stability of central government. Thus, the agreement was reached in exchange for support by the Basque government for the national budget of the central government. More broadly, some authors have suggested (Colomer 2007) that the Spanish electoral system, which could be defined as a half-majoritarian/half-proportional representation system, tends to lead to results in which none of the two major parties has an overall majority. This means that whichever political party wins the elections always needs the support of smaller, and often regional, parties in order to implement its agenda. In most cases, the political party in government relies on the moderate Catalan and Basque nationalists, CiU and the PNV, respectively. As Colomer argues, this process has not only affected

31. The BAC, together with the AC of Navarre, has a unique fiscal framework in the sense that the collection of taxes are carried out directly by Basque administrations. In this case, the provincial councils are endowed with the power to collect taxes, parts of which are later transferred to local councils and the regional government. Thereafter, the Basque government is in charge of negotiating with the central government the sum of money the BAC should pay for the services that are not transferred to the BAC, such as foreign policy, border controls, and so on (Zubiri 2003)

32. AK, adviser to the Spanish government and member of the EU transport commission.

the process of devolution but also the degree of effectiveness with which projects are implemented. This has certainly been the case with the HST.

> Everything is related to the very development of the Statute [of Autonomy]. That is to say, the competencies and the statute have been, that is, I usually say, it is, as if [it were] a "stolen" statute [*estatuto arrancado*]. That is to say, when the statute was finally approved we all believed that it would be implemented literally. We would constitute mixed committees to discuss transferences within six months. What we've achieved after twenty-five years is to constantly argue about what competences belong to whom. You renegotiate what you have already renegotiated. It's as if you have to start all over again every time you sit down at the desk and always regarding something other than the issue at hand. It is always about an exchange for supporting someone-else's candidacy, the budget of the government, etc. . . . always in exchange for something.[33]

Nevertheless, the coming to central power of the PSOE in 2004 can also be seen within the context of a new stage of engagement and cooperation between central government and the BAC (led by the PNV). From the perspective of the Basque government, this normalisation of institutional links was welcome as it created favourable conditions for the re-establishment of the more productive relationships that existed in the past and that were important for the successful completion of large projects such as the regeneration of Bilbao.

## The HST and Inter-scalar Conflicts and Coalitions: Overcoming Local Resistance

The agreement between central government and the Basque government (discussed earlier) also gave the Basque government extended powers to override decisions reached on the local level concerning land use. In practical terms this provided the Basque government with much needed institutional support in overcoming opposition to the HST that it encountered in some of the localities through which the line would run. While both local authorities and the Basque government were employing different tactics in resolving the matter in their favour, given the existing division of powers between regional and local authorities there was an impasse that could not be resolved until the Basque government was given extended

33. AA, former member of and adviser to the Basque government.

powers through the agreement. More specifically, it was allowed to treat the construction of the HST as a public interest project and thus override any local or provincial opposition.

> [T]he subsidiary norm[34] takes between a year and a half and two years. A working group gets together with an architect and a lawyer in order to discuss the type of town we want [for the future]. We started it at the beginning of the year, since the last subsidiary norm dates back to 1989. Many years have passed since and it is essential [that we have a new subsidiary norm] for the good future of this town . . . But if the council does not include land for [HST] infrastructure . . . the provincial government might not approve the norm . . . It's a lot of pressure since the subsidiary norm is about where new houses can be built; what type of housing should be built in ten years' time; how much land should be allocated to the primary sector, etc. . . . Without the subsidiary norm we cannot build more houses, say, because a piece of land is being used for something else . . . the issue is to be able to define the use of land.[35]

Within this context, though, the municipal council in question (Itsasondo, in Gipuzkoa) decided to use its legal authority under the scope of its urban competences as a tactic by which to stop land surveys and tests from being carried out on local municipal and private farmland and thus effectively block the use of land for any other purposes. The latter prevented Basque government contractors from making preparatory works for the construction of the HST:

> [G]eotechnical drilling tests have to be carried out before works begin . . . in order to stop them, the council might require from the surveyor that she produces a permission from the local authority . . . normally, they don't bother with that, and [the surveyors] approach landowners personally . . . however, the landowner has the right to demand a document for temporary land occupation . . . but they never do it since it takes time and, in any case, the local authority may ask them to ask for municipal permission . . . [in any event] they always have to deal with the local authority . . . some local authorities don't bother with that but others do. [Some surveyors] might claim that such permission does not belong to the subsidiary norm of the town council . . . Itsasondo is carrying the

34. The subsidiary norm is a set of laws regarding the use of land within localities. These laws are revised every five or ten years.

35. AL, town councillor in Itsasondo.

> fight to the very end . . . [but it finds that] it needs to renew the subsidiary norm and these are big obstacles for the town.[36]

Thus, after becoming aware of Basque government plans concerning the HST, the local council of Itsasondo passed this information on to local farmers who would be affected by this decision and offered them further advice on the powers that they had to legally refuse access to their land. This included, for example, asking for a certificate from the local council allowing surveyors the right to trespass on private land.

> Whatever work that has to be undertaken in the town, even if it involves a small job such as tailing, has to be reported to the council; we knew that they had plans to carry out land surveys so we demanded that they apply for permission; of course, we refused to give it to them . . . they will have to do it by force . . . These volumes include the detailed actual building of the project. It uses very technical language. It explains the type of machines involved; for how long those machines are going to be used; what type of building materials will be used; land expropriation proceedings: how much land will be expropriated . . . Not all the information is useful: I might not be interested in the type of cement that is going to be used but it is useful to know where an emergency exit is going to go; what land is going to be expropriated, what will happen to the excess of land.[37]

Since the Basque government did not have the competences over decisions concerning the HST (the domain of central government) it could not order the expropriation of or even trespass on private and municipal land. In this sense, the agreement between the Spanish and Basque governments, reached in 2006, was a pivotal point for the development of the HST as it offered a mechanism for financing the project as well as a legal basis on which all existing institutional obstacles, as well as local opposition, could be overcome.

Transport policy and transport infrastructure projects are among the main priorities on the EU policy agenda. In this chapter it was argued that there is a tendency both on the EU and on national levels towards the liberalisation of transport and the specialisation of different modes of transport.

---

36. AH, member of the Assembly Against the HST.

37. AL, town councillor in Itsasondo.

This is justified on the basis of improving economic efficiency and competitiveness. In this context, the HST is categorised as a privately exploitable means of transport that is optimal in connecting major urban areas and covering medium-range distances.

The early 1990s also witnessed a shift in transport policy development in Spain. This shift was marked by the development of the PDI (1994), which stressed the development of urban centres and different modes of connecting them. Thus, the PDI identified three types of connections: (1) intra-city connections (2) suburban connections and (3) interregional connections, based extensively on the development of high-speed trains. In particular, the emphasis was put on expanding the south–north corridor towards Barcelona and the upgrading of the Mediterranean area.

Arguments developed by the Basque government in regard to its strategic interest in communication infrastructures are closely linked to the rationale of many key strategic EU documents and objectives in relation to the notion of sustainable economic development. Indeed, sustainability and environmental impact have become overarching concerns on the EU level. The shifts on both the EU level and within Spain also had an impact on the strategies employed by the Basque government. More specifically, the Basque Y could not be justified as a priority project for either Spain or the EU. The limited powers to carry out such a project led the Basque government to articulate it within several of other policy documents in order to keep it alive. Building coalitions across different institutional levels has been of high significance for generating sufficient support for the HST project. In addition, I argued that when the PSOE won the 2004 general elections in Spain, it had to rely on the support of regionally based parties, such as the PNV, in order to be able to form a stable government. The latter arrangement was instrumental in facilitating the agreement between the central and Basque governments regarding the financing and implementation of the Basque HST.

From the perspective of the Basque government, the HST is more than an infrastructural project and also carries a broader vision for the future development of the BAC. The HST has become an important aspect of the post-Franco nation- and state-building process as imagined by the ruling PNV. This vision for the BAC has more recently been captured within the metaphor of the Basque City, which will be further discussed in the next chapter.

# 7

# The Basque City

The well-known Basque writer Bernardo Atxaga weighed in on the Basque Y in the newspaper *Herria*:

> [W]ithout a doubt I belong to the place of my birth. And I hold a very special relationship with Bilbao. So I do with Morocco. If I had to move to the political terrain, I would not know the type of territorial configuration [such a relationship] should have. I use the notion of the Basque City but only as a metaphor . . . I wish that all the Basque Country would become urbanised because if it doesn't it won't be an interesting place. [This wish] probably puts me in favour of (over)development and it's true. Does it come with a cost? No doubt about it. But I have always been in favour of highways, the Basque Y . . . and as far as I am concerned it is very important to travel from Baiona [Bayonne] to Bilbao in hour or hour and a half . . . let's urbanise the Basque Country, physically too . . . If anyone would argue that a species of squirrel from an area of some mountain would become extinct I would reply "sorry, but the squirrel would have to move somewhere else." *Berria*, 2005.

The imagining of the Basque Country as the Basque City is at the intersection of different policies, strategies and interests of different stakeholders operating on different scales. Indeed, far from taking for granted notions of territoriality, what is needed is the unraveling of the processes of nation and state formation. This is also in the case for the Basque Country, and thus the book seeks to examine the politico-economic forces, institutional processes and cultural imaginaries underpinning the development and evolution of the "Basque Country" as a historically situated entity. Hence, as a national project, it is necessarily open to different possibilities and futures (that is, it is shaped by legacies, but not determined by its past, and is building its future(s)). Furthermore, its restructuring, conflicts and institutionalisations will be necessarily formed according to concrete social relations stretching, developing, breaking and integrating into different territorial formations within and outside its imagined and real boundaries, and expressed through a myriad of concrete projects.

As argued in chapter 2, Basque nationalism as a political programme and political movement emerged during the rapid industrialisation of Bilbao towards the end of the nineteenth century. The pace, nature and impact that such process had in the rapidly growing urban centre of Bilbao (Medrano 1995) led to the development of early Basque national projects as mainly reactionary movements against the forces of industrialisation and capitalism (Corcuera 2004). Thus, in its origins, Basque nationalism was strongly influenced by nineteenth-century conservative intellectual movements associated with ruralism, as the lost paradise of natural order, social cohesion and healthy living, and race, in its generic form as a means to articulating what is "specific and different" (Watson 2003) about the Basque "imagined community." Furthermore, this conservative orientation was coupled with a strong emphasis on religion, specifically Catholicism, as a way to define the Basque national community. In fact, Basque nationalism found the basis of its political support in the rural communities of Bizkaia and subsequently Gipuzkoa (Beltza 1976a). The ideational and political alliance between the urban middle classes (for example, Arana, the founder of Basque nationalism) and the rural population could be seen to a large extent as a response to the aggressive and predatory nature of big industrial capital, the chaotic transformation of Bilbao's urban landscape, as well as the emergence of new secular ideologies such as socialism and communism, which formed the ideological basis of the newly proletarised local and migrant workers' interests, and the perception of displacement and loss. Similar to other nineteenth-century national movements, language and folklore (Hobsbawm 1990) played an important part in the definition of Basqueness. Ethnographic and archaeological works (as undertaken by José Miguel Barandiaran and Telesforo Aranzadi) played an important part in establishing the "scientific" legitimacy to political claims over national and territorial claims. However, and in contrast to Catalonia, an array of economic, political as well as cultural interests remained at best ambiguously linked to the political programme advanced by the newly formed political organisation, the PNV. Indeed, its anti-capitalist and localist programme clashed with the economic and political ambitions of the economic elite, whose interests had far surpassed the boundaries of Basque territories. Furthermore, intellectuals born in the Basque Country (like Miguel de Unamuno and Pío Baroja), were reticent about the scope and reach of cultural production in a context where institutional support for "Basque Studies" (for example, via Euskaltzaindia, the Society of Basque Studies) was confined to a very small intellectual circle, and often associated with learned churchmen (like Barandiaran). This led to appeals for the revival of the Basque language, which had long disappeared from the main urban areas, while only a very limited number of individuals were capable of reading and writing in Basque. Indeed, the standardised version of Basque (Euskera Batua, Unified Basque) only emerged as recently as the 1960s (largely through the efforts of the linguist Koldo Mitxelana), but this could be considered an important milestone towards the consolidation of the Basque nation-building project as it opened up more possibilities for an institutional and cultural universalisation and homogenisation (Gellner 1983). A standardised language is also an important aspect of a claim on high culture, which is one of the central factors for achieving external legitimacy and recognition, and it also allow the formalisation of administrative, political and economic links within a specific territory. Territoriality adds further depth to the existing imagining of the "national space" and offers a more complex set of environments within which conflicts and consensus can be played out, including those about the meaning, nature and boundaries of the national space itself. According to one view of the Basque City idea:

> We also mention Atxaga in one of our texts . . . there were some statements, a couple of months ago, in an interview with him in *Berria* . . . he first starts by using a metaphor . . . the city . . . but he then uses the word "to urbanise" . . . physically to urbanise . . . he has always been in favour of the Basque Y . . . Iñaki Segurola claimed that Atxaga became the spokesperson of the cultural front of capitalism in that interview . . . we demonstrated, on two occasions, as an Assembly, behind the Basque City there is a new playing ground asserting capitalism . . . but that is not just happening with the Basque City . . . this is a universal phenomenon . . . the metropolitan regions or something of that sort . . . it's a model supported and developed by big consultancies and big interests which are introducing a model like this everywhere . . . They are using this notion as a means to justify [this].[1] *AH, member of the Assembly Against the HST.*

Alternatively:

1. AH, member of the Assembly Against the HST.

> It is about consolidating the "city region" as a model for spatial articulation, which blurs the traditional borders between city and territory (countryside) in favour of new, more complex and richer, spaces . . . In a relatively small territory to be able to afford a well-articulated urban system led by three attractive and dynamic cities, with complementary profiles. Overcoming the sterile competition, we have to work towards aspects that reinforce the complementarity between Bilbao, San Sebastián and Vitoria-Gasteiz drawing on the fact that our strength relies on solidarity and territorial cohesion . . . It is about "research, development and innovation" [applicable to territorial planning] but backed by important sectors of our society with different responsibilities who share these ideas and work daily towards the construction of a better territory for our future generations.[2]

Moreover, according to another perspective, "We will create three big monsters in the middle of a desert. There will be macro-cities, that is, the high speed train will have the same effect as the highways had before. I honestly don't know. But to tell the truth, the port would have better chances if a freight railway transport system were developed, since currently [the port] inevitably uses the road."[3]

Chapters 5 and 6 elaborated different aspects of the debates surrounding the restructuring of rail transport and the development of the HST within Spain and the EU, respectively. Here I will focus on the BAC and the main stakeholders that emerged in relation to those debates. These debates, as was the case on the national and supranational levels, are not only related to transport but also make assumptions about the meaning of specific spaces and social relationships and thus are also closely associated with questions of "modernisation," "competitiveness," "economic restructuring" and nation- and state-building. In this sense, different spatial metaphors such as "region," "regionalisation," "rescaling," and so forth have political, economic, ideological, normative and rhetorical aspects that could stand for different sets of relationships and be employed in different strategies across Europe (Paasi 2002).

Accordingly, I will first address the dominant imaginings of Basque nation and state and then examine the different strategies and tactics employed by the key stakeholders. Regarding the former theme, I will

---

2. Sabin Intxaurraga, Basque Minister of Planning and the Environment, in Gobierno Vasco (2002).

3. AM, the Port Authority of Bilbao.

distinguish two dominant imaginings of state and nation within the BAC that could very broadly be associated with the notions of the Basque City and the "Basque Country of localities." The Basque City is predominantly understood as an inter-scalar space closely integrated within both Spain and Europe and is mainly championed by the ruling PNV. In contrast, the "Basque Country of localities" imaginary stresses close interregional and inter-local cooperation, a bottom up integration, short distance travel and general well-being. While the Basque City imaginary is supported by key stakeholders with strong institutional support within the Basque government and the ruling PNV, the "Basque Country of localities" imaginary is supported by only loosely associated movements and associations within the BAC and thus, at present, does not constitute a consolidated alternative political project. The association of ETA with some of the issues taken up by the latter movements is playing an important role in discrediting their legitimacy and is an obstacle to developing a consolidated political alternative to the PNV-led nation and state project (Fernández Duran 2007). I will further argue that both those imaginaries of the Basque Country are closely integrated within global and local flows (both material and symbolic) and thus cannot be easily understood within a traditional-modern-post-modern continuum. Instead, they could be better seen as two different forms of Post-Fordist adaptation, both of which could potentially offer viable alternatives for the future of the Basque Country.

Second, regarding strategy and tactics, I offer a complex and multilayered understanding of the process of nation- and state-restructuring within the Basque Country as imagined by key stakeholders within the BAC. I will focus specifically on the strategies and tactics of the Basque government (led by the PNV, which has emerged as the key player in shaping the nation- and state-building process in BAC), as well as of different social movements, associations and trade unions.

I will detail the discourses and practices of different stakeholders as constantly evolving around a group of objectives that are combined and reconstituted around a set of tactics that operate simultaneously on different levels. The strategies and tactics of different stakeholders are simultaneously institutionalised within different governance regimes, have different temporal horizons and are differently constituted over space (Jessop 2000; Swyngedouw 1997; Brenner 2004). These tactics are made to work together through different institutional arrangements that are potentially contradictory and incompatible but are made to work within specific projects[4] in which different interests are temporarily reconciled within narratives such as the Basque City, "urban region," the Atlantic Arc, the "Euroregion," and so on. In the specific case of the HST it could be argued that a national and EU project has been stabilised at the regional (BAC) scale through, first, its locking into state (PTS, 1987) and EU (ESSEN, 1994) railways and transport strategies.[5]

## Imagining the Basque State and Nation

As argued in chapter 4, discussions about restructuring in Spain are dominated by distinctions of homogeneity and heterogeneity as justifications for coherence. Thus, federalisation could be seen as an attempt to bring more rationality (as well as "historical justice" and political legitimacy) to the "actual" heterogeneity within the territory of Spain. This heterogeneity, it is argued, is institutional, economic, political and interpreted as a legacy from the past (see as well, for example, Medrano 1995). Chapters 2, 3 and 4 looked at the changes in Spain through this perspective. For example, this distinction in the analysis of political and economic changes allows us to understand the apparently different accounts of Catalonia and the Basque Country developed by Colomer (2007) and Atxaga (2005) respectively. In the case of Catalonia, Colomer justifies increased independence on the basis of a claim to the "homogeneity" of the smaller units (which he understands in terms of institutional consolidation, identity, and so on). Consequently, smaller means more homogeneous and thus easier and more efficient to govern.

Regarding the Basque Country, Atxaga uses the same distinction to argue for a Basque City that would unite or, as it were, be an umbrella for essentially heterogeneous parts, "islands," through which the Basque Country is constituted. These approaches naturalise either homogeneity or heterogeneity as a basis for and justifying cohesion and a higher degree

4. For example, the urban regeneration plan of Bilbao (including its port), the HST, Donostia-San Sebastián–Pasaia Bay, the Port of Pasaia, and the logistics centres in Vitoria-Gasteiz.

5. As argued in chapter 5, the HST was, especially after the 1994–1997 period, articulated in relation to different imaginings of the Basque Country through, first, the newly emerging discourses on cities as "polinuclei" cities (Gobierno Vasco 1997, 2002), and with an emphasis on freight and transport sustainability within the EU administration (EC 2001). Second, in relation to the newly emerging (within the BAC) discourse of the Basque City, as well as the emerging long-term vision of the Basque government regarding an economic strategy focused on the BAC becoming a regional transport, logistics and freight hub.

of self-governance. While apparently different, the two approaches are similar in essentialising a distinction between homogeneity and heterogeneity and treating it as "natural" in one way or another. Interestingly, while in the case of Atxaga this leads to a claim of a "cosmopolitan" identity of the Basque City, in the case of Colomer the issue of identity is either irrelevant or leaning towards a sense of belonging to a common culture (ethnic and linguistic community). However, more importantly here, both constitute justifications for essentialising a specific territorial scale, such as the (Basque) city, or the "smaller" unit as somehow privileged.

The broad notion of a "Basque space" has been differently imagined and institutionalised in relation to notions such as country, autonomous community (BAC), region, Euro-region, city, Euro City and Atlantic Arc. The Basque space could be imagined to include the three provinces of the BAC (Gipuzkoa, Araba and Bizkaia), or it could also be seen as the broader Euskal Herria (Basque homeland) also including the neighbouring Spanish autonomous community of Navarre and the French Basque provinces of the Atlantic Pyrenees. These metaphors are to a different extent used by key stakeholders on the national, supranational and subnational levels, and are to a different extent present in the communications, political, economic and administrative exchanges, bargaining, cooperation and conflict that concern the Basque space.

Some of those notions, such as the BAC and Euskal Herria, have only been used more narrowly in defining relations within Spain as well as France. Here the Basque space is institutionalised through the constitutionally defined notion of the BAC. The latter is based on the notion of "historical nationality" (as defined in the Spanish Constitution), and is contested by the radical Basque nationalist view of Euskal Herria as the "historical homeland" of the Basque people where, according to the latter view, a sovereign nation-state should be established. More recently, in 2004 the president of the BAC, Juan José Ibarretxe,[6] attempted to promote what he argued was an intermediate way between the existing autonomy and full independence, what became known as the Ibarretxe Plan. This plan suggested that relations with central government should be redefined in terms of what he called relations of "free association." Ibarretxe envisioned this change as being based on a democratic procedure, but more importantly it also problematised the boundaries of the Basque

6. Leader of the PNV.

space by bringing into the debate the relations between the BAC and the AC of Navarre. To the extent that the Ibarretxe plan was drawing on the existing statutes and the Spanish Constitution, his proposal could be seen as a predominantly political and administrative process of redefining the boundaries of the Basque space. In contrast, the discussions and processes associated with the notion of the Atlantic Arc, for example, are predominantly economic, inasmuch as they focus on the development of an economically competitive area centred on Bilbao and the BAC.

Further, and again in contrast to the "free association" plan, the Atlantic Arc discourse and practices operate at one and the same time on the national, subnational and supranational levels. In the latter sense, the Atlantic Arc is similar to the notion of the Basque City, yet the Basque City is more widely open to interpretation. It incorporates more socially engaged discourses as well as capturing economic and political objectives. The Basque City was first used by the writer Bernardo Atxaga, a central Basque cultural figure (1998, 2005) who linked the notion of the Basque City to an open cosmopolitan identity. While the notion of the Basque City is relatively new, it has rapidly captured the imagination of a broad set of stakeholders with very different agendas and visions for the future of the BAC and the Basque space more broadly.

Indeed, both the Atlantic Arc and the Basque City have been adopted and actively promoted by the Basque government,[7] and both have been creatively used in communicating with diverse audiences with often conflicting interests. They have played a central part in the development of a series of key government documents addressing a wide range of issues, from transport and territorial planning policy (Railway PTS 1997) to territorial restructuring (the Euro City White Book, Diputación Foral de Gipuzkoa 2000) and broad social and economic agenda setting documents (The Basque City, Gobierno Vasco 2002). These have also included cross-border institutional cooperation agreements with neighbouring regions (for example, The Atlantic-Pyrenees Workshop, 1989; Euskadi-Aquitaine Working Committee, 1991; and the Aquitaine-Euskadi Logistic Platform, 2004) as well as inter-institutional exchanges and policy documents between the Basque government and the EU. Thus, the Atlantic Arc and the Basque City also feature prominently within EU documents dealing with

7. The idea of the Basque City within Basque government discourse has been linked to the Euro City notion as well as the significance of the city as a space of Post-Fordist restructuring by linking it to notions of "creativity" and "innovation" (Calzada 2007).

common projects concerning Spain and the Basque Country (for example, the URBAN II funding scheme for the Donostia-San Sebastián–Pasaia Bay project, Plan Urban 2001). "The Atlantic Arc" and the Basque City are discussed within the context of existing EU policies related to regional and urban restructuring under the ESDP. They are associated with EU notions such as "city-region," "urban metropolitan areas," "polynucleated city" and "polycentricity" (Lagendijk 2001; Davoudy 2002) and are integrated into existing EU, national and regional institutional frameworks.

## EU and Spanish Frameworks for City and Regional Development

Chapter 6 argued that, when the Spanish government introduced the Guiding Plan of Infrastructures (PDI) in the early 1990s, this reflected a new focus on cities as the main sites of economic, social and cultural activity (Ordóñez 1993c, 1993d). The introduction of this plan also led to a policy development that addressed the need of intermodality (Rivas 1993: 20). This in turn required a shift from sectoral policy development, which traditionally addressed the problems and needs of a particular mode of transport, to a more multi-sectoral perspective, which would consider the interdependencies of existing modes of transport; a perspective that was most successful at the urban and intra-urban level and of which Bilbao is a good example.

Furthermore, the EU policy development and budgetary arrangement reflected intervention patterns that operated at different scales. Consequently, innovation and technology projects were "regionally" applied to boost and enhance local competitive advantages as well as promote the essential institutional conditions needed to improve the local economy and encourage it to become more competitive vis-à-vis other regions. This coincides with the rise of "region" as a fashionable notion both in European, academic and policy debates in the last twenty years. In this sense, I argued in chapter 1 that the region is assumed to be a new site of "competitiveness," which is often attributed to endogenous regional characteristics. Indeed, such rhetoric has been integrated into the strategies and discourses of regional governments (Giordano and Roller 2002). Yet this stands in contrast to policy documents and strategies (the ESDP, for example), which prioritise the city as a significant player (Sassen 1999). In this context, transport policy was mainly concerned with urban areas as the nodal points of financial capital and concentration of the service sector. That is, as suggested earlier, the coordination of transport at the urban and intra-urban areas reflected an attempt to improve and boost two types of mobility: one limited to the locality and the other between cities located at a middle range distance for a type of worker in the service and financial sectors. In the words of AN, a member of the EU Transport Directorate: "The Basque Country will receive money for projects concerning knowledge and innovation. . . . The Cohesion Funds are what [the Basque Country] should be targeting. The Cohesion Funds are aimed at specific areas and 50 percent goes to the Trans-European networks . . . because as far as I'm concerned the Commission's priority is those two axes [the Atlantic and the Mediterranean corridors]."[8]

Generally, it can be argued that past, present and future feature differently in the dominant imaginings and discourses of cities and regions. Cities look to the "past" in order to imagine their future. For example, in the case of Bilbao, this was based on a perspective from an industrial city whose wealth depended on shipbuilding and the iron and steel industry towards a Post-Fordist city, driven by culture and the creative and service industries (Rodríguez and Martinez 2003; González 2003; Calzada 2007). In contrast, regions compare themselves to other regions, as they are today, in order to imagine their future. In this sense, I argued in chapter 4 that issues such as "institutional thickness," "endogenous skills" as well as "critical mass for the production, reproduction and transmission of knowledge"[9] (Cook, Gómez Uranga and Etxebarria 1998; Cook 2002) have become, since the early 1990s, a part of the dominant discourse in the Basque Country. The latter discourse was represented in key policy and government documents (for example, clusters) (Porter 1990) and was used as a framework through which to understand and promote a series of reforms in the crisis-ridden Basque industrial system. Within this context the HST became a symbol of different political and economic projects as well as discourses and rhetorics about the predominance, complementarities and contradictions of different scales of action. In other words, debates on the building of the HST clearly show the wide variety of tensions and conflicts operating on different scales. As far as the Basque Country is concerned, these conflicts are even more complicated by the high degree of internal heterogeneity (in terms of economic structure) as well as the organisation of capital-labour

---

8. AN, member of the EU Transport directorate.

9. For example, clusters, innovation centres, links between companies and universities, small-medium size enterprises, and so on.

relations among different parts of the Basque Country. In many respects the main economic, political and social conflicts within the BAC criss-cross different scales.

The debates surrounding the future of Bilbao are a good illustration of the complex negotiations, conflicts and different scenarios that were possible for the restructuring of the Basque political, economic and social space. Debates about transport infrastructure and the HST in particular were a central part of the reorganisation of the BAC and the place that Bilbao came to occupy within this process.

## Integrated Transport Systems and Urban Regeneration in Spain: The Case of Bilbao

I have already suggested that the PDI (1993), in contrast to previous developments, tried to overcome sharp dividing lines between different modes of transport and to support policies that favoured integrated transport systems both within and between urban areas. These guidelines were gradually implemented during the 1990s and, at present, transport systems with a high degree of integration already exist within different urban areas across Spain. Indeed, as noted, Bilbao is a good example of such an integrated system

As a result, tram and underground networks were first introduced in Bilbao in the late 1990s, which was a process that was also accompanied by improving and rationalising suburban trains. Further, travel was made easier for passengers by the introduction of an integrated fares system in which travellers could pay a single fare for the use of different modes of transport while the necessary links were also developed in order to ensure a smooth and fast transfer among different modes of transport.[10]

The development of these fully integrated urban and inter-urban systems was dependent on the coordination of different institutional levels where competences, interests and organisational structure would differ. Thus, most of the changes (González 2003) are currently coordinated by a Transport Authority.[11] The company was equally owned by Spanish bod-

10. For example, the Briñas intermodal station, where all modes of transport –interregional bus travel, underground, tram, suburban train, public buses and airport bus– would meet, was developed in Bilbao.

11. For Siemiatycki (2005) the Transport Authority proved to be a good exercise in coordinating the interests and expectations of different stakeholders within a single high significance and impact project, such as that of the Bilbao underground.

ies (INI, Renfe, Feve and the Port) and Basque institutions (the Basque government, the Provincial Government of Bizkaia, the Town Council of Bilbao and, later, the Town Council of Barakaldo), each holding 50 percent of the capital (González 2003: 320). In relation to the development of the public consortium established to coordinate the new development projects in Bilbao, the Bilbao-Ría 2000 consortium, Francisco Fernandez Lafuente (former General Director of Intermodal Transport in Big Cities) stated:

> the objectives of the public company are very wide because, on the one hand, it needs to take into consideration the demands put forward by the MOPT regarding ports, airports, Renfe railways and FEVE and, on the other, it has to pay attention to the Basque government's interests, which is responsible for roads, suburban railway services and the underground. Furthermore, it must also consider the objectives set down by the rest of Basque public administrations at the provincial and local level. [However,] while the authority of the MOPT is of considerable importance but limited, the power of this public company is unlimited and, therefore, it can act upon all transport infrastructures and services if the board of directors would decide to do so (quoted in Ordóñez 1993b: 46).

However, it is the Spanish central government that is in charge of the inter-urban and interregional infrastructure. The latter is stated in the Constitution, with its clear division between central competencies (inter-urban and interregional) and the competencies of the autonomous communities (intra-urban and intra-regional). Such institutional arrangements are an important constraint on the degree to which Spanish cities can "reinvent" themselves. Indeed, the case of Bilbao shows that there are broader structural constrains to the extent to which a city can "reinvent" itself as a post-industrial city (Gibson 2005). Furthermore, urban restructuring is not an independent process, but is necessarily interdependent and co-evolving with broader economic, political and social processes, which in the case of Bilbao are closely associated with the establishment of the BAC, as well as with the ongoing restructuring within Spain and the EU.

### *Two Alternative Futures for Bilbao*

In October 1992, the Ministry of Public Works and Transport (Ministerio de Obras Públicas y Transporte, MOPT), and the Basque public administrations signed an agreement that set down the conditions to constitute a public company called Bilbao-Ría 2000. According to González (2003),

Bilbao was one of the state's urban regeneration priorities, a policy that had started with the cities of Seville and Barcelona.

This sort of regeneration consisted of creating an integrated urban transport system and (re)utilising former industrial land to build a new centre for the arts (the Guggenheim Museum Bilbao), cultural events (The Euskalduna Palace Conference Centre and Concert Hall) and a business centre (the World Trade Centre). In the words of Josu Ortuondo (see Ordóñez 1993b: 46), former mayor of Bilbao, the project sought to create the necessary conditions for a new economy, based on "new technologies," by restructuring the transport infrastructure and regenerating urban spaces, while accompanied at the same time by the improving and rationalising of suburban trains. These developments were contrasted to the former dominance of an urban space subjected to the production of shipbuilding and the iron and steel industries.

The Spanish government had a significant interest in the future development of Bilbao during the entire post-Franco period, and was closely involved in the negotiations over its restructuring. There were major, state-owned, metal and steel industrial sites located in Bilbao, and which constituted over 10 percent of the total employment of the entire sector in Spain. In this sense, as discussed in chapter 5, the economic crisis that Spain went through in the late 1970s was closely associated with the restructuring of Bilbao (one of the major industrial sites in Spain). The ruling (at that time) political party in Spain, the PSOE, had a strong electoral base in Bilbao and thus the rapid restructuring of the city was also of a high political significance. In addition, the PNV, a newly emerging force within the (similarly new) BAC, had relatively weak support in Bilbao, which, given its ambition of becoming the main nationalist party within the BAC, made it of paramount political importance to be seen as an effective player in the restructuring of the city.

However, after the crisis of the1970s and 1980s, Bilbao emerged as a city of only secondary or even tertiary importance in Spain.[12] And as a result, other central government initiatives, such as the new national Railway policy for example, showed little interest in developing any interregional railway connections and/or improving existing railway links and railway infrastructure in northern Spain (see chapter 5). That was the case even for a project such as the regeneration of the Port of Bilbao, where

12. This is in contrast to the dominance of Bilbao as an important industrial and financial city in Spain in the early and mid-twentieth century (see chapter 2).

expansion and modernisation were carried out without taking into consideration equally important aspects of its restructuring such as the development of convenient freight routes to the port.[13]

In this context, Bilbao was a central part of the political and economic stabilisation of the newly established BAC. There were, however, different possible scenarios for the development of the city. First, Bilbao could become, in a similar way to Madrid and Barcelona, a major urban area, in this case, (re)establishing itself as the main city on the Cantabrian coast, thereby becoming the principal capital for the rest of the urban areas along the Cantabrian coastal area and hinterland such as Santander, Logroño, Donostia-San Sebastián and Pamplona-Iruñea. This vision was linked to the emergence of the Atlantic Arc as a new geographical metaphor in contrast to the Mediterranean Arc or corridor. As argued earlier, the Basque government was very active in organising and promoting this new geographical as well as economic and social space. There were, however, different opinions in terms of the emphasis on the feasibility and desirability of the development of Bilbao as a centre of such an Atlantic corridor. For some, Bilbao should become the main urban area of this newly conceived geographical, political and economic space.

> This [the Atlantic Arc] can only become real if other [places also back it]. [For example] La Rioja as well as Santander are looking to develop connections with the Mediterranean area. Why not become the hinterland of Bilbao?! It doesn't make sense to become the hinterland of Barcelona! Let's make a stand [for Bilbao] to become the capital of the Atlantic Arc. But any mention of the Cantabrian coast, no way! What can I say, in my opinion it doesn't make sense to become a second or even a third hinterland tier of Barcelona. I'm a nationalist and I wish Bilbao became the capital of the Atlantic Arc and hence, [the Basque Country] might become a strong euro region.[14]

While the Bilbao and Barcelona areas, as well as the Atlantic and Mediterranean corridors, are discussed as both complementary and competing projects, the centrality of Barcelona and the relatively peripheral position of Bilbao are rarely called in question.

---

13. This may well be the case because the surrounding area of the port consists of a stretch of terrain which has been totally overexploited in terms of housing occupation and land consumption (a legacy of the second industrial wave in the city).

14. AE, member of the Bilbao Chamber of Commerce.

> A good connection should have been developed a long time ago in order to go to Bilbao. Such a corridor would ease the burden on the Port of Barcelona. If Bilbao took charge of the activity generated in the Atlantic Arc and Barcelona that of the Mediterranean Arc, such a corridor would allow both Barcelona and Bilbao to participate in the commercial activities of both the North and the South. One of the claims we put forward in the PEIT [Strategic Infrastructures and Transport Plan] was for the development of a high speed train between Barcelona and Bilbao. What we demand is that there should be a dual infrastructure for passengers and goods in the Ebro corridor . . . In what ways each city will benefit most, this will depend on the strategies that each city and territory develops.15

While projects related to the building of a Mediterranean corridor are supported by a wide group of different stakeholders, the economic and social benefits of building such projects along the Atlantic coast remain uncertain.

> In truth, the French state doesn't want to do anything with the Atlantic Arc either. That is why the French state is talking about short-ship-shipping as an excuse in order to avoid investing in any infrastructure linked to the Pyrenees because to a certain extent, we are competitors in some areas. To put it in a different way, Africa starts in the Pyrenees, and they don't want to be connected with Africa. In short, the Atlantic Arc is a chimera and it's just the Basque Country's political demand. It doesn't contribute in any way to anything; in any case it would [only] benefit, if anywhere, Baiona, Bordeaux and Mont-de-Marsan and all the rest . . . [and] they look to the North, not to us.[16]

The second option is related to the first and extends it, but the emphasis is different. While the first scenario puts the emphasis clearly on the city of Bilbao, the second scenario considers Bilbao as part of a broader Basque project. Thus, the first scenario is favoured by the majority of the Bizkaian institutions, the Port of Bilbao and the Bilbao Chamber of Commerce. This includes support for projects such as building freight corridors towards the Ebro (River) Valley and the Mediterranean zone.

As suggested earlier, the central government did not intend to invest in new railway transport infrastructure or improvements in the existing

15. AD, member of the Barcelona Chamber of Commerce.

16. AE, member of the Bilbao Chamber of Commerce.

railway connections in the northern area of the country (the Renfe railway connections in and out of any of the cities and towns in the BAC, Navarre, and so forth). Nevertheless, Spanish national railway policy in the 1980s did initially envisage a new link from Bilbao to Vitoria-Gasteiz and thereafter to the Ebro (River) Valley. This link was intended as an extension of the existing freight connections to the Port of Bilbao (see figure 5.2). While such a solution was preferred by a number of key players within Bilbao, this did not necessarily mean that they were opposed to alternative solutions involving the development of a HST. The development of a HST and the expansion of existing freight connections could be seen as complementary projects.

> [Someone] was telling me the other day that he had been told that the average speed of transporting goods in Europe was 35–36 Km/h (in contrast to the 18–19 Km/h within the Spanish state). But to even think of changing the speed to 120 Km/h doesn't make sense at all, and besides it is not necessary even under the just-in-time production system. So, what [so-and-so] had in mind was to use the high speed train to transport passengers and, subsequently, free up the rest of the railways for the exclusive use of goods.[17]

Further, the solution that the Basque government found in mid-1990s, which also coincided with a period when EU involvement in the support and financing of HSTs was diminishing and freight railway projects were gaining wider acceptance (see chapter 6), was to propose the alternation of passenger and freight transport using the same HST rail track. This solution was reluctantly accepted by the Port of Bilbao:

> I don't know if it was . . . but he complained that those in the Transport and Public Works Department tossed and turned uncomfortably with the argument because they might have thought that you were siding in favour of those who for other reasons disagree with the project. But I, as an expert, since I am an engineer, there are many arguments for which I'm saying that it's not possible to create a mixed high speed railway for passengers and goods. I'm not saying it for the sake of it. . . . there is no way that those two choices can coexist with each other. Moreover, they are even contradictory in principle . . . the maintenance of railways for the transport of goods is very demanding.[18]

---

17. AM, Port Authority of Bilbao.

18. Ibid.

From early on the Basque government favoured a high speed rail connection among the three provincial capitals (Bilbao, Vitoria-Gasteiz and Donostia-San Sebastián), the Basque Y (see figure 5.5). The building of the HST generally, and the Y shape of the rail track more specifically, had little support either in Spain or in neighbouring France; it was not seen as an economically justifiable project, and the Basque government was faced with dwindling EU support for such projects.[19] Nevertheless, despite all the odds being against the HST project, the Basque government persisted with it and building work started in 2006 (discussed in more detail in chapter 6). One of the clear advantages of this project, from the perspective of the PNV-led Basque government, is the development of a closely integrated Basque economic and political space centred on the BAC. In terms of the future development of Bilbao, the development of a Y-shaped HST connection clearly tips the balance towards the second scenario for Bilbao in which the city becomes an integral part of the BAC. However, the compromise achieved in relation to Bilbao could only partially be replicated with the restructuring of Donostia-San Sebastián. This was well illustrated in the failed attempt of the city to reinvent itself as an important regional player through the development of a Euro City linking Donostia-San Sebastián to the French city of Baiona, and the expansion of the Port of Pasaia. As in the case of Bilbao, the strategies employed by interested parties were played on different institutional levels and criss-crossed local, regional, national and EU borders, and can also be seen as an aspect of the broader PNV-led agenda for building the Basque City.

### *Cross-Border Cooperation: Donostia-San Sebastián–Baiona*

In contrast to Bilbao, the city of Donostia-San Sebastián, despite the elaboration of important policy documents regarding plans for its economic and social restructuring, such as the Euro City White Book (Diputación Foral de Gipuzkoa 2000) and the Mid-term Territorial Plan for the Functional Area of Donostia-San Sebastián (Gobierno Vasco and Diputación Foral de Gipuzkoa 2002), was less successful in implementing such agendas. The creation of stronger links with Baiona was high on the list of priorities for both the local authorities in Donostia-San Sebastián and the Basque

---

19. The EU changed the direction of its policies in the early-to-mid-1990s towards the specialisation of different modes of railway transport amid the growing financing difficulties of the HST.

government. This project was seen as potentially creating new economic opportunities for Donostia-San Sebastián and, from the perspective of the Basque government, constructing cross-border links. The latter offered stronger political ties with the French part of the Basque Country, while also strengthening the international links of the BAC outside of those areas that are mediated by the central Spanish government.

In a similar way to Bilbao, Donostia-San Sebastián has also followed in the footsteps of other cities in actively engaging in the promotion of the city. Thus, the town council became involved in drawing up the Donostia-San Sebastián Strategic Plan (Gobierno Vasco and Diputación Foral de Gipuzkoa 2002), a policy document which set the future aims for the city of Donostia-San Sebastián.[20] According to this policy document, administrative and financial sectors dominate the economic life of the city and constitute 59 percent of the total employment. However, these services are heavily dependent on the main economic centre located in provincial Gipuzkoa. This centre is dominated by the auxiliary automotive and machine tool industrial sectors, which amount to 32 percent of all industrial activity in Gipuzkoa, as opposed to 12 percent that is generated in Donostia-San Sebastián (Gobierno Vasco and Diputación Foral de Gipuzkoa 2002: 12). This document, which was drawn up in collaboration with a wide variety of economic, social and political stakeholders, imagines and proposes projects for the regeneration of the city and its functional area.

Donostia-San Sebastián was partially successful in following the example of Bilbao and other entrepreneurial cities in expanding its cultural sector and attracting external investment in major cultural projects, such as the building of the Kursaal Congress Centre that was designed by the internationally renowned architect, Rafael Moneo, in 1999.[21] However, more ambitious initiatives that could potentially have a lasting effect on the development of the city such as the Donostia-San Sebastián–Baiona Euro City project (Eurociudad Vasca Bayonne-San Sebastián 2003) have been less successful.

---

20. The city of Donostia-San Sebastián, with a population of 185,000 people, has experienced a slow demographic decline and a sharp increase in its elderly population (20% of the population is over 65 years old).

21. Other similar projects, such as the contemporary museum of art, Tabakalera, have been in the making for many years now, and although active, they only attract insignificant events. However, the city has been successful in finding support for major infrastructural projects such as the new Donostia-San Sebastián ring road, major new housing projects (the new Intxaurrondo neighbourhood) and the building of shopping malls in the city.

While the renaissance of the *metropolitan* area of Bilbao is closely linked to removing the port's main facilities from the city centre, the construction of the underground and the relocation of a new urban city centre in Abandoibarra (offering a range of cultural centres and activities), the expansion of the Donostia-San Sebastián *metropolitan* area, like Bilbao, envisages the regeneration of the neighbouring Bay of Pasaia and the reconstruction of its main port facilities away from its current location, along the main towns that surround it.

However, this project has met considerable administrative, legal and investment obstacles. The Bay of Pasaia, a fishing port in decline since the 1980s, has not been able to agglutinate the necessary interest, and political as well as economic power, for a much needed restructuring. Indeed, unlike Bilbao, these initiatives have been local and no private-public agency similar to the Bilbao-Ría 2000 has been created.

In addition, while the Spanish government was keen to invest in the revitalisation of Bilbao, which included improving and expanding the economic activities of the Port of Bilbao through the Cohesion Funds, the Bay of Pasaia was an entirely locally driven project that only received funding from URBAN II programme and local municipalities (Ministerio de Hacienda 2001: 106) after the actual municipalities surrounding the bay[22] came together to present a proposal at the EU level. In this sense, unlike Bilbao, the regeneration of the Bay of Pasaia has not been able to include a specific and mutually agreed project for the future of the port itself, which comes under the jurisdiction of the Spanish state (therefore, it has not benefited from other EU funds, such as the Cohesion Funds, for example). Thus, the URBAN II programme has consisted of a 26 million euro funding which has been spent on the creation of an Eco Boulevard (including cycle lanes), improving road accesses to the cities and towns situated along the bay, and so on. In contrast to the regeneration of Bilbao, the Donostia-San Sebastián–Pasaia Bay project has not received the same institutional and investment support from central and regional governments, and it has been a controversial issue among the different institutional layers within the BAC (local, provincial and regional). Interestingly, in terms of identity and class structure, both spaces differ significantly. While the metropolitan city of Bilbao can be characterised by the

---

22. In addition to Donostia-San Sebastián –including the neighbourhoods of Bidebieta, Herrera, Larratxo and Altza– this also incorporates the towns of Pasaia, Lezo, Errenteria and Oiartzun.

predominance of a PSOE working class and moderate Basque nationalist middle class electoral base, the Donostia-San Sebastián–Pasaia Bay area (if excluding the tertiary and commercial city of Donostia-San Sebastián) is characterised by the predominance of a PSOE working class and radical Basque nationalist working class electorate. The fact that for many years the radical Basque nationalist political party was governing in some of the local councils in this area (such as Pasaia and Lezo) might have something to do with the deadlock over development projects. In addition, inter-governmental disputes (between the Basque government, the Provincial Government of Gipuzkoa and the Port of Pasaia) over the future(s) of the port have not been successful in bringing (a) solution(s) for it. Whereas the Port of Pasaia itself would like to see port activity continue for many years to come, and, certainly, it has been and is an important source of income and employment in the area, it has not been possible to create a project around which investment could be attracted. As in the case of Bilbao, there has been some interest in removing the port (the docks) from the bay itself and rebuilding it behind Mount Jaizkibel, the area adjacent to the port. In addition, local neighbourhood associations have even suggested the creation of cultural infrastructures, such as a museum based on a theme that would encapsulate the history of the past industrial history of the area (based on the port and fishing). This was eventually realised with the creation of Albaola, the Sea Factory of Basques: a cultural space showcasing Basque nautical craftsmanship and technology.

Therefore, the two projects vary significantly in terms of their institutional composition, stakeholders, political situation and social structure. Thus, in the case of Bilbao, the Bilbao-Ría 2000 consortium played a significant role in steering the different social and institutional levels involved towards developing different projects concerning the urban revitalisation strategy. The institutional involvement included 50 percent on the part of central government institutions (including Renfe) and 50 percent on the part of regional and local institutions (including the Basque government, the Provincial Government of Bizkaia and the Town Council of Bilbao). In contrast, as noted, the revitalisation strategy regarding the Donostia-San Sebastián–Pasaia Bay project presented to the URBAN II funding schema counts exclusively on European and local funding. In the latter case, EU institutions were actively involved in the process and played an important steering and mediating role as well as promoting coordination within the functional metropolitan area, by bringing together the municipalities around the URBAN project. Nevertheless, the project could generally be seen as a failure, given the small number of schemes that were implemented and the only very limited impact that they had on the area.[23]

The failed attempt of Donostia-San Sebastián to build a link with Baiona demonstrates that not just any project is possible and that there are limits to the strategic engagement with the interests of different stakeholders. Furthermore, these cases have shown that different institutional arrangements can prove to be important constrains to the degree to which cities can "reinvent" themselves as post-industrial cities.

In a similar way to the integration of Bilbao and the construction of a Y-shaped HST link in the Basque Country, the Donostia-San-Sebastián–Baiona Euro City project was part of a broader PNV-led agenda for restructuring the BAC. This involved the development of multi-layered infrastructural and institutional links among the capitals of the three provinces that were very different from each other: specifically, they were integrated within different markets and characterised by different labour and institutional relationships (chapter 2). It is in this sense that I have argued that this lack of institutional articulation at urban, provincial and regional levels has been largely addressed only since the establishment of the BAC. And it has been shaped mainly by the hegemonic project of the PNV. As such, while all of the projects discussed could be seen as aspects of a broader PNV-led agenda, it is the HST that came to symbolise most potently the internal cohesion, multi-level connectedness and economic promise of the BAC. This imagining of the BAC is of a large metropolitan area: the Basque City.

## The HST: Improving Competitiveness or Social Cohesion?

The Basque government and members of provincial institutions have argued on many occasions that a new railway connection among the three capitals is desirable and would significantly improve currently existing

23. Thus, in the case of Donostia-San Sebastián, the pursuit of URBAN funding can be seen as an interventionist tactic where temporary support was given to local contractors through a city regeneration programme. In contrast to the wide ranging projects in the case of Bilbao, there were far fewer Donostia-San Sebastián–Baiona projects, and they were low profile and low impact. This certainly is not the case for all projects in Gipuzkoa. Indeed, the majority of the clusters supported by the Basque government in its priority sectors (the paper industry, home appliances, the automotive industry, leisure and tourism, piping, added value steel and logistics) (see Porter 1990), as well as those businesses that managed to expand internationally (for example, CAF, the Mondragon Corporation, Irizar and Cia Automotive), are to a large extend located in Gipuzkoa and Bizkaia.

links. Among both supporters and sceptics regarding the question of just how appropriate the HST is, there is agreement that the existing rail connections among the three capitals of the BAC are very poor. There are, however, different emphases and concerns, particularly concerning the economic viability of the HST project, especially given the short distances between each of the three cities and how appropriate it is given the economic needs of the BAC.

Thus, as one argument goes, the economic needs of both the Bilbao area and of the Gipuzkoa region would be best served by upgraded rail links that would improve the freight capabilities of the area. Such an approach would be consistent with the high significance of manufacturing as well as with the more recent government strategy for developing new logistic centres in the BAC. Consequently, "There are areas destined to function as goods distributors and storage places such as those in Irun, Ribavellosa, Agurain, etc. However, connections to the high-speed train (railway) are not expected. At the very least, some talk has been going on around possibly constructing shuttles. The bottom line, nevertheless, is the fact that the high-speed train is not useful to carry goods and all operators and engineers back this opinion."[24]

In addition, given the convenient connections that the HST would build to cities such as Madrid and Barcelona, there is also a concern that the HST, rather than attracting business and investment, could stimulate the exit of some major companies and their relocation to one of the two main cities in Spain. The latter concern is consistent with claims that the HST adds competitiveness to global cities (Torres 2005) and with the changes in other areas in Spain that developed HST connections.[25] In this sense, campaigners against the HST argue that it would only strengthen the position of the two main cities of Spain, which are Madrid and Barcelona:[26]

> The HST cannot be considered in the category of regional and regional investment. [The HST] has been conceived to benefit cities. In spite of this, when every regional and national government "makes a regional" investment (that is, the money spent in a given territory), for example,

24. AE, member of the Bilbao Chamber of Commerce.

25. Thus, for example, since the Seville–Madrid HST link was opened, business people who travelled from Madrid to Seville for work purposes stopped staying overnight in the city, with resultant losses for the hotel and catering sector there. Moreover, since the two cities became so "close," some company headquarters were reported to have been moved to the capital city.

26. Interview with AJ, member of Ecologists in Action.

> they don't say the money invested in the Madrid–Zaragoza train line was spent [in the cities of] Madrid, Guadalajara, Zaragoza and Calatayud. Instead, they say that the money was invested in the province of Guadalajara. It's not the reality of things because the benefits are not [for the province].[27]

It could be argued here that the federal-like structure of Spain, with its relatively powerful autonomous communities (as discussed in chapter 4), creates the conditions for both cooperation and competition between different entities that operate on the intra- and inter- regional levels. However, debates within Spain tend to overemphasise internal changes as well as changes related to the relationship between the ACs and the centre (and the consequences of these processes for the territorial, economic and social cohesion of the country), while paying less attention to equally important developments in the growing importance of mega cities (favoured by global capital). As a result, while uneven regional development continues to be important for understanding the political and economic restructuring of Spain (Linz and Stepan 1996; Moreno 2001), it is also increasingly important to assess those inequalities in relation to the growing power of a small number of strategically positioned global cities.[28]

The HST prioritises long distance travel with a minimum number of intermediate stops and is thus of little benefit for areas that are located close to the rail track. Further, HST projects are very expensive and therefore make any alternative transport projects that might have a stronger local focus unlikely due to lack of funding. What is more, transport projects such as these are physical entities and thus also compete for the physical spaces where they could be located. The latter always necessarily raises social and environmental questions but such issues are even more prominent when the track goes through complex geographical terrains and densely populated areas. The case of Itsasondo, a village in Gipuzkoa directly affected by the HST project, offers a good illustration of the complex interests involved as well as the strategies employed by different

---

27. AK, adviser to the Spanish government and member of the European Transport Commission.

28. Looking at FDI figures, for example, this can be studied on the regional and city level. Yet in some cases, one of those scales would be more appropriate. In the case of the BAC, FDI was relatively evenly distributed in Gipuzkoa, while in Bizkaia it was mostly concentrated in Bilbao. Still further, neither of the two examples is easily comparable to cities like Madrid, Barcelona and Valencia, where the predominant trend is investments in the cities as such (see Ferreiro, Rodríguez and Serrano 1997; Díaz Vázquez 2001, 2004).

stakeholders in either moving forward or creating obstacles for the HST project (discussed in chapter 6).

While the unconnected localities in-between cities and along the rail track get little benefits from the development of a HST, cities that are connected also have the added benefit of additional investment in stations and extra infrastructure that necessarily come with such projects. Thus, the actual location of the HST stations sparked debates of its own among different institutions with jurisdiction over planning matters. In the case of Bilbao, for example, the town council sided with Renfe because the latter had expressed its wish to use Abando railway station to host the new train.[29] This, in turn, would facilitate the revitalisation of neighbourhoods surrounding Abando railway station, which did not benefit from broader investment plans for the urban regeneration of Bilbao. However, the successful regeneration of the Abandoibarra area and its transformation into an international attraction, with its star building, the Guggenheim Museum Bilbao, gave more credibility to the arguments of the Basque government to use the already existing intermodal station there (Termibus) to host the future Basque HST:

> Bilbao Town Council and Renfe push for Abando as the terminus station for the HST. Other services are also located in the Abando Renfe station such as FEVE, Eusko Tren and buses. The Basque government, on the other hand, favours Termibus, which includes the underground station, the tram service, Renfe services, regional and national bus services and the shuttle bus to the airport [the vicinity, Abandoibarra, has already undergone a major regeneration with the building of the Euskalduna Conference Centre and Concert Hall, the Guggenheim Museum, BEC (the Bilbao Exhibition Centre), and so on] . . . The decision over where to build the HST station is made difficult by all the entities involved (including the council). [Franciso Álvarez] Cascos suggested that Renfe should decide the matter, all the rest of the stakeholders in the project rejected it heartedly. Renfe is the station's titleholder . . . [the Ministry of] Public Works wanted the intermodal station to be run by Renfe. But Renfe is just one more operator . . . Logically, Bilbao [the Town Council] is interested in Abando, because, if you notice, the railway is a big obstacle that separates the old quarter and the "traditional centre."[30]

29. Abando used to be the financial centre of the old industrial Bilbao.

30. AE, member of the Bilbao Chamber of Commerce.

Moreover,

> San Mames [near the intermodal station] will become the centre of Bilbao, Bilbao as a metropolis. The rest of the places and spaces integrating the metropolis will be balanced out. Besides, San Mames is where all modes of transport coincide together: underground, tram, railway, urban buses and interregional buses. In terms of location, the HST should arrive at San Mames for two reasons: one, other areas, like Santander, [would also be] connected [to the train]. Two, San Mames, together with the areas of Abandoibarra, Zorrotzaurre, Olabeaga, etc., are becoming the new centre of Bilbao. The articulation of the HST into the Bilbao metropolitan PTP: the objective of the train is to arrive [in the city] and not to interfere, that is, it should not be a divisive element [of the urban landscape]. [The train] should arrive at a certain location from where access to other areas is also provided: say, you arrive on the HST and you are faced with the dilemma [of how] to get to Barakaldo. So the debate centred around which train station is more convenient to host the HST should take into consideration [the fact] that San Mames is already a centre for major transport communications.[31]

Similar debates also emerged in Donostia-San Sebastián, where the then mayor, Odon Elorza (PSOE), made sure that[32] the HST would arrive at Atotxa railway station (which is situated in the city centre). The latter would bring further investments for upgrading the station "according to the level required by the arrival of *a* "HST,"" the development of an underground bus park, as well as facilitating better links between the neighbourhood of Egia and the city centre.[33] The then mayor of Vitoria-Gasteiz, Patxi Lazcoz (PSOE), also associated the arrival of the HST with an opportunity to "bury the rail-lines that to this day divide the city."[34]

---

31. AO, member of the Transport Consortium of Bilbao.

32. "Fomento confirma que el tren de alta velocidad llegará hasta el centro de San Sebastián," Ya.com, 13 July 2006. According to the agreement reached between the Basque Minister of Transport and Public Works, Nuria Lopez de Gereñu; the Secretary of State for Infrastructures, Victor Morlan; the Chief Delegate of the Provincial Council of Gipuzkoa, Joxe Joan González de Txabarri, and the mayor of Donostia-San Sebastián, Odon Elorza, all national destinations –that is, Donostia-San Sebastián–Madrid and Donostia-San Sebastián–Barcelona via Pamplona-Iruñea— will stop in the city centre (Atotxa). While the Madrid–Paris international connection will stop in Astigarraga, a town a few kilometres away to the north of Donostia-San Sebastián.

33. Since the neighbourhood of Egia grew in the 1960s, it was "cut off" from the centre by the rail track and the station on the edge of the district.

34. José María Reviriego, "El tren de alta velocidad es imprescindible para cohesionar Euskadi," El Diario Vasco.com, 24 June 2007.

More generally, city council representatives of the major political parties (the PNV, PSOE, PP and EA) in all three cities welcomed the development of the HST as they all saw this as an opportunity to promote urban regeneration as well as revitalize the tourist sector by providing a better mobility service for tourists. Thus, while the HST clearly offers opportunities to the cities that it connects, it also offers additional benefits of investment and regeneration that usually follow the development of such projects. In addition, the HST is a flagship project, a powerful symbol of development and a site that is likely to raise significantly the international profile of a city as well as attract international attention.

However, looking back at the long period in which the HST project has been developed, it is clear that the priorities and rhetorics of all players (on the regional, national and EU levels) have changed significantly. These have been discussed extensively in the preceding chapters but here it is worth mentioning that, while in the early period of the post-Franco transition the HST was a symbol of the modernisation of Spain and a major preoccupation of the central Spanish government, twenty years later this same concern has become a major preoccupation for the BAC. The two other major benefits that the Basque Y is expected to bring to the BAC are the competitiveness and the social cohesion of the Basque City.

### *Strategies and Tactics in Building the Basque City*

The policies adopted and the coalitions built by Basque government demonstrate the significant role that governments can play in mediating between different interests and strategies operating on different scales, what Jessop (2004) calls meta-governance. In the case of the Basque government these strategies are built around the rhetoric, institutional coalitions and practices involving cities, regions, autonomous communities and the Basque Country as the Basque City. More specifically, Donostia-San Sebastián and Vitoria-Gasteiz, both rather unimportant cities within Spain and Europe, and Bilbao, a city of only secondary importance within Spain, are linked to the HST network, which could largely be attributed to the active involvement of the regional government. As a result, the HST project is one aspect of the development of a dense set of economic and social links among the three major cities in the BAC and linking them to broader Spanish and trans-European networks. Further, there is an expectation on the part of the PNV-led government that the shape that the line will take acts as one of the mechanisms through which the future strategies of Bilbao could be more closely aligned to those of the BAC[35] and over time this integration could lead to the transformation of the Basque Country into the Basque City, which could compete with the two other powerful urban centres in Spain: Madrid and Barcelona (see figure 7.1).

| T0.............. | T1.............. | T2.............. | T3 |
|---|---|---|---|
| Under Franco, Bilbao was a principal industrial centre in Spain. Together with other major cities, it acquired a special status. (see chapter 2) | Bilbao as a tertiary city (After Franco, industrial restructuring, and the constitution of the BAC). See chapter 4. | Bilbao connected to Donostia-San Sebastián and Vitoria-Gasteiz. | The Basque City (?) |

**Figure 7.1.** ????

In this sense the HST agenda of the Basque government is significantly different from those of the Spanish governments and the EU. As mentioned earlier, on the level of central government connections between cities are prioritised. Here, economic development takes precedence and it is articulated within a "Spain of cities" framework. On the European level,

35. On the one hand, projects such as the HST contribute to the stabilisation of specific scales in terms of their legitimisation through financing and institutional development and support (for example, the BAC). However, and contrary to that, these same projects may also contribute towards undermining the longer term stability and coherence of the very same scales that they legitimise over the longer term through enabling alternative strategies. For, example, while the development of a set of projects and programmes for revitalising Bilbao have contributed to the competitiveness of the BAC more generally, this is only as long as Bilbao continues to pursue a Basque City strategy. The latter choice is, however, not irreversible and certainly different options could be available for Bilbao both at present and in the future. In this sense, the successful implementation of large-scale projects such as the HST (as well as the restructuring of Bilbao) under the leadership of the moderate nationalist PNV could be seen as, on the one hand, one aspect of an emerging hegemonic social, political and economic vision for the Basque Country and, on the other, as a process that could enable alternative economic and political projects. In this sense "cohesion" is always also understood through the imagining of different territorial scales that could make a specific reference to, for example, a Basque homeland (within or outside the boundaries of the current autonomous community), specific localities, cities, regions, Spain more broadly, and so on. The meaning of "competitiveness" is also similarly contested.

there are two overlapping discourses: the Europe of Regions and Europe of cities, yet with the latter dominant. More specifically, while the Europe of Regions idea is mostly associated with a social and integrationist agenda, the Europe of cities notion is developed within arguments about competitiveness and is associated with a strong neo-liberal agenda. It could be argued that there are sharper dividing lines between the scales over which economic, political and social issues are articulated within Spain and the EU, as compared to the Basque Country. Thus, one might say that there are two broad economic discourses on Post-Fordist restructuring that are concerned with mostly prioritising financial or production capital, respectively. Therefore, while for finance the primary scale of operation is the city, for production capital it is the region. Both cities and regions could be involved in strategies to become more competitive yet each of them is likely to be dominated by different types of capital as well as capital and labour relations. Further, it can be argued that, whereas the region is about "the flow of knowledge" (innovation, institutional thickness, clusters, and so on), the city is about "the flow of information." There is, then, a reversed relationship between information and knowledge as far as financial and production capitals are concerned. The information driven city also needs mobility and the enabling capacity to allow different information flows, while clusters get their competitive advantage mainly through relationships, building a critical mass of resources and knowledge (Cook and Gómez Uranga 1998). To put it another way, regions are about learning (Morgan 1997). Since the city scale and regional scale constitute different forms of reconciliation of capital and labour, both capital and labour are differently re-territorialised in both cases in what Jessop (2001) calls different spatio-temporal fixes.

In the case of the Basque Country, however, social and economic debates are articulated over less clearly defined scales. Thus, the Basque City (with its pulsating boundaries) appears within debates concerning development, competitiveness and innovation, yet it is also an integral part of Basque social and political projects. Both knowledge and information-centred strategies are possible in the Basque Country and they are both partly represented in the Basque City programme. However, at present, it is the latter that takes priority. A knowledge-centred restructuring would give priority to regions, which in turn would also mean different priorities in terms of transport infrastructure. The HST is unlikely to play such a prominent role in this strategy. Indeed, the future of the BAC as the Basque City has been contested by a set of alternative yet highly fragmented projects that could broadly be referred to as the "Basque Country of localities."

In general, EU spatial policies in relation to cities and regions as well as infrastructure projects have had an important influence on regional planning and territorial policies in Spain and in the Basque Country. Therefore, the Basque City project can be seen as fitting into a vision of a spatially integrated EU dominated by nodes of key metropolitan areas. The PNV project, then, is to transform the BAC into a territory with a population of 2.5 million that is highly institutionally and spatially integrated, and which is networked into the key European and global circuits. On the one hand, the image of the city reflects the priorities in the EU policy agenda and more broadly has come to signify the site of the revival of the new economy: an economy of high added value, which encapsulates aspects of design, innovation, creativity (Calzada 2007) and the growth of financial services. On the other, however, the city also reflects local specificities, agendas and conflicts as well as being a key cite for the global integration of circuits of capital (Harvey 1982, 1989).

As suggested earlier, the Basque City project has political, economic and social implications for the Basque Country, as it is related to a specific vision of Post-Fordist economic restructuring and competitiveness, as well as nation- and state-building. The Basque City project tips the balance towards a higher degree of social cohesion within the territory of the BAC and could potentially lead to strengthening the claim on national sovereignty for the Basque Country. The project, however, also makes a couple of other assumptions that could be divisive along class, locality and industrial sector lines which have been contested in ongoing debates. Thus, first, the Basque City project prioritises a white collar (male) employee in the service industry (as opposed to less mobile workers in the service and manufacturing sectors). Second, it incorporates a vision of the central role of the tourist industry as a priority sector (often justified through the successful urban regeneration of Bilbao and the development of emblematic cultural sites such as the Guggenheim Museum Bilbao). Third, by placing an emphasis on product distribution it prioritises the development of infrastructure that is adequate for this particular sector (as opposed to emphasising manufacturing and regions as a competitive strategy). This coincides with a more recent government strategy for the development of new logistic centres in the BAC. Fourth, this will also have an influence on the territorial organisation of the Basque Country, which is largely made up of small and medium-size towns in which only 20 percent of the people use private cars while 40 percent of car trips are over distances of less than 2 kilometres (Barcena 2005: 124). Finally, and related to the latter, the Basque City project makes a claim on strengthening cosmopolitan identities, which in turn can shape the future of the Basque national project. As argued at the beginning of this chapter, Bernardo Atxaga (2005) identifies the city with a "cosmopolitan identity," a space that can be shared by a myriad of different "islands," without necessarily making a claim of territorial ownership. Further, others such as Bollens (2007: 229) think that "urban areas can constitute unique and essential peace-building resources that can be used to transcend nationalist divides," and, as a consequence, have linked the emphasis on urban projects and urbanisation by the PNV-led government with a strategy to, on the one hand, develop a more modern national identity, and, on the other, overcome more radical nationalist positions that are geographically entrenched in smaller towns located in the countryside (Beck 1999; Bollens 2007).

## *The "Basque Country of Localities"*

When I spoke with AA, I was told:

> I don't see the Basque Y as a transport infrastructure, nor do I see it as a single department project. I see it as the great opportunity to generate a new social, economic and competitive space. I have written elsewhere (I participated in the Basque City book) about Øresund, as an example. . . . The region of Øresund comprises northern Denmark and southern Sweden. Øresund is made up of two different regions, one very rich, the Danish one, and the other, an economically deprived region, the Swedish one. The debate over the bridge has taken many years between two countries with a different history, always at war but with the idea of constructing a bridge. The debate centred on arguments that considered the project a continually failed infrastructure project. Claims were made around the cost of the project, funding possibilities, etc., until the way of looking at it changed. The next idea was to create a new social, economic, business, working [and] university space. Changes in working, residence and housing legislation were made. I think if we could see the project as a wider picture to generate a city-region, we could mobilise all the social elements behind this idea and use, for example, the bond, I talked to you about earlier on. If all of us purchased a bond, with this very act we are backing a project that belongs to the citizen, not to the government or [Álvaro] Amann [the Basque Minister for Transport and Public Works]. In addition, the most advantageous consequences are that the railway can

> be constructed with companies 100% from the Basque Country. It could become, further, an innovation element for local companies and hence to later export such knowledge somewhere else. We could measure the direct and indirect employment it will generate as well as how certain towns will change under such new infrastructure. In addition, you can see other technological applications such as new energy sources, etc., that is, it could become the driving force of the country. Unlike now, when the railways will be brought from somewhere else, as well as the wagons.[36]

The vision held by the Basque government for the future of the Basque Country is strongly contested within the Basque Country (and as evidenced by the above quotation also by members of the government itself). The rather diverse group of environmentalists that has a strong following on the local level, especially in small towns, in all three Basque provinces, opposes this model. They argue that the main focus of the Basque government should be on local issues, on strengthening infrastructural links between neighbouring areas (in contrast to inter-urban links), on support for SMEs and labour associations, and building a "social train." While these coalitions are often referred to as environmentalists, they constitute a very diverse and loosely connected association of groups that are broadly against the building of the HST rail links, yet who do not have a united and clearly defined common agenda.[37] As such, some of these groups operate on the national and global level (for example, Ecologists in Action, Bakeaz, the CCOO trade union, and the IU-EB political party), while others are primarily local (the LAB, EHNE and ELA trade unions, Batasuna, now renamed Sortu and allegedly the political wing of ETA, the Assembly Against the HST, local councils, and so on), and environmental issues are the primary concern for only some of the groups involved. Further, in the case of the Basque Country, Bizkaia, Gipuzkoa and Araba are very different in terms of type of their industrial structure, capital labour relations and links to Madrid and other parts of Spain, which makes coalitions outside the traditional political process difficult and short-lived. As a result, although all these groups have at times worked together, more often than not they have pursued apparently irreconcilable strategies. Indeed, tensions between different campaigning organisations cut across ideological, class and regional lines.

---

36. AA, former member of and adviser to the Basque government.

37. Some of the issues over which all these campaigning organisations agree on are related to the negative environmental impact (energy consumption, noise, the fragmentation of natural habitats, and so on) that the HST will have on the Basque Country.

The Assembly Against the HST was the first social movement to address the issue of the HST and is among the most active and uncompromising groups campaigning against the project. Some of its members had previously been involved in activities to oppose the construction of a dual carriageway to connect Gipuzkoa and Navarre through the Leitzaran Valley. It was this earlier activity, and the awareness that there were government plans for other infrastructural projects that would follow, which led them to reflect on the overall strategy that the government was pursuing. This strategy they understood as one of infrastructural development and economic growth above all other possible objectives and concerns, which also reflected a very specific vision for the restructuring of the Basque Country. In the opinion of one of its members, "after 1991 things were not just about the dual carriageway . . . what really became important was what followed that." Furthermore,

> This is a blasted anecdote . . . when the Euro City project started, it started as the Baiona–Donostia Conurbation . . . which can be traced back to 1993 . . . the period of the diagnostics . . . it's not yet "the Euro City" . . . and the person in charge of that was B.C., the director of the School of Architecture . . . he was a born urbaniser . . . he is in the PNV, in "the name of patriotism" etc. . . . so, in my opinion, since new interests overlapped, within this conception surrounding the metropolis, particularly, [putting an emphasis on] infrastructure, later the Euro City White Book . . . nowhere else is the whole discourse drawing on the need to create the big Atlantic Platform on Transportation better developed . . . Last year, in the BEC , in a joint Aquitaine-Euskadi festival, a photo assembly showed that the Super Port was going to be the key basis of the Euro-region. That is, the Super Port of Pasaia . . . the key basis of the Donostia–Baiona Euro City . . . with a growing importance of transport infrastructure . . . as something inherent to the economy . . . you can already observe new interests . . . and B.C. was a classic urbanist . . . but there are new interests which put forward first the [notion] of an infrastructure hub . . . there are plans to build council houses in Loiola, Martutene [neighbourhoods of Donostia-San Sebastián]. . . but a big chunk of the investment will go to the infrastructures, to the HST.[38]

Thus, members of the Assembly Against the HST believe that opposition to the HST should not be based on developing alternatives to the HST itself, but rather pushing towards the development of alternative models

38. AH, member of the Assembly Against the HST.

of social, territorial and economic integration within the BAC. In other words, at the heart of the Assembly Against the HST position is the idea that the HST is one aspect of a broader social, economic and territorial project that is based on continuous consumption and exploitation of land. They identify this model as one of "developmentalism" (*desarrollismo*) where they believe that the policies of Basque government are aimed at encouraging overdevelopment. This interpretation is well documented in the numerous manifestos and policy reviews developed by the group over the last fifteen years.[39] And these arguments are aligned to broader issues of development, global inequalities, the rural/urban divide and energy dependence (Bermejo 2004).

> We have carried the burden of progress for far too long . . . the villages of the Oria Valley are quite overburdened with infrastructures, whether railways, roads . . . a dumping site was nearby for many years and mining existed for nearly a hundred years . . . And we became aware, I mean, we don't want to pass on the problems to others . . . but we also think that we have already fulfilled the quota . . . for a village like this it is a matter of life or death . . . there are many shafts from mining times underneath the hill behind the town. The hill is [too] fragile to endure a tunnel. We have repeatedly asked the Basque and provincial government to conduct a feasibility study of the hill, since it is prone to landslides . . . An old man in town suggests that there might even still exist shafts underneath the town . . . Our job is not to put forward an alternative; we live in towns and we want to keep them alive . . . we don't agree with the direction society is heading in . . . many times we are told "here come the usual suspects" . . . but we don't agree with blind progress . . . the Basque Country is very small and they are demolishing it . . . there were plans for a quarry, we have been asked for permission but we have always declined it. We organised a meeting at which the town showed up and, as I said earlier, it is quite a worn-out town and it's time to think about our future and the fact that we want another type of future. But the development company's excuse has always been the fact that a huge thing will be coming soon and

39. Based on the PTP of Donostia-San Sebastián, the Assembly Against the HST offers the following staggering data: some data, selected by the review, show that out of 4800 ha of urbanised land, 7600 ha were expected to be urbanised by 2018. The new urbanised 2800 ha would be distributed as follows: big infrastructures: exterior high way and new main road, the HST and Super Port: 680 ha; land for new economic activities: logistics platforms, an industrial estate for distribution, business parks and new commercial estates: 660 ha; low-intensity urban development, as yet undefined: 630 ha.

> this thing will require lots of concrete. These will be the sectors that will most benefit from the project.[40]

Within this discourse there is a mixture of arguments against the HST that combine its potentially damaging impact on tradition, cultural heritage and cohesion as well as questioning its viability as an engineering project.[41] The belief among members of the Assembly Against the HST that the main argument against the HST should be opposition to overdevelopment, broadly defined, became one of the points of confrontation between this group and other organisations (Ecologists in Action, the statewide trade unions, IU-EB, and so on). On the other side of this main divide, members of other campaigning organisations have complained that the position of the Assembly Against the HST is too radical and in the long term their campaign strategy is ineffective and inconsequential. In contrast to this, these other organisations emphasise the development of what they see as a "social train":

> The leitmotiv of the Assembly Against the HST is an emphatic "no" to the HST. Trade unions, left-leaning political parties and we ourselves think that [the pursuit of this objective] is not enough. We should foster a broader debate concerning the type of transport model we'd like [to have]. We should explore different alternatives. In this context, a different network emerged, the "social train" network. We consider that both networks are compatible, although different.[42]

Further, "A degree of progress . . . the social train . . . has to be accepted. Progress is here to stay. Extreme positions, such as those which reject progress completely are unfeasible and undesirable."[43] Representatives of other partner organisations expressed similar views:

> the "Elkarlana foundation" was created. The Assembly Against the HST was also involved . . . but their anti-reformist stand provoked a split with

40. AL, town councillor in Itsasondo.

41. The regular Renfe railway service also passes through the town. He claimed that the village had already had its fair share of transport infrastructures and it was unlikely it could take on any other infrastructure, much less that of the high-speed train. They had already lived in a "building site" for far too many years and the HST would take even more time, with subsequent problems related to noise, dust, dirt, etc. As a result of this, people would be put off from settling in the village (at the time of my interview, brand new quality housing had already been constructed there). Certainly, the informant believed, a project of this size could jeopardise the survival chances of the town.

42. AP, member of Ecologists in Action, local branch.

43. AJ, member of Ecologists in Action.

> the rest of the groups involved. They are against the HST and do not accept any other "alternative." In 1999, the LAB, ELA and HIRU trade unions participated in a workshop about the social train. We all agreed that we don't want the HST. Instead we proposed a social train.[44]

Another major obstacle to developing a common agenda both against the HST and as a broader centre-left alternative to the PNV-led Basque project could be related to the presence of ETA on the left of the political spectrum. Thus, the participation of organisations that were perceived to be associated with ETA or sympathetic to its agenda further weakened the coalition. In this sense, one of the informants complained that getting involved in legal action against the HST (at the request of some of the municipalities affected by the infrastructure itself), where political members of the radical left Basque nationalist political party Batasuna were also involved, made it difficult to develop a strong case against the HST:

> we launched legal action against the HST . . . well, we gathered a legal team hired by the town councils that opposed the HST from the valley of Durango, Gipuzkoa, Elorrio, etc. . . . But we pulled out in the end. You're better off not getting into this sort of thing . . . there is too much politics . . . we had lots of pressure and so we had to bear the consequences . . . there was lots of internal politics, you know, the Batasuna atmosphere, the radical left – as far as I'm concerned they are a bunch of fanatic nationalists. Problems arose when the mayors of some of the town councils involved belonged to Batasuna and when most of the members of the council were in Batasuna . . . It didn't work because, on the one hand, we got involved in the "issue" –and we are against terrorist violence– and, on the other, we had to work with the radical left.[45]

Environmental protection and gender equality are two areas where ETA and its (widely perceived to be) political wing, Batasuna,[46] have always been very active, which in turn makes all debates about related

44. AQ, member of the local agricultural trade union, EHNE.

45. AR, member of Bakeaz, NGO and think tank.

46. Batasuna has remained a general reference for the radical political left in the Basque Country although after it was formally banned by Spanish law in 2003, all its re-incarnations, such as Euskal Herritarrok and ANV, were also quickly banned. Following the permanent ETA ceasefire of January 2011, a new party was founded to represent the radical Basque nationalist left, Sortu, one month later in February 2011. In 2012 it joined other Basque nationalist and left-wing parties to create the EH Bildu coalition, which to date (2015) remains legal and represents the main political expression of radical nationalist sentiment.

issues highly politically charged. As Fernández Duran (2007) argues, as long as ETA exists, the ideals of the radical left will always be associated with ETA and this prevents the development of a consolidated centre-left political alternative for the Basque Country.

The establishment of the BAC in 1983 and the process of its shaping during the post-Franco years demonstrates the complex processes involved in building national and state (-like) institutions. In contrast to accounts that take the notion of region uncritically, here I have argued that regions are constituted in complex ways through competing interests of different stakeholders, priorities, as well as visions of broader social, economic and political configurations. Further, they are shaped, but not determined, by different legacies, as well as emotions and a sense of belonging. In this sense, the question of the competitive advantages of the BAC is not something that is just there and, as it were, waiting to be discovered, but is instead a process in which physical, institutional and social boundaries are negotiated (Paasi 2002). As argued above, the imaginaries developed for the BAC operate within a diverse set of spatial metaphors such as region, the Basque City and Euskal Herria.

The physical and institutional space of the BAC has been shaped by different and often contradictory legacies from the post-Franco transition as well as from earlier periods (Agirreazkuenaga 2011). Thus, the territorial organisation of Franco's Spain, with its emphasis on cities as central administrative, economic and social units (for example, Bilbao, Madrid, Barcelona and Valencia) continued to be important in shaping the internal organisation of the BAC (chapter 3). In contrast, the post-Franco autonomy given to the BAC was based on already existing provincial autonomy that had been erased by the Franco regime. Indeed, the Basque provinces still hold substantial powers vis-à-vis the BAC as a whole. All those institutional formations were constituted by different interests, dominated by different types of capital and capital and labour relations.

Regions, under certain conditions, can acquire substantial powers. In the case of the BAC such powers were acquired due to a combination of factors, such as the substantial autonomy of the BAC, the star-like centre-regions relationships in Spain, the nature of the political process in Spain, as well as the effective use of strategies on the part of the Basque government (both internally and externally). In this sense, although "regions" do not possess regulatory powers in crucial areas such as the labour market[47] and macro-economic policy (Lovering 2001), this does not mean that "regions" are always necessarily powerless.

Furthermore, the political, economic and social organisation of the Basque space; a moderate nationalist project championed by the PNV, although dominant, was faced with some form of loosely organised confrontation within the BAC. More recently, however, while the ideological confrontations remain, the PNV project has been strengthened through its entrenching into a set of diverse institutional networks operating on the national, subnational and supranational level, within which it has been able to successfully operate over a relatively long period of time. The political, economic and social viability of this project remains highly dependent on the continuous ability of the Basque government to operate within these diverse environments in sustaining its claim on the legitimacy of its national project. Economic restructuring, competitiveness, state-building and nation-building are thus closely intertwined in this case without clear priorities, while the boundaries between internal and external legitimacy are highly blurred. The case of the HST demonstrates that the Basque government has been willing to spent substantial amounts of political capital as well as committing substantial financial resources in sustaining a project for which there is little support both inside and outside the BAC and few other justifications than a better territorial integration of the three capitals of the BAC.

This chapter also distinguished between the emergence of two dominant imaginings of the Basque Country and nation that could be associated with the notions of the Basque City and the "Basque Country of localities." These are closely associated with, first, the vision of the ruling PNV for an inter-scalar imagining of the Basque Country within Spain and in Europe and, second, with a vision that prioritises a bottom-up integration, close interregional and inter-local cooperation, short distance travel and well-being. These different Basque projects could be closely associated with specific affiliations related to region, types of labour and capital.

More generally, these two visions could be seen as two different forms of Post-Fordist adaptation, both of which could potentially offer viable alternatives for the future of the Basque Country. Neither of these two

47. This has been a bitterly discussed issue between Basque and central governments and also between different political parties within the BAC. Generally, one can argue that the main Basque-leaning political parties, including Basque trade unions such as ELA and LAB, have demanded that the competencies over the labour market be transferred to the BAC.

Basque national projects draws on an association between state and nation that fit the nation-state ideal-type. Thus, the Basque City imaginary emphasises the significance of territorial cohesion, close integration and centralised authority over the territory of the country, which is combined with a very flexible understanding of different scales, integrated within different institutional frameworks, and led by a highly flexible and strategically astute government. It prioritises the ideal type of a long-distance professional traveller, circulating freely among different urban centres in order to access work and social networks that are highly territorially dispersed, while also offering support to intra-regional capacity building. In this case, belonging to the nation is formalised and mediated through symbols of the state. In contrast, the "Basque Country of localities" operates with a highly flexible and decentralised understanding of identity politics but combined with an imagining of the economy as much more firmly centred on the locality and to an extent sheltered from the influences of global markets. Here, belonging to the nation is more on a meta-level, it is less formalised and closely related to everyday practices and a heterogeneous set of symbols that are dispersed across different localities whose meanings are open to negotiation. These two visions of the Basque Country do not represent a traditional idea of nation and state formation. Both these visions tend to emphasise a different scale for identity, politics and economic integration and, generally, in so doing, they produce and reproduce different rhetoric and discourses that operate at different institutional levels.

# Beyond the Basque City

Academic and media discussions of Basque and Spanish issues tend to start from the question of political violence and ETA, as well as highlighting specific historical legacies, in their efforts to understand the Basque and Spanish nation- and state-building. In contrast, this book has aimed to offer a multi-layered understanding of Basque nation- and state-building as an alternative to the dominance of highly politicised and/or one-sided accounts of these processes. In order to do that, it had to de-naturalise the taken-for-granted Spanish nation-state and discuss its co-evolution with other national projects within Spain. The specific focus on the Basque Country required a further focus on the specific complexities in relation to nation- and state-building in both Spain and the Basque Country over time. These broader aims of the book also offered the background for understanding current debates on the Basque national projects and the complex strategies and coalitions developed by key players in these debates.

By focusing primarily on the post-Franco period, the book aimed at overcoming overly deterministic political or economic-centred interpretations of the transition in Spain and developed an account of their interdependence and embeddedness into global and European transformations. In this sense, centre-periphery debates within Spain and the post-Franco process of regionalisation, it was argued, cannot be understood as following an exclusively "internal to Spain" logic but, rather, need to be understood as an aspect of Post-Fordist restructuring and the changing role and capacity of the nation(al)-state. The latter involved looking at issues of accumulation, capital and class relations, alliances and the processes involved in the contested ideological and rhetorical constructions, as well as the different territorialisations, of the Spanish and Basque nations and states over time. Furthermore, the overemphasis of the post-Franco transition as a 'break with the past' was questioned and the book explored the continuities and discontinuities from the Francoist and the more distant imperial past in terms of uneven development, almost exclusively centre-mediated relations between regions, institutions with overlapping functions, the relative isolation of Spain from major European events and processes and the key role that Franco's regime played in building and consolidating the institutions of the modern Spanish nation-state. However, while the legacies of the Franco and pre-Franco periods were very significant for understanding the present, I also argued that these could not be seen as factors determining a clear path towards the present. Instead, they were discussed as different legacies that contributed to the shaping of the present, where they were a part of diverse strategies of different actors with different objectives.

The imaginings of the boundaries of the Basque Country and the different (and equally feasible) economic and political options available to the city of Bilbao after the death of Franco were some of the examples that illustrated this point. In this sense, institutional restructuring during the post-Franco period was not only about "restoring historical justice," by devolving wide autonomy to the "historical nationalities," but was also a complex process involving the creation of entirely new institutions, the renegotiation of the scope and functions of existing ones, as well as the adaptation of these internal (for Spain) processes to the ongoing process of EU restructuring and expansion.

While detailed discussion of the interdependencies between different factors was important for understanding the complex embeddedness of the post-Franco transition and nation- and state-building in the Basque Country, it also demonstrated the continuing significance of place as a site in which inequalities were reproduced and thus its role as a field of contradictions and conflict. Actual places are not only sites where social relations occur but are also locations where infrastructure is or is not built, and that are connected or disconnected, that are loved, hated and imagined as individual and national homelands, and so on. In this sense, while increased mobility and a growing significance of global networks are certainly changing the nature of relationships between and within places, the latter remains important.

While the main emphasis of this book was to understand Spanish and Basque nation- and state-building and their coevolution, the associated economic and political changes within Spain and the Basque Country were related to ongoing restructuring in the Basque Country, and these processes were related to the changes in the EU and in Spain. For, as I have argued, different strategies were adopted by different players at these levels. More specifically, the lack of support for an industrial policy at the national and on the EU level as well as the withdrawal of such support on the part of governments of EU member states and the increasing emphasis on supply-side intervention contributed to the emergence of cities and regions as major centres of economic activity and investment. Cities, regions and states constitute different spatial scales that favour different types of social and economic relationships, types of capital, labour and capital relations, and that also require different forms of connectivity and infrastructural development in order to thrive in a Post-Fordist environment. Thus, while the city is about mobility, flow, information, and so forth, the region is about thicker sets of social relationships and the enforcement of such ties that will facilitate the transmission of knowledge. The HST is a specific type of transport infrastructure that supports the former, while policies related to the creation of clusters, for example, tend to foster the development of highly embedded relationships involving representatives of different industries, government institutions and research centres.

One of the objectives and challenges facing the Basque government has been to reconcile different legacies, interests and plausible futures in co-shaping Basque institutions and the boundaries and the meanings of the Basque Country. The latter included, for example, the "Basque Autonomous Community" as a political-administrative entity established during the post-Franco transition, the major, and still undergoing restructuring of its industrial base located within the Basque Country and closely linked to Basque identity and sense of pride, and more recently the reinvention of Bilbao as an entrepreneurial city. In this sense, it was argued that the Basque City metaphor attempts to reconcile these different realities and visions. The HST project, with its emphasis on connecting the three Basque capital cities to each other and to other major cities, is an aspect of a more recent discourse encompassing a global and urbanised Basque identity. The latter further emphasises the close integration of the three Basque provinces; it is oriented to the present and prioritises competitiveness; and is in sharp contrast to the alternative visions of a Basque homeland including seven Basque provinces and oriented towards the past.

Further, relationships between and within places continue to be, at least to some extent (although not exclusively), hierarchically structured. Indeed, the debates around the building of the HST in Spain would suggest the relatively peripheral position occupied by Bilbao and the Basque Country relative to Barcelona and Catalonia, for example. It was therefore argued that the Basque Country occupied a semi-peripheral position in both Spain and Europe, which in turn had significant implications for the strategies available to the regional government, particularly in terms of economic restructuring. Specifically, the decline of industry and the weakening of Bilbao as a key industrial centre in Spain, the shift of power from the Atlantic to the Mediterranean area, and the growing significance of large urban areas as opposed to the hitherto unchallenged dominance of national states put the Basque Country in a relatively weak position in terms of the available options for economic and political restructuring. These options were further complicated by the high level of internal heterogeneity among the three provinces constituting the Basque Autonomous Community and the need (on the part of governing coalitions) to balance the divergent interests and expectations of representatives of large and small business, local and immigrant (that is, from other parts of Spain) labour, and so on.

Within this context, the Christian democratic nationalist PNV emerged as a leading political player. Although it mainly represented the interests of the local middle classes and particularly Gipuzkoa-based small businesses and cooperatives, it succeeded in temporarily integrating big business (Beltza 1976a)[1] while not entirely antagonising supporters of "autonomous Spain." Within this context of relative political stability, successive PNV governments in the BAC pursued an economic policy that was far more interventionist than that of the central Spanish government. While very successful in building political and economic alliances at different levels, the Basque political elite was unable to overcome some structural constraints related to the semi-peripheral position occupied by the Basque Country in relation to major European networks.

The latter was well illustrated by the reluctance of virtually all parties (at least at the national level), apart from the PNV-led Basque government, to commit to the building of a HST link to the Basque Country. Indeed, it was argued above that the building of such a link was an entirely unlikely outcome given the lack of interest from other stakeholders and the absence of any convincing economic rationale. The HST line and the Y shape that the rail track will take could therefore be attributed almost entirely to the perseverance, commitment and ability to build coalitions on different levels of the PNV elite for whom the completion of this project was consistent with a much broader political, economic and social agenda that, I argued,

1. Beltza suggests that the big businesses, including the main banks, would prefer to support a project for political autonomy in the Basque Country. This would allow them to have further input into decision-making processes at the local level.

was captured by the Basque City metaphor. This vision combines a political aspect of internal territorial integration where the HST would serve the function of reducing travel times among the three capitals of the Basque provinces, but it will also serve an economic function of creating a large well networked metropolitan space which, it is assumed, will make the Basque Country more attractive to investors. In this sense, in the context of the Basque Country, the HST is both about internal territorial cohesion, building a competitive city-region (the Basque City) and building external links to other key European cities. It was further argued that this vision for Basque nation- and state-building as a Basque City has been contested on different levels by other visions such as a "Europe of regions," "federalist Spain," "the learning regions," an "independent Basque Country," the "Basque Country of localities," and so forth. These different visions, however, only challenge specific (economic, political and social) aspects of the PNV project without offering an overall alternative that would also have support within the Basque Country.

The book has also shown that the state retains a key role in deciding on issues of territorial sovereignty. Although the EU plays a central role in guaranteeing the protection of cultural expression as well as the political and economic rights of minority groups, the powers and repertoire of EU institutions are limited regarding issues of territorial sovereignty. In the case of the Basque Country, this is seen in the better reception given to metaphors with stronger economic than political connotations such as the Basque City, "Basque region," or the Atlantic Arc.

While some of these themes were discussed throughout the book, others were primarily addressed in specific chapters. Thus, chapter 1 offered a general theoretical overview of the literature on Post-Fordist restructuring and established the broad theoretical and conceptual framework within which Basque and Spanish restructuring could be understood. Chapter 2 and 3 identified the key legacies from the Franco and the pre-Franco periods. It was argued that these included the strong outward orientation and the weak links between different parts of Spain, the central importance of Madrid as a centre mediating and steering these relationships, highly uneven-development and markedly urbanised regional areas in political and economic terms. In chapter 4 these legacies were further discussed within the context of the post-Franco transition where I looked at different aspects of the political and economic crisis in Spain and argued that these processes were closely interrelated with restructuring within Europe. This is in contrast to dominant interpretations of the crisis in Spain where the main emphasis is on the political changes within the country: "the Spanish transition" was seen as mainly a political crisis that was overcome "successfully" with the completion of what is usually referred as "political devolution" (autonomy). As far as Basque nation- and state-building is concerned, the "successful" end of the political restructuring made any claims for further devolution problematic.

Chapters 5 and 6 then focused on discussions around the building of a HST to illustrate the complex interdependencies, contradictions and complementarities on the institutional level as well as among different stakeholders. These chapters outlined major developments on the regional, national and supranational levels by shifting the emphasis between different periods (1986–1992 and after 1993) and scales, (specifically, Spain in chapter 5 and the EU in chapter 6). It was argued that over time there was a strengthening of the neo-liberal agenda both at the EU level and within Spain (although not to the same extent in the Basque Country), which in relation to the ongoing HST project was reflected in the growing emphasis on competitiveness in Europe as well as, from a Spanish perspective, integration with Europe rather than within Spain. These chapters also offered a detailed elaboration of the complex relationships between scale, territorial sovereignty, and the plausible and actual strategies adopted by different stakeholders. This theme was further developed in chapter 7, where the main focus was on the Basque Country. It was argued that in the Basque Country the HST project had an important political-integrative aspect and was closely associated with the PNV-led Basque nation-building project. The latter was built on imagining the Basque Country as a city with integrated dense transport infrastructures prioritising fast connections between distant urban areas, which is in contrast to what I called the "Basque Country of localities," which prioritises the preservation of small communities, building bottom-up connections between neighbouring localities and short-distance travel. While these two visions for the Basque Country are very different, I argued that neither of them fit the nation-state ideal-type and cannot be easily identified as traditional, modern or post-modern because both are very highly integrated into global symbolic and material networks.

I further argued that the consolidation of an alternative vision for the future of the Basque Country is currently difficult and unlikely. This is to a large extent due to the activities of ETA, which have been often associated with, for example, preserving local specificity and the natural environment, as well as a strongly anti-HST rhetoric and activity. Any involvement of ETA has defined such areas as "ETA domains" and thus, by association, discredits the activities of other organisations that might have such agendas. Thus, in December 2008, ETA killed Inaxio Uria, the owner of Altuna y Uria, a Basque company that was directly involved in the construction of the HST. It was not the first time that ETA had taken steps to oppose environmentally controversial projects in the BAC (although this is not necessarily the only reason for this specific assassination). Earlier examples included the construction of the nuclear plant in Lemoiz (Bizkaia), in the early 1980s, and, later, in the early 1990s, the development of the Leitzaran dual carriageway that linked Gipuzkoa and Navarre. ETA stated its opposition to the development of the Basque Y HST project on a number of occasions. Thus in July and in August 2008 ETA released statements that: "Each of these vast cement based projects buries our homeland project."[2]

After the latest ETA assassination in December 2008, representatives of the "Stop the HST!"("AHT Gelditu!") coalition, formed by a host of political, social and other civic organisations actively campaigning against the HST, immediately condemned the actions of ETA:

> The killing of the businessman, Inaxio Uria, has caused anger among us and we wish to condemn ETA's involvement in this issue. We would like to highlight that any opposition to the HST has to be resolved on the principles of mobilisation, resistance and civil disobedience. In contrast to an armed solution, we firmly believe that popular involvement holds the key to stop the HST once and for all. We demand that ETA ceases to be involved in this social and environmental conflict.[3]

As argued above, then, radical and/or pro-independence violence has been over the years closely intertwined and associated with social and environmentalist movements as well as anti-modernisation agendas. This has made it difficult for a consolidated centre-left agenda to emerge as an alternative project to the PNV-led nationalist agenda. This is because many of the possible themes and issues in which such a centre-left platform could develop are too closely associated with the activities of ETA. The same statement released by the "Stop the HST!" coalition also observed that:

At the same time, we urge the political authorities to reflect upon the causes that have led to this current situation and that they do not use this

2. Quoted in Berria.info, 9 December 2008.

3. Ibid.

attack and the wide popular opposition that the HST project has generated in order to criminalise the entire popular movement against the HST as if it were part of the fight against ETA. In this sense, at the same time, we firmly reject the attitude of those who have taken advantage of these circumstances in order to delegitimise any opposition to the HST and have used it to defend any project that would provoke economic, social and environmental damage."[4]

After ETA's ceasefire in 2011, it could have been expected that the changed political scenario would open up the possibility for developing a new centre-left coalition that would include the PSOE, the radical Basque nationalist left and other left-orientated parties such as the United Left (Ezker Aniztua-Izquierda Unida), thus potentially weakening the PNV-led national project. Contrary to this, however (although similar to developments in Catalonia), the post-ETA context and the emergence of Bildu (which draws together several pro-self-determination groups, including Eusko Alkartasuna) has reinforced, rather than disrupting and reshaping, old coalitions such as that between the PSOE and the PNV, and even made a PNV-PP coalition also plausible. Indeed, it could be argued that the current climate of crisis in the Basque Country has led to a sharpening of politics along identity and economic lines. In terms of the future of the HST link in the Basque Country, while the PP and PSOE nationally have shown little enthusiasm for the Basque Y project, on the regional level both parties, together with the PNV, have organised a programme of economic rationality and pragmatism by which existing infrastructure projects (including those of the HST and the Port of Pasaia) are seen as integral parts of the future economic success of the Basque Country.

Furthermore, while predictions are always necessarily a dangerous territory, it could be argued that, given that the main sentiments behind the continued support for ETA from a substantial part of the population in the BAC are closely linked to the issue of allowing ETA prisoners to serve out their sentences in or close to the Basque Country (that is, as opposed to the current Spanish penal policy of ETA prisoner dispersion in jails throughout Spain), if such demands were met then support for an ETA-defined agenda could decrease significantly. If this issue was resolved, however, then this could potentially weaken the PNV-led nationalist project and also facilitate the consolidation of the aforementioned potential

4. Ibid.

centre-left coalition (similar to processes that took place in Catalonia). Certainly, none of these parties (with the exception of the PSOE) supports the Basque Y project. In this sense, different imaginaries of the future of the Basque Country as a Basque City or as a "Basque Country of localities" are related to developments with ETA, yet, and importantly here, are not overdetermined by such developments. While the existence of ETA and political violence are important aspects that shape the direction of Basque nation- and state-building, these are only some of a multiplicity of factors, and not necessarily the most important ones.

# Bibliography


Agirre Kerexeta, I. (1989). "El País Vasco ante los ejes de comunicación y desarrollo europeos." Lección Inaugural del Curso Académico, Universidad de Deusto, 1989–90.

Agirreazkuegana, J. (2011). *The Making of the Basque Question: Experiencing Self-government, 1793–1877*. Reno: Center for Basque Studies, University of Nevada, Reno.

Aglietta, M. (1979). *A Theory of Capitalist Regulation: The US Experience*. London: NLB.

Agnew, J. (1994). "The Territorial Trap: The Geographical Assumptions of International Relations Theory." *Review of International Political Economy* 1(1): 53–80.

Agnew, J.A., and Corbridge, S. (1995). *Mastering Space: Hegemony, Territory and International Political Economy*. London: Routledge.

Agranoff, R. (1994). "Comunidades: Asymmetrical Federalism in Spain: Design and Outcomes." Paper presented at the XVIth World Congress of the International Political Science Association, Berlin, 21–25 August.

Ahedo, M. (2004). "Cluster Policy in the Basque Country (1991–2002): Constructing "Industry-Government" Collaboration through Cluster-associations." *European Planning Studies* 12(8): 1097–1113.

Ahedo, M. (2006). "Business Systems and Cluster Policies in the Basque Country and Catalonia (1990–2004)." *European Urban and Regional Studies* 13(1): 25–39.

AHTaren Aurkako Asanblada (2000). *AHTaren aurkako borroka dela eta: Zenbait ekarpenen bilduma*. N.p.: AHTaren Aurkako Asanblea.

AHTaren Aurkako Asanblada (2002). *Alegaciones de la Asamblea Contra el TAV al Plan Territorial Parcial (PTP) de Donostialdea-Bajo Bidasoa*. N.p.: AHTaren Aurkako Asanblea.

Aja, E. (1999). *El Estado autonómico: Federalismo y hechos diferenciales*. Madrid: Alianza Editorial.

Aja, E. (2000). "Los problemas actuales de articulación del Estado autonómico." *Revista de Occidente* 229(June): 35–54.

Aja, E. (2003). "La reforma constitucional del Senado." *Revista de Occidente* 271(December): 39–63.

Aja, E. (2004). "Spain: Nation, Nationalities, and Regions." In J. Loughlin (ed.), *Subnational Democracy in the European Union: Challenges and Opportunities*. Oxford: Oxford University Press.

Albaladejo, P. F. (1994). "Cities and the Spanish State." In C. Tilly and W.P. Blockmans (eds.), *Cities and the Rise of States in Europe A.D. 1000 to 1800*. Boulder: Westview Press.

Albarracín, J., et al. (1993). *La larga noche neoliberal: politicas economicas de los ochenta*. Madrid: ICARIA.

Albrechts, L., and Coppens, T. (2003). "Megacorridors: Striking a Balance between the Space of Flows and the Space of Places." *Journal of Transport Geography* 11(3): 215–224.

Alcaide Gónzalez, R. (2005). "La Vía estrecha en Cataluña: industria, ocio y servicio público." In M. Muñoz Rubio (ed.), *Historia de los ferrocarriles de vía estrecha en España*. Madrid: Fundación de los Ferrocarriles Españoles.

Alcaide Inchausti, J. (2003). *Evolución económica de las relaciones y provincias españolas en el siglo XX*. Bilbao: Fundación BBVA.

Álvarez Junco, J. (1996). "The Nation Building Process in Nineteenth-century Spain," In C. Mar-Molinero and A. Smith (eds.), *Nationalism and the Nation in the Iberian Peninsula: Competing and Conflicting Identities*. Oxford: Berg.

Amin, A. (1994). *Post-Fordism: A Reader*. London: John Wiley & Sons.

Amin, A., and Robinds, K. (1990). "The Re-emergence of Regional Economies? The Mythical Geography of Flexible Accumulation." *Environment and Planning D: Society and Space* 8(1): 7–34.

Amin, A., and Thrift, N (1995a). "Globalisation, Institutional Thickness and the Local Economy." In P. Healey et al. (eds.), *Managing Cities: The New Urban Context*. Chichester, NY: J. Wiley.

Amin, A., and Thrift, N. (1995b). *Globalization, Institutions, and Regional Development in Europe*. Oxford: Oxford University Press.

Amin, A., and Tomaney, J. (2002). *Behind the Myth of European Union: Prospects for Cohesion*. London: Routledge.

Anderson, B. (1991). *Imagined Communities: Reflections on the Origin and Spread of Nationalism*. London and New York: Verso.

Antolín Iria, J.E. (2000). "El debate del tren de Alta Velocidad dentro del sistema ferroviario vasco." *Euskonews & Media* (online journal) 80, 26 May–2 June.

Apeldoorn, B. (2002). *Transnational Capitalism and the Struggle over European Integration*. New York and London: Routledge.

Arboníes, A. L., and Moso, M. (2002). "Basque Country: The Knowledge Cluster." *Journal of Knowledge Management* 6(4), 347–355.

Areso, J. (1989). "El Gobierno impulsará el corredor subcantábrico y el eje Lisboa-Valencia." *El Diario Vasco*, 19 September.

Arestis, P., and Paliginis, E. (1995). "Divergence and Peripheral Fordism in the European Union." *Review of Social Economy* 53(2): 261–284.

Aretxaga, B. (1999). "A Hall of Mirrors: On the Spectral Character of Basque Political Violence." In W.A. Douglass et al. (eds.), *Basque Politics and Nationalism on the Eve of the Millennium*. Reno: Basque Studies Program.

Arocena, P. (2004). "Privatisation Policy in Spain: Stuck between Liberalisation and the Protection of Nationals' Interests." CESifo Working Paper Series No. 1187, May.

Arrighi, G. (1985). *Semiperipheral Development: The Politics of Southern Europe in the Twentieth Century*. London: Sage Publications.

Atxaga, B. (2005). *Lekuak*. Iruña: Pamiela.

Atxaga, B., and Schommer, A. (1998). *Euskal Herria gaur*. Bilbao: Caja Laboral-Euskadiko Kutxa.

Baena del Alcazar, M. (1994). *Curso de ciencia de la administración*. Madrid: Tecnos.

Balcells, A. (1996). *Catalan Nationalism: Past and Present*, ed. and intro. Geoffrey J. Walker, trans. Jacqueline Hall with collaboration of Geoffrey J. Walker. New York: St. Martin's Press.

Balfour, S. (1989). *Dictatorship, Workers, and the City: Labour in Greater Barcelona since 1939*. Oxford: Oxford University Press.

Balfour, S. (1997). *The End of the Spanish Empire, 1898–1923*. Oxford: Oxford University Press.

Balfour, S. (2000). "Spain from 1931 to the Present." In R. Carr (ed.), *Spain: A History*. Oxford: Oxford University Press.

Balfour, S. (2001). "War, Nationalism and the Masses in Spain, 1898–1936." In E. Acton and I. Saz (eds.), *La transición a la polítca de masas*. Valencia: Universitat de València.

Balfour, S., and Quiroga, A. (2007). *The Reinvention of Spain: Nation and Identity since Democracy*. Oxford: Oxford University Press.

Banyuls, J., and Recio, A. (2012). "Spain: The Nightmare of Mediterranean Neoliberalism." In S. Lehndorff (ed.), *A Triumph of Failed Ideas: European Models of Capitalism in the Crisis*. Brussels: ETUI.

Barandiaran, A. (2005). "Literaturan zein bizitzeko eran ez dut kide handirik ikusten Euskal Herrian." *Berria*, 18 December: 40–41.

Barcena, I. (2005). "European Governance and Green Social Movements: Transportation and GMO Policies in Spain." *Human Ecology Review* 12(2): 120–132.

Barea, I., and Barea, A. (1945). *Spain in the Post-war World*. London: Fabian Publications.

Barea, J., Dizy, D., and Ruiz, O. (2007). "The New Model of the Railway Industry in Spain within the European Framework." *Annals of Public and Cooperative Economics* 78(3): 353–380.

Bartle, I. (2002). "When Institutions No Longer Matter: Reform of Telecommunications and Electricity in Germany, France and Britain." *Journal of Public Policy* 22(1): 1–27.

Beck, J.M. (1999). "The Continuity of Basque Political Violence: A Geographical Perspective on the Legitimisation of Violence." *GeoJournal* 48(2): 109–121.

Bel, G. (2010). *España. Capital Paris*. Barcelona: Destino.

Bel, G. (2012). *Infrastructure and the Political Economy of Nation Building in Spain, 1720–2010*, trans. William Truini. Brighton: Sussex Academic Press.

Beltza (1976a). *Nacionalismo vasco y clases sociales*. San Sebastian: Txertoa.

Beltza (1976b). *El nacionalismo vasco 1876–1936*. San Sebastian: Txertoa.

Beltza (2012). *ETAren estrategiarn armatuaren historiaz*. Baiona: Maiatz.

Bermejo, R. (2004). "Análisis de rentabilidad del proyecto de la 'Y' vasca y bases para una estrategia ferroviaria alternativa." *Bakeaz* 63: 1–15.

Bermeo, N. (1994). "Sacrifice, Sequence, and Strength in Successful Dual Transitions: Lessons from Spain." *The Journal of Politics* 56(3): 601–627.

Blanning, T. (2007). *The Pursuit of Glory: Europe 1648–1815*. London: Allen Lane.

Blinkhorn, M. (1980). "Spain: The 'Spanish Problem' and Imperial Myth." *Journal of Contemporary History* 15(1): 5–25.

Blinkhorn, M. (1975). *Carlism and Crisis in Spain, 1931–1939*. Cambridge: Cambridge University Press.

Blyton, P., and Martinez Lucio, M. (1995). "Industrial Relations and the Management of Flexibilty: Factors Shaping Developments in Spain and United Kingdom." *The International Journal of Human Resource Management* 6(2): 271–291.

Bohle, D. (2006). "Neoliberal Hegemony, Transnational Capital and the Terms of the EU's Eastward Expansion." *Capital & Class* 30(1): 57–86.

Bollens, S. (2007). "Urban Governance at the Nationalist Divide: Coping with Group-based Claims." *Journal of Urban Affairs* 29(3): 229–253.

Borja Álvarez, A. (1996). "Política industrial en la Comunidad Autónoma Vasca 1996–1999." V Jornadas de Economía Crítica, Santiago de Compostela, 17–18 May.

Borja Álvarez, A. (1998). "Sistema formativo y tejido productivo vasco. Retos ante el siglo XXI." In A.G. Arizkun and M. Gómez Uranga (eds.), *Soberanía económica y globalización en Euskal Herria*. Bilbao: Fundación Manu Robles-Arangiz.

Börzel, T. A. (2000). "When Europe Hits Home: Europeanization and Domestic Change." *European Integration online Papers (EIoP)*, at file:///C:/Users/samsung/Downloads/SSRN-id302768.pdf, last accessed 2/10/2015.

Börzel, T. A. (2001). *Shaping States and Regions: The Domestic Impact of Europe*. Cambridge: Cambridge University Press.

Börzel, T. A. (2002). *States and Regions in the European Union: Institutional Adaptation in Germany and Spain*. Cambridge: Cambridge University Press.

Bourne, A. (2001). "Centre and Periphery in the European Union: The Domestic Politics of Basque Activism in Europe." ECPR Joint Workshops Sessions, Workshop No 4: Centre and Periphery, Grenoble, April.

Bourne, A. (2003). "European Integration and Conflict Resolution in the Basque Country, Northern Ireland and Cyprus." *Perspectives on European Politics and Society* 4(3): 392–415.

Boyd, C.P. (1979). *Praetorian Politics in Liberal Spain.* Chapel Hill: University of North Carolina Press.

Boyd, C. P. (1997). *Historia Patria: Politics, History, and National Identity in Spain, 1875–1975*. Princeton: Princeton University Press.

Boyer, R. (1979). *The Regulation School: A Critical Introduction.* New York: Columbia University Press.

Brenan, G. (1990). *The Spanish Labyrinth: An Account of the Social and Political Background of the Spanish Civil War.* Cambridge: Cambrige University Press.

Brenner, N. (1998). "Between Fixity and Motion: Accumulation, Territorial Organization and the Historical Geography of Spatial Scales." *Environment and Planning D: Society and Space* 16: 459–481.

Brenner, N. (1999). "Globalisation as Reterritorialisation: The Re-scaling of Urban Governance in the European Union." *Urban Studies* 36(3): 431–451.

Brenner, N. (2004). *New State Spaces: Urban Governance and the Rescaling of Statehood.* Oxford: Oxford University Press.

Brenner, N., Peck, J., and Theodore, N. (2010). "Variegated Neoliberalization: Geographies, Modalities, Pathways." *Global Networks* 10(2): 182–222.

Brenner, N., and Theodore, N. (ed.) (2002). *Spaces of Neoliberalism: Urban Restructuring in North America and Western Europe.* London: Blackwell Publishing.

Breuilly, J. (1993). *Nationalism and the State.* Manchester: Manchester University Press.

Broncano, C.P. (2003). "La constitución de 1978." *Anuario de la Facultad de Derecho* 21: 453–465.

Burdiel, I. (1998). "Myth of Failure, Myth of Success: New Perspectives on Nineteenth-century Spanish Liberalism." *The Journal of Modern History* 70(4): 892–912.

Cabrera, M., and Del Rey, F. (2007). *The Power of Entrepreneurs: Politics and Economy in Contemporary Spain*, trans. Robert Lavigna. New York and Oxford: Berghahn Books.

Callahan, W.J. (1984). *Church, Politics, and Society in Spain, 1750–1874*. Harvard: Harvard University Press.

Calzada, I. (2007). "Euskal Hiria: Construyendo la ciudad-red creativa vasca." Paper presented at the Creative Capital Summer School, 23–25 July.

Campos, J. (2006). "The End of an Era." In J.A. Gómez-Ibáñez and G. de Rus (eds.), *Competition in the Railway Industry: An International Comparative Analysis*. London: Edward Elgar Publishing.

Campos, J. (2008). "Recent Changes in the Spanish Rail Model: The Role of Competition." *Review of Network Economics* 7(1): 1–17.

Cantos, R., and Maudos, J. (2001). "Regulation and Efficiency: The Case of European Railways." *Research Part A: Policy and Practice* 35(5): 459–472.

Carballo, A. (1990). "Cinco documentos de la Comunidad Europea preparan la liberalización del tren europeo." *Vía Libre* 312 (January): 5–8.

Carr, R. (1980). *Modern Spain (1875–1980)*. Oxford: Oxford University Press.

Carr, R. (1982). *Spain, 1808–1975*. Oxford: Oxford University Press.

Carr, R., and Fusi Aizpurua, J.P. (1981). *Spain, Dictatorship to Democracy*. London and Boston: Allen & Unwin.

Casalls, X. (2007). "Monarquia y democracia: Qué ocurre con el rey?" Seminar, Aberdeen University. Unpublished material.

Chari, R. S. (1998). "Spanish Socialists, Privatising the Right Way?" *West European Politics* 21(4): 163–179.

Chari, R.S. (2004). "The 2004 Spanish Election: Terrorism as a Catalyst for Change?" *West European Politics* 27(5): 954–963.

Chari, R.S., and Heywood, P. (2009). "Analysing the Policy Process in Democratic Spain." *West European Politics* 32(1): 26–54.

Cilleruelo Carrasco, E. (2005). "I+D+i en la Comunidad Autónoma del País Vasco." *Revista de Investigación en Gestión de la Innovación y Tecnología* (online journal) 32 (October).

Clark, R. P. (1979). *The Basques: The Franco Years and Beyond*. Reno: University of Nevada Press.

Closa, C., and Heywood, P. (2004). *Spain and the European Union*. London: Palgrave Macmillan.

Cobanera, A. (2002). "Desindustrialización y regeneración económica del País Vasco. Acciones de reconversión del Gobierno Vasco y SPRI." In J.H. Zubizarreta (ed.), *Desindustrialización y regeneración socio-económica*. Bilbao: Euskal Herriko Unibertsitatea.

Colino, C. (2008). "The Spanish Model of Devolution and Regional Governance: Evolution, Motivations and Effects on Policy Making." *Politics & Society* 36(4): 573–586.

Colino, C. (2009). "Constitutional Change without Constitutional Reform: Spanish Federalism and the Revision of Catalonia's Statute of Autonomy." *Plubius: The Journal of Federalism* 39(2): 262–288.

Collinge, C. (2005). "The *Différance* between Society and Space: Nested Scales and the Returns of Spatial Fetishism." *Environment and Planning D: Society and Space* 23: 189–206.

Colomer, J.M. (1998). "The Spanish 'State of Autonomies': Non-institutional Federalism." *West European Politics* 21(4): 40–52.

Colomer, J. M. (1999). "The Spanish 'State of Autonomies': Non-institutional Federalism." In P. Heywood (ed.), *Politics and Policy in Democratic Spain*. London: Frank Cass Publishers.

Colomer, J.M. (2007). *Great Empires, Small Nations: The Uncertain Future of the Sovereign State*. New York and London: Routledge.

Comín, F. (2000). "Los mitos y los milagros de Suanzes: la empresa privada y el INI durante la autarquía." *Revista de Historia Industrial* 18: 221–245.

Conversi, D. (1990). "Language or Race? The Choice of Core Values in the Development of Catalan and Basque Nationalism." *Ethnic and Racial Studies* 13(1): 50–70.

Conversi, D. (2002). "The Smooth Transition: Spain's 1978 Constitution and the Nationalities Question." *National Identities* 4(3): 223–244.

Cooke, P. (2002). *Knowledge Economies: Clusters, Learning and Cooperative Advantage*. London and New York: Routledge.

Cooke, P., et al. (2004). *Regional Innovation Systems: The Role of Governance in a Globalised World*. London: Routledge.

Cooke, P., Uranga Gómez, M., and Etxebarria, G. (1997). "Regional Innovation Systems: Institutional and Organisational Dimensions." *Research Policy* 26(4): 475–491.

Cooke, P., Uranga Gómez, M., and Etxebarria, G. (1998). "Dimensiones de un sistema de innovación regional: organizaciones e instituciones." *Ekonomiaz* 41: 46–67.

Corcuera Atienza, J. (2004). *The Origins, Ideology, and Organization of Basque Nationalism, 1876–1903*, trans. Albert Bork and Cameron J. Watson. Reno: Center for Basque Studies, University of Nevada, Reno.

Cox, K., and Mair, A. (1991). "From Localised Social Structures to Localities as Agents." *Environment and Planning A* 23: 197–213.

Crespo, M., et al. (1981). *La economía vasca durante el franquismo*. Bilbao: La Gran Enciclopedia Vasca.

Crespo, T. (2008). "Una revitalización con plan: El Casco Viejo de Vitoria, la bahía de Pasaia, Bilbao La Vieja y Basauri-Arrigorriaga compiten con sus proyectos por los fondos Urban de la UE en el periodo 2007–2013." ElPais.com, 3 March.

Davoudi, S. (2002). "Polycentricity: What does it mean and how is it Interpreted in the ESDP?" Paper presented at the EURA conference, "Urban and Spatial European Policies: Levels of Territorial Government," Turin, 18–20 April.

Davoudi, S. (2006). "Polycentric Development and Metropolitan Governance." Paper presented at the Euskal Hiria Kongresua, 20–21 November, Bilbao.

de Rus, G., and Inglada, V. (1997). "Cost Benefit Analysis of the High-speed Train in Spain." *The Annals of Regional Science* 31(2): 175–188.

del Aguila, R., and Montoro, R. (1984). *El discurso político de la transición española*. Madrid: Centro de investigaciones Sociológicas (CIS).

Delaney, D., and Leitner, H. (1997). "The Political Construction of Scale." *Political Geography* 16(2): 93–97.

del Val, Y. (1993). "La CE creará el Fondo de Inversiones para la financiación de infraestructuras." *Vía Libre* 349 (February): 27.

del Val, Y. (1998). "Bruselas publica un documento en el que analiza la aplicación de directiva 91/440: La Comisión Europea propone que los ferrocarriles abran un 25% de sus redes a nuevos competidores." *Vía Libre* 411 (July–August): 4–8.

Desfor, L. (1998). *Symbol and Ritual in the New Spain: The Transition to Democracy after Franco*. Cambridge: Cambridge University Press.

Díaz Vázquez, R. (2001). *Inversión extranjera directa en España: Patrón de localización regional*. Departamento de Fundamentos del Análisis Económico e Historia e Instituciones Económicas. Vigo: Universidad de Vigo.

Díaz Vázquez, R. (2004). "La inversión extranjera directa en Madrid." *Revista de Estudios Regionales* 71: 59–84.

Díez Medrano, J. (1995). *Divided Nations: Class, Politics, and Nationalism in the Basque Country and Catalonia*. Ithaca: Cornell University Press.

Díez, M., and García Artetxe, I. (1990). "La Política tecnológica vasca en la década de los ochenta." *Ekonomiaz* 19: 140–153.

Dillon, M., and Reid, J. (2000). "Global Governance, Liberal Peace, and Complex Emergency." *Alternatives-Social Transformation and Humane Governance* 25(1): 117–143.

Diputación Foral de Gipuzkoa (2000). *El libro blanco de la Eurociudad Vasca*. San Sebastián: Diputación Foral de Gipuzkoa.

Doherty, A., and Hoedeman, O. (1994). "Misshaping Europe: The European Round Table of Industrialists." *The Ecologist* 24: 135–141.

Dunford, M., and Kafkalas, G. (eds.) (1992). *Cities and Regions in the New Europe: The Global-Local Interplay and Spatial Development Strategies*. London: Belhaven Press.

Elguea, B. (2006). "Álava inaugura la mayor plataforma logística de transporte del País Vasco." Diariovasco.com, 26 January.

Elliot, J.H. (1989). *Spain and its Worlds 1500–1700*. New Haven and London: Yale University Press.

Elliot, J.H. (1992). "A Europe of Composite Monarchies." *Past and Present* 137: 48–71.

Encarnación, O. G. (1997). "Social Concertation in Democratic and Market Transitions: Comparative Lessons from Spain." *Comparative Political Studies* 30(4), 387–419.

ERT (European Roundtable of Industrialists) (1984). *Missing Links: Upgrading Europe's Transborder Ground Transport Infrastructure*. Brussels: ERT.

Escribano Collado, P. (1985). "La Constitución Española." *Revista Española de Derecho Constitucional* 5(15): 271–274.

Esdaile, C. (2000). *Spain in the Liberal Age: From Constitution to Civil Wars*. Oxford: Blackwell.

Eskisabel, S. (1990). "Euskal Herriko burdinbideetako," at http://zientzia.eus/artikuluak/euskal-herriko-burdinbideetako/, last accessed 2/10/2015.

Esping-Andersen, G. (1990). *The Three Worlds of Welfare Capitalism*. Cambridge: Polity Press.

Esteban, M., Rodríguez, A., Moreno, J., Altuzarra, A., and Larrañaga, J. (2009). "La evaluación de la Política Regional Europea. Análisis empírico de las metodologías aplicadas." *Investigaciones regionales* 14: 157–184.

Etxebarria Kerexeta, G., and Franco Ibarzabal, H. (2000). "Euskal Herriko errepide Sarea." *Euskonews & Media* (online journal) 80, 26 May–2 June.

Etxebarria Kerexeta, G., and Franco Ibarzabal, H. (2003). "Reflections on Urban Revitalisation Strategies in Old Industrial Regions: The Case of Bilbao." Paper presented at the Special Session "Economic Development in European Cities," European Association for Evolutionary Political Economy 2003 Annual Conference, Maastricht, the Netherlands, 7–10 November.

Etxezarreta, M. (1991). *La restructuración del capitalismo en España, 1970–1990*. Barcelona: ICARIA.

European Commission (1993). *Growth, Competitiveness, Employment: The Challenges and Ways Forward into the 21st Century*. Luxembourg: Office for Official Publications of the European Communities; Brussels: European Commission.

European Commission (1997). *High-level Group on Public-private Partnership Financing of Trans-European Transport Network Projects*. VII/321/97 EN, May 1997. Brussels: European Commission.

European Commission (2001). *EU White Book on Transport*. Brussels: European Commission.

European Council (1994a). *European Council in Corfu: Presidency Conclusions*. Brussels: European Council.

European Council (1994b). *European Council in Essen: Presidency Conclusions*. Brussels: European Council.

European Council (1995). *Trans-European Networks: Report. Group of Personal Representatives of the Heads of State or Government*. Luxembourg: Office for Official Publications of the European Communities.

Fernández Duran, R. (2007). "ETA legitima al estado policial y refuerza a 'España' y al capital," at http://www.rebelion.org/noticia.php?id=52632, last accessed 2/10/2015.

Fernández Duran, R. (1999). "Movilidad motorizada, globalización económica y proyecto europeo: Un análisis crítico de las Políticas de transporte de la UE." *Inguruak* 24: 23-36.

Ferreiro, J., Rodríguez, C., and Serrano, F. (1997). "The Role of Foreign Direct Investment in an Old Industrial Region: The Case of the Basque Country and Japanese FDI." *European Planning Studies* 5(5): 637–657.

Ferreiro, J., and Serrano, F. (2001). "La tercera vía Española: entre el liberalismo de los ochenta y la socialdemocracia clásica." *Problemas del Desarrollo* 32(125): 161–199.

Fishman, R. M. (1982). "The Labor Movement in Spain: From Authoritarianism to Democracy." *Comparative Politics* 14(3): 281–305.

Fishman, R. M. (1990). "Rethinking State and Regime: Southern Europe's Transition to Democracy." *World Politics*, 42(03): 422–440.

Font, J., Gutierrez, R., and Parrado-Diez, S. (1999). *Intergovernmental Partnerships at the Local Level in Spain: Mancomunidades and Consortia in a Comparative Perspective*. Paris: OECD.

Foweraker, J. (1987). "Corporatist Strategies and the Transition to Democracy in Spain." *Comparative Politics* 20(1): 57–72.

Fraile, P., and Escribano, A. (1998). "The Spanish 1898 Disaster: The Drift towards National-protectionism." *Revista de Historia Económica* 16(01): 265–290.

Franco Ibarzabal, H. (2004). *Garraio-azpiegiturako politikak eta lurralde-eredua. Euskal Herriko kasurako aplikazioa*. Ekonomia Aplikatuaren Saila 1. Bilbao: Euskal Herriko Unibertsitatea.

Fraser, R. (1976). "Spain on the Brink." *New Left Review* I/96 (March–April): 3–33.

Galfarsoro, I. (2001). "Nazioa eta narrazioa kulturala global berrian: Euskal identitate modernoaren eraikuntza eta Ezker Abertzalearen politika lokala." *Adierazpen Diasporikoak*, at http://ibs.lgu.ac.uk/forum/MNANA.html, last accessed 30/05/2003.

García Álvarez, J. (2002). *Provincias, regiones y comunidades autónomas. La formación del mapa político de España*. Madrid: Temas del Senado.

García de Enterría, E. (1972). *La administración española de ciencia administrativa.* Madrid: Alianza.

García de Enterría, E. (1976). "Los aspectos básicos de la cuestión regional en España." *El País,* 24 September.

García Delgado, J. L. (1986). "Estancamiento industrial e intervencionismo económico durante el primer franquismo." In J. Fontana (ed.), *España bajo el franquismo.* Barcelona: Critica.

García Delgado, J.L., et al. (2005). *Lecciones de economía española.* Madrid: Civitas.

Gatti, G., Irazusta, I., and Martinez Albeniz, I. (2005). *Basque Society: Structures, Institutions, and Contemporary Life.* Reno: Center for Basque Studies, University of Nevada, Reno.

Gellner, E. (1983). *Nations and Nationalism.* Oxford: Blackwell.

Gellner, E., et al. (1986). *Patronos y clientes: en las sociedades mediterráneas,* trans. Jesús Manuel Fernández. Madrid: Ediciones Júcar.

Geradin, D. (2002). *The Liberalization of Postal Services in the European Union.* The Hague: Kluwer Law International.

Gereffi, G., and Memerevic, O. (2003). *The Global Apparel Value Chain: What Prospects for Upgrading by Developing Countries.* Sectoral Studies Series. Vienna: United Nations Industrial Development Organization.

Gibson, M. (2005). "Is it Bye-Bye, Bilbao, and Hello, Bottom Line?" *The Wall Street Journal Europe,* June 3.

Giddens, A. (1985). *A Contemporary Critique of Historical Materialism,* vol. 2: *Nation and Violence.* Cambridge: Polity Press.

Gill, S. (1998). "European Governance and New Constitutionalism: Economic and Monetary Union and Alternatives to Disciplinary Neoliberalism in Europe." *New Political Economy* 31(1): 5–26.

Giner, S. (1982). "Political Economy, Legitimation and the State in Southern Europe." *The British Journal of Sociology* 33(2): 172–199.

Giner, S., and Sevilla, E. (1984). "Spain: From corporatism to corporatism'." In A. Williams (ed.), *Southern Europe Transformed.* London. Harper & Row.

Giordano, B., and Roller, E. (2001)."Catalonia and the 'Idea of Europe': Competing Strategies and Discourses within Catalan party politics." *European Urban and Regional Studies* 9 (2): 99–113.

Giordano, B., and Roller, E. (2004). "'Té para todos?' A Comparison of the Processes of Devolution in Spain and the UK." *Environment and Planning A* 36: 2163–2181.

Givoni, M. (2006). "Development and Impact of the Modern High-speed Train: A Review." *Transport Reviews* 26(5): 593–611.

Gobierno Vasco (1988). *Plan económico a medio plazo 1989–1992*. Vitoria-Gasteiz: Servicio Central de Publicaciones del Gobierno Vasco.

Gobierno Vasco (1989). *Plan Programa Europa 93*. Vitoria-Gasteiz: Servicio Central de Publicationes del Gobierno Vasco.

Gobierno Vasco (1994). *Plan económico a medio plazo 1994–1997*. Vitoria-Gasteiz: Servicio Central de Publicaciones del Gobierno Vasco.

Gobierno Vasco (1997). *Avance del plan territorial sectorial de la red ferroviaria*. Vitoria-Gasteiz: Servicio Central de Publicaciones del Gobierno Vasco.

Gobierno Vasco (2002). *Euskal hiria*. Vitoria-Gasteiz: Servicio Central de Publicaciones del Gobierno Vasco.

Gobierno Vasco and Diputación Foral de Gipuzkoa (2002). *Plan territorial parcial Donostia-San Sebastian, avance*. N.p: Diputación Foral de Gipuzkoa, Departamento de Obras Hidráulicas y Urbanismo; Gobierno Vasco, Departamento de Ordenación del Territorio y Medio Ambiente.

Gobierno Vasco and Diputaciones Forales (1996). *Euskadi XXI: Plan interinstitucional de infraestructuras y revitalización de áreas desfavorecidas*. Vitoria-Gasteiz: Presidencia del Gobierno Vasco.

Goikoetxea Martínez, A. (2007). *Euskal Herria estado-nación en el Siglo 21: Una nueva arquitectura socio-Política*. Arrasate-Mondragón: Euskal Herria Siglo 21.

Gómez-Ibáñez, J. A., and de Rus, G. (eds.) (2006). *Competition in the Railway Industry: An International Comparative Analysis*. London: Edward Elgar Publishing.

Gómez Uranga, M. (1991). "La internacionalización de la industria española: un proceso acelerado." In M. Etxezarreta (ed.), *La reestructuración del capitalismo en España, 1970–1990*. Barcelona: ICARIA.

Gómez Uranga, M. (2003). *Basque Economy: From Industrialization to Globalization*, trans. Ana Olabe. Reno: Center for Basque Studies, University of Nevada, Reno.

Gómez Uranga, M., and Etxebarria, G. (1993). "Networks and Spatial Dynamics: The Case of the Basque Country." *European Planning Studies* 1(3): 299–318.

Gómez Uranga, M., and Etxebarria, G. (2000). "Panorama of the Basque Country and its Competence for Self-government." *European Planning Studies* 8(4): 521–536.

Gómez Uranga, M., Franco Ibarzabal, H., and Etxebarria, G. (1998). "Las redes de Infraestructura y el desarrollo regional." In A.G. Arizkun and M. Uranga Gómez (eds.), *Soberanía económica y globalización en Euskal Herria*. Bilbao: Manu Robles-Arangiz Institutoa.

González, S. (2003). "La Política de escalas en Bilbao: La construcción socio-Política de un área metropolitana." PhD thesis, Universidad del País Vasco-Euskal Herriko Unibertsitatea.

González, S. (2006). "Scalar Narratives in Bilbao: A Cultural Politics of Scales Approach to the Study of Urban Policy." *International Journal of Urban and Regional Research*, 30(4): 836–857.

Graham, H. (1999). "'Against the State': A Genealogy of the Barcelona May Days (1937)." *European History Quarterly* 29(4): 485–542.

Graham, H. (2004). "The Spanish Civil War, 1936–2003: The Return of Republican Memory." *Science & Society* 68(3): 313–328.

Graiño, S. (1988). "Julián García Valverde frente a los periodistas: Salto cualitativo en el tipo de tren y empresa." *Vía Libre* 298 (November): 17.

Granell, F. (2001). "Europe's Evolving Economic Identity: Spain's Role." In R. Gillespie, *Spain: The European and International Challenges*. London: Frank Cass.

Grugel, J., and Rees, T. (1997). *Franco's Spain*. London: Arnold.

Guillen, M.F. (2001). *The Limits of Convergence: Globalization and Organizational Change in Argentina, South Korea, and Spain*. Princeton: Princeton University Press.

Gunther, R. (1992). "Spain: The Very Model of the Modern Elite Settlement." In J. Higley and R. Gunther (eds.), *Elites and Democratic Consolidation in Latin America and Southern Europe*. Cambridge: Cambridge University Press.

Gutiérrez, J., González, R., and Gómez, G. (1996). "The European High-speed Train Network: Predicted Effects on Accessibility Patterns." *Journal of Transport Geography* 4(4): 227–238.

Gutiérrez, J., Monzón, A.J., and Piñero, J.M. (1998). "Accessibility, Network Efficiency, and Transport Infrastructure Planning." *Environment and Planning A* 30(8): 1337–1350.

Harman, C. (1988). *The Fire Last Time: 1968 and After*. London: Bookmarks.

Harriague, X. (2008). "Inazio Uriaren hilketa AHTrekin lotua baldin bada, erran nahiko luke ETAk Lemoizko zentral nuklearrelpaisean eta Leitzarango autobidean erabilitako estrategiari ekin diola." Berria.info, at http://www.berria.info/papera_inprimatu.php?htmla=BERRIA/y2008/m12/d20081209/p00010005.html, last accessed 9/12/2008.

Harrison, J. (1974). "Catalan Business and the Loss of Cuba, 1898–1914." *The Economic History Review* 27(3): 431–441.

Harrison, J. (1976). "Big Business and the Failure of Right-wing Catalan Nationalism, 1901–1923." *The Historical Journal* 19(4): 901–918.

Harrison, J. (1978). *An Economic History of Modern Spain*. Manchester: Manchester University Press.

Harrison, J. (1983). "Heavy Industry, the State, and Economic Development in the Basque Region, 1876–1936." *The Economic History Review* 36(4): 535–551.

Harrison, J. (1995). *The Spanish Economy: From the Civil War to the European Community*. Cambridge: Cambridge University Press.

Harrison, J. (2006). "Economic Crisis and Democratic Consolidation in Spain, 1973–82." *Working Papers in Economic History*. Universidad Carlos III de Madrid.

Harvey, D. (1982). *The Limits of Capital*. New York: Verso.

Harvey, D. (1989). *The Urban Experience*. Oxford: Blackwell.

Harvey, D. (2003). *A Brief History of Neoliberalism*. Oxford: Oxford University Press.

Harvey, D. (2006). *Spaces of Global Capitalism*. New York: Verso.

Heiberg, M. (1989). *The Making of the Basque Nation*. Cambridge: Cambridge University Press.

Held, D. (1988). "Farewell Nation State." *Marxism Today* (December): 12–17.

Herranz-Locán, A. (2005). "The Regional Distribution of Spanish Transport Infrastructure (1860–1930)." Paper presented at the VIII Congreso De la Asociación Española de Historia Económica, Santiago de Compostela, Coruña and Vigo, 13–16 September.

Herranz-Locán, A. (2006). "Railroad Impact in Backward Economies: Spain, 1850–1913." *The Journal of Economic History* 66(04): 853–881.

Heywood, P. (1995). *The Government and Politics of Spain*. London: Macmillan Press.

Heywood, P. (1998). "Power Diffusion or Concentration? In Search of the Spanish Policy Process." *West European Politics* 21(4): 103–123.

Hirst, P. (1997). "The Global Economy-Myths and Realities." *International Affairs* 73(3): 409–425.

Hirst, P., and Thompson, G. (1996). *Globalisation in Question: The International Economy and the Possibilities of Governance*. Cambridge: Polity Press.

Hobsbawm, E. (1990). *Nations and Nationalism since 1780*. Cambridge: Cambridge University Press.

Hobsbawm, E. (1996). "Ethnicity and Nationalism in Europe today." In G Balakrishnan (ed.), *Mapping the Nation*. London and New York: Verso.

Holl, A. (2007). "Twenty Years of Accessibility Improvements: The Case of the Spanish Motorway Building Programme." *Journal of Transport Geography* 15: 286–297.

Holman, O. (1989). "In Search of Hegemony: Socialist Government and the Internationalization of Domestic Politics in Spain." *International Journal of Political Economy* 19(3): 76–101.

Holman, O. (1996). *Integrating Southern Europe: EC Expansion and the Transnationalisation of Spain*. New York: Routledge.

Holman, O. (2004). "Integrating Peripheral Europe: The Different Roads to 'Security and Stability' in Southern and Central Europe." *Journal of International Relations and Development* 7(2): 208–236.

Houtum, H., and Lagendijk, A. (2001). "Contextualising Regional Identity and Imagination in the Construction of Polycentric Urban Regions: The Cases of the Ruhr Area and the Basque Country." *Urban Studies* 38(4): 747–767.

Ibarretxe, J.J. (2002). "Ibarretxe ante el Parlamento Vasco: 'Pacto para la convivencia'." El Mundo.es, at http://www.el-mundo.es/documentos/2002/09/espana/ibarretxe.html.

Irigoin, A., and Grafe, R. (2008). "Bargaining for Absolutism: A Spanish Path to Nation-state and Empire Building." *Hispanic American Historical Review* 88(2): 173–209.

Jáuregui, G., Castells, J.M., and Iriondo, X. (1997). *La institucionalización jurídica y política de Vasconia*. Zarautz: Eusko Ikaskuntza.

Jensen, A., and Richardson, T. (2007). "New Region, New Story: Imagining Mobile Subjects in Transnational Space." *Space and Polity* 11(2): 137–150.

Jensen, G. (2000). "Military Nationalism and the State: The Case of Fin-de-siècle Spain." *Nations and Nationalism* 6(2): 257–274.

Jenson, J. (1991). "All the World's a Stage: Ideas, Spaces and Times in Canadian Political Economy." *Studies in Political Economy* 36: 43–72.

Jessop, B. (1990). *State Theory: Putting the Capitalist State in its Place*. Oxford: Blackwell.

Jessop, B. (1992). "Fordism and Post Fordism: A Critical Reformulation." In A. J. Scott and M. Storper (eds.), *Pathways to Industrialisation and Regional Development*. London: Routledge.

Jessop, B. (1993). "Towards a Schumpeterian Workfare State? Preliminary Remarks on Post-Fordist Political Economy." *Studies in Political Economy* 40: 7–40.

Jessop, B. (1994). "Post-Fordism and the State." In A. Amin (ed.), *Post-Fordism: A Reader*. Oxford: Blackwell.

Jessop, B. (1995). "Towards a Schumpeterian Workfare Regime in Britain? Reflections on Regulation, Governance, and the Welfare State." *Environment and Planning A* 27: 1613–1626.

Jessop, B. (1997). "Capitalism and its Future: Remarks on Regulation, Government and Governance." *Review of International Political Economy* 4(3): 561–581.

Jessop, B. (1999). *Crisis del Estado de bienestar. Hacia una nueva teoría del estado y sus consecuencias sociales*, prol. J.I. Bula, trans. A. Supelano Sarmiento. Santa Fe de Bogotá, Colombia: Siglo del Hombre.

Jessop, B. (2000). "The Crisis of the National Spatio-temporal Fix and the Tendential Ecological Dominance of Globalizing Capitalism." *International Journal of Urban and Regional Research* 24(2): 323–360.

Jessop, B. (2001). "On the Spatio-temporal Logics of Capital's Globalisation and their Manifold Implications for State Power." Working

Paper, Dept. of Sociology, Lancaster University, at http://www.comp.lancs.ac.uk/sociology/soc072rj.html.

Jessop, B. (2002a). *The Future of the Capitalist State.* Cambridge: Polity Press.

Jessop, B. (2002b). "Liberalism, Neoliberalism, and Urban Governance: A State-theoretical Perspective." *Antipode* 34(3), 452–472.

Jessop, B. (2004). "Multi-level Governance and Multi-level Metagovernance." In I. Bache and M. Flinders (eds.), *Multi-level Governance.* Oxford: Oxford University Press.

Jessop, B. (2008). *State Power.* Cambridge: Polity Press.

Jessop, B. (2010). "The 'Return' of the National State in the Current Crisis of the World Market." *Capital & Calss*, 34(1): 38–41.

Jessop, B., and Sum, N.L. (2000). "An Entrepreneurial City in Action: Hong Kong's Emerging Strategies in and for (Inter)Urban Competition." *Urban Studies* 37(12): 2287–2313.

Jonas, A. (1994). "The Scale Politics of Spatiality." *Environment and Planning D: Society and Space* 12: 257–264.

Jones, M. (1997). "Spatial Selectivity of the State? The Regulationist Enigma and Local Struggles over Economic Governance." *Environment and Planning A* 29: 831–864.

Jones, M. (1998). "Restructuring the Local State: Economic Governance or Social Regulation?" *Political Geography* 17(8): 959–988.

Jones, M. (2001). "The Rise of the Regional State in Economic Governance: 'Partnerships for Prosperity' or New Scales of State Power?" *Environmental and Planning A* 33: 1185–1211.

Keating, M. (1996). *Naciones Contra el Estado: el nacionalismo de Cataluña, Quebec y Escocia*, trans. Jordi Beltrán. Barcelona: Arial.

Keating, M. (1998). *The New Regionalism in Western Europe: Territorial Restructuring and Political Change.* Cheltenham: Edward Elgar.

Keating, M. (2001). *Plurinational Democracy: Stateless Nations in a Post-sovereignty World.* Oxford: Oxford University Press.

Keating, M. (2003). "Plurinational Democracy and the European Order." Jornadas de Estudio Sobre la Propuesta del Lehendakari, UPV-EHU/IVAP, Donostia-San Sebastián, 4–7 February.

Keating, M., and Bray, Z. (2006). "Renegotiating Sovereignty: Basque Nationalism and the Rise and Fall of the Ibarretxe Plan." *Ethnopolitics* 5(4), 347–364.

Keating, M., and Wilson, A. (2009). "Renegotiating the State of Autonomies: Statute Reform and Multi-level Politics." *West European Politics* 32(3): 536–558.

Keyder, C. (1985). "The American Recovery of Southern Europe: Aid and Hegemony." In G. Arrighi (ed.), *Semiperipheral Development: The Politics of Southern Europe in the Twentieth Century*. London: Sage.

Koch, M. (2005). "Wage Determination, Socio-economic Regulation and the State." *European Journal of Industrial Relations* 11(3): 327–346.

Kok, W., et al. (2004). *Facing the Challenge: The Lisbon Strategy for Growth and Employment*. Luxembourg: Office for Official Publications of the European Communities.

Kumar, K. (1995). *From Post-industrial to Post-modern Society: New Theories of the Contemporary World*. Oxford: Blackwell.

Lamikiz, A. (2002). "Ambiguous 'Culture': Contrasting Interpretations of the Basque film *Ama Lur* and the Relationship between Centre and Periphery in Franco's Spain." *National Identities* 4(3): 291–306.

Le Galès, P., and Lequesne, C. (eds.) (1998). *Regions in Europe*. London: Routledge.

Letamendia, F. (1994). *Historia del Nacionalismo Vasco y ETA*, vol. 1: *ETA en el Franquismo (1951–1976)*. San Sebastian: R&B.

Letamendia, F. (2013). *Dos ensayos vascos: fin de ETA y resolución del conflicto: respuestas a la crisis*. Madrid: Fundamentos.

Letona, X., and Eizagirre, E. (2005). "Euskal Y-a, 194 kilometroko trenbide faraonikoa." *Argia* (online journal) 1987, at http://www.argia.eus/argia-astekaria/1987/euskal-y-a-194-kilometroko-trenbide-faraonikoa, last accessed 17/06/05.

Levi-Faur, D. (2003). "New Regimes, New Capacities: The Politics of Telecommunication Nationalisation and Liberalisation." In L. Weiss (ed.), *States in the Global Economy: Bringing the Domestic Institutions Back In*. Cambridge: Cambridge University Press.

Lieberman, S. (1995). *Growth and Crisis in the Spanish Economy 1940–93*. New York and London: Routledge.

Linz, J.J. (1996). "Hacia la consolidación democrática." *La Política: Revista de estudios sobre el estado y la sociedad* 2: 29–50.

Linz, J.J., and Stepan, A. (1996). *Problems of Democratic Transition and Consolidation: Southern Europe, South America, and Post-communist Europe*. Baltimore and London: Johns Hopkins University Press.

Lipietz, A. (1982). "Towards Global Fordism." *New Left Review* 132(2): 33–47.

Lipietz, A. (1987). *Mirages and Miracles: The Crisis of Global Fordism.* London: Verso.

Llera, F., Mata, J., and Irvin, C. (1993). "ETA: From Secret Army to Social Movement: The Post-Franco Schism of the Basque Nationalist Movement." *Terrorism and Political Violence* 5(3): 106–134.

Logan, J. R., and Molotch, H. L. (2007). *Urban Fortunes: The Political Economy of Place.* California: University of California Press.

López III, F. (1990). "Bourgeois State and the Rise of Social Democracy." In R.H. Chilcote et al. (eds.), *Transitions from Dictatorship to Democracy.* New York and London: Crane Russak.

López, I., and Rodríguez, E. (2010). *Fin de ciclo. Financiarización, territorio y sociedad de propietarios en la onda larga del capitalismo hispano (1959–2010).* Madrid: Traficantes de Sueños.

López Novo, J. (1995). "Empresarios y relaciones laborales: una perspectiva histórica." In F. Miguélez and C. Prieto (eds.), *Las relaciones laborales en España.* Madrid: Siglo Veintiuno de España Editores.

Lovering, J. (1999). "Theory Led by Policy? The Inadequacies of the 'New Regionalism' in Economic Geography Illustrated from the case of Wales." *International Journal of Urban and Regional Research* 23(2): 530–554.

Lovering, J. (2001). "The Coming Regional Crisis (and how to avoid it)." *Regional Studies* 35(4): 349–356.

Lozano, P. (1992). "José Borrell, Ministro de Obras Públicas y Transportes: 'Para 1993 la prioridad es el Madrid-Barcelona'." *Vía Libre* 339 (April): 10–11.

Lozano, P. (1993). "José Borrell, Ministro de Obras Públicas y Transportes: 'Desde hace un año disfrutamos de una oferta ferroviaria propia del siglo XXI'." *Vía Libre* 352 (May): 7–9.

MacLeod, G. (2001). "New Regionalism Reconsidered: Globalization and the Remaking of Political Economic Space." *International Journal of Urban and Regional Research* 25(4): 804–829.

MacLeod, G., and Goodwin, M. (1999). "Reconstructing an Urban and Regional Political Economy: On the State, Politics, Scale, and Explanation." *Political Geography* 18: 697–730.

Maíz, R., Caamaño, F., and Azpitarte, M. (2010). "The Hidden Counterpoint of Spanish Federalism: Recentralization and Resymmetrization in Spain (1978–2008)." *Regional and Federal Studies* 20(1): 63–82.

Malefakis, E. (1970). *Agrarian Reform and the Peasant Revolution in Spain: Origins of the Civil War*. New Haven: Yale University Press.

Mangen, S. (2001). *Spanish Society after Franco: Regime Transition and the Welfare State*. Basingstoke: Palgrave.

Maravall, J.M. (1982). *The Transition to Democracy in Spain*. Spain: Croom Helm.

Martin, B. (1990). *The Agony of Modernization: Labor and Industrialization in Spain*. Ithaca: ILR Press.

Martín Urriza, C. (1996). "Breve historia de las privatizaciones en España." *Cuadernos de Relaciones Laborales* 8: 131–145.

Martínez Alier, R., and Roca, J. (1987). "Spain after Franco: From Corporatist Ideology to Corporatist Reality?" *International Journal of Political Economy* 17(4): 56–87.

Martínez-Herrera, E. (2002). "Nationalist Extremism and Outcomes of State Policies in the Basque Country, 1979–2001." *International Journal on Multicultural Societies* 4(1): 16–40.

Martínez Lucio, M. (1995). "Interpreting Change: Debates in Spanish Industrial Relations." *European Journal of Industrial Relations* 1(3): 369–383.

Massey, D. (1984). *Spatial Divisions of Labour: Social Structures and the Geography of Production*. London: Macmillan.

Mayer, M. (1994). "Post-Fordist City Politics." In A. Amin (ed.), *Post-Fordism: A Reader*. Cambridge: Blackwell.

McVeigh, P. (1999). "Is Spain Still Different? From Franquismo to Neoliberalism in Democratic Spain." ECPR Workshop no. 26, "National Models and Transnational Structures: Globalisation and Public Policy," University of Mannheim, Mannheim, 26–31 March.

Medrano, J.D. (1994). "Patterns of Development and Nationalism: Basque and Catalan Nationalism before the Spanish Civil War." *Theory and Society* 23(4): 541–569.

Medrano, J.D. (1995). *Divided Nations: Class, Politics, and Nationalism in the Basque Country and Catalonia*. Ithaca: Cornell University Press.

Mees, L., et al. (2001). *El péndulo patriótico. Historia del Partido Nacionalista Vasco, II: 1936–1979*. Barcelona: Crítica.

Meijers, E., and Romein, A. (2003). "Realizing Potential: Building Regional Organizing Capacity in Polycentric Urban Regions." *European Urban and Regional Studies* 10(2): 173–186.

Ministerio de Fomento (2006). *PEIT: Strategic Infrastructures and Transport Plan 2005–2020*. Madrid: Ministerio de Fomento.

Ministerio de Hacienda (2001). *Programa Iniciativa Comunitaria URBAN. San Sebastián - Pasajes 2001-2006.* Madrid: Miniesterio de Hacienda.

Molero, J. (2001). "Industrialisation and Internationalisation in the Spanish Economy." Instituto Complutense de Estudios Internacionales, Working Paper 28.

Montero, M. (2005). *La California del Hierro. Las minas y la modernización económica y social de Vizcaya*. Bilbao: Beta III Milenio.

MOPT (Ministerio de Obras Públicas y Transporte) (1994). *Plan director de infraestructuras 1993–2007*. Madrid: MOPT.

Moreno, L. (2001). *The Federalization of Spain*. London and Portland, OR: Frank Cass.

Moreno, L., and Sarasa, S. (1992). "Génesis y desarrollo del Estado del bienestar en España." Instituto de Estudios Sociales Avanzados, *Documentos de trabajo*: 92-13.

Morgan, K. (1997). "The Learning Region: Institutions, Innovation and Regional Renewal." *Regional Studies* 31(5): 491–503.

Morgan, K. (2004). "Sustainable Regions: Governance, Innovation and Scale." *European Planning Studies* 12(6): 871–889.

Moso, M., and Olazaran, M. (2002). "Regional Technology Policy and the Emergence of an R&D System in the Basque Country." *Journal of Technology Transfer* 27(1): 61–75.

Moulaert, F., Swyngedouw, E., and Wilson, P. (1988). "Spatial Responses to Fordist and Post-Fordist Accumulation and Regulation." *Papers of the Regional Science Association* 64(1): 11–23.

Muñoz, A. (1999). "Redefining Euskadi as an Autonomous Community and Participant in the Construction of Europe." In W.A. Douglass et al. (eds.), *Basque Politics and Nationalism on the Eve of the Millenium*. Reno: Basque Studies Program.

Muñoz Rubio, M. (1991). "50 años de Renfe." *Vía Libre* 324 (January).

Muro, Q., and Quiroga, R. (2004). "Building the Spanish Nation: The Centre-Periphery Dialectic." *Studies in Ethnicity and Nationalism* 4(2): 18–37.

Murphy, B. (1999). "European Integration and Liberalization: Political Change and Economic Policy Continuity in Spain." *Mediterranean Politics* 4(1): 53–78.

Nadal, J. (1975). *El fracaso de la Revolución industrial en España, 1814–1913*. Barcelona: Ariel.

Nairn, T. (1974). "Scotland and Europe." *New Left Review* I/84: 57–82.

Navarro, M. (1989). "Política de reconversión industrial en España." *Información Comercial Española*, January: 45–69.

Navarro, M. (1990). *La Política de reconversión: balance crítico*. Madrid: Eudema Actualidad.

Navarro, M. (1992). "Actividades empresariales de I+D y Política tecnológica del Gobierno Vasco." *Ekonomiaz* 23: 118–159.

Navarro, V. (1997). "The Decline of Social Democracy: The Spanish Experience 1982–96." *Socialist Register* (online journal) 33.

Navarro Arancegui, M. (1994). *La crisis de la industria manufacturera en la CAPV*. Bilbao: Manu Robles Arangiz Institutoa.

Novo López, P. (2005). "Luces y sombras de una red ferroviaria en el País Vasco." In M. Muñuz Rubio (ed.), *Historia de los ferrocarriles de vía estrecha en España*. Spain: Fundación de los Ferrocarriles Españoles.

Núñez Seixas, X.M. (2001). "The Region as Essence of the Fatherland: Regionalist Variants of Spanish Nationalism (1840–1936)." *European History Quarterly* 31(4): 483–518.

Núñez Seixas, X.M. (2005) "From National-Catholic Nostalgia to Constitutional Patriotism: Conservative Spanish Nationalism since the early 1990s." In S. Balfour (ed.) *The Politics of Contemporary Spain*. London: Routledge.

Obermauer, A. (2001). "National Railway Reform in Japan and the EU: Evaluation of Institutional Change." *Japan Relway and Transport Review* 29: 14–31.

O'Connor, J. (2001). *The Fiscal Crisis of the State*. New Brunswick, NJ: Transaction.

O'Donnell, G., Schmitter, P. C., and Whitehead, L. (eds.). (1986). *Transitions from Authoritarian Rule: Southern Europe*. Baltimore: John Hopkins University.

OECD (Organisation for Economic Co-operation and Development) (1996). *Networks of Enterprises and Local Development: Competing and Co-operating in Local Productive Systems.* Paris: OECD.

Olaizola, J. (2006). "La nueva red ferroviaria, una deuda histórica." *Euskonews & Media* (online journal) 371, 24 November–1 December.

Ordóñez, J.L. (1993a). "Francisco Fernandez Lafuente, Director General de Intermodal del Transporte en las Grandes Ciudades: 'Bilbao-Ría 2000 no tiene límites en los proyectos de transporte'." *Vía Libre* 350 (March): 43–44.

Ordóñez, J.L. (1993b). "Josu Ortuondo Larrea, Alcalde de Bilbao: 'Abandoibarra será el corazón económico del futuro Bilbao'." *Vía Libre* 350 (March): 46.

Ordóñez, J.L. (1993c). "Un plan diseñado en la búsqueda del reequilibrio territorial y medioambiental." *Vía Libre* 352 (May): 10–11.

Ordóñez, J.L. (1993d). "El PDI es un documento para el debate social sobre infraestructuras." *Vía Libre* 352 (May): 18.

Paasi, A. (2001). "Europe as a Social Process and Discourse: Considerations of Place, Boundaries and Identity." *European Urban and Regional Studies* 8: 7–28.

Paasi, A. (2002). "Place and Region: Regional Worlds and Words." *Progress in Human Geography* 26(6): 802–811.

Pastor, A. (1992). "Estrategias de Política industrial." In E. Albi Ibañez (ed.), *Europa y la competitividad de la economía española.* Barcelona: Ariel.

Payne, S. (1971). "Catalan and Basque Nationalism." *Journal of Contemporary History* 6(1): 15–51.

Payne, S. (1984). *Spanish Catholicism: A Historical Overview.* Wisconsin: University of Wisconsin Press.

Peck, J., and Tickell, A. (1992). "Local Modes of Social Regulation? Regulation Theory, Thatcherism and Uneven Development." *Geoforum* 23(3): 347–363.

Peck, J., and Tickell, A. (1994). "Searching for a New Institutional Fix: The After-Fordist Crisis and Global-Local Disorder." In A. Amin (ed.), *Post-Fordism: A Reader.* Cambridge: Blackwell.

Peck, J., and Tickell, A. (1995). "The Social Regulation of Uneven Development: 'Regulatory Deficit', England's South East, and the Collapse of Thatcherism." *Environment and Planning A* 27: 15–40.

Peck, J., and Tickell, A. (2002). "Neoliberalizing Space." In N. Brenner and N. Theodore (eds.), *Spaces of Neoliberalism.* Oxford: Blackwell.

Pérez Díaz, V. (1993). *The Return of Civil Society: The Emergence of Democratic Spain.* Harvard: Harvard University Press.

Perkmann, M., and Sum, N. (eds.) (2002). *Globalization, Regionalization and Cross-border Regions.* Basingstoke: Palgrave Macmillan.

Peters, D. (2003). "Cohesion, Polycentricity, Missing Links and Bottlenecks: Conflicting Spatial Storylines for Pan-European Transport Investment." *European Planning Studies* 11(3): 317–339.

Petras, J. (1990). "Spanish Socialism: On the Road to Marbella." *Contemporary Crises* 14(3): 189–217.

Petras, J. (1993). "Spanish Socialism: The Politics of Neoliberalism." In R.H. Chilcote and J. Kurth (eds.), *Mediterranean Paradoxes: The Politics and Social Structure of Southern Europe.* London: Berg.

Pike, A., Pose, A.R., and Tomaney, J. (2006). *Local and Regional Development.* London: Routledge.

Piore, M., and Sabel, F. (1984). *The Second Industrial Divide: Possibilities for Prosperity.* New York: Basic Books.

Plan Urban (2001). *Bahía de Pasaia San Sebastián-Pasaia 2001-2006*, at www.bahiadepasaia.com, last accessed 2/10/2015.

Porter, M. (1990). *The Competitive Advantage of Nations.* London: Macmillan.

Porter, M. (2002). *Competitiveness and the Role of Regions.* Institute for Strategy and Competitiveness. Harvard: Harvard Business School.

Portilla, M., et al. (1995). *Ferrocarriles y desarrollo. Red y mercados en el País Vasco 1856–1914.* Bilbao: Universidad del País Vasco.

Poulantzas, N. (1976). *Las crisis de las dictaduras: Portugal, Grecia, España*, trans. Tununa Mercado. Madrid: Siglo Veintiuno.

Poulantzas, N. (1978). *State, Power, Socialism*, trans. Patrick Camiller. London: Verso.

Prados de la Escosura, L. (1988). *De imperio a nación: Crecimiento y atraso económico en España (1780–1930).* Madrid: Alianza Editorial.

Preston, P. (1986). *The Triumph of Democracy in Spain.* London: Routledge.

Preston, P. (1990). "Spain." In A. Graham and A. Seldon (eds.), *Government and Economies in the Postwar World*. London: Routledge.

Prieto del Campo, C. (2005). "A Spanish Spring?" *New Left Review* 31 (January–February): 43–68.

Reviriego, J.M. (2007). "El tren de alta velocidad es imprescindible para cohesionar Euskadi." Diariovasco.com, 24 June.

Richards, M. (1996). "Constructing the Nationalist State: Self-sufficiency and Regeneration in the Early Franco Years." In C. Mar-Molinero and A. Smith (eds.), *Nationalism and the Nation in the Iberian peninsula*. Oxford: Berg.

Richards, M. (1998). *A Time of Silence: Civil War and the Culture of Repression in Franco's Spain*. Cambridge: Cambridge University Press.

Richardson, T. (1997). "The Trans-European Transport Network: Environmental Policy Integration in the European Union." *European Urban and Regional Studies* 4(4): 333–346.

Ringrose, D. (1996). *Spain, Europe and the "Spanish Miracle" 1700–1900*. Cambridge: Cambridge University Press.

Rivas, J.C. (1993). "El ferrocarril debe especializarse y coordinarse con otros medios: la intermodalidad, clave para el futuro sistema de transportes." *Vía Libre* 352 (May): 20.

Rivas, J.C. (1997). "El 'sorprendente' éxito de 5 años de AVE." *Vía Libre* 398 (May): 10–11.

Rodríguez, A., and Martínez, E. (2003). "Restructuring Cities: Miracles and Mirages in Urban Revitalization in Bilbao." In E. Swyngedouw and A. Rodríguez (eds.), *Urbanizing Globalization: Urban Redevelopment and Social Polarization in the European City*. Oxford: Oxford University Press.

Rodríguez, A., Martínez, E., and Guenaga, G. (2001). "Uneven Redevelopment: New Urban Policies and Socio-spatial Fragmentation in Metropolitan Bilbao." *European Urban and Regional Studies* 8(2), 161–178.

Rodríguez, A., Swyngedouw, E., and Moulaert, F. (2003). "Urban Restructuring, Social-political Polarization and New Urban Policies." In F. Moulaert, A. Rodríguez, and E. Swyngedouw (eds.), *The Globalized City: Economic Restructuring and Social Polarization in European Cities*. Oxford: Oxford University Press.

Rodríguez, G. (2004). *El Estado del bienestar en España: debates, desarrollo y retos*. Madrid: Editorial Fundamentos.

Roldan, S., Muñoz, J., and Serrano, A. (1977). *Qué es el capitalismo español*. Madrid: La Gaya: Ciencia.

Roller, E. (2004). "Conflict and Cooperation in EU Policy-making: The Case of Catalonia." *Perspectives on European Politics and Society* 5(1): 81–102.

Romero González, J. (2002). "Nationalities and Regions in Spain: The Limits of the Autonomic State." http://www.lib.byu.edu/~rdh/wess/iber/autonomy.html, last accessed 3/2/05.

Romero González, J. (2004). "Spatial Planning and Multilevel Coordination in Spain." *Quaderns de Política Económica* 6 (January–April): 19–35.

Romero González, J. (2005). "El gobierno del territorio en España. Balance de iniciativas de coordinación y cooperación territorial." *Boletín de la A.G.E.* 39: 59–86.

Romero Salvadó, J. (1996). "The Nation-building Process in Nineteenth-century Spain." In C. Mar-Molinero and A. Smith (eds), *Nationalism and the Nation in the Iberian Peninsula*. Oxford: Berg.

Romero Salvadó, J. (1999). *Twentieth-century Spain: Politics and Society in Spain 1898–1998*. Basingstoke: Palgrave Macmillan.

Romero Salvadó, J., and Smith, A. (eds.) (2010). *The Agonony of Spanish Liberalism: From Revolution to Dictatorship 1913–23*. London: Palgrave Macmillan.

Ross, C. J. (2000). *Spain 1812–1996*. London: Arnold.

Ross, J. F. (1998). *Linking Europe: Transport Policies and Politics in the European Union*. London: Praeger.

Royo, S., and Christopher, P. (eds.) (2003). *Spain and Portugal in the European Union: The First Fifteen Years*. London: Frank Cass and Co.

Ruipérez, J. (2002). "Los principios constitucionales en la transición Política: teoría democrática del poder constituyente y cambio jurídico-político en España." *Revista de estudios políticos* 116: 25–84.

Ruiz del Árbol, A. (1987). "En Julio pueden empezar las obras." *Vía Libre* 281 (June): 10–12.

Ruiz del Árbol, A. (1988a). "La industria nacional de material rodante esta en condiciones de responder a las exigencias de Renfe." *Vía Libre* 288 (January): 20.

Ruiz del Árbol, A. (1988b). "Un trayecto complicado: Del PTF al 21-0." *Vía Libre* 298 (November): 19.

Sánchez Albornoz, N. (1968). *España hace un siglo: una economía dual.* Madrid: Alianza.

Sánchez Albornoz, N. (ed.) (1985). *La modernización económica de España, 1830–1930.* Madrid: Alianza.

Sanz Aldúan, A. (2000). "El mito de las redes transeuropeas: transporte y sostenibilidad en la Unión Europea." Seminario sobre Las redes transeuropeas (RTE) y el modelo federal de la UE, una visión desde Euskadi, Bilbao, 20–22 January.

Sassen, S. (1999). "Whose City is it? Globalisation and the Formation of New Claims." In A.F. Foo and B. Yuen (eds.), *Sustainable Cities in the 21st Century.* Singapore: National University of Singapore.

Sayer, A. (1989). "Postfordism in Question." In B. Jessop (ed.), *Regulationist Perspectives on Fordism and Post-Fordism.* Cheltenham: Elgar.

Sayer, A. (1992). *Method in Social Science: A Realist Approach.* London: Routledge.

Schubert, A. (1990). *A Social History of Spain.* London: Unwin Hyman.

Schubert, A., and Álvarez, J.J. (2000). *Spanish History since 1808.* London: Arnold.

Schwartz, P., and González, M.J. (1987). *Una historia del Instituto Nacional de la Industria (1941–1976).* Madrid: Tecnos.

Scott, A.J. (1988). "Flexible Production System and Regional Development: The Rise of New Industrial Spaces in North America and Western Europe." *International Journal of Urban and Regional Research* 12(2): 171–186.

Segura, J. (1992). "La competitividad industrial de la economía española." In E. Albi Ibañez (ed.), *Europa y la competitividad de la economía española.* Barcelona: Ariel.

Segura, J., et al. (1989). *La industria española en la crisis, 1978–1984.* Madrid: Alianza.

Share, D. (1988). "Spain: Socialists as Neoliberals." *Socialist Review* 18(1): 38–67.

Shaw, M. (2000). *Theory of the Global State: Globality as Unfinished Revolution.* Oxford and New York: Cambridge University Press.

Siemiatycki, M. (2005). "Beyond Moving People: Excavating the Motivations for Investing in Urban Public Transit Infrastructure in Bilbao Spain." *European Planning Studies*_13(1): 23–44.

Smith, A. (1986). *The Ethnic Origins of Nations*. Oxford: Blackwell.

Smith, A. (2004). "Regions, Spaces of Economic Practice and Diverse Economies in the 'New Europe'." *European Urban and Regional Studies* 11(1): 9–25.

Smith, N. (1991). *Uneven Development: Nature, Capital, and the Production of Space*. Oxford: Blackwell.

SPRI (1992). *Una visión para el futuro*. Vitoria-Gasteiz: Servicio Central de Publicaciones del Gobierno Vasco.

Storm, E. (2004). "The Problem of the Spanish Nation-building Process around 1900." *National Identities* 6(2): 143–156.

Storper, M. (1995). "The Resurgence of Regional Economies: Ten Years Later the Region as a Nexus of Untraded Interdependence." *European Urban and Regional Studies* 2(3): 191–221.

Storper, M. (1997). *The Regional World: Territorial Development in a Global Economy*. New York and London: Guilford.

Storper, M., and Scott, A.J. (1989). "The Geographical Foundations and Social Regulation of Flexible Production Complexes." In J. Wolch and M. Dear (eds.), *The Power of Geography: How Territory Shapes Social Life*. Winchester: Unwin Hyman.

Storper, M., and Walker, R. (1989). *The Capitalist Imperative: Territory, Technology, and Industrial Growth*. Oxford: Blackwell.

Suárez, A. (1989). "Paris-Londres-Madrid unidos por el TGV." *Vía Libre* 300 (January): 5–6.

Suárez, A., and Ruiz del Árbol, A. (1988). "En espera de la decisión y de los pedidos." *Vía Libre* 299 (December): 15–16.

Suárez, A., del Val, Y., Ruiz del Árbol, A., and Graiño, S. (1988). "Cinco ofertas para la alta velocidad española." *Vía Libre* 293 (June): 15.

Suárez, F. (1988). *La crisis del antiguo régimen en España (1800–1840)*. Madrid: Ediciones Rialp.

Swyngedouw, E. (1992). "The Mammon Quest, 'Glocalisation', Interspatial Competition and the Monetary Order: The Construction of New Scales." In M. Dunford and G. Kafkalas (eds.), *Cities and Regions in the New Europe: The Global-Local Interplay and Spatial Development Strategies*. London: Belhaven Press.

Swyngedouw, E. (1997). "Neither Global nor Local: 'Glocalization' and the Politics of Scale." In K. Cox (ed.), *Spaces of Globalization: Reasserting the Power of the Local*. New York: Guilford.

Swyngedouw, E. (1999). "Modernity and Hybridity: Nature, *Regeneracionismo*, and the Production of the Spanish Waterscape." *Annals of the Association of American Geographers* 89(3): 443–465.

Swyngedouw, E. (2004). "Globalisation or 'Glocalisation'? Networks, Territories and Rescaling." *Cambridge Review of International Affairs* 17(1): 25–48.

Swyngedouw, E. (2007). "TechnoNatural Revolutions – The Scalar Politics of Franco's Hydro-social Dream for Spain, 1939–1975." *Transactions, Institute of British Geographers* 32(1): 9–28.

Swyngedouw, E., Mouleart, R., and Rodríguez, A. (2002). "Neoliberal Urbanization in Europe: Large-scale Urban Development Projects and the New Urban Policy." *Antipode* 34(3): 542–577.

Tamames, R. (1986). *The Spanish Economy: An Introduction*. London: C. Hurst & Co.

Tayfur, M. F. (2003). *Semiperipheral Development and Foreign Policy: The Cases of Greece and Spain*. Aldershot: Ashgate.

Thomas, K. (2000). "Creating Regional Cultures of Innovation? The Regional Innovation Strategies in England and Scotland." *Regional Studies* 34(2): 190–198.

Thomson, G. (2010). *The Birth of Modern Politics in Spain: Democracy, Association and Revolution, 1814–1875*. Basingstoke: Palgrave Macmillan.

Toharia, L. (1988). "Partial Fordism: Spain between Politics." In R. Boyer (ed.), *The Search for Labour Market Flexibility: The European Economies in Transition*. Oxford: Clarendon.

Torres, V. (2005). "¿Ave o ferrocarril?" *Habitat* (online journal) 28 (January).

Tortella Casares, G. (1994). *El desarrollo de la España contemporánea. Historia económica de los siglos XIX y XX*. Madrid: Tecnos.

Tortella Casares, G. (2000). *The Development of Modern Spain: An Economic History of the Nineteenth and Twentieth Centuries*, trans. Valerie J. Herr. Boston: Harvard University Press.

Totoricaguena, G.P. (2004). *Identity, Culture, and Politics in the Basque Diaspora*. Reno: University of Nevada Press.

Trans-European Networks, (1996). *Community Guidelines for the Development of the Trans-European Transport Network.* Decision No 1692/96/EC of the European Parliament and the Council of 23 July 1996 on Community guidelines for the development of the trans-European transport network. Brussels: European Commission.

Tratado de la Unión Europea (1997). *Tratado de la Unión Europea.* Madrid: Editorial Civitas.

Unanue, J. (2002). *Las relaciones laborales en Euskal Herria. Apuntes históricos y análisis de su evolución desde la transición Política.* Bilbao: Fundación Manu Robles-Aranguiz Institutua.

Urry, J. (2007). *Mobilities.* Cambridge: Polity Press.

Valls, L. (2004). "EU Cross-border Cooperation Policy in Spain: A Comparison of Interreg III A in the Two Frontiers." *Ritsumeikan International Affairs* 2: 115–139.

Van Houtum, H.R., and Lagendijk, A. (2001). "Contextualising Regional Identity and Imagination in the Construction of Polycentric Urban Regions: The Cases of the Ruhr Area and the Basque Country." *Urban Studies* 38(4): 747–767.

Van Miert, K. (2003). *Report of the High Level Group on the Trans-European Transport Network.* Brussels: European Commission.

Vickerman, R. (1997). "High-speed Rail in Europe: Experience and Issues for Future Development." *The Annals of Regional Science* 31(1): 21–38.

Viñas, A. (2001). "The Enlargement of the European Union: Opportunities and Concerns for Spain." In R. Gillespies (ed.), *Spain: The European and International Challenges.* London: Frank Cass.

Watson, C. (2003). *Modern Basque History: Eighteenth Century to the Present.* Reno: Center for Basque Studies, University of Nevada, Reno.

Watson, C. (2007). *Basque Nationalism and Political Violence: The Ideological and Intellectual Origins of ETA.* Reno: Center for Basque Studies, University of Nevada, Reno.

Weber, E. (1976). *Peasants into Frenchmen: The Modernization of Rural France, 1870–1914.* Stanford: Stanford University Press.

Weber, M. (1978). *Economy and Society,* vol. 1, ed. Guenther Roth and Claus Wittich, trans. Ephraim Fischoff et al. Berkeley: University of California Press.

Whitfield, T. (2014). *Endgame for ETA: Elusive Peace in the Basque Country.* London: C. Hurst & Co. Publishers.

Wise, M. (2000a). "The Atlantic Arc: Transnational European Reality or Regional Mirage?" *Journal of Common Market Studies* 38(5): 865–891.

Wise, M. (2000b). "From Atlantic Arc to Atlantic Area: A Case of Subsidiarity against the Regions?" *Regional Studies* 34(9): 865–873.

Woodworth, P. (2001). *Dirty War, Clean Hands.* Cork, Ireland: Cork University Press.

Woodworth, P. (2004a). "The War against Terrorism: The Spanish Experience from ETA to Al-Qaeda." *Journal of Iberian Studies* 17(3): 169–182.

Woodworth, P. (2004b). "Spain Changes Course: Aznar's Legacy, Zapatero's Prospects." *World Policy Journal* 21(2): 7–26.

World Bank (1963). *The Economic Development of Spain.* Baltimore: The Johns Hopkins Press.

Wright, A. (1977). *The Spanish Economy 1959–1976.* London: Macmillan.

Yago, G. (1983). "The Sociology of Transportation." *Annual Review of Sociology* 9: 171–190.

Zallo, R. (2001) *The Basque Questions and Disputes*, http://ibs.lgu.ac.uk/forum/zallop.htm, last accessed 10/12/01.

Zubiri, I. (2003). "El sector público del País Vasco en la actualidad." *Ekonomiaz* 53: 60–103.

Zulaika, J. (2006). *ETAren hautsa.* Irun: Alberdania.

## Non-Bylined Newspaper Articles

### *Newspapers in Spain*

*Cinco Días* (1988). "Si en el TAV francés vinieran los miembros de ETA, firmaría la compra," 25 November.

### *Newspapers in Basque Country*

*Berria* (2008). "AHT Gelditu!-ko zenbait kidek hilketa gaitzetsi dute," 9 December.

*El Diario Vasco* (1989). "Atienza asegura que Bilbao debe competir con las grandes urbes españolas – de cara al año 2005," 8 June.

——(1989). "El Consejo de Aquitania y el Gobierno Vasco crean una comisión del 'eje Atlántico," 3 September.

——(1989). "En Bruselas se cuestionan la conveniencia de financiar infraestructuras en el Plan de Reconversión Vasco," 6 September.

*Diario Vasco* (1989). "Tavernier: no existirá el eje atlántico si no hay relaciones entre Aquitania y País Vasco," 17 September.

——(1989). "El Gobierno impulsará el corredor subcantábrico y el eje Lisboa-Valencia," 19 September.

——(1989). "Landaburu: No descarto financiar infraestructuras en al País Vasco," 21 September.

——(1989). "Ruiz de Alegría: Nadie cuestiona la validez del acuerdo en infraestructuras con Madrid," 23 September.

——(1989). "Cooperación transfronteriza: el día 4 será firmado un acuerdo País Vasco-Aquitania," 23 September.

——(1989). "El País Vasco y Aquitania desarrollaran acciones conjuntas a nivel Europeo," 29 September.

——(1989). "Barrionuevo pide a la CE dos salidas para el TAV: Irún y Port Bou," 3 October.

——(1989). "Los socialistas franceses reclamaron un mayor protagonismo en la co-operación Euskadi-Aquitania," 4 October.

——(1989). "Jáuregui afirma que antes de fin de año la CE aprobara que el TAV pase por la frontera de Irun," 14 October.

——(1989). "Barrionuevo defiende ante la CE la conexión del TAV por Irún," 17 October.

——(1989). "CAF firma con Alstom el contrato para construir los trenes de alta velocidad," 31 October.

——(1989). "El País Vasco formará próximamente parte de la Asociación de Regiones Fronterizas Europeas," 3 November.

——(1989). "CE: informe encargado por la Comisión recomienda inversiones en infraestructuras en el País Vasco," 22 November.

——(1989). "La Comunidad Europea financiara proyectos de infraestructura en el País Vasco," 23 November.

——(1990). "Atienza quiere aplicar para las zonas vascas el modelo norteamericano de reindustrialización," 26 April.

——(2006). "Acuerdo entre los gobiernos central y vasco para construir la 'Y' vasca por 4.178 millones," 24 April.

——(2007). "ELA se mantiene como primera fuerza sindical del País Vasco, con el 40% de la representación," 8 February.

### *Specialised Railway Journal in Spain*

*Vía Libre* (1987). "Aprobado el proyecto ferroviario más importante del siglo: El PTF diseña el ferrocarril español del año 2000," 280 (May): 8–10.

——(1987). "El nuevo futuro del ferrocarril necesita el apoyo de la gran familia ferroviaria," 281 (June): 7-9.

——(1987). "Nuevo material ferroviario español," 285 (October): 9–17.

——(1988). "Antonio Monfort: Es posible una variante a 250 km/h entre Zaragoza y Barcelona," 289 (February).

——(1988). "Gonzalo Martín Baranda: Pronto habrá un TALGO a 200 km/h," 289 (February).

——(1988). "25 Ramas y 70 locomotoras para Alta Velocidad a Concurso," 289 (February): 16.

—— (1988). "Instalaciones: Un aspecto prioritario," 289 (February): 21–22.

——(1988). "Congreso de los diputados," 291 (April): 6.

——(1988). "Alstom solo comprará Ateinsa y Maquinista si gana los dos concursos," 292 (May).

——(1988). "Italia se presenta a los dos concursos," 292 (May).

——(1988). "Clave en lo político," 294 (July): 25.

——(1988). "Finalizada la negociación alemana con el INI," 297 (October): 9.

——(1992). "Un futuro de nuevas realizaciones," 339 (April).

### *Websites*

*http://aei.pitt.edu/browse/* (Archive of European Integration, University of Pittsburgh website)

*http://www.bakeaz.org/* (NGO, think tank, website)

*http://bilbaoport.es/* (Port Authority of Bilbao website)

*http://www.cambrabcn.org/* (Barcelona Chamber of Commerce website)

*http://www.camarabilbao.com/* (Bilbao Chamber of Commerce website)
*http://europa.eu.int/* (Gateway to the European Union website)
*htt://www.euskadi.net/* (Basque government website)
*htt:/www.feve.es/* (Spanish Narrow Gauge Railways website)
*http://www.fomento.es/* (The Spanish Ministry of Development website)
*http://www.pl-ae.com/* (Aquitaine-Euskadi Logistic Platform website)
*http://www.renfe.es/ (*Spanish National Railway Network website)
*http://www.sindominio.net/ahtez/* (Assembly Against the HST website)
*http://skyscraperpage.com/* (Urbanism forums website)

# Index

Made in United States
Cleveland, OH
05 November 2026

47772444R00199